M000289889

STEPHEN ROACH

Accidental Conflict

AMERICA, CHINA, AND THE CLASH
OF FALSE NARRATIVES

Yale

UNIVERSITY PRESS

NEW HAVEN & LONDON

Copyright © 2022 by Stephen Roach. All rights reserved.
This book may not be reproduced, in whole or in part, including
illustrations, in any form (beyond that copying permitted by Sections 107
and 108 of the US Copyright Law and except by reviewers for the public
press), without written permission from the publishers.

Yale University Press books may be purchased in quantity for
educational, business, or promotional use. For information, please e-mail
sales.press@yale.edu (US office) or sales@yaleup.co.uk (UK office).

Set in Scala and Scala Sans type by Integrated Publishing Solutions.
Printed in Great Britain.

Library of Congress Control Number: 2022937754
ISBN 978-0-300-25964-3 (hardcover : alk. paper)

A catalogue record for this book is available from the British Library.

10 9 8 7 6 5 4 3 2 1

For my students

CONTENTS

PREFACE AS SEQUEL

MY PREVIOUS BOOK, *Unbalanced: The Codependency of America and China*, ended with a warning that now seems painfully obvious. I feared the codependent economic relationship between America and China might go terribly wrong. Unfortunately, that is what happened. The open conflict now evident between the world's two most powerful nations is the outgrowth of an inherently precarious codependency.

We should have seen it coming. Relationship conflict arises when there is a profound shift in the terms of engagement between two partners. When *Unbalanced* was published in 2014, the two nations were at a fork in the road. One path would be delineated by what I called an asymmetrical rebalancing—where one partner changed and the other didn't. The other, more symmetrical path would be forged by the willingness of both partners to change. The asymmetrical path was a recipe for conflict. Symmetry would avoid conflict and allow each nation to meet its growth and geostrategic challenges in a collaborative spirit that bordered on harmony. The choice was theirs.

There is no dark secret as to what happened: China changed while America remained stuck in its ways. In part, this shift stemmed from China's inevitable growth challenges. A spectacular takeoff of 10 percent annual economic growth from 1978 to 2007 took its economy to a critical threshold. With per capita income having risen more than tenfold over that period,

China was rushing headlong toward the challenging zone of the "middle-income trap," where setbacks are more the rule than the exception.

For China, this was a clarion signal to change. And that is exactly what it did. With prescient foresight, or serendipitous good fortune, China embarked on the road to rebalancing, shifting its sources of economic growth away from an increasingly unstable external sector toward internal private consumption and indigenous innovation. But the changes in China have gone far beyond economic rebalancing—there has also been an equally dramatic and worrisome tilt in its political economy of power and ideology. With the United States clinging to a timeworn growth model and increasingly consumed by social and political polarization, the die was cast: a destabilizing dynamic between the two nations has led to a full-blown trade and technology war.

This tilt in the relationship dynamic underscored the paradox of the Next China—that China's emergence as a major engine of global economic growth turned into an uncomfortable ascendancy for established world powers. But it did more than that. It also unmasked the great American paradox of a savings-short global power that had long prospered well beyond its means. Conflict took on a life of its own, bringing an increasingly treacherous endgame into focus. Notwithstanding the darker warnings of history, the rising power was indeed clashing with the incumbent hegemon.

It didn't have to go this way, and there is still a chance to avoid the worst-case outcome. The big question is whether both powerful nations have the vision and, ultimately, the political will to resolve this conflict before it is too late. As Henry Kissinger has put it, the United States and China are now in the "foothills" of a new cold war. Predictably, codependency has entered the danger zone of conflict escalation. For America and China, a new framework of engagement and coexistence is an increasingly urgent priority. And so we begin where *Unbalanced* left off.

Introduction: Expedience

HISTORY IS LITTERED WITH FALSE NARRATIVES. From the flat earth theory and the Ptolemaic system of cosmology to tales of UFO sightings and the "Big Lie" of election fraud promulgated by former President Donald Trump and his supporters, twisting facts to tell a convincing story has long been central to the human condition. So it is with the false narratives about each other that China and America have embraced.

The distinction between a true and a false narrative is often tricky to make. Veracity is ultimately determined by time. Just as new discoveries correct bad science, "fake news" can be fact-checked, and political detours can avoid dead ends. Yet dislodging a false narrative can be exceedingly difficult. Fact-based counterarguments, as reactions to America's post-Trump political adventures attest, may not be enough. Repetition of a lie often breeds conviction. And technology-enabled repetition takes on new meaning in an era dominated by online social networks. If left unchallenged, the false narrative can become self-fulfilling—at least until experience makes it untenable. Until that moment of reckoning, however, the false narrative can take on a life of its own, shaping the very history from which it has emerged.

For most in the United States there is nothing false about the profusion of negative stories on China. They resonate with a broad cross-section of the American public. In mid-2021, fully 76 percent of Americans had an unfavorable view of China, according to the Pew Research Center. This is a stunning increase of 29 percentage points since the United States launched a trade war with China in 2018, and it represents the most negative US public opinion toward China since the inception of this survey in 2005.

China suffers from a similar malady. While it has long sought to replicate the strength of the US economy and to rival America's hegemonic global role, China sees the United States through its own biases. It fears that America wants to contain its growth and development. It extrapolates the trade war of 2018–21 into the future, convinced that it will remain in the crosshairs of a protectionist and increasingly nationalistic United States.

At the same time, many in China have embraced the narrative of America in decline—especially after nearly two decades of crises and instability. China's ultimate false narrative of America—the ideological triumph of socialism over capitalism—underscores a very different aspect of conflict between the two nations. It pits one system against the other, leaving little room for compromise on deeply entrenched values. As long as the Communist Party controls China, it can't afford to let go of this ideologically expedient narrative.

Dueling false narratives spell nothing but trouble for this deeply conflicted relationship. America's fixation on the China threat is on a collision course with China's focus on the American threat. In both cases, the fears underlying these false narratives may feel perfectly legitimate, providing justification for strong actions. The dueling false narratives of the United States and China have, indeed, led to very real conflict.

How did it get to this point? The simple answer is misplaced fear—the most corrosive ingredient in any relationship, human or economic. In the United States, those fears are rooted in the economic angst of American workers and families over the chronic job and wage pressures that have sapped vitality from a once proud US manufacturing sector. These fears coincide with an outsize foreign trade deficit, which for many symbolizes a leakage of jobs to overseas producers that can undermine any nation's sense of self. That China's dramatic rise as an economic power accounts for the largest portion of the US trade deficit is especially grating given that many low-cost Chinese-made products appear to replace the very goods that American workers once produced at home.

This narrative has the added allure of its own strain of political expedience. US politicians—Republicans and Democrats alike—have been quick to connect the dots and add an important twist: America's economic carnage, they claim, is not only traceable to Chinese trade, it also reflects unfair, abusive, and often illegal economic aggression by the Chinese state. This amounts to an existential threat to the cherished American Dream and US global leadership.

This dark narrative works especially well for US politicians looking to duck responsibility for the plight of American workers. It lets them off the hook for the very real pain felt in countless communities across the nation. It deflects attention from decades of government budget deficits that have sapped domestic US saving, giving rise to the dreaded trade deficits that politicians are quick to pin on China. The combination of self-inflated economic angst and political expediency makes for a compelling story. It fulfills the classic conditions of a powerful false narrative. And it has taken on a life of its own.

The same thing is happening in China. The trade war with the United States has played to the dark side of a long-insecure Chinese leadership. China's so-called century of humiliation, which began with the Opium Wars in the mid-nineteenth century, left deep scars of wounded pride and national pain that have conditioned the Chinese public and leaders of the Chinese Communist Party to fear that the West might well attack again. In the grip of such wrenching insecurity, these expectations leave the country ripe for its own politically expedient false narratives.

All this paints a picture of accidental conflict, the collision that didn't have to happen were it not for the mutual expedience of a confluence of false narratives. This has taken the conflict between the United States and China decisively into the danger zone. As president, Donald Trump provided catalytic support to conflict escalation, but his was by no means the sole voice linking long-simmering economic pressures with the toxic politics of nationalism. In the world according to Trump, the China threat is the single greatest obstacle to making America great again. The tariff war, an outgrowth of this line of reasoning, has taken the world's two most powerful nations to the brink of a full-blown economic rupture.

Surprisingly, Trump's successor, Joe Biden, has done little to dispel this narrative. Again, the reason is political expediency. While the two presidents have very little in common, they are both captives and protagonists of America's false narratives on China that have so inflamed public opinion.

This troubled relationship has roots in some of the most contentious issues shaping the global economy. The rise of China is itself a double-edged sword. On the one hand, the Chinese economy of the not-so-distant future—call it the Next China—is likely to be increasingly consumer-led, services-based, and innovation-driven. It has the potential to provide the largest source of growth in global aggregate demand in the first half of the twenty-first century. The positive take on this development is that rapid expansion in the markets of the Next China would offer great opportunity for other nations to share in the benefits of China's burgeoning middle class. And who is better positioned than the United States and its vast collection of world-class companies to reap those benefits?

But the other edge of the sword is equally sharp. There is widespread concern, especially today in the United States, that the benefits of a rising China may come at great expense to American citizens as well as to those in the world's other major economies. Fears of lost jobs and repressed wages, the ultimate economic sacrifice for any nation, are central to those concerns.

Adding to fears of economic insecurity is the extraordinary confluence of two black swan events—low-probability shocks that actually came to pass in a shortly compressed period of time. First came the Covid-19 pandemic in 2020. While most major economies, especially the United States and Europe, appear to be on the road to post-Covid recovery, China continues to struggle with new variants of the virus. In all instances, the impacts of the shock are likely to cast a long shadow over behavioral patterns of individuals, companies, and public finance. The pandemic-battered post-Covid world will need to learn to live with the virus and its aftershocks, as well as the fear that gripped us in 2020 and 2021. A shot in the arm won't erase that.

The second shock, the Russo-Ukrainian War, came a mere two years later in early 2022. On the surface, this seemed like a classic great power clash between the United States and the Russian Federation. But China, which had just signed a new "unlimited" partnership agreement with Russia, was quickly caught in the crossfire. If it held to that agreement by maintaining, or even increasing, support to Russia, China risked being judged guilty by association in the eyes of the West. Such a verdict would not be without sanctions-like penalties that would only intensify conflict between the United States and China.

If one nation struggles more than the other in the aftermath of these twin shocks, it will only further inflame the blame game that is already well under way. US politicians, for example, can't seem to let go of the narrative of Covid-19's Chinese origins. If the disease started in Wuhan, goes the argument, China must deserve blame for its effects, both those already suffered and those that might yet occur. Never mind the politicized denial that inhibited America's own Covid response throughout 2020. It was more expedient to pin the problem on someone else. And that someone, of course, is China. Similarly, while China played no role in starting the war in Ukraine, it risks blame if it condones, let alone assists, the dangerous military aggression of its newfound Russian partner.

How this will all play out is anyone's guess. There is no lack of alternative narratives, especially with the economy. Volatile stock markets long for the instant gratification of a vigorous economic recovery. Rising inflation and interest rates threaten that optimistic outcome, as do the mounting perils of war and great power conflicts.

Whatever the eventual outcome, escalating tensions between the world's two leading powers are likely to have enduring impacts. The contrast between differing economic models of the two nations is not just about ideology but also about very different time horizons. The economic translation of "American exceptionalism" is spend now, save later. Largely because of that, the United States has long lacked a solid foundation of domestic saving—the seed corn of economic growth for any nation.

China, taking a longer-term perspective, has drawn heavily on its surplus saving to support the massive investments its spectacular development has required—new capacity, infrastructure, a deepening of human capital, and now a quest for home-grown, or indigenous, innovation. The big question for China is whether it can pivot toward more of a US-style consumer model. An equally large question for the United States is whether it can become more like China in restoring its saving capacity to fund the investments it needs for future growth.

Meanwhile, the results speak for themselves. America, fixated on short-term results, has let its saving and international imbalances intensify. Lacking domestic savings yet wanting to invest and grow, the United States has borrowed heavily from the rest of the world to fund that growth. Yet to attract foreign capital, America has had to run chronically large deficits in its balance-of-payments and foreign trade positions. This contrasts sharply with China's emphasis on saving as the foundation of future growth. But China's excess saving brings its own set of problems: it has given rise to vast trade surpluses that spawn allegations of unbridled Chinese mercantilism and unfair trading practices.

The lens of codependency brings this contrast between the two nations' economic value propositions into sharper focus. In the 1980s and 1990s, the needs of the Chinese and US economies dovetailed perfectly. Coming off two decades of instability, the battered Chinese economy desperately needed a new source of growth. America was struggling in the aftermath of a wrenching stagflation—the confluence of sluggish economic growth and rising inflation. Shifting its manufacturing to China allowed US companies to cut costs and boost profitability while keeping prices in check and thereby allowing American consumers to enjoy rising living standards. For a fleeting moment in the late 1990s and early 2000s, this marriage of convenience was a blissful outcome for both nations. Chinese economic growth surged as the United States offered a major source of demand for Chinese exporters. And American consumers enjoyed a great expansion of purchasing power that low-cost imports from China provided.

But that was then. Now we are seeing a classic clash of codependency. China has moved up the value chain, making more advanced products and developing new industries that the United States wants to claim as its own. The US public, gripped by economic angst and with its leaders unable or unwilling to promote change, clings to the politically expedient characterization of China as an existential threat to America's future prosperity.

In the end, the world's response to the transitional imperatives of the Next China may be decisive in resolving the battle of competing narratives. Getting its economy right is essential for China to hit its own development targets as well as to resolve its relationship conflicts with others. Its focus on artificial intelligence as the linchpin of indigenous innovation is key to its audacious goal of achieving great power status by 2049. This poses a special challenge: is China strong enough to pull off such a transformation without reforming its debt-intensive state-owned enterprises or developing a modern, open financial system, including a fully convertible currency?

Similar questions can be asked of the United States. Can it continue to grow without addressing its saving challenge? Lacking in saving and the investment and research that saving supports, can the United States maintain its edge on the frontier of innovation? America needs to strengthen its economy, not just recapture a modern version of an earlier magic. It has to anticipate a very different future, one that undoubtedly includes an important role for a rising China. The resolution of the US-China conflict will depend critically on how both nations address daunting growth challenges, separately and together.

Conflict resolution is all the more urgent in today's anxious and uncertain climate. The concurrent challenges of post-pandemic global healing and renewed military conflict in Europe are complicated by the confluence of breakthrough technological change, political upheaval, periodic bouts of financial instability, and newfound fears over health and climate security. A profusion of false narratives can deflect attention away from tackling these tough problems.

But for both the United States and China, the greatest danger of false narratives lies in the dark recesses of political expedience. What plays well politically may be more of a raw power play than an ideal economic or geostrategic strategy. As the false narratives spawned by the seduction of political power become ever more deeply entrenched, the vicious cycle of accidental conflict becomes exceedingly difficult to break. The real risk is that the temptations of the false narrative may not be dislodged by any experience-based correction that follows. Conflict resolution is vital to preventing permanent damage from the clash of false narratives between America and China. A new approach is desperately needed.

PART ONE

ON RELATIONSHIPS

FOR MODERN CHINA, THE RELATIONSHIP dynamic with other major nations has always been in tension with its economic growth strategy. Mao Zedong, the revolutionary founder of the People's Republic of China (PRC), proposed an unsustainable combination: a political and ideological revolution without economic support. Initially ensnared in a contentious alliance with the Soviet Union, Mao's China lacked the support of a strong and reliable ally. As Mao's life was ending, in the mid-1970s, a weakened and isolated China, suffering the aftermath of the upheavals of the Great Leap Forward and the Cultural Revolution, was trapped in a tightening vise of social and political turmoil. Something had to give.

It took a post-Mao leadership struggle and the ascendancy of a pragmatic Deng Xiaoping for China to chart a new path. Out of necessity in the chaos following two decades of instability under Mao, Deng emerged as the architect of the defining transition of modern China under the credo of "reforms and opening up." The opening-up meant a break from Maoist isolationism and tethered the Chinese economy to the rest of the world, transforming it into the greatest beneficiary of a new and powerful wave of globalization.

China was not alone in seeking partnership as a means toward solving serious economic problems. Partly by accident, partly by design, China and the United States came together in a shared journey. Just as China was searching for a new growth recipe in the late 1970s, so too was America, which was gripped by a punishing stagflation—mounting inflation and slowing growth.

China came to America's rescue on several fronts. It offered cheaper products to American consumers, expanding their weakened purchasing power in a time of soaring inflation and increasingly stagnant wages. It provided demand for dollar-based financial assets, which the United States, short of savings and desperate for foreign funding of its budget deficits, sorely needed. And China offered a new market for growth-constrained corporate America, quietly emerging as the United States' third largest and fastest-growing export market.

America, for its part, provided a quick fix for the increasingly precarious state of the Chinese economy. US demand for Chinese goods enabled China to successfully execute its export-led development strategy, which boosted economic expansion at an unprecedented pace of 10 percent annual growth for three decades. Export production required massive investments in factories, distribution centers, and infrastructure, all of which added fuel to China's growth juggernaut.

Over time, the attraction between the two needy partners deepened, and its benefits became increasingly important to both nations. By the late 1990s, their marriage of convenience had morphed into a full-blown economic codependency.

Despite its good fortune, China has struggled to manage the give and take of relationships with the world at large and with the United States in particular. Its powerful export-driven growth, turbo-charged by accession to the World Trade Organization in 2001, led to internal macroeconomic imbalances and external tensions with its trading partners, both of which cast doubt on the sustainability of the Chinese growth miracle.

A codependent economic relationship with the United States framed the sustainability question in a different light. The huge saving and trade imbalances between the United States and China ultimately put the world's two largest economies on a collision course. China's new powerful leader framed conflict in a different light. Xi Jinping's depiction of the Chinese Dream—driven by a sense of rejuvenation and the goal of great power status by 2049—was increasingly seen by the United States as a threat to its post–World War II hegemony and prosperity.

The early bliss of convenience segued uncomfortably into the conflict phase of codependency. As a reactive, blame-prone mindset took hold in both nations, their codependency became destabilizing. First came the trade war, followed by a tech war and then the early skirmishes of a new cold war. Undermined by the viral spread of false narratives, the Chinese and American Dreams faced a dangerous clash. A ruptured relationship was in desperate need of repair.

1

Shared History

GIVEN THAT ITS CIVILIZATION GOES BACK some four thousand years, China's overlap with the 250-year-old American experiment may look like a rounding error. But there can be no mistaking the rich shared history between the two nations. As the United States came of age as an industrial power in the nineteenth century and then as a global hegemon in the aftermath of World War II, its relationship with a reawakened and rising China has grown to be a defining feature of the modern world order.

The past fifty years have been especially challenging for both economies. While each has faced innumerable problems at home, the global context has been especially vexing. The oil shocks and Great Inflation of the 1970s, the Asian financial crisis of the late 1990s, the Global Financial Crisis of 2008–9, and the Covid and Ukrainian shocks of the early 2020s are visible signs of an increasingly crisis-prone world. The cross-border linkages of globalization have spared no nation from the impacts.

The Chinese word for crisis, *wéijī* (危机), conveys both danger and opportunity. For China and the United States, that duality has led to important shifts in their economic strategies that have left them accident-prone and vulnerable to conflict.

China entered the twentieth century on a trajectory of demise. While its collapse during the late Qing dynasty reflected economic and political pressures, it was largely foreign military actions, bookended by the Opium Wars of the mid-nineteenth century and the Japanese invasion in the 1930s, that

earned this era the label "century of humiliation." Not only was China defeated in those conflicts, parts of the nation were occupied repeatedly by
foreign imperialists—first Great Britain, then Japan, and finally the former Soviet Union. Humiliation is a gentle way of depicting the bruising of
China's national ego. It suffered not only a loss of geographic territory but
a diminished sense of self.[1]

The United States largely remained on the sidelines. The second Opium
War coincided with its Civil War, when some even feared that Great Britain
might once again turn its sights on its newly vulnerable former colony.[2]
While it remained neutral during the outbreaks in China, the United States
was quick to seize on the economic advantages that arose from the forced
British opening of Canton trade.[3] Nor did the United States intervene to
stop Japan's invasion of the Chinese province of Manchuria in 1931.[4] Not
until the attack on Pearl Harbor a decade later, precipitating America's own
war with Japan, did it ally itself with China.

That alliance was short-lived. In the immediate aftermath of World War
II, it was shattered by the revolutionary ascendancy of Chinese communist
leadership under Mao Zedong and soon gave way to overt conflict after war
broke out on the Korean peninsula in 1950. The Korean War itself was a
visible, if paradoxical, manifestation of emerging vulnerabilities in the relations between what was now a new nation, the People's Republic of China,
and the relatively old United States. Ironically, as China and the USSR joined
forces in waging battle against the United States in Korea, the Soviet Union
had replaced Japan as the foreign occupier of Manchuria.[5]

With the cease-fire in the Korean War in 1953, tensions in the US-China
relationship were subsumed within the Cold War between the United States
and the Soviet Union, which had begun in 1947. The Sino-Soviet military
alliance in the Korean conflict, combined with Mao's deepening reliance on
Soviet economic assistance in the 1950s, left little doubt in the United States
as to where China stood in the new postwar global power struggle. China
and the Soviet Union had forged an ideological and military compact that
posed an increasingly worrisome threat to a victorious but still insecure
United States.[6]

Though triumphant in World War II and having battled to a tie in the
Korean War, the United States was increasingly weary of conflict. Wars had

become the norm in a still vulnerable world. Notwithstanding the threat of mutual destruction in the nuclear age, there was nothing comforting about a cold war that could easily spark a hot outbreak. Amid that tension, any hopes for a productive US-China relationship during the 1950s and 1960s were quashed.

Setting the Stage: The Chinese Perspective

With the world divided by Cold War loyalties, the United States and China were on very different paths, with competing visions of history that had little in common. For China, that history, at first dominated by an ideological revolution, was also a time of political and military partnership with the Soviet Union that had no answers for its struggling economy.[7] The American post–World War II experience was very different: having suffered little damage, the United States found itself leading the reconstruction of a war-torn world, which presented an extraordinary opportunity for economic ascendancy.

Yet in one of the classic ironies of history, neither of those paths was sustainable.

Mao Zedong's considerable talents ran to politics, polemics, and ideology rather than economic development. As China's revolutionary leader from 1949 to 1976, he pushed the embryonic Chinese economy to the brink of collapse. During Mao's leadership, China's economic growth rose and fell in fits and starts. His two riskiest domestic experiments, the Great Leap Forward of the late 1950s and the Cultural Revolution of the 1960s and '70s, brought wrenching political instability and left the economy in near shambles.[8]

That condition wasn't entirely evident from China's aggregate economic statistics. While its inflation-adjusted (or real) gross domestic product expanded by about 6 percent a year from 1952 to 1977, that wasn't nearly fast enough to lift the nation out of poverty. By 1976, when Mao's death brought an end to the Cultural Revolution, fully 35 percent of total Chinese output was still concentrated in the agricultural sector, where labor productivity was less than 20 percent of that in the services sector and only about 12 percent of productivity in the manufacturing sector.[9] This unbalanced growth struc-

ture was stacked against prosperity. As a result, China had become vulnerable to its own strain of "hysteresis"—projecting a tough legacy of economic
performance into the future.[10] With fully three-fourths of the rural Chinese
population mired in poverty, China could not afford to stay this course.[11]
Without a fundamental shift in the structure of its economy, a still impoverished nation was destined for more social and political turmoil. Something had to give.

Predictably, all of this posed enormous challenges during the post-Mao
leadership struggle.[12] China was desperate for a new recipe for economic
development—in essence, a new source of economic growth. With the population left exhausted and disgruntled by the ideological chaos of Maoism
and with economic failure an urgent threat, China's leaders had no choice
but to look to external demand to provide economic growth. That not only
required an important transition in its growth model, it brought the rest of
the world squarely into China's growth equation.

In 1978, the diminutive and previously oft-maligned Deng Xiaoping
emerged on top from China's power struggle and seized the opportunity
to spur economic revival. He ushered in a fact-based assessment of the
economy that led to a call for "reforms and opening up." His emphasis on
development over ideology stood in sharp contrast to Mao's focus on revolutionary ideology over development.

The new emphasis came through loud and clear in Deng's famous December 1978 speech to a Party "work conference," held on the eve of China's
so-called Third Plenum of the Eleventh Central Committee of the Chinese
Communist Party.[13] The speech marked a major turning point for a nation
that had been convulsed by two decades of social, political, and economic
chaos. Deng drew a clear line in contrasting Mao's leadership with his own,
stressing that "[t]he Cultural Revolution has become a stage in the course
of China's socialist development." In other words, it was over. It was time
to turn away from revolutionary zeal and take on the heavy lifting of building economic prosperity.[14]

Deng urged the assembled cadres to emancipate their minds by "seeking
truth from facts." His approach, conveyed through firm and consistent political messaging, was not just clear-eyed but also pragmatic. His stress on

"uniting as one" implied that China would continue under the collective leadership of Party governance. But the strategic focus on "modernization," probably Deng's most enduring legacy, drew together the values of hard work, a pioneering spirit, and the oversight of competent officials in pursuit of forward-looking opportunities.[15]

The payback was quick and powerful but not without considerable pushback from the deeply entrenched vested interests of the Mao era.[16] But following his call for reform, Deng persevered and set the Chinese economy on a powerful growth trajectory. Real gross domestic product grew by nearly 10 percent a year over the next thirty-five years. That was more than 55 percent faster than the pace achieved under Mao. Adjusting for China's population growth, the acceleration was even sharper—8.5 percent annual growth in GDP per capita post-1978, versus just 3.6 percent under Mao. By 2020, following the hyper growth of the "Deng takeoff," China's real GDP per capita was fully four times higher than it would have been had the country grown at the rate it did under Mao Zedong.[17] Modern China had risen to the challenge of its first transition imperative.

Deng's hyper-growth recipe was not just a convenient solution to China's economic woes. It also addressed a key shortcoming: the economy was not generating enough jobs to employ its vast reservoir of impoverished surplus labor. China was, and still is, in the midst of a historic migration from the countryside to urban population centers. Its economy was moving away from labor-intensive agricultural activities to the more efficient manufacturing sector. Faster economic growth was the only way for China to absorb all the workers flooding from farms into the cities. In effect, its surplus-labor economy had to run faster on the treadmill in order to maintain social stability and raise national living standards.

This phase of China's growth—the development takeoff—did not occur in a vacuum. Under Deng's guidance, the focus was initially on the supply side of the economy. His stress on "four modernizations" underscored the need for the simultaneous development of industry, science and technology, national defense, and modern agriculture.[18] The strategy spoke little of the demand side. For a still impoverished nation, where output in 1980 was less than $500 (in US dollars) per person, internal demand was wishful thinking.[19] So China turned to the rest of the world to support the supply-side focus of Deng's growth strategy. The transition would not have suc-ceeded without this shift to external demand.

Thirty years later, China's economy faced another key transition. The hyper-growth antidote to China's surplus labor problem raised important questions about the staying power of the Deng Xiaoping economic miracle. In a now celebrated press conference following the conclusion of the Na-tional People's Congress in March 2007, Premier Wen Jiabao expressed concern that problems might be brewing beneath the surface of China's seemingly all-powerful growth machine. After a thirty-year growth miracle, he said, the Chinese economy risked becoming increasingly unstable, un-balanced, uncoordinated, and unsustainable.

Later dubbed the "Four Uns," Wen's critique sparked intense internal debate over China's growth strategy.[20] Hyper growth—Deng's 10 percent solution—might have been the correct strategy for staving off economic failure following the Great Leap Forward and the Cultural Revolution. But the recipe had outlived its usefulness, spawning a wide range of problems that increasingly required attention.

Wen Jiabao had a fair point. The imbalances he mentioned included China's excesses of domestic saving and fixed investment, which had risen to 50 percent and 40 percent of GDP, respectively. Similarly, China's cur-rent account imbalance—a nation's broadest measure of its international position vis-à-vis the rest of the world—was moving toward a record sur-plus of 10 percent of its GDP in 2007.[21] Compared to those of other major economies, China's imbalances were in a league of their own.

Internally, meanwhile, the Chinese economy was increasingly unstable—too much investment and exports and not enough internal private con-sumption. And the central government, despite its historical affinity with central planning, was losing control of an increasingly fragmented, uncoor-dinated system of governance dominated by provincial and city power blocs.

But the most telling aspect of the Four Uns critique was Wen's concern over sustainability. In alluding to excess resource consumption, especially coal-fired energy, he drew immediate attention to China's horrific envi-ronmental degradation and pollution—not just the dirty air that its people breathe but also the filthy water they drink. Sustainability also touched on growing inequalities in the distribution of income and wealth, a develop-ment greatly at odds with the aspirations of Xi Jinping's yet-to-be-articulated Chinese Dream that I will come to shortly. Wen's critique underscored the long-neglected first word in the nation's very name: People's Republic of China.

The Four Uns framed an important strategic tradeoff for Chinese eco-nomic development. Deng's approach focused on the quantity of economic growth as the answer to Maoism's failures. While hyper growth worked as an immediate fix—a fix that lasted for a generation—it created a new set of problems, from imbalances and inequities in the economic structure to the diminished quality of China's air and water. Although he never said it explicitly, Wen was arguing for a fundamental rethinking of the balance be-tween quantity and quality in the Chinese growth model. What worked for Deng Xiaoping, he thought, would not work in the future.

Wen's critique was remarkably prescient. A year and a half later, in 2008, when the Global Financial Crisis erupted, an unprecedented contraction in global demand posed a dire threat to the export-led Chinese economy. This was an important wake-up call for a nation that had taken the world's sup-port for granted.

As the greatest beneficiary of the powerful globalization and trade liber-alization that underpinned the explosion in world trade, China had watched its exports soar to an unheard-of 35 percent of GDP by 2007. That was fully 15 percentage points above the share just six years earlier, when China had entered the World Trade Organization. During that six-year period, from 2001 to 2007, China's overall GDP rose at a 10.8 percent annual rate, the strongest six-year burst of the Deng Xiaoping growth miracle.[22] There could be little doubt that Deng's hyper-growth solution was unusually dependent on export demand from foreign markets.

The Global Financial Crisis drew that support into serious question. That was particularly evident during the sluggish post-crisis recovery in the world economy that was accompanied by a flattening out of global trade as a share of world output—a dramatic break from the pre-crisis trend of record in-creases in trade.[23] These events called into question the staying power of China's export-led growth strategy; so did early signs of emerging trade frictions and protectionism.

Wen's Four Uns not only underscored the tradeoff between the quantity and quality dimensions of the Chinese growth gambit, they raised profound questions about China's economic ties to an increasingly crisis-prone world. Once again, as in the late 1970s, an economic transition had put pressure on the relationship underpinnings of China's growth strategy. But there was no turning back for Deng Xiaoping's hyper-growth strategy—or so it seemed.

Yet over the next decade, China struggled to change. The global climate remained precarious and rife with trade tensions, and China's progress on the rebalancing campaign was mixed at best. The economy was still top-heavy in exports and investment, and deficient in domestic demand, especially private consumption. In 2017, China faced yet another key transition point in its development. Unlike Wen Jiabao, who framed China's transition imperatives from an analytical perspective, China's new leader, Xi Jinping, spoke more about ideology.[24]

That combination—ideology and a powerful leader—is not without irony. In many respects, it hearkens back to the days of Mao Zedong. But whereas Mao opted for ideology over prosperity, Xi's approach has been very different. The transition of 2017 was all about injecting socialist dogma into China's growth and development equation but with an important twist: unlike Mao, who tore up China's pre-revolutionary script of private ownership, Xi built on the analytics of Wen's case for structural rebalancing. But he added an ideological overlay, dubbed "Xi Jinping Thought." In his judgment, analytics alone were not compelling enough to take China to the Promised Land. The nation had the right economic strategy, he argued, but lacked the will to put it into practice.[25] Implementation was the problem, and for Xi, the Party and its ideological underpinnings were the key to a more effective and disciplined implementation.

Xi's approach was far more comprehensive than Wen's rebalancing campaign. It was presaged by a nationalist appeal to the great dream of the Chinese people that he espoused when he first assumed office in November 2012 as general secretary of the Chinese Communist Party. That was followed by an unprecedented anti-corruption campaign, and by warnings about the perils of an ossified Party structure. A year later, a comprehensive reform agenda—the so-called Third Plenum reforms of 2013—hinted at much more to come.[26] But as with Wen's rebalancing strategy, implementation was also a problem for Xi's reforms. Much of the action plan remained on hold.[27] A new and more disciplined approach was needed.

Xi outlined that approach on October 18, 2017, at the opening session of the CCP's Nineteenth Congress. In a ponderous speech of well over three hours, he laid out a new Party-centric vision of China's future. Like Deng Xiaoping's historic but far more succinct speech some thirty-nine years earlier, Xi's offered a comprehensive approach.[28] It placed the economic challenge within a "five-sphere integrated plan"—political, cultural, economic, social, and ecological. The "four-pronged strategy" for economic policy featured supply-side structural reforms as the immediate task: reducing excess capacity, eliminating the overhang of excess homebuilding, reducing debt, or deleveraging, and cost-cutting. Warning yet again of complacency, Xi demanded unrelenting focus on China's "Three Critical Battles"—de-risking (avoiding dangerous and unnecessary risks), poverty alleviation, and pollution control.[29]

Much of the plan was repetition—a sloganized reworking of proposals that had been on the Chinese policy agenda for years. This was particularly true of initiatives aimed at economic rebalancing, which dated back more than a decade to the Four Uns. Under Xi, Wen Jiabao's consumer-led rebalancing strategy was rebranded as "dual circulation," a concept I will discuss in Chapter 9.[30] The 2017 version was more up to date, focusing on innovation, clean energy, eco-friendly urbanization, family planning policy, and a long list of other reforms.

Xi also extolled the virtues of the "mixed-ownership model"; paradoxically, this provided unwavering support for China's all powerful state-owned enterprises while at the same time reaffirming commitment to the decisive role of markets in the economy, stressing people over bureaucracy, collectivism over individualism. All in all, the far-ranging agenda of 2017 was effectively one-size-fits-all. But there was no new strategic breakthrough that might transform the Chinese economy into a higher-quality growth experience.

And yet Xi's speech to the Nineteenth Party Congress was historic in one critical sense: it put forward a comprehensive implementation strategy. After years of unmet promises, reform fatigue had set in, and Xi believed the only

way to restore reform momentum was a major emphasis on the enhancement of Party-based governance. The five-year anti-corruption campaign
launched in 2012 suddenly made sense. A corrupt Party was incapable of
effectively implementing new policies; anti-corruption was seen as the means
to a disciplined and focused implementation of the reforms urgently required for a fair and prosperous society.[31]

This may have sounded like a rehashing of socialist jargon that had long
dominated major Party meetings. But this time it was really something rad-
ically different. Xi had recognized that China's economic strategy, however
correct it might be in theory, had ended up having no teeth in practice. The
Party, whose 95 million members made it the largest political organization
in the world, was the only institutional mechanism able to bridge the gap
between theory and practice. An uncorruptible Party held the key to implementation—long the missing piece in China's development strategy. For
Xi, Party reform was everything. This was the crux of what quickly became
known as Xi Jinping Thought. For China, it ended up being the country's
most radical change in a generation.

Xi Jinping Thought was framed around an important reworking of one
of the key pillars of Chinese socialism—the Marxian notion of the *principal
contradiction*. Initially couching the idea as a dialectical critique of the social
struggles of capitalism, Marx argued that the failure to resolve these struggles could lead to instability, systemic failure, and possibly revolution.[32] In
1982, Deng Xiaoping grounded the ideology of reforms and opening-up in
this Marxian notion as the need to resolve the contradiction between "the
people's growing and material needs and the backward level of social production." Thirty-five years later, China was no longer backward and that
view was out of date.

Xi Jinping Thought was premised on a bold first revision to China's principal contradiction. In his 2017 speech, Xi proposed that China's principal
contradiction should now be framed as "between unbalanced and inadequate development and the people's ever-growing needs for a better life."[33]
Both Deng's and Xi's versions of the contradiction were people-centric, but
the backward economy of Deng's time had been superseded by the challenges of imbalances and inadequacies in the much more highly developed Chinese economy of the twenty-first century. Xi Jinping Thought thus

brought the dialectic of Party ideology into better alignment with the rebalancing strategy of Wen Jiabao. This combination of analytics and ideology dispelled any doubt as to where the nation was headed.

The overarching message of Xi Jinping Thought was unmistakable: his focus was not about moving in a new direction but about holding firm to a comprehensive reform agenda. This required a revamping of the Party as the means of implementation, as well as a projection of Party governance and leadership power that China had not seen since the days of Mao Zedong.

Consistent with the Marxian notion of the principal contradiction, Xi couched his imperatives in urgent terms, as if the Chinese system was on the brink of catastrophic failure. It would take strong authoritarian leadership, his supporters argued, to avoid such a dire endgame.[34] The Party responded to Xi's message by elevating his stature to a degree not seen since Mao's time. The very label *Xi Jinping Thought* says it all; only Mao had had the word "thought" attached to his ideological imprint before. Deng Xiaoping Theory paled in comparison, as did, even more so, the "Three Represents" of Jiang Zemin and the "Scientific Development" of Hu Jintao.[35]

This elevation of Xi's message was in keeping with his earlier designation by the Party as a *core leader*—a term previously reserved only for Mao.[36] This culminated in the well-advertised shift in leadership succession formalized in March 2018. The ten-year, two-term limit on presidential tenure that governed peaceful succession in China's two recent leadership transitions—from Deng to Jiang in 1992 and from Jiang to Hu in 2003—was abandoned. Xi Jinping effectively was made president for life.[37]

What matters most for the future is what Xi Jinping does with this power. The rhetorical goal is clear: achieving the status of a Great Socialist Nation by 2049, the centenary of the People's Republic of China. The question is the means, not the end.

By all indications, these means are far more muscular than at any point since the Mao era, both in Xi's internal command of China and also in his outward projection of power. The low-profile "hide and bide" approach espoused by Deng Xiaoping is no longer deemed appropriate.[38] Xi's leadership has both an inward focus—power consolidation, anti-corruption, and countering any threats to social unrest, such as those currently in Xinjiang and previously in Tibet—and important outward-facing elements: the Belt and Road Initiative as well as power projection in the South China Sea, Hong Kong, and Taiwan.

But this exercise of power by China's most powerful leader since Mao has led to a new strain of conflicts. Once again, China's transition has raised profound questions about its relationship with others. Can Xi solidify the power needed to implement reform without being tempted by the excesses of power projection that have undermined authoritarian regimes for centuries?[39]

Setting the Stage: The American Perspective

Like China, the United States has faced several key economic transitions since the end of World War II, all of which had important implications for its role in the world. As with China, three transitions stand out—the Great Inflation of the mid-1970s, the shift to an asset-dependent economy in the late 1990s and early 2000s, and the trade protectionism that has been especially evident since 2016. Each of these transitions is deeply rooted in the shifting tradeoffs of America's ever-challenging political economy. And they have all inexorably led toward conflict with China.

Economists still debate the causes of the Great Inflation of the 1960s and '70s. The factors at work ranged from a synchronous boom in the world economy to shortages and double ordering of key industrial materials and commodities, to the quadrupling of oil prices following the OPEC embargo in the aftermath of the 1973 Yom Kippur War. Sagging productivity and inflation-indexed labor compensation added to pressures on the cost side of the equation. And policy blunders compounded the problem. The Federal Reserve, incorrectly diagnosing the initial inflationary upsurge as transitory, failed to tighten monetary policy until it was far too late.[40] Meanwhile, fiscal authorities mistakenly believed they could finesse a classic "guns and butter" tradeoff—spending aggressively on the Vietnam War while also funding the Great Society.[41]

The results speak painfully for themselves. Inflation, as measured by the Consumer Price Index, which went from just 1 percent in the early 1960s to 5.5 percent by the end of that decade, surged to 10 percent in 1974–75, and then peaked at 13.5 percent in 1980.[42] It took a new and tough chairman of the Federal Reserve, Paul Volcker, to raise interest rates enough to bring runaway inflation under control. The Fed's benchmark policy interest rate, the federal funds rate, was pushed to a record 19 percent by early 1981, sending the US economy into its then steepest recession since the end of World War II.[43]

At the time, this was the greatest test for the modern, post–World War II US economy. The pressures of rising inflation, high interest rates, and sluggish expansion of consumer incomes led to a pronounced weakening of economic growth. This era of "stagflation"—unusually weak economic growth coupled with high inflation—led to a major rethinking of America's economic strategy.[44] Tightening monetary policy was only part of the solution. By the early 1980s, with the US economy increasingly desperate for new sources of support, politicians responded with tax cuts and a push for deregulation in the hope of restoring vitality to an unencumbered free market system.

It wasn't enough. As it turned out, the United States was just like China in one critical respect—it needed a new source of growth. But this was not easy to uncover. Unlike China, the United States viewed foreign trade as a threat to its prosperity, symbolized by a growing trade deficit that had opened in the early 1980s. Blaming that problem on an overvalued US dollar and alleged unfair trading practices of a mercantilist Japanese economy, the United States orchestrated the so-called Plaza Accord of 1985, forcing Japan to raise the value of its currency and accept restrictions on US imports of Japanese-made goods.[45]

That wasn't enough either. The dollar came down, the Japan threat was defanged, but the US economy still struggled. Eventually, China stepped up and delivered just what the United States needed: cheap goods, benefiting American consumers, and readily available capital, an important source of budget deficit financing for the US Treasury. US merchandise imports from China rose from just $1 billion in 1980 to $12 billion by the end of the decade—and currently stand at over $500 billion.[46] Chinese purchases of long-term US debt have followed an even steeper growth trajectory, rising from only around $200 million in 1989 to about $1.1 trillion in 2021.[47]

That was only half the story of America's search for growth in the 1980s.

The other half reflects the powerful impacts of the Fed's easing of monetary policy as inflationary pressures subsided. After reaching a record level of 19 percent in 1981, the federal funds rate was gradually lowered until, by late 1986, it was below 6 percent—and the US economy predictably responded with a strong recovery. It was, indeed, "morning again in America," as President Reagan, taking credit for what the Federal Reserve had done, proclaimed to a relieved nation.[48] The American public had discovered the power of the interest rate lever in shaping the downs and the ups of the US economy.

The purging of the Great Inflation was a mixed blessing. It did surprisingly little to support the American middle class; median wage income entered a decades-long period of stagnation from which it has barely recovered. But the swift reduction in interest rates unlocked the door to a powerful shift in the structure of the US economy, from income-driven growth to asset-dependent growth. That allowed wealthy investors to reap a bonanza, as the value of financial assets, both stocks and bonds, surged in response to a powerful disinflation and an associated plunge in interest rates.

That was icing on the cake—for those who could afford it. Asset owners took advantage of what economists have called "wealth effects"—in effect, spending a portion of what they believed would be a permanent appreciation in their assets' value. Financial market deregulation added an important new twist, enabling homeowners to take out second mortgages and draw down newly established home equity credit lines in order to extract purchasing power from their largest asset holding—their homes. They then used that newfound purchasing power to support personal consumption. In other words, frothy financial markets and the asset appreciation they generated filled an important void left by stagnant wages. Notwithstanding the mounting inequality that arose from these developments, a new source of economic growth had finally been uncovered. By the late 1990s, the transition from the income- to the asset-based economy was complete.

Alas, that didn't work out so well either. Increasingly frothy US financial markets formed successive bubbles in stocks, residential property, and ultimately credit itself. Unfortunately, income-stretched American consumers had gotten used to supporting their lifestyles from the confluence of psychological wealth effects and the direct extraction of capital gains on their housing investments. When those bubbles burst—equities in 2000, property in 2006, and credit in 2008—asset-dependent American consumers were left in the lurch and pulled back sharply on spending. These spending adjustments were relatively small after the dotcom bubble burst in 2000. But after the housing bubble popped a few years later, followed by credit soon after, the ensuing consumer recession was the worst on record.[49] The United States was, and still is, in need of a new source of growth.

The Political Economy of Saving Disparities

This brief recapitulation of the Chinese and US economies over the past forty-five years has an important recurring theme—both nations are constantly searching for new sources of economic growth. The challenge for America was very different from that confronting China in one critical respect: America is a wealthy nation trying to do too much with too little—in effect, living beyond its means. China, by contrast, was unable or unwilling to share the dividends of its newfound growth with its vast population of potential consumers. This led to profound saving disparities between the two nations that have had lasting and important implications.

These saving contrasts are stark by any standard. China is the largest saver in the world and America is the most saving-deficient economy in the world. While the saving gap has narrowed a bit in recent years, the disparity remains enormous. In 2021, total domestic saving in China was 45 percent of its GDP, nearly two and a half times the 19 percent rate in the United States. Looked at in US dollar terms, the gap is equally large: Chinese domestic saving was $7.5 trillion in 2021, compared to just $4.6 trillion in the United States.[50]

Domestic saving is a broad measure that includes the combined saving of households, businesses, and governments. Chronic government budget deficits in the United States are a major drag on domestic saving, but individuals and businesses also save considerably less than their Chinese counterparts. China is a high saver pretty much across the board—excess saving among corporations and households is only minimally offset by government-sector deficits.

The figures cited above represent what is called gross saving—saving that includes the depreciation (wear and tear as well as obsolescence) of each nation's aging capital stock. Stripping out depreciation provides a measure of net saving, the money that presumably is left over to fund the actual growth in a nation's productive capacity. In the United States, the net domestic saving rate was just 3.2 percent of national income in 2021, half the 6.3 percent norm of the final three decades of the twentieth century. That leaves America with very little domestic saving available to fund growth in its economy.

While there are no official estimates of the net saving rate in China, there are good reasons to believe it is in the 20 to 30 percent range, or some 7 to 10 times that in the United States.[51] This extraordinary differential in net saving rates has important implications for the two nations' relative growth prospects. China is much better able to fund investment in productive capacity, research and development, and human capital—all of which bear critically on productivity, indigenous innovation, and competitiveness. Savings-short America is at a distinct disadvantage on all these counts.

These saving disparities do not arise out of thin air. For the United States, federal budget deficits are a major culprit, but so is the asset-dependent US economy. Asset holders, especially freewheeling American consumers, had become convinced that continued appreciation of their stock market and real estate holdings could take the place of saving out of labor income. In response, the income-based personal saving rate plunged from about 13 percent of disposable personal income in late 1982 to just 2.5 percent in mid-2005, at the height of the housing bubble. In the new asset economy, there apparently was no need to save the old-fashioned way.

There is, however, an important catch. Any economy—even the ever-creative asset-dependent US economy—needs saving in order to invest and grow. Over the long haul, asset-dependent saving doesn't provide that support—especially if it is underpinned by bubbles, which eventually burst. That became glaringly evident in the early 2000s. The declines in income-based saving, in conjunction with seemingly chronic government budget deficits, pushed overall domestic saving into negative territory from 2008 to 2010, from which it had recovered to only a 3.2 percent rate by 2021.[52]

At this point, America's relationship with other nations comes into play. Lacking in saving but still wanting to invest and grow, the United States must import surplus saving from abroad. And to attract the foreign capital, it must then run balance-of-payments deficits with the rest of the world that are invariably accompanied by trade deficits. Given the size of the US economy and the scale of its saving shortfall, these trade deficits can be very large, involving a multiplicity of America's trading partners as detailed in Chapter 4.

This takes us to a critically important consequence of the trade deficits that have arisen out of the shortfall of domestic saving. Americans don't like trade deficits and for good reason. On one obvious and important level, trade deficits are emblematic of leakages in any economy. They represent a loss of output, jobs, and income growth to trading partners, replacing economic activity that could have occurred at home. US politicians have repeatedly seized on the distaste for this leakage as justification for anti-trade agendas that promise to plug the leak and bring jobs back home. Ronald Reagan and George H. W. Bush prosecuted this case against Japan. Donald Trump took this argument to an entirely new level, promising to Make America Great Again by launching a trade war against China.

Well-practiced in spin and motivated by political expedience, US leaders have left out a crucial part of the story: they are to blame for the largest portion of America's domestic saving shortfall. Government budget deficits show up in the national income accounts as negative saving. America's federal government has recorded budgetary shortfalls every year since 2001, and in fifty-four of fifty-nine years since 1962.[53] Without these persistent deficits, there would be considerably less need for foreign capital, and for trade deficits as the price for receiving that capital. US politicians implicitly argue that America can have its cake and eat it too—that is, they support eliminating trade deficits by any means possible, including an overt trade war, while perpetuating the very spending that gives rise to the trade deficits in the first place. US politicians prefer to proclaim their innocence and pin the blame on others—Japan in the 1980s, and China today.

This unwillingness to accept responsibility for the consequences of profligacy has been an especially easy sell in the arena of public opinion.[54] But there is an important economic context to this development. The shift in America's saving posture is part of a broader continuum. The disinflationary dividends of the 1980s and 1990s had a disproportionate impact on asset markets and on wealthy asset holders. The gains that accrued in the asset economy were used to support both current consumption and asset-based saving.

US politicians were delighted with the initial impacts of this shift, which allowed Americans to live beyond their means, as delineated by the econ-omy's internal income-generating capacity. But as pressures began to build on the middle class, there was a decided populist shift in US politics that has given rise to trade frictions and protectionism. Saving, or the lack of it, emerges as a major culprit in America's saga of relationship conflict, which now has China in its crosshairs.

China's saving story is at the other end of the spectrum. It has far too much saving and needs to figure out a way to put its surplus saving to work, both to drive its economy and to reduce tensions with the United States and other nations.

In the 1980s, of course, China needed plenty of saving to fund its ambi-tious development agenda. In the wake of the Cultural Revolution, the Chi-nese landscape was littered with crumbling factories and roads.[55] It lacked the modern productive capacity and infrastructure required for assembly and distribution to customers at home and abroad. That had to change quickly if China was to fulfill the export requirements of Deng Xiaoping's reforms.

Thanks to its savings, it did. China's domestic saving rate, which amounted to 33 percent of its GDP in 1980, rose consistently throughout the decade and into the early 1990s, hitting 43 percent in 1994.[56] China stood out among developing economies in seizing the saving opportunity. In 1980, its domestic saving rate was about 30 percent larger than that of the broad aggregation of emerging and developing economies. By 1994, its saving rate was nearly double that of the entire developing world. In the early years of its development takeoff, that saving provided China with the wherewithal for the massive investments required of its export-led growth strategy. Eco-nomics teaches us that saving must always equal investment, and China put that truism to work.

But then China's saving strategy went awry. Aggressive reforms of state-owned enterprises were put in place in the late 1990s. This triggered two major developments that affected national saving—layoffs of over 40 million workers and the dismantling of the "iron rice bowl" that had given its labor force cradle-to-grave social benefits, ranging from shelter and food to education and medical care. The near-elimination of those benefits, under the guise of state-owned enterprise reforms in the late 1990s, was equivalent to a major loss of state-supported saving. That unleashed a powerful surge of fear-driven, precautionary saving to compensate for the benefits formerly provided by the state. And China's domestic saving rate, after coming down a bit in the late 1990s and early 2000s, then soared to 52 percent in 2008.[57]

This was a very destabilizing outcome. By opting for precautionary saving, Chinese households diverted their wage earnings away from discretionary consumption of items like cars, furniture, appliances, and luxury goods. The long-sought goal of consumption-led growth was stymied. The private consumption share of Chinese GDP fell instead of rose, dropping from 46 percent in 2000 to just 34 percent in 2010. China's current account surplus soared to a record 9.9 percent of GDP by 2007, as its surplus saving far outstripped domestic investment.[58] This was the largest international imbalance in the world at the time, prompting many to accuse China of being a destabilizing influence on the eve of the Global Financial Crisis of 2008–9.[59]

Beyond its effects on international finance, China's surplus saving was destabilizing for another reason. It exacerbated the country's relationship problems with the rest of the world. Just as America's shortfall of saving has consistently spawned trade deficits with about one hundred nations around the world, China's saving led to trade surpluses with nearly 160 countries.[60] Aided by a tightly managed currency and accused of unfair trading practices, surplus-prone China was cast in the same role Japan was in the 1980s—that of a currency-manipulating mercantilist. Unwittingly, or perhaps with malicious intent (as many in the West saw it), China's surplus saving posture soured its relationships with the rest of the world.

Whither Saving?

The saving disparities between the United States and China shed considerable light on the relationship problems that have come between the two nations. China plays a key role in filling America's saving void. Prone to surplus saving, China sells its products all over the world, both directly and through its participation in a vast network of global supply chains. For years, the United States was China's biggest foreign customer. How those deficits and surpluses get parsed out among trading partners, let alone measured accurately in a supply-chain connected world, is a complex process that we will return to in Chapter 4.

But recognition of the problem does not guarantee resolution. It is perfectly logical to urge China to save less and America to save more, but it is far tougher for either nation to do that. That seems especially true of the years immediately ahead. In the post-Covid era, America's saving problem is going from bad to worse. With over $7 trillion of fiscal stimulus enacted since 2020, US budget deficits have soared to 15 percent of GDP, enough to push overall public debt up to an average of 103 percent of GDP in the five years ending in 2031, close to the record of 106 percent hit in 1946 in the immediate aftermath of World War II.[61] In the zero-interest environment long perpetuated by an overly accommodative Federal Reserve, the interest expenses of servicing that debt have been negligible, and, consequently, there has been little pressure for fiscal discipline. America's savings hole grew deeper as a result. That might change as the Fed now moves to normalize interest rates to counter mounting inflationary pressures, but congressional resistance to federal budget control remains strong.

In the meantime, low savings will also make the US current account deficit exceptionally large for that same foreseeable future. As a result, trade deficits will remain a serious, even a growing problem for the United States. Contrary to accepted political wisdom, trade wars with individual countries cannot solve multilateral trade deficits with many countries that arise from saving problems. Politicians who promise otherwise, without addressing the saving problem, indulge in the economic version of "whack-a-mole"— squeezing one nation's deficit while another one pops up. First it was Japan, now China. The follow-up question for savings-short America is who will be next.

China has an equally daunting saving problem to address. For years it has stressed "saving absorption"—the need to draw down surplus saving in order to fund an inadequate social safety net that, if realized, would reduce precautionary saving and unlock discretionary consumption, driving the consumerism of Chapter 9. Yet progress has been painfully slow. After peaking at 51.6 percent in 2008, China's domestic saving rate has declined only a bit, to a still lofty 45 percent in 2021. That remains about 11 percentage points higher than the average for all developing and emerging economies.[62]

China knows what it needs to do to temper the stresses that arise from its surplus saving bias. It is sitting on a reservoir of fuel that could hold the key to its ever-elusive new source of growth. If, for example, China brought its gross saving rate down to the average of other developing countries, that would free up $1.7 trillion that could be applied to bolstering its porous social safety net.[63] The dividends of saving absorption could, of course, be considerably larger if China, as a self-proclaimed moderately well-off society, lowers its saving rate still further, to the 20 percent average for advanced economies. It is also in a position to use saving absorption as an instrument of goodwill in addressing its seemingly chronic relationship problems. The increased domestic consumption that would result from reduced precautionary saving would be a bonanza for its major trading partners, including the United States.

There is no secret about what it would take to spark saving absorption in China. Government policy should aim at rebuilding the social safety net that was largely dismantled in the late 1990s. Households would then be able to look to the future with much greater confidence—precisely the incentive they need to divert wage earnings out of fear-driven precautionary saving into discretionary consumption as I stress in Chapter 9. A number of proposed reforms are, in fact, aimed at addressing retirement, healthcare, and other aspects of the social safety net. But China has a long history of over-promising on these reforms. Will it be any different this time?

Knowing the possibility and seizing the moment are two different matters. In clear recognition of this disconnect, Xi Jinping Thought purportedly takes the task of Chinese reformers to a new level. Tackling the saving problem would be an excellent stress test of this new approach to governance. Not only would it boost the long-needed rebalancing of the domestic economy, it would put China in a much better position to address the relationship problems that surplus savers always seem to attract.

2

From Convenience to Codependency

JUST AS THE INTERPERSONAL CONNECTION feeds the human spirit, relationships between economies have long been central to growth and prosperity. There can be no denying the complexity of these interactions in an increasingly globalized world. The political economy of transnational engagement, always a delicate balance, is even more delicate today.

Central to this dilemma is the tradeoff between growth and trade. Politics can not only expand growth opportunities by creating powerful economic unions, as exemplified by the United States and the European Union, it can also spur the mutual gains of trade liberalization. But politics can also drive disunion, as the breakup of the former Soviet Union attests, and spark trade conflicts like the devastating global trade war of the 1930s. The US-China conflict is deeply rooted in the political economy of the balance between growth and trade.

To be sure, trade is not what it used to be. What started out as the relatively simple cross-border exchange of goods that, in the nineteenth century, formed the basis of David Ricardo's theory of comparative advantage—the essential justification for the mutual benefits that rise from trade between nations—has evolved into incredibly complex multi-country assembly and production platforms known as supply chains, or, more formally, global value chains.[1] With this complexity come relationship complications that can exacerbate tensions between nations.

That is especially true of the United States and China. Recent transitions in both economies have destabilized many aspects of their relationship. Transitions not only change the rules of engagement between trading partners but can easily be mistaken for threats that pit one partner against the other. Accidental conflicts can, and do, arise as a result.

The US-China conflict is, first and foremost, a relationship conflict. As in most human relationships, the two nations came together recognizing the benefits of mutual attraction. Over time, the innocence of that first connection led to a deepening and yet more challenging partnership. But something was always missing—mutual trust. We will explore the US-China trust deficit in more detail later in this book, but suffice it to say that there can be little doubt of its importance. Absent trust, the give and take of normal frictions between partners can escalate into blame, scorn, and outright conflict. Without trust, the possibility of a breakup or rupture becomes very real.

This raises important questions about the character of the economic relationship between the United States and China. What is it about the relationship that is so threatened by economic transitions? Why have these threats escalated into outright conflict? Can this vicious cycle be arrested before it is too late?

The New Paradox of Global Trade

Modern economies are far from self-contained. They often lack key resources—raw materials or well-educated, highly-trained labor—so they trade with others to make up for those deficiencies. Ricardian principles of comparative advantage tell us there is great benefit from drawing on the intrinsic strengths and resource endowments of others. It is the essence of the "win-win" mantra that has long been associated with the collective benefits of increased trade between nations. Taking advantage of this is as much a political decision as an economic one.[2]

Yet there has been a revolution in cross-border trade. David Ricardo's classic example of England and Portugal trading cloth and wine for mutual benefit made sense in its day, but not today. Trade is no longer concentrated solely in the cross-border exchange of finished goods that are produced in one country and sold to another. In fact, the very concept of the finished good has changed forever.

From Ricardo's time until about the 1960s, the finished good was basically the output of a domestically contained production process involving some combination of a nation's labor and capital, or workers and raw materials. Today, the finished good comes off an assembly line as the piecemeal combination of numerous components, with inputs from many intermediate production and assembly platforms around the world. This multistage, multination assembly and production process is very different from Ricardo's concept of the vertically integrated manufacturing plant contained within one nation.

The global value chain (GVC), which knits together production and assembly, inputs and components from many nations, is an outgrowth of breakthroughs in information and telecommunications technologies, sharply reduced transportation costs, and a rethinking of the logistics of product-flow connectivity. It has turned the very concept of global competition inside out. This has important implications for all transnational economic relationships, especially the one between China and the United States.

Economist Richard Baldwin assesses GVCs in the context of major shifts in globalization that he dubs "unbundlings."[3] The first unbundling arose when the self-contained village was able to obtain food and other necessities from outside its own geographic area—essentially separating, or unbundling, consumers from producers. As physical transportation costs declined, especially shipping and rail in the nineteenth century, this process of exchange spread to trade between nations.

Baldwin traces the second unbundling to the technology- and logistics-induced fragmentation of the production process into components and parts that are ultimately assembled as finished goods. This is when GVCs essentially separated, or unbundled, producers from nation-states. Whereas the first unbundling fostered competition between nations, the second has led to a denationalization of global competition.[4]

These unbundlings underscore one of the great paradoxes of the US-China trade conflict. National trade statistics are out of sync with GVCs. A product is counted as a finished good when it leaves the final point of assembly for its end-market destination. At the port of embarkation, it is valued at the cumulative factory cost, irrespective of the transformations that occurred at earlier stages of production and assembly in other nations. This means national statistical systems make no allowances for fragmented production and assembly that take place up and down the intermediate stages of the global value chain. Trade statistics, originally designed for bundled, self-contained nation-states, have not been unbundled in an era of GVCs.

The Apple iPhone is the most celebrated example of this. Most iPhones are assembled in Zhengzhou, China, and shipped to the United States from Shanghai at a factory cost of some $240 per unit. With annual domestic sales of about 60 million units, the US statistical system uses that $240 unit cost in valuing the iPhone made-in-China piece of the overall US trade deficit at nearly $17 billion. Yet the actual production that occurs in Chinese factories adds only about $8.46, or 3.5 percent, to the average unit cost of an iPhone.[5] The bulk of the value added comes, in order of importance, from components made in Japan, Taiwan, and Korea, which collectively account for about 55 percent of the iPhone's total factory cost.

The iPhone is the quintessential GVC-enabled product. Yet the US statistical system completely misses this point—as do American politicians. Donald Trump, threatening a new round of tariffs in his trade war in 2019, insisted that "Apple makes its product in China."[6] It would have been more accurate for the president to have said that Apple *assembles* its products in China.

This is not just statistical nitpicking. According to published US trade statistics, China exported some $506 billion of merchandise to the United States in 2021.[7] Yet many of those exports are not goods that were wholly produced in China. Instead, they reflect value added from other nations—components and parts that themselves often originate from complex transnational supply chains. The final products that get shipped from China to the United States come off a Chinese *assembly* line, not a production line. GVCs have effectively transformed China from the factory of the world to the assembly line of the world. That means the made-in-China portion of exports to the United States is considerably less than $500 billion.[8]

Nevertheless, the ever-contentious US-China merchandise trade deficit, which US government statisticians report was $355 billion in 2021, is what gets the headlines in the very public debate over Chinese trade practices. According to official statistics published by the US Department of Commerce, China accounted for 32 percent of the total merchandise trade deficit in 2021, easily the largest piece of America's outsize trade gap.[9] Never mind that China's share has come down in recent years for a variety of reasons, the most important being, of course, the imposition of steep tariffs by the Trump administration starting in 2018. China is vilified for the leakages of output, jobs, and incomes that its alleged unfair trading practices are presumed to impose on the United States.[10] But a significant portion of that blame is exaggerated, as it reflects components, inputs, product design, and other value-added activities that actually come from other nations.

It is now possible to measure GVC-related distortions to trade between nations. Researchers from the Organization for Economic Cooperation and Development (OECD) and the World Trade Organization (WTO) have jointly developed a statistical framework that isolates the value added at different stages in the GVC process; for Chinese exports to the United States, they estimate the overstatement could be as large as 35 percent.[11] That means a more accurate assessment of China's share of the total US merchandise trade deficit could be closer to 20 percent than the 32 percent currently indicated from published government statistics. That is still a large number, but it represents far less leakage than American politicians might want to admit. Like it or not, a key piece of evidence in the case against China is based on an antiquated statistical measurement system that is out of sync with the new reality of GVC-enabled global trade.

This mismatch between widely accepted statistical "evidence" and real-world global trade tells us a great deal about the relationship between the United States and China. Much of the value of foreign products that flow through China on their way to the United States actually represents the production of other nations. Who are those nations? How do they fit into the US trade puzzle? What do they have to say about the true character of the US-China trade relationship? If the trade conflict is to be a "just war"—defensible on moral and ethical grounds—we need objective, fact-based answers to these questions.

Marriage of Convenience

The relationship tale began with Deng Xiaoping's visit to the United States in early 1979. It was the first official mission of a Chinese state leader since the People's Republic of China was founded in 1949. What started out as a formal visit to Washington DC ended up as a sampling of Americana. Deng traveled to Georgia, Texas, and Washington State, visiting companies, inspecting US technology, and dabbling in cultural activities. The photograph of a four-foot-eleven-inch Deng wearing an oversize Stetson cowboy hat while attending a rodeo in Houston made many newspapers' front pages.[12] Despite protests and even an assassination attempt, he gave the mystique of China a very human, almost endearing flavor.

One of the less appreciated but perhaps the most important stops on Deng's tour was his visit to Seattle, Washington, on February 3–4, 1979. Not by coincidence, his plane landed at Boeing Field just south of the city. While in Seattle he met briefly with Henry Kissinger, who had become an old friend of China's after orchestrating President Nixon's historic visit there in 1972. But Deng had come to Seattle for a more important reason. China's economic takeoff needed planes, and as the world's largest aircraft manufacturer, Boeing was eager to pursue the commercial bonanza that a new customer like China might provide.[13]

Sunday afternoon, February 4, was reserved for a field trip to Everett, Washington, twenty-five miles north of Seattle. Deng spent several hours touring Boeing's vast 747 aircraft factory and assembly line.[14] China had already placed orders for three of the aircraft, with promises of more to come. Fascinated by modern technology, especially after a visit to the Johnson Space Center in Houston the day before, Deng saw the 747 through the lens of his newly articulated vision of China's growth potential.

He spent three hours in a golf cart touring Boeing's Everett facility—far more than the thirty minutes he had allotted to Kissinger earlier that day—and was clearly enthralled by what he saw. One observer noted that he "looked just like a little kid."[15] But that childlike fascination had lasting implications. Neither Boeing nor Deng knew at the time that China would become one of the company's largest customers over the next two decades. Nor did US politicians or policymakers appreciate the possibilities for America's largest export business, commercial aircraft.

At the time, back in 1979, there was virtually no cross-border trade between the United States and China. The combined total of exports and imports between the two nations amounted to just $4 billion in US dollars, a fraction of the more than $662 billion of peak value hit in 2018.[16] In 1979, bilateral trade between the two nations was dominated by American purchases of Chinese-made textile products (clothing) and children's toys. US exports to China largely consisted of agricultural products, especially corn, soybeans, and wheat. From the American perspective, imports far outweighed exports—US-China trade was in deficit by about $3 billion. This amounted to a little over 10 percent of the total US trade deficit, which had been fluctuating in a narrow range for several years. It wasn't a particularly big deal at the time. The United States, unworried about trade deficits in general, paid little attention to the Chinese portion of the imbalance.

When Deng Xiaoping boarded his plane (a Boeing 707) to return to China on February 4, he was immediately thrust back into the full agenda that awaited him at home. He had woken up in Seattle that morning with a bad cold and a fever, but as his plane rose in a driving rainstorm from the same Boeing Field where it had landed forty hours earlier, he had an inkling of the opportunities that might arise from partnership with the United States.[17]

So did America. In early 1979, the US economy was mired in "stagflation," and President Jimmy Carter, even before the Iranian hostage crisis later that year, was hanging on for his political life. The United States was searching for a new answer to its mounting economic predicament, while careening toward a full-blown geopolitical crisis. A month before Deng's arrival, Carter had granted full US diplomatic recognition of the People's Republic of China, and he went on to sign a trade and investment accord during the Washington DC leg of Deng's trip. Totaling eight days, including the forty fateful hours in Seattle, the historic visit of Deng Xiaoping left Americans hoping that China could help the United States as well.

Deng's visit was a beginning. Richard Nixon and Henry Kissinger had broken the diplomatic ice with Mao Zedong and Zhou Enlai in the early 1970s, but the economic relationship between the two nations remained largely dormant. Slowly, that began to change in the aftermath of Deng's American tour. By 1985, total US-China trade (exports and imports combined) had increased to about $8 billion, and in 1989, a decade after the visit, trade between the two nations hit $18 billion, with US imports from China exceeding its exports by $6 billion—a bilateral trade imbalance that would only grow larger in the years to follow.

There were also important shifts in the composition of these trade flows. America's appetite for Chinese products broadened out. In addition to clothing and toys, it began buying an increasingly sophisticated array of machinery and other capital equipment, as well as motor vehicle parts, consumer appliances, and key strategic materials such as rare earths, which are essential for the production of batteries and electronics.[18] While imports of Chinese products rose more rapidly in the 1980s than American exports to China, there was a comparable upgrade in the quality of US product flow to Chinese markets. Aircraft led the way: Boeing's order book from China was brimming. The four aircraft on order during Deng Xiaoping's Everett inspection tour in 1979 have since expanded to over two thousand Boeing planes currently in service in China.

The modern US-China economic relationship thus began as a relatively innocent marriage of convenience between two struggling economies. For a while, this paid off handsomely. China needed external demand to support its new export-led development strategy. Exports rose from 6 percent of its GDP in 1980 to 15 percent by 1990 before exploding to a 37 percent share by 2009. The United States was China's biggest foreign customer during this period, accounting for nearly 20 percent of the cumulative growth in Chinese exports from 1984 to 2007.[19]

The United States also benefited substantially from the relationship. With consumer incomes under pressure, low-cost Chinese goods allowed hard-pressed Americans to expand their purchasing power. Adjusted for inflation, disposable (after-tax) personal income rose at a 3.2 percent average annual rate in the 1980s and 1990s; this reflected the positive impacts of a powerful disinflation that pushed the overall consumer price index (CPI) inflation rate down from 13.5 percent in 1980 to just 2.2 percent by 1989.[20] Were it not for China and its impact on globalization, US disinflation would have been less pronounced, and the resulting increase in real, or inflation-adjusted, after-tax disposable income of American workers would have been considerably smaller.[21]

A competitively challenged corporate America also benefited from the boost in earnings that came from low-cost Chinese inputs. The after-tax share of US corporate profits held relatively steady at 5.2 percent of total domestic US income between 1980 and 1999.[22] Absent cost efficiencies arising from the outsourcing of high-cost domestic production to China, along with purchases of cheaper Chinese-made machinery and other factor inputs, there is good reason to believe that these profits would have been pushed sharply lower. It wasn't just a coincidence that a sharp expansion of trade occurred right after Deng Xiaoping's visit. Two needy partners each provided just what the other required at an opportune moment in their shared history.

Codependency

Over the years, the connection deepened. What was at first convenient eventually became essential for both countries to satisfy their increasingly urgent growth imperatives. US demand for Chinese-made products was the anchor of the relationship. Not only did this fuel China's export-led economic growth but it also underpinned the flows of financial capital between the two nations. For China, the importance of this linkage goes back to two important lessons that it learned from the Asian financial crisis of the late 1990s: currency stability is critically important for developing economies, and so are the foreign exchange reserves required to defend currencies during periods of economic turmoil.

China was able to sidestep the sharp devaluations that took down other rapidly growing Asian economies during that crisis. Its relatively closed capital account shielded its embryonic financial markets from global turmoil, preventing its currency from being attacked by speculators.[23]

Eventually, financial reforms, including a gradual opening of its capital account and shifting to a market-determined exchange rate, became important elements of China's development agenda. Ever-cautious Chinese officials have long stressed that any such adjustments should be gradual and tightly managed. That meant Chinese currency managers would keep much of their foreign exchange reserves in dollar-based financial assets like US Treasury securities in order to hold the renminbi in a tightly controlled range versus the dollar.[24] Since the late 1990s, when China had less than

$200 billion in currency reserves, it has boosted the overall value of its official foreign exchange reserves to over $3.2 trillion; while this is down from the $4 trillion high of 2015, it remains more than ample to defend the currency from speculators and shield China's economy from a loss of export momentum that might arise during a global crisis.[25] China needed US dollars to execute this strategy.

The United States is a major beneficiary of China's preference for dollar-denominated assets. In large part, as we saw in Chapter 1, that is because the United States lacks the domestic saving it needs to fund its budget deficit, fixed investment, and, ultimately, economic growth. By investing heavily in dollar-based assets, China is effectively lending a significant portion of its surplus saving to a savings-short United States. Chinese Treasury holdings of long-term US Treasury securities are currently around $1.1 trillion, slightly below Japan's stake of $1.3 trillion.[26] Most believe China keeps about 60 percent of its foreign exchange reserves in dollar-based assets, which would imply total holdings of US securities—Treasuries, agency credits (Fannie Mae, Freddie Mac, and Ginny Mae), corporate bonds, equities, and short-term deposits—in the $1.8 trillion range, more than 60 percent higher than what is captured in US Treasury statistics.[27]

The United States also benefits from China's rapidly growing demand for US export products. In 2000, China accounted for just 2 percent of total US merchandise exports. Over the next two decades, US exports to China grew at an average rate of 12 percent a year, faster than export growth to any other country. By 2021, China accounted for nearly 9 percent of total US merchandise exports, exceeded only by America's two neighbors, Canada (18 percent) and Mexico (16 percent).[28] As America's third largest and most rapidly growing export market, China has played a strong, though largely unappreciated, role in supporting US manufacturers and their workers. Yet many prominent politicians believe incorrectly that China is a small and relatively inconsequential market for US exports.[29]

Consequently, there is a compelling case for viewing the US-China relationship through the lens of an economic codependency. China depends on the United States for export demand and for financial support of its currency. The United States depends on cheap Chinese imports to buttress consumer purchasing power and business profits, and also depends increasingly on Chinese demand for US exports. And the United States needs Chinese capital to compensate for its profound shortfall of domestic saving. By 2010, this had become a robust two-way relationship, with both nations benefiting from their dependency on the other.[30]

Codependency is also a visible manifestation of China's broader relationships with the rest of the world. The Chinese economy has become tightly woven into the fabric of an increasingly globalized world. But the weave is not without some important loose threads. Starting in the late 1990s, a series of global crises raised fundamental questions about the staying power of globalization. Contrary to the promises of a new source of resilience, globalization promoted a contagion of cross-border dislocations in financial markets and global trade flows that became a new source of vulnerability to interdependent economies. China, mindful of any source of vulnerability, especially after the Global Financial Crisis of 2008–9, began to rethink its excessive reliance on the global economy, on globalization.

This rethinking gave rise to China's new strategic focus on self-sufficiency—a shift away from external demand toward new sources of internal demand, such as consumer spending. As noted in Chapter 1, Premier Wen Jiabao planted the seeds of this rethinking with his famous "Four Uns" critique in 2007. Xi Jinping then crystallized, or rebranded, this effort in 2019 as a "dual circulation" strategy, featuring support from both internal and foreign demand.

These efforts pose a major challenge to US-China codependency. By boosting internal consumption, they have the potential to reduce China's surplus saving, which would then exacerbate pressures on savings-short nations like the United States. For the United States, whose aspiration to grow without saving had led it to count on borrowing some of China's surplus, Chinese self-sufficiency was not without potentially serious consequences.

The tensions now in play in the US-China conflict are an outgrowth of these contrasting perspectives. For China, growth and development have long been of paramount importance to the rejuvenation of a once powerful nation plagued by a legacy of instability. Initially, it turned to its trading partners in the West to support that rejuvenation. This worked especially well for the United States, which had growth problems of its own. But then China began to rethink its strategy. That reassessment has destabilized the

connections that underpinned a deepening codependent relationship between the United States and China. It sowed the seeds of the conflict to
come.

Transition Conflicts

The evolution from convenience to codependency did not come out of
thin air. It arose from key transitions in both the US and Chinese economies that reflect the shifts from one phase of economic activity to another.
Transitions are inherent in the natural process of growth and development,
but in this case, they have unsettled the relationship between two codependent partners. Understanding the complexities of relationship transitions
is key to unlocking the forces at work in the US-China conflict.

In broad terms, the transition from convenience to codependency reflects an important change in the depth of the relationship between partners. The convenient relationship reflects *shallow* economic connections, in
which cross-border trade and capital flows make up relatively small shares
of each partner's external linkages. A loss of partner support from shallow
connections is largely inconsequential. Codependency, by contrast, is underpinned by *deep* economic connections in which partners are linked by disproportionately large shares of their total trade and capital flows. With deep
connections, partner support becomes strategically important for both nations. A loss of that vital support is threatening and potentially destabilizing.

Conflict rarely arises from disturbances to the shallow connections of a
convenient relationship. They are bumps in the road or, at worst, a minor
detour. Disruptions to the deeper connectivity of codependency have far
more significant impacts on trade or capital flows, or both. Partners that
are heavily reliant on such external support also tend to have unstable economies—such as the saving imbalances that afflict both the United States and
China; these imbalances can make disruptions of deep connections very
destabilizing. That is especially the case for an asymmetrical disruption—a
transition in one economy that is not matched by comparable adjustments
in the other. Such an outcome changes the terms of engagement between
two partners in a relationship, an especially threatening development that
plays on mutual vulnerabilities.

When we see it through this distinction between shallow and deep connections, the US-China conflict comes into sharper focus. While the nations have very different economic systems, they are similar in one critical respect: they developed deep connections with each other in order to address important economic challenges. Both countries have sought external solutions to internal growth problems. And that is where the problems have arisen for both—their external responses to transition imperatives have been directed at each other.

Framing its strategy through Deng Xiaoping's mantra of "reforms and opening up," China drew heavily on the deep connection of receptive US demand to boost its exports, which in turn set off an extraordinary burst of Chinese growth and development. From the US perspective, a deep connection with China enabled America to solve three major economic problems—expanding hard-pressed consumer purchasing power by substituting low-cost goods from China for higher-cost goods made at home; funding outsize budget deficits with Chinese capital; and boosting US economic growth by sharp increases in exports to China. Without these deep connections, there is no telling how long China's growth shortfall or US stagflation might have persisted.

In the late 1970s and early 1980s, both nations initially faced transitional imperatives—reforms and opening-up for China, and stagflation in the United States. And both, in embracing external solutions to these transitional challenges, were willing to share the mutual benefits—a classic "win-win." Transitions and the deep connection of their resolutions were well aligned with both nations' strategic aspirations.

That moment of mutual gratification didn't last. Persistent saving divergences eventually destabilized the relationship, and mutual gratification gave way to conflict. America's trade deficit, an outgrowth of a pernicious US saving shortfall in confluence with China's chronic saving surplus, became a flashpoint between the two nations.

Yet saving disparities were the tip of a much bigger iceberg. For both nations, economic and trade conflicts have been exacerbated by mounting social tensions. The United States and China both suffer from a form of middle-class angst. In America, it shows up as stagnant real wages, mounting inequality, and what has been dubbed the "deaths of despair" (from suicide, drugs, and alcoholism).[31] In China it is manifested through the pressures of absorbing surplus labor from the countryside, an aging population, and inadequate social safety nets. Now both nations face the enduring stresses of the post-Covid era and the risks of escalating global turmoil stemming from a war in Europe. Growth, which has been under pressure in both economies for the past decade, is likely to remain just as challenging in the years ahead. These multiple layers of tension—economic, social, political, and geostrategic—compound the complexities of relationship conflict.

This conflict will further complicate both nations' economic problems. China remains reliant on the United States as an important, albeit somewhat diminished, source of growth for its exports. If US tariffs continue to constrain China's exports to the United States, China will need another source of growth to fill the void, just as it did during the Deng Xiaoping era. At the same time, the US economy is also facing increasingly stiff headwinds from declining productivity growth, a range of demographic issues, and rising debt. It too needs yet another new recipe for economic prosperity. Add in the shared problems of inequality, education, climate change, health, and systemic racial (US) and ethnic (China) biases, and there is little doubt that both nations once again face major strategic challenges to their economic growth strategies.

But can they resolve those dilemmas in the midst of conflict? It will obviously be much tougher for the United States and China to solve their problems by putting conflict aside and turning back toward each other. The United States, which once welcomed low-cost imports from China, now views Chinese sourcing as a threat that must be countered. China views the United States as fixated on containing its development aspirations, a threat that it believes must be countered. Threats and counterthreats make conflict resolution all the more difficult.

All this underscores the likely persistence of a precarious balancing act between external and internal demand that ultimately needs to be addressed by both nations. In one respect, the persistence of that tension exacerbates an already vicious cycle. Yale historian John Gaddis suggested that Mao's practice of "picking fights abroad was a major way to maintain unity at home."[32] Is that still the case for Xi Jinping? Is it also true of America?

The impulse toward national unity motivated to engage in a just adversarial battle could provide an important element of support for both combatants in the current trade war. Does the nationalistic fervor instilled by Xi Jinping require a relationship conflict as the price, or even the catalyst, for success? Were Donald Trump's protectionist tactics really necessary to muster the political support needed to Make America Great Again?

There can be no mistaking the perceived urgency to act. For both nations, challenges to economic growth seem particularly daunting. Under Xi Jinping, growth in Chinese per capita GDP has slowed to just 6.1 percent a year, well below the 8.9 percent average of China's three preceding administrations (Deng, Jiang, and Hu) but certainly better than the 3.6 percent growth trajectory under Mao.[33] It will be up to Xi to convince the Chinese people that a slower growth trajectory is well worth the sacrifice if it represents a long-needed reorientation away from quantity and toward the quality of the growth experience.

America faces similar problems. For entirely different reasons, per capita real GDP growth in the United States has slowed to just 0.6 percent a year since 2007 in the aftermath of the Global Financial Crisis—only about a quarter of the 2.3 percent pace from 1950 to 2006.[34] Time and again, slow growth has exposed economic and social ills at low tide, adding further fuel to conflicts like trade wars. It will be up to US leaders to address America's formidable growth challenges.

Despite these tough questions, there is also hope. Nations pushed to the brink can draw on survival instincts and leadership to find a new way. Deng Xiaoping played that role as a visionary leader in China at a time of great national distress. Paul Volcker did the same as a fiercely independent and disciplined central banker at one of America's most challenging economic junctures.[35] While the two systems of governance are very different, at critical moments they have both been heavily influenced by the interplay between the political economy and the imperatives of prosperity. Can that happen again?

The Relationship Framework

Economic codependency has a deeper meaning that goes beyond quantifying the empirical linkages between partners. With its shallow connections, a marriage of convenience is an expendable relationship with a disarmingly casual sense of commitment. Partners can take it or leave it—they are not lost if it ends. Codependency is far more serious and based on deeply meaningful connections.[36] Partners are heavily invested in each other and reliant on each other's support. As I underscore later in this book, in a codependent relationship, termination—the breakup—has potentially devastating consequences. That is very much the risk for the United States and China, the world's two leading economies who are now embroiled in the classic conflict phase of codependency.

It is a stretch, of course, to apply the diagnostics of human pathologies to economic relationships. Psychology is the study of the human mind and its actions, while economics is the study of the allocation of scarce resources at the individual (micro) and economy-wide (macro) levels. The high priests of economics—usually frustrated mathematicians in disguise—typically look down on the psychological aspects of economic analysis.[37] As in physics, "mathiness" has long been the language of success in economics.[38] Fuzzy concepts like human desires, narratives, and relationships don't lend themselves easily to mathematical modeling. Since they are hard to model algebraically, they are invariably "assumed away" by economists who prefer to characterize individuals and firms as "rational decision makers" operating under conditions of "perfect information."[39] Of course, the very real imperfections of life can hardly be assumed away. Behavioral economics, a newer field, attempts to address this shortcoming of mainstream economics by stressing the impacts of cognitive and emotional factors on economic decision making.[40] Although a few of its practitioners have received great recognition, behavioral economics largely remains an arcane offshoot of traditional economics.

The economic translation of the psychology of codependency is compelling, nevertheless. Codependency is described in the American Psychiatric Association's *Diagnostic and Statistical Manual of Mental Disorders (DSM)* as a "relationship addiction" that often involves putting a lower priority on one's own needs while being excessively concerned with the needs of others.[41] The *DSM* goes on to note the progressive nature of relationship addiction by underscoring an escalating path of conflict that conforms to a "defensive functioning scale" of codependency. What starts as a highly adaptive relationship ultimately ends with a full-blown rupture, the breakup actions of "defensive dysregulation."[42]

It may be a stretch to view America and China from this perspective. Table 1 takes a stab by presenting a synthesis of the psychological and political-economy perspectives of US-China codependency. At a minimum, it is a useful organizing framework for many of the developments, which we will explore in Parts II and III of this book, that underly the false narratives of accidental conflict between the two nations.

Table 1 matches up seven key milestones on the road to US-China conflict escalation with the *DSM* equivalent designation on the defensive functioning scale. The "X" under the two country columns indicates which nation is responsible for sparking conflict at each stage in the conflict continuum. A row with a "double X"—one for each country—designates shared culpability, tit-for-tat retaliation, or both. There is no attempt to render a verdict on fault by calculating a final score of the "blame game"; the *DSM* scale is more about successive steps in a progression of conflict escalation than a ranking of conflict culpability.

The equivalence is far from perfect. In the chapters ahead, I will detail more nuanced aspects of the road to conflict escalation. But it makes good sense to step back and think about the conflict-prone codependent relationship in which this escalation is taking place. Three characteristics of this relationship appear to have put the two nations on a collision course.

First, codependency is inherently *reactive*, with two vulnerable nations quick to respond to the other's cues. From either side, a loss of sustenance from the other tends to get amplified or exaggerated. A savings-short US economy lacks a certain sense of economic self. As such, it feels threatened when China aims to draw down its own surplus saving or divert its surplus capital away from dollar-based investments—the very things America needs the most from China. Similarly, China, lacking in its own internal support of consumer-led growth, feels threatened when the United States puts tariffs on China's exports or sanctions on its most important companies, such as Huawei. China relies heavily on the external demand of American consumers for its products, and on US markets to be receptive to its companies.

Second, codependency tends to evoke *asymmetrical* responses. Often, only one of the partners recognizes the need to change. For economies, self-help

Table 1. Framing the Conflict

DSM Defensive Functioning Scale	United States	China	US-China Conflict Milestones	Conflict Origins
High adaptive level	X	X	Marriage of convenience	Arose from US stagflation and Chinese instability following Great Leap Forward and Cultural Revolution; seeking new sources of growth
Mental inhibitions		X	Rejuvenation	Outgrowth of nationalistic Chinese Dream stemming from "century of humiliation"
Minor image-distorting level		X	Xi Jinping Thought	Less a major strategic breakthrough and more about revisionist ideology and reform implementation; elevates Xi to Mao status
Disavowal	X		Bilateral deficit fixation	More a reflection of macroeconomic saving shortfalls than unfair trade practices
Major image-distorting level	X		USTR Section 301 report	Allegations based on flawed logic and weak evidence; like Japan in the 1980s, politics of blame
Action level	X	X	Trade/ Tech war	Reflects deep existential fears: Chinese fear of US containment and US fear of China's tech dominance
Defensive dysregulation	X	X	Cold War 2.0	Early signs in rhetoric and actions (i.e., tit-for-tat blacklisting); "foothills" of Cold War 2.0

Source for DSM Defensive Functioning Scale: American Psychiatric Association, *Diagnostic and Statistical Manual of Mental Disorders,* 4th and 5th eds. (Washington DC: American Psychiatric Publishing, 2003 and 2013).

might involve a more sustainable growth strategy. In China, this could mean saving less, consuming more, and being more disciplined in implementing economic reforms. In the United States, it might entail living within its means, saving more, and using that saving to fund investment in new capacity, infrastructure, and human capital.

Asymmetry creates problems when one partner changes while the other doesn't. For example, if China finally delivers and shifts its growth structure toward private consumption, services, indigenous innovation, and less surplus saving while the United States attempts to stay the course on consumer-led, savings-short, deficit- and debt-intensive growth, the relationship will be destabilized. A rebalanced Chinese economy, less predisposed toward exports of goods and surplus financial capital, will no longer be able to provide what its needy American partner has come to expect. Conflict arises from the actionable consequences of such asymmetry.

Of course, there is more to asymmetrical relationship shifts than just economics. Shifting political forces are especially noteworthy today, not just in the United States where many believe that democracy is under serious attack but also in China where, as we will see shortly, the political calculus has changed dramatically under Xi Jinping.[43] It is hard to say which political shift is greater—both have the potential to end up as seismic shocks. At this point, it is safe to conclude that the interplay between the political economy of both nations has also proved to be very destabilizing for Sino-American codependency.

Third, codependency is a *progressive* disorder. That is the whole point of Table 1's attempt to align the metrics of the DSM defensive functioning scale with the milestones of the US-China conflict. Since codependency is a reactive disorder, an asymmetrical shift can easily lead to friction and tensions. Changes in one partner's economic growth strategy can be interpreted, or literally felt, as a threat to the other. Lacking in self-confidence, the vulnerable partner counters the threat by blaming the other and evoking a defensive sense of victimization, fueling progressive conflict escalation.[44]

These behavioral responses do not come out of thin air but are an outgrowth of the narratives that underpin human behavior. In the next chapter, I will examine the critical role of the narrative in sparking and propagating economic and political conflict between the United States and China.

In assessing relationship risk, it is critical to determine the veracity of any threat, the validity of the true narratives, and the weakness of the false narratives that destabilize interactions. Sorting out fact from fiction reveals the motives that drive conflict. But irrespective of motive, the implications are clear: the progressive escalation of actions and reactions is inherent to the pathology of codependency—in economies as well as in individuals. What started out as presidential campaign bluster in 2016 has morphed into a trade war, a tech war, and now perhaps a cold war. Predictably, each partner denies culpability and blames the other for the conflict. Escalation has become self-reinforcing, and quite possibly self-defeating.

While it may be a stretch to psychoanalyze economies, there can be no mistaking the dangers of an inherently unhealthy relationship disorder. Social science, whether it is economics or psychology, places great emphasis on diagnosis as the first step to conflict resolution and eventual recovery. Is codependency the correct diagnosis for a deeply troubled US-China relationship? If so, what does that diagnosis tell us about the cure?

3

Two Dreams

STUDYING RELATIONSHIP CONFLICTS can be depressing. Even in the dismal science of economics, there is always a brighter side to the story. Relationships need not end in a downward spiral of conflict. There will always be bumps in the road, but the combination of mutual trust and a willingness to imagine and accept change offers opportunities for conflict resolution and self-improvement—essential for a lasting and rewarding relationship. That is true of human beings as well as nations and their economies.

National dreams speak to possibilities. The American Dream and the Chinese Dream, both rooted in folklore and history, are uplifting expressions of national ethos. The historian James Truslow Adams is credited with popularizing the American Dream during the Great Depression, in 1931.[1] Xi Jinping introduced the modern concept of the Chinese Dream in late 2012, when he first assumed leadership of the Chinese Communist Party.[2] The American Dream was initially more of a literary notion describing a sociocultural phenomenon, whereas the Chinese Dream was a political statement of national purpose by an ambitious new leader.

Both dreams were meant to instill national pride and offer a sense of direction, but there is an important difference of focus. The American Dream speaks of personal opportunity, whereas the Chinese Dream speaks of a nationalistic rejuvenation of a great nation. There is also a difference in context.[3] The American Dream was framed during the worst years of depression, at a time of grave national despair. The Chinese Dream was first expressed at a time of rising national strength.

The two dreams are important to the relationship debate. They speak to matters of individual and national empowerment, freedom and upward mobility, and the balance between strength at home and outward-facing power. They are statements of national values and purpose that draw on the aspirations of two distinct cultures with very different histories.

We know from experience and common sense that dreams are not to be taken literally. They are mixtures of fantasy and bits of reality floating around in the human subconscious.[4] But as political and social statements, the American and Chinese Dreams are grounded in perceptions of reality. To the extent that they reflect each nation's core values, they qualify as national narratives. From a relationship perspective, the challenges arise from the intersection between the two dreams. Do they combine to promote conflict resolution, or work at cross-purposes, exacerbating conflict? Viewing the two national dreams as narratives deepens our understanding of the US-China conflict.

National Visions

In its current form, the Chinese Dream was first articulated by Xi Jinping on November 29, 2012, two weeks after he was installed as general secretary of the Chinese Communist Party. He and other members of China's top leadership, the Standing Committee of the Politburo, were touring the "Road to Rejuvenation" exhibit at the National Museum of China, prominently situated on Tiananmen Square in Beijing. The visit was a carefully choreographed leadership moment.

The massive exhibit, which took up an entire wing of the world's largest museum, started out by telling the story of China's "century of humiliation." Through photographs, documents, and commentary, the first half of the exhibition painted a tragic picture of a proud nation's defeat and occupation by foreign powers in the nineteenth and early twentieth centuries. The second half, accompanied by stirring patriotic music, featured rejuvenation—China's courageous response to the humiliation of invasion and occupation. It extolled the virtues of a nation that overcame adversity, rose up in revolution, and emerged as the People's Republic of China, strong and determined to apply the lessons of one of the most painful periods of its history.

Filled with patriotic fervor after viewing the exhibition, Xi turned to the assembled media and proclaimed, "Realizing the great rejuvenation of the Chinese nation is the greatest dream of the Chinese nation in modern times."[5]

This was not a casual throwaway line. It almost sounded like a national oath of allegiance. Xi's words were focused and deliberate, aimed at making an important political point. The statement was featured prominently in the national media and quickly became seen as a solemn promise to China and the world, emblazoned on mugs, plaques, and posters for all to see (and, of course, buy). It eventually sparked a nationalistic zeal that had not been seen in China since the Cultural Revolution ended in the mid-1970s.

Xi's initial account of the dream was subsequently expanded. An English-language translation of the more complete version reads as follows:

> The Chinese dream, after all, is the dream of the people.
> We must realize it by closely depending on the people.
> We must incessantly bring benefits to the people.
>
> Realizing the great renewal of the Chinese nation is the
> greatest dream for the Chinese nation in modern history.[6]

The years following Xi's introduction of the dream have seen an outpouring of commentary.[7] The addition of the first three lines—a people-centric prelude to Xi's initial statement—is especially noteworthy. The Chinese nation is, after all, the *People's* Republic of China. Framing a national dream without reference to the first word in the country's name would send the wrong message, emphasizing national power over the needs of the people. It could easily be interpreted as a belligerent threat issued by the determined and tough new leader of a rising nation, unconnected to the aspirations of its citizens. The insertion of the first three lines was an attempt to correct that impression. The Chinese Dream is not only about power but about marshalling that power to address the needs of ordinary Chinese people.[8] That correction has been drawn into sharp question by Xi Jinping's subsequent ascendancy as China's most powerful leader since Mao Zedong, a point I will take up in Part III of this book.

For Xi Jinping, this expanded version of the Chinese Dream has become an all-encompassing mantra—a touchstone for his connection to the Chinese populace, and a nationalistic rallying cry. The dream is at once a political statement, a social goal, and an economic target. It offers both inward- and outward-facing implications. It is aligned with the notion of a shared prosperity to China's ambitious development trajectory, initially toward a moderately well-off society and eventually to a Great Socialist Nation. Perhaps most significantly, it underscores China's determination to reclaim its former stature among the leading nations of the world. All this and more, in the name of rejuvenation.

For a rising China, rejuvenation has important geostrategic implications in areas such as military power and alliance building. Xi Jinping's commitment to modernizing the People's Liberation Army (PLA) is particularly important in this respect.[9] The same is true of alliances. The Belt and Road Initiative, Xi's signature foreign policy effort, has China investing in—and exercising influence over—more than one hundred forty nations with a $30 trillion pan-infrastructure program encompassing Asia, large portions of Africa, and Europe, and now reaching into South America.[10] Rejuvenation also has important implications for the domestic economy. China currently accounts for about 19 percent of global output, making it the largest economy in the world by one measure (purchasing-power parity). But that figure is only about half the 35 percent share it held in the mid-nineteenth century. China still has a considerable distance to travel on the road to rejuvenation before it can recapture its earlier position of global economic leadership.[11]

At the same time, the stress on rejuvenation as the essence of the Chinese Dream risks sending a very different message—that China also views itself as having been a hapless victim of foreign mistreatment and subjugation. Had that not occurred, goes this line of reasoning, it would have no difficulty today in maintaining its stature as the world's leading nation. This view presumes that China bears no responsibility for the extraordinary fall from power that occurred during the civil unrest and subsequent demise of the Qing dynasty in the early twentieth century.[12] It also lets China off the hook for the technological autarky that prevented history's leading innovator—from ancient times through the seventeenth century—from participating in the Industrial Revolution of the eighteenth and nineteenth centuries.[13] By fixating on rejuvenation without accepting responsibility for its own plight and subsequent destiny, China risks blaming others for problems of its own making, and embedding a false sense of conflict into the core of the Chinese Dream. As we shall see, it is hardly alone in this tendency.

The American Dream, by contrast, was framed not by a political leader but by a writer and historian, James Truslow Adams. In *Epic of America,* Adams wrote:

> The American dream is that dream of a land in which life should be richer and fuller for every man, with opportunity of each according to his ability or achievement.
>
> It is not a dream of motor cars and high wages merely, but a dream of social order in which each man and each woman shall be able to attain the fullest stature of which they are innately capable and recognized by others for what they are.
>
> . . . If the American dream is to be a reality, our communal spiritual and intellectual life must be distinctly higher than elsewhere, where classes and groups have their separate interests, habits, markets, arts and lives.
>
> . . . If we are to make the dream come true, we must all work together, no longer to build bigger, but to build better. There is a time for quantity and a time for quality.[14]

Written in 1931, this was a rallying cry for national optimism in the depths of despair. The US economy was in the midst of its sharpest economic contraction in its history, which would reduce real GDP by 26 percent from 1929 to 1933 and push the national unemployment rate up to 25 percent.[15]

Undaunted by this grave moment of national self-doubt, Adams urged confidence and hope. For the downtrodden American populace, his words were inspirational, almost spiritual. His invocation of ability-based rewards, social benefits over material wants, and the rejection of class distinctions spoke of an America as the land of great opportunity for all. It was a noble and powerful message at a time of extraordinary hardship and great national need.

Adams's vision would be challenged repeatedly in the decades to follow. Later developments in the United States, especially mounting inequalities in gender and race, middle-class wage stagnation, a multitude of social tensions, and the cravings of an increasingly materialistic society, made his idealistic views look almost naïve. Even so, the dream of a better future became a constant rallying cry for the nation during its toughest moments. And it offered a rich template of possibilities for what could be imagined, if not achieved, under more ideal circumstances.

Nations can hardly be criticized for dreaming of sustained prosperity, of the better life. It is extremely rare, however, that they can all pull it off at once. For many reasons—economic, social, political—paths diverge, leaving many dreams shattered while others are close to realization. The Chinese Dream and the American Dream reflect the two nations' sharply diverging trajectories over past centuries. Yet there are also some striking similarities. Like Xi's vision, the American Dream can also be framed from both inward- and outward-facing perspectives. The introspective implications have been shaped by a generational progression in living standards, great progress in eradicating poverty and disease, and the material trappings of wealth—provided, as Adams insisted, those rewards are aligned with ability and effort.

As seen from the outside, the American Dream has long been couched in terms of the nation's opening its borders to foreign immigrants. Viewed from the inside looking out, America's military supremacy speaks for itself.[16] From either perspective, the American Dream has long stood for the concept and ideals of opportunity and strength of national character as protected under the rule of law, with an emphasis on fair outcomes.

Adams's portrayal of a nation seeking quality over quantity also resonates with strategic challenges currently facing China. There is a time, Adams stressed in his portrayal of the United States, to emphasize each. The same is true in China. The hyper-growth recipe of Deng Xiaoping has given way to the slower, higher-quality growth prescriptions of Wen Jiabao and Xi Jinping. As economies develop and mature, they are expected, almost beckoned, to focus more on quality. In the end, for both nations, there is far more to the dreams of prosperity than growth for the sake of growth. Adams stated that explicitly, while Wen and Xi admitted it implicitly.

Neither dream, of course, comes with a guarantee of realization, especially when relationship conflicts put pressures on both nations. Seen through the lens of codependency, the aspirations of the Chinese Dream may be at odds with those of the American Dream. The friction comes from the core of the dreams—people-centric aspirations of two very different nations at different stages in their economic development, each with an unfortunate tendency to blame others for its problems. With codependency already spawning tensions and conflicts over saving and trade imbalances, the growth underpinnings of both the United States and China are more precarious—complicating the promises of their national dreams.

Significantly, national dreams are intended to be forward-looking in their messaging of aspirational goals. Anchored in moments of great despair and humiliation, the national dreams of America and China both offer uplifting trajectories intended to leave their difficult histories behind. The two dreams are works in process. As a once poor, now middle-income society, China still has much to accomplish in its development and quest for prosperity. As a wealthy nation, the United States faces tough structural headwinds to maintain its prosperity and stay the course of economic growth.

We should not think of these dreams solely in economic terms. A nation's aspirations can be shattered if its economic trajectory is misaligned with its political system. Governance and leadership can be decisive in nurturing the political economy of national dreams.

Rethinking Prosperity

Neither the American nor the Chinese Dream is a static snapshot of where the respective nations stand today. Nor are they backward-looking celebrations of what has already been accomplished—America's fifteenfold increase in per capita income over the last 150 years or China's twenty-five-fold increase over the past forty years.[17] The dream is a forward-looking vision of the possible, no matter how tough or uncertain the prospects of achieving it.[18]

Economists, politicians, and policymakers tend to quantify the realization of dreams by a nation's gross domestic product, or GDP. There are well-known flaws in this approach, both as a measure of past performance and as a gauge of what lies ahead. The international system of national income accounts has long been criticized for ignoring negative externalities such as environmental degradation, traffic congestion, litter, worker safety, chemical and nuclear waste, and climate change.[19] Aggregate GDP also tells us little about the distribution of national income. It is blind to considerations of equity and equality. Significantly, GDP-based metrics tend to place greater emphasis on the quantity of economic growth (its scale and speed) than on the quality of that growth.

These important drawbacks aside, the GDP filter sheds much light on a nation's aspirational growth trajectory. It draws out the key dimensions of credibility and feasibility, versus the possibilities by which dreams are typically framed. Dreams are fantasy on one level but provide the basis for a reality check on another level.

For China, the reality check will come from its efforts to transform a powerful growth model along the lines of the rebalancing envisioned by Wen Jiabao. If it can deliver on this daunting and complex transformation, it could triple or quadruple per capita incomes between 2021 and 2049, and the centenary goal of the Great Modern Socialist Nation would be within sight.[20] Realizing the Chinese Dream probably requires nothing less.

A similar reality check looms for the American Dream, especially in light of the American economy's relatively sluggish performance of late. After fifty years of 3.7 percent real GDP growth from 1950 to 1999, growth slowed to just 2 percent between 2000 and 2021. Had the US economy stayed, instead, on its 3.7 percent growth trajectory, by 2021 real GDP would have been $8.5 trillion, or 44 percent, higher than it actually was.[21]

This shortfall poses an obvious and important dilemma: Can the American Dream continue to be realized if the US economy is growing at just 2 percent a year? Or does it require a return to the heady 3.7 percent growth path of yesteryear? Is there an acceptable compromise?

It is reasonable to surmise that for much of the population, 2 percent growth no longer solves the equation for realizing the American Dream. Lifting the economy's longer-term growth rate back into an intermediate range—somewhere in the 2.5 percent to 3 percent vicinity—seems like a far more acceptable outcome. How can this be done?

The answer opens up a wide range of possibilities. Ultimately, it involves resurrecting the country's increasingly anemic productivity growth, long recognized as the pivotal source of economic progress. Labor productivity growth in the nonfarm business segment has slowed to just 1.1 percent a year over the 2011–21 period—basically a halving of the 2.3 percent rate recorded from 1950 to 2010.[22] Consistent with the Adams version of the American Dream, economic theory stipulates that over the long haul, workers are paid in accordance with their marginal productivity contribution. Unfortunately, the post-2010 slowdown in labor productivity has left American workers unable to reap the rewards of their long-held dreams.

Economists have debated productivity for decades. There is general agreement that business investment in new technologies is key to equipping workers with tools they need to be more efficient, smarter, and more creative in their daily tasks. That shifts the focus to America's saving challenge, the wherewithal of any nation's internal capacity to fund its capital investments. Yet America's recent saving performance is deficient not only when compared with its own history but even more so when compared with China. For the United States, subpar saving is a bad dream come true.

Economic dreams, of course, are not just about national averages. As Adams stressed in his case for the American Dream, equity and fairness matter a great deal. That is also very much the case in China, where the debate over inequality has taken on new importance. That raises critical questions about disparities in the income and wealth distribution as impediments to realizing both the Chinese and the American Dreams. Inequalities within national populations tend to foster resentments and undermine harmony, and may ultimately corrode the national unity that shared dreams require.

There can be no mistaking the growing concentration of income and wealth in both the United States and China. As of 2015 (latest available data), the top decile of the Chinese income distribution accounted for 41.7 percent of total income.[23] While that's down slightly from the peak of 43 percent in 2011, and below the 46 percent share of the United States in 2015, it is well above the 31 percent average share China recorded in the 1980s and 1990s. A comparable skewing is evident in both nations' wealth distributions. In 2015, the upper decile of the Chinese wealth distribution owned a record 67 percent of total wealth, a dramatic increase from the 42 percent aver-

age share from 1980–99 and closing in on the 73 percent wealth share of
America's upper decile in 2015.[24]

Rising inequality in a developing country like China is very different
from its equivalent in a wealthy nation like the United States. As Deng Xiaoping counseled in the 1980s, early-stage economic development should
not be expected to spread its benefits evenly across all strata of society.[25] He
stressed China's eventual need to shift the rewards of economic growth
from the early beneficiaries of development to the segments of society that
initially had been left behind. This was an obvious but important point.
It should hardly be surprising if the initial dividends of prosperity in any
developing nation accrue disproportionately to the more highly educated,
technically adept, geographically advantaged segments of the workforce.
The hope is that development and poverty alleviation eventually spread to a
broader cross-section of the population.

This sequencing of economic development as stressed by Deng is the
focus of Xi Jinping's recent "common prosperity" campaign, which underscores the need to reverse the widening disparities of China's income and
wealth distribution.[26] There are signs that China's income and wealth distribution has been shifting geographically as the initial gains in eastern
urban areas have begun to spread to the rest of the country.[27] Yet Xi's new
emphasis on common prosperity, which will be taken up in Part IV of this
book, has caused consternation around the world.[28] For a Chinese nation that
has seen rising inequality in its overall distribution of income and wealth,
the new common prosperity campaign implies something more.

Unlike Deng, Xi's emphasis has been less on geography and more on the
shifting character of the Chinese wealth distribution. With good reason. By
2015, total Chinese wealth had risen to 7.1 times the level of income generation.[29] That is far in excess of the ratio of 4.7 in the United States, and fully
65 percent higher than the average wealth-to-income ratio of 4.3 that China
recorded in the 1980s and 1990s. While the surging Chinese real estate
market appears to have been particularly important in pushing up the pace
of wealth creation in relation to income generation, there was nothing common about China's newfound prosperity.[30] Rising wealth inequality had become a glaring excess in the so-called harmonious society.

This development underscores the split character of the economic rewards associated with the Chinese Dream. The material trappings of asset ownership associated with urbanization and land reforms have far exceeded the gains in labor income generation stemming from increased employment and higher real wages. In this important respect, the Chinese Dream mirrors shifts evident in other increasingly asset-dependent economies around the world. By taking aim at the excesses of wealth creation, Xi Jinping's new focus on common prosperity marks an abrupt break from the past four decades. It could well reframe the aspirational objectives of the Chinese Dream.

Rising inequality also threatens the American Dream, but for different reasons. The growing bias away from shared prosperity in the United States is traceable to many factors, including a weakened public education system, urban and social decay, substance abuse, deteriorating family structures, and a system that has skewed rewards away from labor and increasingly toward owners of capital. While a rising tide of rapid economic growth never lifts all boats equally, the post-2000 growth slowdown has certainly exacerbated social inequities and, for many, drawn the promises of the American Dream into serious question.[31]

Any national dream conveys optimism about the future, but there are of course no guarantees. Nor is there any guarantee that two nations enmeshed in a codependent economic relationship will both realize their respective dreams. My previous book, *Unbalanced*, argued that the best chance at shared prosperity would come from a synchronous rebalancing in the economic structures of the United States and China. That has yet to happen.

Ultimately, the codependency framework suggests that the shared needs of the US and Chinese economies are both a blessing and a curse. For years, relationship benefits far outweighed the costs, providing mutual reinforcement of both nations' growth imperatives and support to the realization of their national dreams. Each economy relied on the other to help fulfill its growth aspirations. Initially, it was a marriage of great convenience.

But in the end, the marriage was neither convenient nor sustainable. Conflict is now the new norm, and it has the potential to draw both the Chinese and the American Dreams into serious jeopardy. Few saw this coming. In my 2014 book, I referred to such a possibility as only a "bad dream"— noting, optimistically, that bad dreams rarely come true. Unfortunately, as

I warned in a fictional account of a bad-dream sequence, there are rare exceptions—like trade wars—when bad dreams could actually come to pass. My nights are now restless with the cold sweats of that earlier dream.

National dreams are cut from different cloths. Their contexts are very different for America and China—a wealthy incumbent power and a rapidly rising, increasingly prosperous emerging power. Yet despite important differences in the systems that govern both the growth and distribution of economic gains, they share one critical challenge—solving a daunting growth problem without imposing hardship on others. The United States and China rely on different dreams to guide their journeys. Fulfillment of one dream need not preclude fulfillment of the other.

Narrative Identity and Conflict

The origins and history of the American and the Chinese Dreams reveal much about the ethos of the two nations. But they raise deeper questions: What is the purpose of a national dream? How does it fit into the broader discourse of politics, society, and economics?

There are, of course, no simple answers. Dreams can convey unifying, patriotic aspirations for nations, mantras for politicians, incentives for entrepreneurs and risk-takers, and promises of opportunity and fairness that offer hope to ordinary people. They can also touch on relationship issues arising between countries. But whatever the focus, the national dream is basically a story, a narrative of the possible.

Yet a national narrative, with all it stands for, is far from a simple story. Academic psychologists define "narrative identity" as an imagining of the future based on an autobiographical reconstruction of the past.[32] This resonates with our previous discussion of the historical roots of the American and Chinese Dreams. For both nations, the aspirations encapsulated in their dreams were conditioned by hard experiences—the Great Depression for America, the century of humiliation for China. In both cases, overcoming these experiences of adversity has shaped the hopes and dreams of a more uplifting future.

The problem lies in the role this reconstruction of the past plays in shaping forward-looking narratives. While time heals many wounds, it also has a habit of blurring and distorting people's memories. For China, rejuvenation lies at the core of its national narrative. Yet as I argued above, China's sense of rejuvenation can cut both ways—as a positive force in urging the nation to overcome its "century of humiliation" and as a negative force in blaming others for self-inflicted problems. The same is true of the American narrative—a Great Depression that took an unprepared nation by surprise, but a national carnage that can also be seen as a self-inflicted collapse following the speculative excess that fueled the Roaring Twenties, which, as many have argued, set the stage for the disaster to come.[33]

This contrast between different reconstructions of history is crucial to the distinction between true and false narratives. I will argue in Parts II and III of this book that the United States and China have come into conflict in large part because each has allowed its narrative identity to be unduly shaped by false narratives, which have arisen primarily out of misplaced and distorted views of their histories.

As Robert Shiller, the champion of narrative economics, has admitted, academic economists often slight the role of narrative in assessing economic problems.[34] Yet Shiller believes that narratives deserve attention because of their impact. They offer a story line that guides reaction, creates support for action, and shapes outcomes. The appeal of a narrative arises from its ability to address an important problem, condition the subsequent debate, and influence the public response.

The narrative's influence on public discourse can spread very rapidly. We can glean insights into this spread from epidemiology, which stresses that the spread of infectious diseases reflects two key considerations—vulnerability of exposed populations and transmissibility.[35] Covid-19 is an obvious and very topical case in point. As a novel coronavirus, for which no natural immunities exist, it was primed to attack a highly vulnerable population. And it became evident very quickly that Covid is highly contagious through airborne particulates.

The US-China conflict is an outgrowth of viral narratives. It plays to the vulnerability of national dreams, the perception of existential threats to each nation's aspirational trajectory. Without their dreams, nothing would be threatened. The vulnerability arises out of the conflicts of codependency and the risks those conflicts pose to the realization of each country's dream.

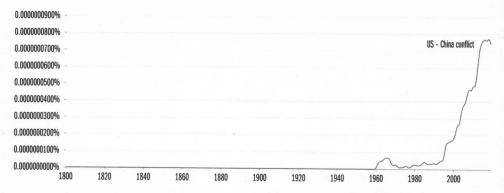

Figure 1. "US-China Conflict"; Google Ngram Book Search from 1800 to 2019. Google Books Ngram Viewer, http://books.google.com/ngrams.

Viral spread, illustrated in Figure 1 by the frequency at which the phrase "US-China conflict" has been used over time as captured by the Google Ngram filter, is a function of the messenger (the "Trump effect" at its peak) and the medium (politicized social networks).[36] Timing and context have played important catalytic roles in compounding this combination of vulnerability and spread. Slower economic growth, the interplay of American populism and Chinese nationalism, and the Covid-related global growth shock have elevated the narrative of US-China conflict to near epidemic proportions. As Shiller points out, the broad constellation of these concerns—especially their self-reinforcing collective impact—is what makes a narrative viral. The conflict between the United States and China touches on the powerful undercurrent of anxiety in both nations.

Epidemiology tells us that contagion eventually fades. As we have learned with Covid, infectious diseases can be arrested by either herd immunity or medical intervention—limiting spread by the creation of natural antibodies that are spawned by the infection of a large segment of the population, or by a vaccine that stops infection in its tracks.

This is where the comparison breaks down. As the Google Ngram search results on the US-China conflict imply, there is no natural immunity against economic problems like middle-class angst and trade wars. Nor, I will argue, do the policy remedies offered to address those problems qualify as economic vaccinations against relationship conflict.

The main arguments of this book hinge on the critical distinction between true and false narratives. Time is the ultimate test of the veracity of any narrative, but it may take a long time for the test results to become available. Meanwhile, considerable damage can be done by the persistent impacts of false narratives that lead to social anger and bad policies. The "Big Lie" of the 2020 US presidential election is the most glaring case in point.

The Big Lie is not an outlier. It turns out that public opinion is far more receptive to falsehoods than to truth. This key point was substantiated in a fascinating 2018 study conducted by researchers from the MIT Media Lab.[37] They examined the differential diffusion of some 126,000 rumors spread on Twitter through 4.5 million tweets and retweets from 2006 to 2017—a period that predates the Big Lie of 2020 and 2021. Rumors were classified as true or false based on the consensus of six independent fact-checkers. The overall results were clear: Twitter-based dissemination of false rumors far outweighed retweets of true stories by six to one.

But the devil of the MIT study is in its detail: the granular characteristics of public receptivity to false rumors. The research team explored several different dimensions of rumor spread—*size* (the number of viewers involved in the cascading circulation of a Twitter-generated rumor over time), *depth* (the number of retweet hops), *breadth* (the maximum number of viewers at any point in time), and *speed* (the time it took to reach "structural virality"). On all four counts—size, depth, breadth, and speed—the diffusion of falsehoods exceeded that of true stories.

These results held across all major information categories. But there is an important twist that bears critically on our assessment of relationship conflicts: the MIT team found that the dissemination of *political false rumors* was at the top of the heap in all dimensions of rumor spread, far outweighing fake news accounts of terrorism, natural disasters, science, urban issues, and finance.

The study also showed that while the use of machine- or robot-generated messages accelerated spread, they had the same impact on the spread of true and false rumors. But since false rumors were retweeted six times more often than true stories, the difference must lie with those individuals who made the conscious decision to propagate the lies. Contrary to widespread impressions, the responsibility for disproportionate dissemination of false narratives lies with human intervention, not with "bots."[38]

Despite the emergence of the truth squad as a new cottage industry of fact-checkers, the viral explosion of false narratives tends to build on itself, with repetition amplified by politics, personalities, and social media. As a result, a false narrative may persist long after it has been disproved by either facts or events.[39]

From the standpoint of relationship conflicts, the false narrative's durability may be one of its most vexing characteristics. Fact-checkers counted 30,573 lies spoken by Donald Trump during his presidency.[40] Yet according to polling data, as of mid-2021, nearly 40 percent of all American voters and almost 75 percent of Republicans still believed his biggest lie—that the November 2020 election was rigged.[41] Not only does the false narrative take on a life of its own, but corrections ring on deaf ears.

This tendency can be illustrated by another Ngram word-search analysis that examines the spread of narratives surrounding the extreme volatility of share prices of Internet companies in 2000. As Figure 2 indicates, the viral attraction to the narrative of ever-increasing "Internet stock prices" dissipated on its own when these prices, which reached record highs in March 2000, fell by an average of 60 percent over the subsequent six months.[42] This was just as epidemiology would have predicted. At the same time, fixation on the notion of a "dotcom bubble" remained an enduring topic of discussion.

This is a perplexing development on one level. The explosive rise of Internet stock prices had led to the expansion of the dotcom bubble and the related false narrative of a "new paradigm" of productivity-enhanced economic growth as proselytized by highly influential people, including former Federal Reserve Chairman Alan Greenspan.[43] Yet when those same share prices collapsed in 2000 and invalidated a key element of that narrative, fixation on the dotcom bubble barely skipped a beat. Clinging to a shattered dream has long been a feature of irrational exuberance in financial markets.[44] With the United States and China both steeped in denial over self-generated sources of conflict, the same could well be the case for the false narratives that have now tainted a once constructive, or at least convenient, relationship.

What is it about human nature that craves the false narrative? While the

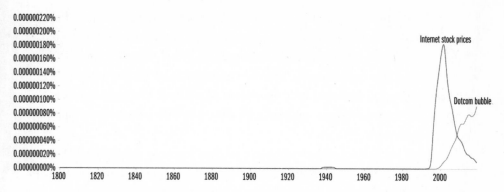

Figure 2. "Dotcom Bubble" vs. "Internet Stock Prices"; Google Ngram Book Search from 1800 to 2019. Google Books Ngram Viewer, http://books.google.com/ngrams.

answers are complex and possibly unknowable, the MIT study gives an important hint. A decomposition of rumor spread—measured by calibrating the "information distance" between rumor tweets and their pre-tweet history—identified the "novelty factor" of false rumors as one of their most appealing characteristics. This may reflect the very human inclination to be thrilled, or as Shiller suggests, to be titillated by the shock value of the unconventional. He adds that the persistence of a false narrative may also be related to the behavioral tendencies of reciprocity and vengeance, underscored by an unwillingness to let go of an accusation and an eagerness to extract punishment or revenge, irrespective of adverse economic consequences.[45]

All of this is relevant for assessing the shock value of the relationship disturbances that have come to characterize the conflict phase of US-China codependency. As America's former "tweeter-in-chief," Donald Trump (before he was banned from Twitter) quickly grasped the amplified impact of a political false rumor in shaping public opinion. Moreover, since the circulation of highly viral political false rumors is traceable more to conscious transmission between individuals than to dissemination by robots, this suggests the US-China conflict is less a machine-driven outcome than one aligned with the extreme rhetoric of its antagonists, which Trump was more than happy to provide. Third, the false rumor has a lasting impact on public opinion, a verdict that resonates with America's record levels of anti-China sentiment.[46]

Whatever the reasons, the false narrative has become an essential element of the social and political discourse, not just in the United States but also in China. Its impact on public opinion can hardly be overstated. False narratives not only destabilize societies in the narrow sense, with lasting impacts on domestic discourse. The false narrative also exaggerates each nation's fear of the other—especially in the case of an inherently unstable economic codependency.

Parts II and III of this book focus on the false narratives the United States and China have directed at each other. I will argue that the false narrative is the crux of their escalating relationship conflict. They drive each nation's perception of the other and distort and destabilize the interplay between them. That has led to erroneous impressions that have become deeply entrenched on both sides of the relationship. False narratives impugn the motives and intentions of each nation in the eyes of the other, coming across as threats that play to the vulnerabilities of national dreams. Most importantly, false narratives set the stage for accidental conflict.

While this is a worrisome development, it is not an entirely surprising one for a codependent relationship. Conflict is inherent whenever two partners engage in asymmetrical behavior. False narratives exacerbate that conflict, turning normal frictions into perceived existential threats, leading to a progressive conflict escalation. But there is an important new twist: the hyper-speed of narrative transmission due to a nearly instantaneous dissemination on vast social networks. That means the impact of false narratives is now of an entirely different order. America and China both need to own up to the urgency of this threat before it is too late. Unmasking the false narratives that have sparked this conflict is an important first step toward resolution.

But by no means would it guarantee a happy ending. Correcting false narratives, or even containing their viral spread, is not a sufficient antidote for poisoned public opinion. The US-China conflict is now in the danger zone. At this point, damage control is not enough—a new framework of engagement is desperately needed.

PART TWO

AMERICA'S FALSE NARRATIVES OF CHINA

THE RELATIONSHIP NARRATIVE IS UNIQUE. Unlike self-focused first-hand accounts, the relationship narrative not only chronicles the behavior of others but stresses the interplay between partners. Perceptions are often biased and distorted, as narratives of others are typically framed on the basis of how we see ourselves. Assessing the motives and actions of partners through the lens of our own experiences is difficult in human relationships but vastly more complex in national relationships. Liberal democracies with common economic, social, and political values find it hard to identify with and assess illiberal authoritarian regimes. The relationship narratives of the United States and China suffer greatly from this perspective bias.

The tendency toward false narratives has long been one of the most corrosive features of the Sino-American relationship. The problems rarely originate from direct people-to-people interactions such as educational exchanges and tourism. But the impacts of government policies on public opinion are a different matter.

Underpinning many of America's false narratives of China is the China-collapse scenario. Like most modern economies, China has its share of potential systemic risks—from debt overhangs and asset bubbles to inequality and environmental degradation. But concerns in the United States run deeper, since many are convinced that China's one-party authoritarian socialist state will ultimately be brought down by social unrest. The key word is "ultimately." That such an upheaval has yet to occur is considered no guarantee that it won't happen in the future.

China has defied that dire endgame because its leadership has adeptly managed the critical balancing act of its political economy—stability versus growth. This strategy has successfully delivered economic development and prosperity in accordance with Chinese values—or, as Party rhetoric has it, Chinese characteristics. That argument falls on deaf ears in the United States.

America has long held the view that China's internal problems will be aggravated by external pressures until the system becomes untenable and the government collapses. That is how the previous collision between two incompatible systems, the Cold War between the United States and the former Soviet Union, ended. With tensions between the United States and China now strikingly reminiscent of that earlier period, many believe that a new cold war signals the beginning of a comparable endgame.

The war in Ukraine is a new and worrisome complication, especially if China aligns itself with Russian aggression in accordance with the "unlimited partnership" agreement reached between Vladimir Putin and Xi Jinping in February 2022. But there is an important twist to a new cold war whether it involves one or two adversaries for the United States. America's economic strength in waging the first cold war should not be conflated with its much weaker economic position heading into conflict with China, either alone or with Russia as its partner. There is no guarantee that the economic triumph of the United States in the first cold war is a template for the outcome of a second one.

The US-China trade war, initiated by Donald Trump and sustained by the

Biden administration, provides an important real-time example of the false narratives underpinning external pressure on China. America has long worried about large bilateral trade deficits as costing it output, jobs, and income. Just as Japan was considered the culprit thirty years ago, China is vilified as the threat today. Yet to the extent that America's bilateral trade deficits are a symptom of its shortfall of domestic saving, trade conflicts can also be viewed as an outgrowth of false narratives and a foil for the deeper political clash between two systems.

But bilateral trade imbalances are just the tip of the iceberg of America's allegations of China's unfair trading practices—from theft of intellectual property and forced technology transfer to unfair government subsidies of its state-owned enterprises and aggressive cyber espionage. The recent Covid blame game, along with human rights concerns over Chinese actions in Xinjiang and Hong Kong, have exacerbated this suspicion. All this takes public impressions of the China threat to a much higher order, increasingly characterized as an urgent challenge to American values. Yet here as well, the allegations rest on weak evidence and a profusion of false narratives. The false narrative is a convenient excuse for America's unfortunate tendency to duck responsibility for its own problems and instead prosecute the propaganda war of an increasingly treacherous blame game.

The perceptions arising from these false narratives, central to America's current anxiety over China, have given rise to a trade war, a tech war, and the early stages of another cold war. This fits the ominous script of the "Thucydides Trap"—the historical tendency of military conflicts between rising and ruling powers. Whispers of a hot war are hardly surprising in such a climate. The Russo-Ukrainian War has elevated those whispers to a shout. Against the backdrop of rising tensions in the Taiwan Straits and South China Sea, the chance of an accidental clash between America and China is growing.

Why must the United States always flirt with conflict to defend its core principles and universal values? Are the threats real or imagined? While America triumphed in the two world wars of the twentieth century and the Cold War that followed, subsequent adventures have backfired—largely because they have been justified by false narratives. From the domino theory of Vietnam, to the weapons of mass destruction in Iraq, to the post-9/11 imperative of nation building in Afghanistan, accidental conflict has become the rule, not the exception. Is the United States making the same tragic mistake in escalating conflict with China?

4

Bilateral Bluster

The 1982 murder of Vincent Chin in Detroit, Michigan, symbolizes
the impact false narratives can have on a nation's social fabric and
political economy. After a bar fight at a bachelor party eight days
before his wedding date, Chin, a twenty-seven-year-old American
citizen born in China and gainfully employed as a draftsman, was
beaten to death by two US autoworkers who were angry over Japan's
supposed threat to their livelihoods. Chin was a tragic victim of
racial and economic profiling—murdered by two men who were
unable or unwilling to make the distinction between a Japanese
and a Chinese person. For them, blaming Asians was all that
seemed to matter.

DONALD TRUMP FIGURED OUT very quickly that narratives require a large
megaphone to influence national sentiment and policy. But a loud voice,
even amplified through Twitter, is not enough—it needs a grievance to in-
cite debate. For Trump, the grievance was China.

Robert Lighthizer was the perfect messenger to prosecute that complaint.
Trained as a lawyer, he had been on the front line of America's trade skirmishes for nearly thirty years. As deputy US trade representative in the early
1980s, he had led the charge against Japan, focusing on a wide range of
alleged unfair trading practices. That earlier combat service was just what
Donald Trump was looking for as he set his sights on China. He appointed
Lighthizer as the eighteenth US trade representative in early 2017.

Lighthizer's marching orders followed the story line of a classic false narrative. As president, Trump was intent on governing by his 2016 campaign credo, "Make America Great Again." The task, as he saw it, was to resurrect a once proud economy from its glorious past—a rejuvenation mission, in some respects, not much different from Xi Jinping's Chinese Dream. To do that, Trump argued, it was necessary to remove the obstacles in America's way. He fixated on China as the most formidable obstacle to America's economic renewal.

On one level, it was a compelling case. Trump's image of the America of yesteryear was framed around a once vibrant manufacturing sector that, in the early 1950s, employed one of every three workers. By contrast, the American manufacturing sector of 2017, when Trump's term in office began, employed only one of every twelve workers, often in aging, antiquated factories. The gaping foreign trade deficit, Trump argued, was a corrosive symptom of America's economic capitulation to China. Not only did China account for by far the largest portion of the US trade deficit, it was accused of using underhanded and illegal practices to achieve this result.

America could not be made great again, Trump insisted, until China stopped robbing American communities and workers of their well-deserved livelihoods. The major difference between Trump and his like-minded predecessors who shared similar views on America's China threat was that he was determined to do something about it. China would change its behavior immediately, he promised, or pay a steep price for its transgressions. So America's newly installed forty-fifth president gave Lighthizer his first assignment: make the case against China—develop a narrative for action.

Lighthizer's Macro Folly

Robert Lighthizer's earlier experience with Japan served him well as he set about this task. Just as he did in the 1980s, he relied on the little-used Section 301 of the US Trade Act of 1974 to make the case against China.[1] In March 2018, the Office of the US Trade Representative (USTR) produced a 182-page "Section 301" complaint that contained detailed allegations of wide-ranging unfair trading practices by China—especially those pertaining to innovation policy, forced technology transfer, intellectual property rights protection, unfair industrial policies, and cyber espionage. Supported by 1,139 evidence-packed footnotes and five appendices, Lighthizer's complaint quickly became the foundational justification for the trade war that was about to begin.[2] It was the essence of Trump's anti-China narrative.

Before we dive into the details of the Lighthizer report, it is important to review the background. The Section 301 complaint pertains to the legality of Chinese trading and economic practices. The allegations are important because they raise fundamental questions about America's macro narrative. How serious is the US trade problem? And how do we assess the role China has played in causing it?

As I argued in Chapter 1, America's trade deficit with China is symptomatic of a much deeper problem: a chronic shortfall of domestic saving. The anemic 2.9 percent net domestic saving rate that prevailed in 2016 when Trump was elected—far below its 7 percent average from 1960 to 2006—left the United States with little choice but to borrow surplus saving from abroad to fund its economic growth. That meant it had to run a chronic balance-of-payments deficit in order to attract the foreign capital. Behind every balance-of-payments deficit is a multilateral trade deficit, an imbalance with a broad cross-section of a nation's trading partners. This isn't an esoteric economic theory. It is an arithmetic accounting identity that applies to any nation.[3]

The United States is no exception to this rule. In 2021, America's multilateral merchandise trade deficit consisted of bilateral deficits with 106 countries, slightly above the average of 100 bilateral deficits over the past decade, 2012 to 2021. China is the statistical villain in this trade carnage. As the overall trade imbalance between the two nations deepened over decades, the Chinese share of the total US deficit grew to a peak of 48 percent in 2015. Over the ten years ending in 2021, China accounted for an average of 43 percent of the total US merchandise trade gap, slightly more than the combined 40 percent share of the next eight largest deficit nations (Mexico, Japan, Germany, Italy, India, South Korea, Canada, and Taiwan).[4]

In recent years, China's share of the overall US trade gap has started to shrink. By 2021 it had fallen to 32 percent, down from the 48 percent peak in 2015 and the lowest since 2008, when it was also 32 percent. That shrink-age is largely an outgrowth of the high tariffs the Trump administration imposed on China in 2018–19, actions we will explore shortly. However, while a reduction in the Chinese share of America's multilateral trade defi-cit is superficially gratifying and in line with the Trump-Lighthizer narra-tive, it is basically meaningless for the overall US economy.

The main reason is that the macroeconomic saving imbalance that caused the trade deficit in the first place has gone from bad to worse—a net do-mestic saving rate that fell from an already depressed 3.2 percent in the first quarter of 2017, when Trump entered office, to just 2 percent in 2020, when his term ended. In a climate in which saving declines, bilateral trade pro-tectionism backfires. Putting pressure on just one trading partner without addressing the underlying saving problem does nothing to reduce the over-all trade deficit. Like whack-a-mole, it only diverts the imbalance from one country to others.

America's recent imposition of tariffs and other sanctions on China shows how this trade diversion plays out. In 2020, the final year of the Trump administration, America's bilateral merchandise trade deficit with China was $108 billion less than it had been in 2018; this "improvement" largely reflected the impacts of Trump's tariffs and Covid-19. But the trade deficit with America's other trading partners expanded by $151 billion over the same period. Particularly sharp deterioration was evident in America's trade deficits with Vietnam, Mexico, Taiwan, Singapore, India, South Korea, and Hong Kong.[5]

Adding together the narrowing of the US-China trade deficit with the wid-ening of the deficits in those benefiting from diversion produces perhaps the most scathing indictment of the Trump-Lighthizer narrative: America's overall merchandise trade deficit has since hit a record of nearly $1.1 tril-lion in 2021, fully $197 billion larger than in 2018 when Trump's trade war began. As the national income-accounting identity implies, the best a savings-short US economy can hope for by squeezing one partner is a diversion of trade deficits to other partners. Blaming China for the US trade deficit is a triumph of political rhetoric over arithmetic. The overall trade deficit, the source of the political angst over the plight of beleaguered American work-ers and their once proud manufacturing companies, got worse, not better.

There is another, equally insidious aspect of this trade diversion. Replacing the Chinese portion of the trade gap with deficits from other nations was the functional equivalent of a tax hike on American companies and consumers. In part, that is because China is a relatively low-cost producer compared with many of the higher-cost beneficiaries of trade diversion.[6] Couple that with the tariff hikes on Chinese imports imposed by the United States—yet another cost increase for US companies and consumers—and the benefits that purportedly arose from squeezing China, according to the Trump-Lighthizer narrative, essentially vanish.

Finally, it is important to stress that under current circumstances, US trade deficits are likely to become even more problematic in the years ahead. To the extent that the US saving shortfall is going from bad to worse in the face of a Covid-related explosion of federal budget deficits, the argument for a bilateral fix looks all the more farfetched.[7]

The macroeconomic case underpinning the Trump-Lighthizer China trade narrative is deeply flawed. As we turn to a more detailed assessment of the key structural allegations in the Section 301 report, it is important to keep in mind that the basic narrative itself is false, based on a major conceptual error. It reflects a politically expedient claim that asserts the impossible— a bilateral solution to a multilateral problem.

On one level, this shouldn't be a surprise—Lighthizer does trade law, not economics. Yet he had the support and counsel of the Trump administration's full complement of economic advisors. Unfortunately, this team was co-opted by politics and missed the basic point.[8] Because it ignored macroeconomics, the essence of Trump's case against the Chinese trade deficit was, in the end, nothing more than bluster.

Forced Technology Transfer

> The Chinese government reportedly uses a variety of tools . . . in order to require or pressure the transfer of technologies and intellectual property to Chinese companies.
> —March 2018 USTR Section 301 report (p. 5)

Forced technology transfer has become the poster child of the US-China economic conflict. In its most basic sense, it refers to China's alleged coercion of American companies to turn over their proprietary technologies as the price for doing business in Chinese markets. This is a very serious charge. It strikes at the core of innovation-based American competitiveness. Forced transfer would give China direct access to advanced technologies developed in the United States, in effect allowing Chinese companies to sidestep any heavy lifting of their own. It is the equivalent of intellectual property theft.

Two key issues need to be addressed in order to assess this claim—the platform on which the transfer allegedly occurs and the forcing mechanism that would coerce a US company to turn over its core technology to a Chinese company.

The transfer is alleged to take place within the structure of joint-venture (JV) arrangements—legally negotiated, contract-bound partnerships between foreign companies and their domestic partners. JVs have a long history in the business world, dating back to ancient trading enterprises in Egypt, Phoenicia, Babylonia, and Syria.[9] China and many other countries, including the United States, have supported JV structures as models to encourage the growth and expansion of new businesses. Currently, more than 5,600 JVs are operating in China, compared to some 200,000 JVs and strategic alliances that have been set up around the world since 1985.[10]

Significantly, US and other multinational corporations willingly enter these legally negotiated arrangements for commercially sound reasons— not only to establish a toehold in China's rapidly growing domestic markets but as a way to cut global production costs by drawing on lower-cost offshore Chinese production and assembly platforms. Contrary to the impression conveyed in the Section 301 report, US companies are far from innocent victims of JV arrangements. They knew what they were getting into and did so of their own volition.[11]

Nor is there any dispute about the transfer of ideas or sharing of common resources that occurs in joint ventures. A JV entails a comingling of people, business strategies, operating platforms, product designs, and yes, production technologies. The goal is for partners to build a strong and competitive business that can stand on its own. The advantage of having a domestic partner in any country is hardly controversial; local knowledge—of markets, supply networks, distribution channels, and regulatory requirements—is critical for uninformed foreign entrants. But the charge in the Section 301 report is not about the voluntary sharing between partners. The allegation is *coercion*—squeezing a contractually bound partner into giving up something it otherwise would not surrender. Related to this allegation is the presumption that sophisticated US multinationals are dumb enough to turn over core proprietary technologies voluntarily to their Chinese partners.

Believe it or not, it turns out that the USTR had no hard evidence to back up this key aspect of the allegation. It admitted this in the text of the Section 301 report, confessing that since the coercion purportedly takes place in the form of oral instructions behind closed doors, there is no hard evidence to support the allegation.[12] The USTR opted, instead, to substantiate the charge through implicit evidence from proxy surveys on technology transfer conducted by trade organizations like the US-China Business Council. The Section 301 report cited evidence from the 2016 USCBC survey (released in 2017) in which respondents complain of discomfort with China's treatment of their proprietary technology.

Once again, the devil is in the detail. In the 2016 USCBC survey that was available when the Section 301 report was prepared, only 19 percent of respondents claimed that they had been pressured to transfer technology to their Chinese JV partners; that means, of course, that 81 percent of companies reported no such coercion.[13] But whatever the motive behind the transfer—forced or unforced—most US businesses did not view it as a serious threat. In a follow-up USCBC survey released in 2018, 99 percent of the respondents indicated that there had been no meaningful deterioration in intellectual property protection over the preceding year.[14] In other words, not only did the USTR lack hard evidence to substantiate the charge of forced transfer, the soft evidence it offered to validate the consequences of the allegation was far from compelling.

There are far deeper problems with Lighthizer's case for forced technology transfer as a leading example of unfair Chinese trading practices. For starters, joint ventures, as a structure for foreign investment in China, have been on the wane, a trend that is likely to accelerate. Such activity peaked in China in 2003 with the completion of close to 950 JVs by Fortune-500 global multinationals; over the 2016–20 period, the annual deal flow had been more than cut in half, to fewer than 400 new JVs per year.[15] Chinese statistics show that from 2017 to 2019 (the most recent years of available data), investments in wholly owned foreign enterprises outweighed those in equity joint ventures by nearly three to one in the value of these projects and by an even larger margin in the number of deals.[16]

Moreover, China's newly enacted Foreign Investment Law, which came into force in 2020, calls for the progressive elimination of foreign ownership caps in many key industries—including oil and gas exploration, nuclear fuel production, and many segments of finance. That would further reduce the need for joint ventures and encourage foreign companies to establish wholly owned enterprises in China by direct acquisition.[17] Lighthizer's fixation on the Chinese JV is yesterday's news.

Yet another serious problem with this high-profile aspect of the Lighthizer case is that it ignores China's explicit recognition of the legitimacy of technology transfer and its willingness to pay a considerable sum for the privilege. According to Nicholas Lardy of the Peterson Institute for International Economics, in 2020 China paid out nearly $38 billion in licensing fees for the use of foreign intellectual property, nearly three times the amount of such payments it made a decade earlier and fourth in the world behind Ireland, the Netherlands, and the United States.[18] This is contrary to Lighthizer's inference that forced transfer is the functional equivalent of theft. China, the suspect in this purported transgression, is in fact paying considerable sums for legitimate and perfectly legal technology licensing arrangements—just like most other major countries around the world, including the United States.

The USTR's Section 301 allegations of China's forced technology transfer do not stand up to scrutiny. Contrary to widespread perceptions, the poster child of the US-China conflict does not deserve a special place on the wall of trade infamy. US allegations of China's forced technology transfer are a classic and enduring false narrative.

Intellectual Property Theft

> The scale of international theft of American intellectual property (IP) is unprecedented . . . China is the world's largest source of IP theft.
> —"The IP Commission Report" (May 2013, updated 2017)

The accusation of forced technology transfer pertains to the means to an end. The end is the intellectual property embedded in purportedly stolen new technologies. The allegation of intellectual property theft—China's ultimate act of larceny in the Information Age—is taken as a given by much of the American public and by others around the world.[19] According to a 2019 statement of former US Secretary of Defense Mark Esper, China is guilty of the "greatest intellectual property theft in human history."[20]

This was a critical piece of the Trump anti-China campaign. Previous leaders had allowed America to be fleeced of its most precious assets by the Chinese, went the gospel according to Trump, but he insisted that he would put a stop to it. Even with Trump out of office, the seemingly historic magnitude of the alleged theft remains central to the relationship narrative that still divides the United States and China.

Like most narratives, this one also comes with its own fact-based evidentiary support. The most widely cited body of evidence was assembled by the seemingly illustrious IP Commission, which bills itself as "an independent, bipartisan initiative of leading Americans" from all walks of life. This commission was co-chaired by two renowned US public servants, Admiral Dennis Blair (ret.), a former director of national intelligence, and Jon Huntsman Jr., ex-governor of Utah and former ambassador to China and Russia.

In a 2017 update to its original report, the commission estimated that intellectual-property theft cost the US economy somewhere between $225 billion and $600 billion annually, an exceptionally broad range.[21] Trade secrets purportedly stolen via industrial and state-sponsored espionage, forced technology transfer, and other surreptitious means accounted for between 80 to 90 percent of the estimated total, with the remainder coming from counterfeit and pirated hardware and software. Consistent with Esper's inflammatory accusation, China was singled out as the major villain in this crime.

The veracity of these claims is dubious. The estimate of stolen trade secrets, the lion's share of IP theft allegations highlighted in the USTR's Section 301 report, is especially dubious. As with the claim of forced technology transfer, there turn out to be no hard data to support the claim on the magnitude of stolen trade secrets. The IP Commission rests its case on a study spearheaded by PricewaterhouseCoopers LLP (PwC), which relies on questionable "proxy modeling" techniques, attempting to estimate the value of lost GDP arising from stolen trade secrets. It does so by constructing statistical linkages to data on nefarious activities such as narcotics trafficking, corruption, occupational fraud, and illicit financial flows.[22] The PwC team found that the scale of such activities—their "proxies" for IP loss— could reduce US GDP by a range of 1–3 percent. So they waved their wand and concluded that proxy modeling suggests a comparable range for America's GDP loss due to IP theft.

But our focus is on China, and here is where the evidentiary support of the IP Commission conclusions completely breaks down. Its only hard estimates of dollar-based IP theft are derived from data provided by the US Customs and Border Patrol (CBP), which reported $1.35 billion in seizures of counterfeit and pirated goods in 2015 (three years before the Section 301 complaint was filed). Yet another model—this one constructed by researchers at the OECD—was used to inflate this figure to an estimate of total IP theft in the United States.[23] In effect, the IP Commission is balancing its major conclusion on the head of a pin, using a relatively small $1.35 billion CBP data point to arrive at its $225 billion to $600 billion range for total US IP theft. This is a staggering leap of faith.

But it gets even worse. Believe it or not, the IP Commission relied on yet another "model," this one from the Business Software Alliance, to allocate 61 percent of this concocted estimate of total US IP loss to the Asia Pacific region.[24] And then the final step: 87 percent of the Asia Pacific total was attributed to Greater China—52 percent to the mainland and 35 percent to Hong Kong. Nor is there any documentation on how those attributions to and within Greater China were made.

All this raises serious questions about the "impeccable evidence" that purportedly quantifies the Chinese share of stolen US trade secrets, which, again, accounts for most of the IP Commission's assessment of America's alleged IP losses. The commission demands an extraordinary leap of faith to accept its notorious claim of Chinese intellectual property theft, a claim that basically relies on models built on models of models—models that in all cases are of dubious quality in their own right. This approach goes beyond the norms of a typical false narrative. It does not come close to doing justice to adjudicating claims about such a critically important issue.

Industrial Policy and the Tech Predator

> USTR determines that the Chinese government directs and unfairly
> facilitates the systematic investment in, and acquisition of, U.S. com-
> panies and assets by Chinese companies, to obtain cutting-edge
> technologies and intellectual property (IP) and generate large-scale
> technology transfer in industries deemed important by state indus-
> trial plans.
> —March 2018 USTR Section 301 report (p. 65)

The USTR's Section 301 complaint also indicts China's seemingly unique
approach to industrial policy: state-directed subsidized support to targeted
industries. Not only does this aspect of the narrative allege unfair government support of advanced-technology industries—implying that China does
something other responsible nations do not—it also accuses China of an
unusually aggressive outbound investment campaign ("going out" in the
Chinese vernacular) aimed at acquisitions of leading US technology companies. What China can't do at home, goes the argument, it will accomplish
through predatory activity abroad—especially in the United States. China
was accused by the USTR of using state support to snatch competitive
supremacy from free and open market-based systems that are supposedly
playing by very different, and of course fair, rules.

China makes no bones about its long-standing support of industrial policy. Since the era of Soviet-style central planning in the 1950s, state-directed
support of industrial development—especially targeting those areas the
government wants to champion and then providing funding mechanisms
to hit those targets—has long been an active element of China's economic
strategy. In the past decade, several high-profile industrial policy initiatives
have been prominently featured in its various five-year plans. In the technology area they include an early focus on "strategic emerging industries"
(2010), followed by more formal plans such as Made in China 2025 (2015),
the Internet Plus Action Plan (2015), and the New Generation AI Development Plan (2017); there are also a profusion of industry-specific plans covering government support for advanced industries such as electric vehicles,
renewable energy, robotics, biotechnology, information technology, integrated circuits, and aviation. Other efforts, especially the pan-regional Belt

and Road Initiative, also smack of industrial policy, but they are less germane to the debate over Chinese technology strategy raised by the USTR's Section 301 complaint.

The Made in China 2025 campaign struck an especially raw nerve when it was rolled out. It was seen in the United States as *prima facie* evidence of China's devious plot to attain global dominance in the great industries of the future: autonomous vehicles, high-speed rail, advanced information technologies and machine tools, exotic new materials, biopharma and sophisticated medical products, as well as new power sources and advanced agricultural equipment. Implicit in the US response is the accusation that China is taking aim at future industries that America has claimed as its own. Peter Navarro, former Trump administration trade advisor, famously claimed that "China has targeted America's industries of the future . . . if China successfully captures these emerging industries, America will have no economic future."[25]

Several questions arise: How unique is China's industrial policy strategy? The USTR makes it sound as if China alone engages in such efforts. What is China trying to accomplish with industrial policy? The Chinese make it clear that their industrial policies are focused on enhancing indigenous innovation by developing domestic capacity in the design and production of new technologies. The USTR, along with Navarro and Trump, characterize this as an existential threat of the same magnitude as earlier threats by the former Soviet Union. The Chinese see it as a critical development imperative. Is there a right and wrong here?

The Section 301 report throws down the gauntlet in addressing the first of these questions, stating unequivocally that "Unlike China, the United States does not have a broad-based industrial policy."[26] Because of that, the USTR concludes, China has a distinct and unfair advantage over the United States. Yet contrary to USTR assertions, China is hardly alone in the art and practice of industrial policy. At one time or another, most major advanced economies have deployed similar tactics with similar objectives. That includes the United States.

President Dwight Eisenhower, in his 1961 farewell address, first drew attention to America's powerful military-industrial complex as the linchpin of far-flung US efforts at state-sponsored, taxpayer-funded innovation.[27] The

United States does it through the Defense Advanced Research Projects Agency (DARPA), housed in the Pentagon and created by Eisenhower in 1958 following the 1957 launch of the Sputnik satellite by the Soviet Union.

With America's total military budget now in excess of $700 billion—more than the defense budgets of China, Russia, the United Kingdom, India, France, Japan, Saudi Arabia, and Germany combined—DARPA and related science and technology efforts by the Defense Department enjoy sizable public funding.[28] This support has played an important role in the development of many major US technological advances, such as NASA-related spinoffs, the Internet, the global positioning system (GPS), breakthroughs in semiconductors, nuclear power, imaging technology, and a broad array of pharmaceutical innovations including "operation warp speed," which led to spectacular innovations in Covid-19 vaccine development.[29]

These breakthroughs have come largely from proactive government support to defend America's innovation leadership. As this book goes to press, the US Senate and the House of Representatives have passed separate versions of targeted assistance to the domestic semiconductor industry and to other US companies that are thought to be feeling the heat of Chinese competition. And tightened regulatory oversight of alleged foreign technology threats—through expanded powers of the multi-agency Committee on Foreign Investments in the United States (CFIUS) as well as through multilateral efforts like the recently proposed joint US and European Trade and Technology Council—are further highly visible manifestations of American industrial policy.[30]

Nor has the United States been alone in embracing industrial policy as a linchpin of national economic strategy. It was central to Japan's so-called plan rational development state, which underlaid the country's rapid growth in the 1970s and 1980s.[31] The Ministry of International Trade and Industry perfected the art of state-subsidized credit allocation and tariffs to protect Japan's sunrise industries; in 2021, its successor, the Ministry of Economy, Trade and Industry, proposed a "new axis in economic and industrial policy" featuring targeted efforts in new technologies, strategic goods, regulations, and systems aligned with societal goals such as climate change, security, and inequality.[32]

Germany took a similar route with its impressive *Wirtschaftswunder*, augmented by strong state-directed support for the *Mittelstand* of small and medium-size enterprises; its more recent *Industrie 4.0* (2013) is comparable in focus and scope to China's Internet Plus plan.[33] And France's well-known model of "indicative planning," which dates back to President Charles de Gaulle's Fifth Plan of 1966–70, specifically emphasized a "fusion of economic and political power" that merged the French industrial system with the state.[34]

Yet the USTR goes even further, indicting Chinese industrial policy as the instrument of predatory acquisitions of American technology companies through its "going out" campaign of foreign direct investment in the United States. These efforts are depicted as a unique state-directed and -funded plan aimed at gobbling up innocent and unprotected newly emerging US companies and their proprietary technologies. The Section 301 report devotes more than twice as many pages to charges concerning China's supposed external technology theft via offshore acquisitions as it does to internal transfers through JVs and alleged unfair licensing practices. This accusation is framed as a blatant grab by China for America's most precious assets as the world's leading innovator. Based mainly on a case-by-case assessment of several Chinese acquisitions of US technology companies, the report concludes, "USTR determines that the Chinese government directs and unfairly facilitates the systematic investment in, and acquisition of, US companies and assets by Chinese companies, to obtain cutting-edge technologies and intellectual property."[35]

Here again, a strong and unequivocal accusation is not well supported by fact. An annual tally of outbound mergers and acquisitions activity from China into the United States conducted by the American Enterprise Institute reveals that there were only seventeen such transactions in the technology sector between 2005 and 2017, the years immediately preceding Lighthizer's Section 301 investigation.[36] By contrast, there were fifty-two deals in the real estate sector. Moreover, the deal count of Chinese acquisitions of US technology companies over this period also lagged transactions in finance, energy, transportation, and entertainment. These are not exactly the footprints of an aggressive predator, fixated on stalking Silicon Valley in search of juicy, vulnerable technology targets.

The conclusion that emerges is that China's industrial policy efforts are neither unique nor unusually focused on leading-edge American technology companies. That brings up the deeper question of intent: What does China hope to accomplish with its technology-focused industrial policies? And does the United States, specifically the USTR, have a legitimate basis for questioning that intent?

The answer to these questions hinges on the key role that technological breakthroughs and innovation play in economic development. In early-stage development, poor, backward countries typically rely on imports of technologies developed by more advanced nations. Over time, as developing nations adapt these technologies to the growing needs of their companies and people, they usually make a transition from imported to indigenous innovation. This entails a shift in focus from importing technologies to breakthroughs developed at home—in research labs, companies, entrepreneurial start-ups, and universities.

Many believe that this shift from imported to indigenous innovation marks a critical transition in economic development. As a developing economy approaches the frontier of innovation established by advanced economies, making that shift becomes all the more important. Failure to do so is often associated with the "middle-income trap," the tendency of developing nations to slow down when they reach the middle-income threshold.[37] While there is intense debate over the empirical validity of this argument, there can be no doubt that indigenous innovation is ultimately a significant objective for any nation.[38] And, as the following chapter of this book argues, it certainly makes great sense to view China as being on the cusp of this critical transition.[39]

Yet the USTR's Section 301 report repeatedly depicts China's emphasis on indigenous innovation as a dire threat to America. This accusation is less about allegations of theft and more about an audacious sense of entitlement. From Robert Lighthizer to Peter Navarro to Donald Trump, the inference is that China is not entitled to develop its own organic system of technological change and innovation. Its success is viewed as equivalent to a claim on the same future that America sees as its own. While the USTR had every right to question the legal and moral integrity of the *means* to China's push for indigenous innovation—and, unfortunately, did a poor job of making that case—it has no place questioning the right of any nation to aspire to innovation-based prosperity. Notwithstanding the USTR's anti-China bluster, the United States does not have a monopoly on indigenous innovation.

Cyberhacking

China's cyber activities targeting U.S. companies pose significant costs on U.S. companies and burdens U.S. commerce.
—March 2018 USTR Section 301 report (p. 176)

Cyber espionage is the third leg of the USTR's case against China. There can be no mistaking the evidence underscoring the major role played by China's People's Liberation Army (PLA) in cyber intrusions directed at US commercial interests. These problems were so serious that President Barack Obama presented detailed top-secret evidence of state-sponsored computer hacking to President Xi Jinping at the so-called Sunnylands Summit in June 2013.[40]

Apart from the subsequent publicity stunt of a Pennsylvania grand jury indictment of five PLA officers on charges of cyberhacking in May 2014, this confrontation had positive results, at least for a while. It sparked two years of negotiations and led to agreement on a joint US-China cyber accord in 2015.[41] Since then, most reports point to a reduction in Chinese incursions.[42] Ironically, most of the evidence cited in the 2018 USTR report that documented China's nefarious cyber activities predates the 2015 accord.

The Section 301 report is filled with examples of alleged abuses by Chinese companies and China's unfair policies and regulatory constraints. This is especially the case in the section covering cyber-enabled theft of intellectual property, which details complaints raised by SolarWorld, US Steel Corporation, Allegheny Technologies Inc., United Steelworkers, Westinghouse, and Alcoa. Special emphasis was placed on a 2013 report by the cybersecurity firm Mandiant that detailed the cyberhacking activities of a Shanghai-based unit (APT1) of the PLA.

The seventy-five-page Mandiant report reads like science fiction. It details the schematics of the hackers' keystrokes, identifying the hackers by nickname (UglyGorilla, SuperHard, and DOTA), and pinpointing the headquarters address of PLA cyber unit 61398 on Datong Road in Shanghai, Pudong. It is highly effective in providing an insider's intimate account of state-sponsored Chinese cyberhacking. But like the USTR's Section 301 report, it suffers from the flaw of attempting to draw macro inferences from micro examples. A key example is the assertion that the APT1 unit was a threat group that "targeted at least four of the seven strategic emerging industries (SEIs)" that have been the focus of Chinese industrial policy since 2010.[43] On closer inspection, however, this assertion lacks support: the overlap between the industry composition of the Mandiant attack data and China's SEI targets is wide of the mark.[44]

That gets to a deeper point, a major methodological deficiency of the USTR's approach in assessing the China threat. In a large economy like China or the United States, one can always find examples of misbehavior. But it is irresponsible to frame broad allegations of unfair trading practices on the basis of selective lists of anecdotes, however compelling. That is true of forced technology transfers, outbound investment, industrial policy, and cybersecurity. This is a major methodological shortcoming of the USTR report.

Notwithstanding this mismatch between cyberattack allegations and the substantiating evidence, there can be little doubt about the severity of the problem for the US-China relationship. China and the United States are both facing increasingly serious cybersecurity problems. State and nonstate actors in both nations have repeatedly penetrated each other's Internet infrastructures, with lasting and costly disruptions to companies, consumers, and overall economic activity. As I will discuss in Chapter 13, the recent outbreak of ransomware, with hackers attempting to monetize these disruptions, only compounds this problem.

As economic systems become increasingly digitized, these disruptions will undoubtedly grow even more consequential—but will almost certainly have a greater impact on the growth potential of the Chinese economy than on the US economy. This disparity is partly because the growth in the digital share of the Chinese economy is starting from a lower base than in the United States; International Monetary Fund (IMF) estimates put a broad measure of China's digitized share of GDP currently around 30 percent, versus about 60 percent for the United States.[45] Yet by 2030, IMF forecasts call for near parity of digital shares in the two economies, at around 70 percent. That estimate implies a 40-percentage-point increase in the Chinese share, four times the 10-point increase expected in the United States.

The IMF's prediction underscores the possibility that, compared with the United States, China is likely to have a more digitization-intensive growth trajectory over the coming decade. Such an outcome is certainly consistent with the broad thrust of China's industrial policy programs, including Made in China 2025, Internet Plus, and the New Generation AI Development Plan. Successful execution of these ambitious plans will be thwarted by escalating cyber conflict. Largely for that reason, China is more vulnerable to economic disruptions arising from cyber conflict with the United States or other nations. From the standpoint of its growth potential, China has far more at stake than anyone in getting cybersecurity right.

The danger of cyber conflict underscores the insidious nature of the problem. Both the United States and China engage in hacking and are doing so at a dramatically increasing rate. Yet neither nation seems to have much control over the breadth and depth of these activities. Getting cyber right is an urgent imperative for both nations, as well as for the relationship between them. In the end, as I emphasize in Chapter 13, it is less about blame and more about collective resolution of a shared problem.

Finally, I should note that the USTR devoted just twenty pages of its 182-page Section 301 report to cyber issues—less than one-quarter the space it gave to intellectual property problems associated with China's "going out" strategy and only half the space it devoted to forced technology transfer. Apparently, in making its case against China, the USTR thought it had bigger fish to fry.

Lessons of Japan

"When governments permit counterfeiting or copying of American products, it is stealing our future, and it is no longer free trade."
—Ronald Reagan, September 23, 1985

We've seen this movie before. President Reagan delivered those words following a meeting of leading international finance ministers held at New

York's Plaza Hotel on September 22, 1985. The "Plaza Accord," which had just been signed by the United States, Japan, Germany, the United Kingdom, and France, effectively forced Japan to boost the value of its currency, the yen. That agreement was aimed at providing relief for a sharply overvalued US dollar, which was widely thought to be inflicting economic damage on the United States by crimping the competitiveness of a beleaguered American manufacturing sector.

In the 1980s, Japan was widely portrayed as America's greatest economic threat—not only because of allegations of intellectual property theft by President Reagan and others but also because of an outsize bilateral trade imbalance. In its standoff with the United States, Japan blinked, and ultimately paid a steep price for doing so—it made a series of subsequent policy blunders that led to the expansion and then bursting of large asset bubbles, followed by deflation and at least three "lost" decades of economic stagnation.[46] Today, the same plot now features China.[47]

Leaving aside the objectionable mercantilism practiced by both countries, Japan and China have something else in common: they both became targets of America's unfortunate habit of scapegoating others for its own economic problems. Like blaming Japan in the 1980s, China bashing today is an outgrowth of America's increasingly insidious macroeconomic imbalances. In both cases, a dramatic shortfall in domestic saving spawned current account and trade deficits in the United States, setting the stage for its battles with Asia's two economic giants.

When Reagan took office in January 1981, America's net domestic saving rate stood at 7.8 percent of national income, and the current account was basically in balance. Within two and a half years, following Reagan's wildly popular tax cuts, federal budget deficits exploded and the domestic saving rate plunged to 3.7 percent. As a result, the current account and merchandise trade balances moved into what would become perpetual deficits.[48] The national income identity between saving and investment held. Lacking in domestic saving, America faced a serious trade problem largely of its own making.

Yet the Reagan administration was in denial. There was little appreciation of the link between saving and trade imbalances. Instead, the blame was pinned on Japan, which accounted for 42 percent of US merchandise trade deficits in the first half of the 1980s.[49] Japan bashing then became the rage, supported by a wide range of grievances raised over unfair and illegal trade practices. Leading the charge was a young deputy US trade representative named Robert Lighthizer, who had discovered the miracle cure for trade disputes—Section 301 of the US Trade Act.[50]

Fast-forward nearly thirty years and the similarities are painfully evident. Unlike Reagan, President Trump did not inherit an economy with an ample reservoir of saving. When Trump took office in January 2017, the net domestic saving rate was just 3 percent, well below half the rate at the start of the Reagan era. But like his predecessor, who had waxed eloquent about "morning in America," Trump also pushed for large tax cuts—this time to "make America great again."

The result, a predictable widening of the federal budget deficit, more than offset the temporary surge in private saving that normally accompanies a maturing economic expansion. As a result, the net domestic saving rate actually fell to 2 percent of national income by 2020, keeping America's international balances—both the current account and merchandise trade deficits—deep in the red.

And China was then cast in the same role that Japan was made to play in the 1980s. On the surface, today's threat seems more dire. At its peak in 2015, China accounted for 48 percent of the US merchandise trade deficit, compared to Japan's 42 percent share in the early 1980s; as was noted earlier, however, China made up precisely the same 42 percent share of the total US trade deficit over the decade ending in 2021 as Japan did thirty years earlier.[51] That is as close as it ever gets to an ah-ha moment for the wounded victims of unfair trade. Through the American lens, the Asian trade villains had turned out to be statistically identical twins.

Yet just as today's outbreak of China bashing conveniently ignores America's saving shortfall, the same was true of Japan bashing in the 1980s. That was a serious mistake then and is even more so today. The United States was able to squeeze Japan but could not reduce its overall trade deficit. When Ronald Reagan came into office in 1981, the merchandise trade deficit was 0.8 percent of US GDP; when he left office, in January 1989, the gap had expanded to 2.3 percent. Unsurprisingly, Japan's bilateral portion of the US overall trade deficit was diverted elsewhere, in part, to higher-cost trading partners such as Germany.[52] Trade diversion away from Japan in the late 1980s reflected the strengthening of the yen that arose from the Plaza Accord, not unlike the trade diversion away from China that has recently been sparked by Trump's tariffs. The bilateral fix for a multilateral problem failed against Japan in the 1980s, just as it is failing against China today.

When Trump summoned the same Robert Lighthizer to lead the charge against China, the intervening decades seemed to have taught his USTR very little. Lighthizer was just as clueless about the macro argument in 2018 as he was in 1985. In both instances, US denial bordered on delusion. Back in the 1980s, basking in the warm glow of untested supply-side economic theories—especially the cult-like belief that tax cuts would be self-financing— the Reagan administration failed to appreciate the links between budget deficits and trade deficits.[53] Today, the seductive power of low interest rates, coupled with a new strain of voodoo economics called Modern Monetary Theory, was equally alluring for the Trump administration and for a bipartisan consensus of China bashers in Congress.[54]

The macroeconomic constraints on a savings-short US economy are ignored for good reason: there is no political constituency for reducing trade deficits by cutting budget deficits and thereby boosting domestic saving. America wants to have its cake and eat it too, with a health-care system that swallows 18 percent of its GDP, defense spending that exceeds the combined sum of the world's next seven largest military budgets, and tax cuts that have reduced the GDP share of federal government revenue well below the average of the past fifty years.[55] Saving, if it entails forgoing any of these excesses, is considered almost un-American.

This remake of an old movie is wearing thin. Once again, the United States has found it far easier to blame others—Japan then, China now—than to live within its means. But the sequel could have a very different ending. China, which has studied the lessons of Japan very carefully, is unlikely to acquiesce to America's bilateral bluster. That raises an even deeper question: why does the United States always seem to need a scapegoat when addressing its economic challenges?

This answer is deeply rooted in saving—or in the case of the United States, the lack thereof. Saving disparities, an inherent source of conflict between codependent economies, also cause important divergences in economic growth. Saving supports investment in productive capacity, infrastructure, and human capital. Nations that save too little can either curtail that investment and the growth potential it supports or borrow surplus saving from others to fill the void.

China, with its vast reservoir of surplus saving, has yet to face the full ramifications of this choice. The United States, with its secular decline in domestic saving, has opted for the latter option, complete with the multilateral trade deficits that follow from that choice. But the United States doesn't like large bilateral trade deficits any more than other nations do. It didn't like them with Japan in the 1980s, and it doesn't like them with China today. But it also doesn't like to save. So it has no alternative but to turn to low-cost foreign producers to fill the gap between what it saves and what it spends. Trade deficits are a painfully visible manifestation of America's myopic unwillingness to save for the future. The real threat is not a bilateral imbalance with one country—Japan then, China now—but a domestic saving shortfall that has given rise to America's multilateral trade deficits with many countries.[56]

The trade bluster the USTR aimed at China rests on a combination of shaky evidence and flawed analytics. The USTR's Section 301 complaint is a biased political document that has further inflamed anti-China sentiment in the United States. It is a visible manifestation of a codependency gone terribly wrong, with savings-short America increasingly seeing itself as a victim.

Like the rest of us, the Chinese are tough competitors who don't always play by the rules. For that, they need to be held accountable. But the case made by the USTR, as well as the tariffs that rested on this case, were politically compromised attempts to co-opt trade policy in order to duck accountability for self-inflicted problems. With Trump's trade war having backfired for entirely predictable reasons, America's false narratives about Chinese trade transgressions will likely have important and lasting economic consequences. Unwilling or unable to have learned the lessons of Japan some thirty-five years ago, the United States, by scapegoating China, is making the same mistake today.

Ronald Ebens, a Chrysler plant supervisor, and Michael Nitz, his stepson and a laid-off autoworker, were initially charged with the second-degree murder of Vincent Chin. They were able to cut a deal with the prosecutors and pleaded guilty to a lesser crime of manslaughter. In the end, Ebens and Nitz served no time in jail; they were put on probation for three years, fined $3,000 each, and ordered to pay $780 in court costs. They were later charged in federal courts for civil-rights hate-crime violations. Nitz was acquitted on those charges. Ebens's initial conviction was overturned on appeal, and he was subsequently cleared of all charges.

The death of an innocent young Chinese-American in a tragic and outrageous act of Japan bashing was an ugly chapter in a long history of blame with impunity, a painfully visible manifestation of America's attraction to false narratives. The appalling outbreak of anti-Asian hate crimes in 2021–22 raises the very real question of whether the United States has ever learned the lesson of Vincent Chin.

5

Huawei as a Trojan Horse

SHENZHEN, ONCE A SMALL FISHING VILLAGE straddling the Pearl River Delta near Hong Kong, didn't exist as an urban center thirty-five years ago. Nor did its most celebrated business, Huawei. Today, Shenzhen is an ultramodern metropolis with a population of thirteen million, and Huawei, with nearly two hundred thousand employees, is China's leading technology company. In our saga of relationship conflict, China and Huawei's shared story is less about scale than about fear. For America, Huawei has become public enemy number one in the tech war with China—the architect and producer of modern weapons of mass destruction that could lead China to victory in the decisive battles of cyber warfare.

The fear is largely based on a false narrative taken to the extreme. Unraveling the case of Huawei requires not only a careful look at the Chinese company but an examination of the sources of America's own technological anxieties. My argument, in a nutshell, is that the United States has dropped the ball on technology leadership while exaggerating the threat it faces from a powerful adversary. The example of Huawei is a case study in conflict escalation.

Huawei does not have a perfectly clean slate. Over its thirty-five-year history, it has faced a scattering of charges ranging from software piracy and possession of stolen property to industrial espionage and, more recently, international sanctions violations. Yet this record is far from unique. It actually puts Huawei in a league with American tech giants like Intel, Cisco,

Google, and Apple, all of which have been accused of similar misconduct in the Information Age. Nor is Huawei's record out of line with the long history of industrial espionage that embroiled Great Britain and the United States in the late nineteenth century.

Anxieties surrounding Huawei are grounded less in the company's missteps than in a projection of its intent. As the world's leading developer and producer of 5G telecommunications equipment—a new generation of mobile, wireless, cellular-based technologies—Huawei is feared for how it might convert that platform into an instrument of cyber warfare.[1] It would be relatively simple, goes the argument, to create a "backdoor" in the global 5G infrastructure through which to deploy cyber weapons against China's adversaries around the world, especially in the United States. Huawei is portrayed as the mythical Trojan Horse in the coming cyber war.

That fearsome image is aligned with the background of Huawei's founder, Ren Zhengfei. Born in 1944, Ren, like many young Chinese men of his generation, served in the People's Liberation Army. During his nine-year military career, he started out as a civil engineer and eventually gravitated toward technology, rising to the level of deputy regimental chief (without military rank).[2] The fear in this case comes right out of the script of Hollywood movies—once in the PLA, always in the PLA.[3] At the command of the state, goes the claim, the good soldier Ren won't hesitate to lead Huawei into battle.

The paranoia comes from pulling the narratives together—Huawei's alleged backdoor potential and Ren's PLA background. The company's murky ownership structure compounds the fear. Taken together, these factors dispel any doubt over intent and capability, a lethal combination that has sparked wars in the past.[4] In the eyes of a vulnerable United States, the Huawei threat is no different. Circumstantial evidence is apparently more than enough to make the case, and another narrative based more on presumption than hard evidence has now become accepted wisdom in the United States.

The presumption-based threat is key to our assessment of America's false narratives of China. By now, given the weak evidence behind America's Section 301 allegations of unfair Chinese trading practices, this story should have a familiar ring. The Trump administration staged an aggressive preemptive attack on Huawei in 2018, first blacklisting the company through the rarely used Commerce Department "entity list" and then moving aggressively to put similar sanctions on the firm's supply-chain network, including US companies that had been providing Huawei with critical semiconductor inputs. By disabling the Trojan Horse, goes the argument, the United States can protect itself from a dire threat, prevent China from gaining a stranglehold on the world's communication technology, and perhaps even return to dominating the industry.

If it were only that simple.

The Rising Innovator

Huawei represents one of greatest fears afflicting the United States—the fear that America's role as the world's leading innovator will be supplanted by an unfriendly adversary. Innovation is not just a means to military superiority. By driving technological change, it also underpins productivity growth, the essential building block of national prosperity. For that reason alone, the battle for innovation leadership has long been decisive in great power struggles and international economic competition. As the global hegemon, long acclaimed as the world's leading innovator, America views a rising China as a serious threat on both counts.

Yet America's fears of Huawei are as much a function of the surprisingly fragile US leadership position in innovation as they are a reflection of any specific challenge posed by China. To understand the case America has assembled against Huawei, I start with a careful assessment of how both the United States and China fit into a dynamic and rapidly changing global innovation race.

The best yardstick for that race is the Global Innovations Index (GII), a comprehensive measure of the innovative prowess of over 130 leading nations.[5] The most recent GII shows that China is rapidly closing the gap. Over the past decade, its GII ranking has increased from forty-third in the world in 2010 to twelfth place in 2021.[6] It ranks first among the world's so-called upper-middle-income nations, and now scores slightly higher than Japan, long a powerful force in global technology, which ranked thirteenth in 2021. The United States has remained in the top five since 2013 and was third in 2021, behind Switzerland and Sweden.

A wealth of detail buried in the overall GII rankings offers further insight into China's growing prowess as an emerging leader in innovation. The recent improvement has been especially evident in the so-called output-based components of the GII—in essence, the *results* of innovative activities within a country.[7] China ranks particularly high in areas like knowledge creation, industrial design, and patents and trademarks; overall, on the output side of the GII innovation equation, China ranked seventh in 2021, only three places behind the United States, which was in fourth place.

China lagged in GII inputs—the enabling elements of innovative activities such as institutional support (regulatory and government oversight), Internet and telecom connectivity, and market sophistication. China's overall score on the input-based GII components put it in twenty-fifth place out of 132 countries in the world in 2021, well behind the United States (third), South Korea (ninth), Japan (eleventh), Germany (fourteenth), and Israel (eighteenth).

This dichotomy between a relatively high GII output ranking and lagging inputs reveals an important characteristic of China's recent innovation dynamic: it has been able to draw concrete applications benefits from a still relatively underdeveloped innovation infrastructure. That puts it near the top in the GII ranking of "innovations efficiency"—innovations output ranking relative to inputs. At the same time, that status raises questions about whether China will be able to maintain its impressive momentum if it continues to lag in laying the foundation on the input side of the equation.

The GII results draw attention to the most important aspect of China's progress in innovation—converting its scarce resources, especially a relatively new emphasis on the human capital of its potentially vast population of knowledge workers, into engineering and leadership positions in many advanced technology businesses. The results speak for themselves—China now has a long list of world-class companies in leading-edge industries, ranging from e-commerce and financial technology to life sciences and autonomous vehicles. Perhaps most importantly, these breakthrough applications all benefit from China's stunning progress in artificial intelligence—the new catalyst of innovation. That's why the United States is so worried. The combination of AI and Huawei only compounds America's fear of China as a rising technological threat.

A New AI Superpower?

AI sparks as well as fuels innovation. It draws on a powerful combination of developments in both the capacity and speed of information processing, the "big data" of large and rapidly expanding digitized experience-based observations, and the "neural" deep learning networks of processing machines. Machine learning, whether it is *unsupervised* pattern recognition processing, *supervised* category-based predictions, or *reinforced* rules-based decision making, is the essential characteristic of machine-driven, or artificial, intelligence.[8]

There has been an important evolution in the mix of the building blocks of the AI era; paybacks have shifted from theory to practice. The science of creating the powerful new algorithms that originally launched machine learning has now become less important than the measurable benefits associated with the problem-solving applications of those algorithms. AI is no longer an industry in itself but is more an infrastructure that knits together and drives other industries.

Dr. Kai-Fu Lee, a China-based venture capitalist who was born in Taiwan, educated in the United States, and worked in Silicon Valley, argues persuasively that this shift in AI from theory to application plays precisely to China's strengths.[9] The mathematical and computational models of deep-learning algorithms were largely developed in the United States, Canada, and the United Kingdom. While China pushed ahead and eventually attained global leadership in AI research and patents, it remained largely an observer and copycat in this first phase of AI. While far from a finished product, Lee argues, the bulk of this initial theoretical effort is now relatively complete and readily available as "open science" on open-architecture Internet-based research platforms.[10]

These platforms gave China its critical entry point into what Lee dubs the "Age of Implementation"—the development of new applications-driven businesses spawned by China's vast Internet-based marketplace. Big data is China's comparative advantage in this transition, facilitated by a surveillance state that has compromised privacy for the sake of control and is more than willing to extract unprecedented volumes of data from what is now by far the largest Internet community in the world.[11]

This shift in AI-enabled innovation from theory to application follows an earlier transformation of the Information Age from hardware to software.[12] While China did not have an inherent first-mover advantage in either of those stages, its opportunities in AI applications are very much aligned with Kai-Fu Lee's thesis. The emergence of powerful "platform companies" such as Tencent's WeChat, Alibaba and Ant, Baidu, ByteDance's Toutiao, Xiaomi, and Meituan, just to name a few, testifies to the extraordinary potential of China's AI-enabled applications businesses.

But now there is a new and important catch to this development. Recent Chinese regulatory actions have focused on constraining some of the activities of China's Internet platform companies. These regulatory actions demonstrate the government's growing discomfort with the social and political implications of platform-based content like gaming and music.[13] I will discuss China's shifting tradeoff between AI and social stability in the second half of this book. But, at a minimum, this development certainly draws into question an important aspect of what had been until recently China's seemingly open-ended AI-enabled transformation.

Notwithstanding these developments, the Chinese government has remained firmly committed to big data and its potential applications in business and defense, as well as the interplay between crime enforcement and social control.[14] Xi Jinping has stressed this from the start, emphasizing back in 2013 that "The vast ocean of data, just like oil resources during industrialization, contains immense productive power."[15] The July 2017 rollout of the "New Generation AI Development Plan," discussed in Chapter 4, was followed by several developments that drew attention to the big data piece of AI. In his October 2017 address to the Nineteenth Party Congress, Xi emphasized the link between big data and the real economy—giving strong top-down encouragement to the push for data-driven applications.[16] A couple of months later, Xi again endorsed the effort by chairing a special Politburo study session on China's national big data strategy, stressing yet again "integrated development of the digital economy and the real economy."[17]

There was prompt follow-up from Chinese regulators, especially by the National Development and Reform Commission, the Ministry of Industry and Information Technology, and the Ministry of Education.[18] A 2020 RAND Corporation study drew attention to China's focus on data-driven public security applications—especially its controversial social credit system that "scores" individual behavior against Communist Party standards, as well as the growing use of facial recognition systems in surveillance-based crime enforcement—and to a wide range of military applications such as data-driven analysis of foreign military activity, targeting of enemy assets, data-intensive procurement and equipment maintenance systems, war gaming, and personnel and training. The RAND study concluded that China takes a "whole of government" approach to big data analytics.[19]

No such formal commitment exists in the United States—at least not yet. While US Internet-based companies have similar opportunities to move into newly digitized markets, they suffer from one critical deficiency compared with China—the lack of scale in big-data support.[20] Data privacy concerns constrain data collection, and big-data-based analytics are accordingly limited, even for anonymized databases. China has already captured, copied, and created a much larger critical mass of high-quality big data than anything assembled in the United States.[21] US data analytics are largely confined to private commercial applications, relying on the scalable tactics of data extraction employed by Google, Facebook, and Amazon. Harvard professor Shoshana Zuboff has dubbed this "surveillance capitalism," stressing the AI-enabled behavioral modifications that have become aligned with the monetary objectives of America's data-driven Internet businesses.[22]

But that's where the similarities between the American and Chinese approaches end. China's national focus on big data analytics goes well beyond the private sector efforts in the United States. Moreover, survey data indicate a much greater acceptance of big data extraction by the Chinese public than in the United States.[23] China is thus well positioned, over time, to draw the greatest leverage from the data- and applications-driven paybacks of artificial intelligence. The United States has belatedly recognized China's AI threat, a warning recently underscored by the National Security Commission on Artificial Intelligence; in the words of Graham Allison and Eric Schmidt, chair of the commission, China is already a "full-spectrum peer competitor of the United States in commercial and national security applications of AI."[24] Further narrowing of the US-China innovation gap seems highly likely as a result.

In the end, China, the United States, or any other nation must ensure that the machine learning of AI is aligned with the norms and values of its society.[25] Failure to do so is a recipe for tech backlash and social instability. In the rush to embrace artificial intelligence, the significance of the letter "A" is often swept aside. AI mimics, but does not replicate, human emotion and intelligence. The role of AI in relationship conflicts may well hinge on that critical distinction.

The Threatened Innovator

Just as China wrote the book on ancient innovation, the United States has played the same role in modern times. From Benjamin Franklin and Thomas Edison to Henry Ford and Steve Jobs, the genius of invention has long been the spark of US economic prosperity. That genius, however, did not come out of thin air. It was the outgrowth of a strong commitment to education, a spirit of scientific discovery, entrepreneurial passion and risk-taking, a supportive institutional partnership between government and private enterprise, and intense competition. While some argue that America's best days as an innovative society are behind it, new breakthroughs in life sciences, alternative energy, and yes, AI, may say otherwise.[26]

Whatever the verdict, China's push for indigenous innovation has injected a new insecurity into America's economic equation. It's not just the trade conflict. The innovation race underscores yet another layer of tensions between the world's major economic powers. That raises two related possibilities: Does the battle for innovation leadership spell prosperity for the winner and decline for the loser? Or is there room at the top for more than one innovative leader?

The dilemma is deeper than this contrast between zero-sum and win-win perspectives might suggest. As we saw in Chapter 4, the USTR's Section 301 allegations depict China as an illegitimate innovator aided by massive intellectual property theft, forced technology transfer, abusive industrial policy practices, and cyberhacking. President Trump's trade war made this argument actionable, as did his tech war focused on Huawei.

That much of the Section 301 complaint is wide of the mark, however, shines a light on the other side of the US-China innovation conflict—America's macroeconomic vulnerability. Has the confluence of weak saving and large trade deficits stressed in Chapter 4 exacerbated America's anxiety over China as a "full-spectrum" AI competitor? Has the resulting bilateral bluster obscured far deeper problems afflicting US innovation strategy?

These questions suggest that we should stop viewing the United States as a victim in the innovation conflict and consider America's role as the protagonist. We need to ask whether the trade war is a smokescreen meant to deflect attention from problems of America's own making—in this case, a diminished capacity for innovation. This ties directly back to our earlier analysis of America's chronic saving shortfall. Lacking domestic savings, the United States has underinvested in many areas—especially manufacturing capacity, infrastructure, and human capital. Moreover, pressured by inadequate saving, the United States has not only failed to fund urgently needed education reform—the genius piece of the innovation equation—but has increasingly underinvested in research and development (R&D), the pipeline of future innovation.

While overall R&D has remained relatively stable over the past decade as a share of US GDP, at about 2.75 percent, there has been an ominous shift in the mix. A far greater portion of America's R&D outlays is now funded directly by the business sector rather than by the federal government. Business R&D, which was relatively stable at 1 percent of GDP through the 1970s, had doubled to nearly 2 percent of GDP by 2017.[27] While that is an impressive accomplishment, private-sector efforts understandably tend to be more commercially oriented than basic research activities of the scientific community. The result is that America's R&D has shifted away from "R" in favor of "D."

The decline in federal R&D outlays is particularly noteworthy. Federally sponsored R&D surged from 0.7 percent of GDP in 1953 to 1.9 percent of GDP by 1965, an outgrowth of the Pentagon's DARPA-driven responses to Sputnik. Since then, and after the United States won the race to the moon, it has been all downhill. The federal government's share of US R&D spending fell from a peak of 67 percent of the total in 1964 to a 25 percent share by 2000, and it has continued to fall further. By 2017, federally funded R&D had returned to the 0.7 percent share of GDP last seen in the early 1950s.[28]

Particularly worrisome is a sharp decline in US R&D devoted to basic research and experimental development. These categories of R&D are critical drivers of innovation, largely earmarked to government and academic laboratories involved in the theoretical and experimental research of pure science. Many of these projects lead to dead ends; they seldom offer immediate commercial payback but instead yield discoveries that find commercial application years or decades later. The basic research portion of R&D is the seed corn of innovation.

Basic research programs reflect collaborative synergies between government funding and university execution. In 2017, for example, the US federal government funded about 42 percent of all basic research, while institutions of higher education were responsible for running and executing 48 percent of the projects. With basic and experimental research having remained relatively stable at just under 20 percent of overall US R&D spending since 2000, this trend is best interpreted as a constant slice of a shrinking pie.[29]

The shift in the mix of overall R&D—diminished federally funded basic research combined with increasingly commercialized emphasis by businesses on development—is the real problem. Significantly, that shift is tightly aligned with America's saving problem. The decline in the federal government's R&D share of US GDP that began in 1965 coincides almost precisely with the onset of the chronic downtrend in domestic saving. The net domestic saving rate peaked at 7.2 percent of national income in the fourth quarter of 1964, the same moment when the government R&D share of GDP also hit its high. Moreover, the subsequent decline in the domestic saving rate, from its late 1964 high to just 2 percent of GDP in 2020, closely matches the downtrend in this key component of R&D.

Maybe this is a coincidence. But there is good reason to believe that the two trends—saving and federal government R&D—are related. At the height of the Cold War, facing the technological threat of a post-Sputnik Soviet Union, America considered innovation of great national importance. Then complacency set in and priorities shifted. The United States went to the moon, the Soviet Union started to crumble, and military adventures in Vietnam chewed up an increasing portion of the federal budget. R&D was marginalized, and a key source of American innovation began to decay.

China can hardly be blamed for this problem, which is entirely America's own making. But that is precisely what the USTR's Section 301 allegations aimed to do. If the US innovation potential is compromised by Chinese actions on forced technology transfer, intellectual property theft, or industrial policy, then it would be reasonable to conclude that much of America's innovation problem is made in China. Yet that is the opposite of the truth.

Blaming China is one thing, even if that blame rests on false narratives. But doing so misses the more important aspect of the two nations' innovation competition: China is going the opposite way from the United States on R&D. This should not be surprising given the diverging saving patterns, with Chinese surplus saving positioned to fund an increase in R&D while America's deficit in saving has been accompanied by the declining research portion of R&D.

As the world's largest saver, China certainly has the wherewithal to support R&D-intensive growth. By 2017, its total R&D outlays of some $496 billion (expressed in purchasing-power parity terms) exceeded those of the European Union and were just 10 percent below the R&D spending levels of the United States. As a result, China's R&D intensity, expressed in terms of the share of GDP, has risen from 1.5 percent to 2.4 percent of GDP over the decade ending in 2020. While that still falls a bit short of the current US share of 2.75 percent, an extrapolation of recent trends suggests convergence is likely at some point in the next few years.[30]

But China's innovation push goes well beyond its superior saving position. As noted earlier, it is a strategic outgrowth of a well-telegraphed shift from imported to indigenous development that has brought it very close to the frontier of innovation. China's space program is a case in point, with its *Chang'e-5* mission to the moon, its *Tianwen-1* exploration of Mars (with a follow-up manned mission to Mars by 2033), and its new *Tiangong* space station. Recent developments in radio astronomy, quantum computing, deep-sea exploration in the manned submersible *Fendouzhe*, and hypersonic missile development all reflect world-class paybacks from China's focus on basic research.[31]

According to Wang Zhigang, China's minister of science and technology, the basic research portion of total Chinese R&D outlays now exceeds 6 percent.[32] While that figure reflects a doubling of such spending during the Thirteenth Five-Year Planning period (2016–20), the basic research portion of total Chinese R&D spending remains less than half the US share of nearly 17 percent. That should provide some comfort to those who fear the immediacy of China's innovation threat. China still has a long way to go in closing the basic research gap with the United States.[33] But unless things change, that day will come, most likely sooner rather than later.

The bottom line: America has an innovation problem, and by embracing the false narrative of China as an illegitimate innovator, it is refusing to accept responsibility for the macroeconomic imbalances that have put pressure on its investment imperatives, including the R&D spending that underpins innovation. In failing to face up to its shortcomings as a savings-short nation, the United States is either unable or unwilling to support the innovation it needs for lasting prosperity. That leads us to what is by now an all-too-familiar question: why is America so eager to blame China for its own deficiencies?

Tech Conflict and Reshoring

In the end, the veracity of the evidence didn't matter. The vulnerable innovator took strong action against the rising innovator. The tariffs the Trump administration imposed on China in 2018 predictably escalated into retaliatory actions by both sides. US tariffs on Chinese imports went from 3 percent in 2017, before the trade war started, to 21 percent by the end of 2019. China responded by raising tariffs on US exports from 8 percent to 22 percent over the same period.[34] Other than fueling animosity, these tariff actions accomplished very little. As noted earlier, the bilateral US-China trade imbalance narrowed, but America's multilateral trade deficit, most recently encompassing 106 countries in 2021, continued to widen.

Ignoring the futility of this approach, the United States upped the ante by launching a full-blown tech war with China. Huawei was the primary target. Despite the lack of hard evidence of a threat, the "backdoor" potential of Huawei's 5G platform products was labeled a major US national security risk. This was an important piece of the case made by US Trade Representative Robert Lighthizer. It was one thing to frame Section 301 allegations as a conceptual case against China, and quite another to take targeted action against an individual high-profile Chinese company.

Initially, the approach was to blacklist Huawei, effectively closing off its strategic access to US markets. The company was placed on the "entity list" administered by the Bureau of Industry and Security (BIS) of the US Department of Commerce. The entity list was designed as a mechanism to prevent US exports from being diverted into production of weapons of mass destruction by America's adversaries. Foreign companies that are placed on the list have to apply for a supplemental license, subject to review by the BIS, in order to receive US products. While not an outright ban on access to US suppliers, placement on the entity list signals that such a ban is likely to come in the future.

In the first decade after it was created in 1997, the entity list was hardly used; only about two hundred foreign companies, mostly those involved in aerospace, chemicals, logistics, and technology (other than telecommunications), were designated targets. Beginning in 2008, however, a growing recognition that the entity list could be used more aggressively in addressing security, trade, and foreign policy concerns led to a sharp increase of foreign companies being placed under its purview; by early 2017, the entity list boasted about seven hundred companies. In light of the growing use of the list during both the Obama and Trump administrations, the BIS quickly complied with a May 2019 presidential executive order recommending Huawei's inclusion. As the Huawei battle escalated, the entity list expanded sharply, reaching nearly fourteen hundred companies by late 2020.[35]

That effectively put a chokehold on Huawei's most critical input, the design and production of high-end semiconductor chips made in America. Without those chips, Huawei's production of its world-leading 5G telecommunications equipment as well as its smartphones, at the time the second most popular in the world, would be stymied. Despite years of effort, China remains several generations behind US semiconductor companies such as Qualcomm, Intel, Applied Materials, Lam Research, and KLA-Tencor, as well as chip-design companies such as Cadence Design Systems, Synopsys, Ansys, and Mentor Graphics (now owned by Germany's Siemens but still with large operations in the United States). These companies are vital to the design and production of more advanced central processing units (CPU), graphics processing units (GPU), and field-programmable gate arrays (FPGA)—the lifeblood of Huawei's global product flow.[36]

But that wasn't enough for the Trump administration's tech war. After placing Huawei on the entity list, it threatened licensing restrictions on a wide network of US companies connected to Huawei's global supply chain. Then the administration, quick to recognize the potential of this approach, broadened out the tech war by using the entity list to address other complaints against China.

For example, in an effort to target Chinese companies allegedly tied to surveillance of Uyghur Muslim minorities in Xinjiang Province, the entity list was expanded to include Chinese companies involved in video surveillance (Hikvision and Dahua), voice recognition (iFlytek), data forensics (Xiamen Meiya Pico Information), nanotechnology (Yixin Science and Technology), and artificial intelligence (SenseTime). These early efforts have since been expanded; by late 2021, more than two hundred Chinese technology companies had been placed on the US entity list.[37] This not only supported America's concerns over Chinese human rights violations but also took aim at China's newly emerging AI-focused tech companies that were leading the innovations battle with the United States. This represents a dramatic expansion of the entity list that goes well beyond its original intent as a safeguard against foreign threats from weapons of mass destruction.

America's tech conflict with China now strikes at the heart of the new networks that underpin global trade and globalization. This "weaponization of supply chains," as it has become known, is far more potent in addressing foreign threats than bilateral tariffs. Not only do company-specific sanctions intensify bilateral conflict between the United States and China, through supply-chain connectivity they potentially add a new source of instability to the linkages of an interdependent, globalized world.

This gets back to the point I made in Chapter 2 about the increased role of global value chains in driving world trade and economic growth. The explosive growth in GVCs over the past twenty-five years has made the world more tightly woven together than ever before. A recent IMF study found that GVCs accounted for 73 percent of the total growth in global trade between 1993 and 2013.[38] With the expansion of global trade itself, accounting for 70 percent of the increase in world GDP over that same period, GVC linkages qualify as an increasingly crucial engine of global growth.[39]

The damage the world economy could suffer from the weaponization of supply chains should not be minimized. Efficiency dividends—lower input costs and associated reductions in product prices—will be especially hard hit. In times of stress, the weak link in a supply chain—the choke point—can unmask the tradeoff between efficiency and bottlenecks. Professors Henry Farrell and Abraham Newman have developed a network-based theory of globalization that stresses the critical role of supply chains in both eliminating slack and serving as instruments of weaponized pressure between nations.[40] In Chapter 11, I will argue that this weaponization, not just of supply chains but also of dollar-based cross-border financial flows, has materially increased both the risks and the consequences of a cold war between the United States, China, and now Russia.

But there is a more immediate impact to consider. Take away supply chains, which have played a key role in holding down inflation and expanding household purchasing power in the United States, and we risk many macro fundamentals being turned inside out.[41] At a minimum, trade will get diverted to higher-cost foreign producers. Over time, the "ultimate fix" of such "reshoring" would return output to higher-cost domestic production platforms. Lacking the efficiency dividends of lower costs, both companies and consumers would end up paying more for less. Living standards would suffer.

China could be hit especially hard by an unwinding of global supply chains. Following its accession to the World Trade Organization in late 2001, Chinese GDP growth averaged 9 percent a year for eighteen years while urban employment expanded by two hundred million and the number living in poverty was reduced by more than five hundred million. By no coincidence, China's economic growth in the aftermath of WTO accession was largely export-led, and increasingly driven by GVCs.

Political leaders have increasingly bought into the idea that network effects can now provide a new dimension of leverage to economic and foreign policy that can be adroitly deployed in times of pressure. The weaponization of supply chains, as an outcome of the US-China conflict, has spurred widespread demands for the "supply-chain liberation" of reshoring to bring offshore production back home. The "friend-shoring" of restricting supply chain access to coalitions of like-minded national alliances has taken on new importance in the Russo-Ukrainian War. The networks of globalization, once a powerful force of economic, financial, and political integration, are now at risk of becoming new sources of fragmentation and divisiveness.[42]

But the geopolitics of deglobalization come with their own set of complications. It turns out that GVCs are not easily malleable. Companies cannot quickly redirect sourcing from one supplier to alternatives in other foreign markets. Recent research underscores this "stickiness" of GVCs.[43] So too does the experience of Apple, long noted for its supply-chain prowess. Before he became CEO of Apple, Tim Cook was the company's chief operations officer, charged with supply chain management. It took him years to reengineer the iPhone supply chain.[44] Adjusting supply chains is far from the flick of a switch that many politicians assume.

Globalization is under attack in many quarters today. The supply chain—the knitting together of heretofore fragmented components of production, assembly, and distribution—has become the platform of the modern global economy. GVCs not only employ the latest advances in technology and logistics, they also offer increasingly efficient and near instantaneous delivery of both goods and services. That efficiency dividend has been drawn into sharp question by the supply-chain shock of 2021 in the wake of the pandemic.[45] Initially incorrectly diagnosed as transitory, this disruption only underscores GVCs' central role as an engine of global commerce. Dismantling or weaponizing supply chains—no matter who does it—puts all these hard-won gains at risk.

As I noted earlier, trade conflicts are hardly new. Countries have long battled over industrial prowess and its supporting technologies. At one level, today's battles are strikingly reminiscent of nineteenth-century conflicts in the early stages of the Industrial Revolution, when the United States, as a rising power, was aggressive in poaching workers, smuggling machines, abusing patent protection, and stealing industrial designs from Britain.[46] While the weapons of these battles are different, the stakes are just as high—innovation-led growth, productivity, and ultimately economic prosperity. That is the bottom line of the trade war that has now morphed into a tech war.

Helen of Troy

Let's return to the saga of Huawei and its purported role as the Trojan Horse. According to ancient Greek mythology, the Trojan Horse was the decisive weapon in the battle of Troy. Virgil writes that after a ten-year siege, the Greek army abandoned its camp and sailed away—apparently heading home but in fact anchored out of sight in a nearby harbor—leaving behind a large wooden horse-like structure, secretly containing thirty Greek warriors, presented as a gift to Troy.[47] The Trojans, overcoming their misgivings, pulled the giant horse inside the city gates. That night, the hidden warriors crept out through a secret door, opened the gates, and allowed the waiting Greek army to enter and sack the city, ending the Trojan War.

Homer's *Odyssey* offers a very different narrative.[48] Helen, daughter of Zeus and proclaimed the most beautiful of all women, was either abducted or seduced into seeking refuge in Troy. The Greeks, with their Great Horse, went into battle to rescue her. Helen, acting out of conflicted loyalties, resisted rescue, and figured out the secret of the Trojan Horse. Speaking in Greek, she circled the horse three times, enticing the lonely soldiers and luring them out the secret door. The tortured soldiers were slain and the battle for Troy raged on. The disheartened Helen was returned to Sparta to face a death sentence.[49]

Huawei, cast as the modern-day Trojan Horse in the US-China conflict, has been brought inside the gates but encircled, prevented from opening the backdoor on its 5G infrastructure that would let it seize control of America's telecommunications platforms.

Does the mythical story apply to Huawei? The answer goes to the heart of the case against it—intent. There is plenty of reason to doubt the company's sense of global citizenship. Earlier lawsuits and legal actions by Cisco (2003), Motorola (2010), and T-Mobile (2019) cast considerable suspicion. Lingering concerns over Huawei's murky ownership structure have reinforced the presumption that it is inseparable from the Chinese state.

The latest twist came in 2018 when Huawei was accused of violating US sanctions against Iran, which led to Canada's arrest and a nearly three-year confinement of Chief Financial Officer Meng Wanzhou (the daughter of Huawei CEO and Chairman Ren Zhengfei). While the charges against her made no mention of backdoor espionage, they compounded the company's image problem, raising further suspicions of intent. If a company does business with the purported enemy, the reasoning went, then it could easily be willing to launch a cyberattack on the United States. It did not seem to matter that US authorities have a long history of ignoring far more blatant sanctions violations by leading American financial institutions.[50]

Egged on by the inflammatory rhetoric of Donald Trump, who loudly pulled out of the previous administration's nuclear agreement with Iran, the American public had no problem voicing near unanimous condemnation of Huawei as a threat to US national security. Yet the charges against the company were eventually settled out of court with no connection made to the backdoor allegations, and Meng Wanzhou's "deferred prosecution agreement," reached with US authorities in September 2021, made absolutely no mention of industrial espionage.[51]

To this day, there remains no hard evidence to support the key allegations surrounding the backdoor weapon—basically, the secret code embedded in operating software that would enable the Chinese government (acting through Huawei) to bypass security controls in order to gain access to a computer system or capture encrypted data. Such intent is almost impossible to prove or disprove, but its prominence in the public discourse adds a worrisome dimension of fear to an already contentious trade conflict.

It turns out there is only one public account of the existence of a Huawei backdoor. Vodafone, Europe's largest telecom provider, disclosed in 2011 that it had found vulnerabilities in the Huawei-installed software of its fixed-line network in Italy that could have potentially compromised security of home Internet routers and optical service nodes that directed traffic through broadband network gateways.[52] At Vodafone's request, Huawei eventually removed the vulnerabilities. At no point was there any report of suspicious data capture or systems-control activity that exploited these backdoors. Vodafone was satisfied with this outcome and has since increased reliance on Huawei as its fourth largest supplier of equipment, behind Apple, Nokia, and Ericsson. There was no sign that any backdoor vulnerability was weaponized. This all occurred ten years before the USTR framed its Section 301 allegations.

Does that mean that Huawei could not create such a backdoor and turn it into a weapon of cyber warfare? Of course not. What this incident does indicate is that a backdoor can be uncovered by cybersecurity experts in a host country. Presumably, it also means existing cybersecurity protocols can provide early warning of any backdoors, allowing breaches to be neutralized before they might be put into action in cyber combat. In Vodafone's case, it is important to stress that despite the apparent vulnerability of Huawei's Italian operating system, no nefarious state-sponsored acts were detected.

Despite the lack of evidence that Huawei poses a lethal threat to America's telecommunications infrastructure, the fervor against the company has only intensified. An important reason for this growing animosity ties back to a theme I addressed in Chapter 4. Just as a savings-short United States has fixated on China to mask its shortfall in the investment needed to sustain long-term economic growth, the fixation on Huawei may be masking America's inability to mount an effective presence in the 5G business.

That raises a key question: If 5G is such an important platform that it revolutionizes all aspects of telecommunications, from Internet and telephone service to video and e-commerce, where was corporate America in meeting this competitive challenge? The short answer can be found in the sad tale of the demise of Lucent. Lucent, which had been carved out of the Bell Systems after the US government's breakup in 1984, housed one of the world's leading research platforms, Bell Laboratories.[53] While Lucent, in partnership with Canada's Nortel, had incumbent advantage in the prior development of early-generation 3G networks, it dropped the ball on 5G, largely for short-term financial reasons.[54] Lucent's subsequent struggles are well known—in 2006 it was taken over by France's Alcatel, which in turn was absorbed by Nokia in 2016.

The rest is history. Huawei, Ericsson, and Nokia now dominate the 5G business, collectively accounting for over 80 percent of the global market. American companies are nowhere to be found. Contrary to US assertions, Huawei's 5G leadership is not just due to subsidized Chinese state lending.[55] Huawei's massive R&D budget, more than $22 billion in US dollars in 2021 and double that of its 2015 budget, is comparable to the R&D spending of US tech leaders Amazon and Alphabet and well above that of Apple; in addition, more than half of Huawei's total workforce of nearly two hundred thousand employees is involved in research.[56] Largely through those efforts, Huawei leads the world in the 5G patent race, an essential element of a powerful commercialization strategy.[57]

Huawei's success raises the distinct possibility that America's opposition could be less about unsubstantiated fears of the dreaded backdoor and more about competitive insecurity and politicized anti-China vengeance. The pre-emptive US attack aimed at undermining Huawei as the world leader in 5G has allowed friendly European alternatives (Ericsson and Nokia) to grab market share, encouraging some to believe that this may possibly create an opening for a US company to enter the 5G market.

All this is not to say that Huawei does not have a serious problem. To be caught in the crossfire of a trade dispute is one thing, but to be the lightning rod of a tech conflict is another matter altogether. Rather than get in front of the problem, Huawei has consistently played defense in reacting to allegations lodged by the United States and its allies. It has met concern and criticism with a combination of obfuscation, disdain, and arrogance. When confronted with detailed evidence regarding Cisco's 2007 charges of software piracy embedded in one of its routers, Chairman Ren smugly offered a one-word retort, "Coincidence."[58] Huawei has an unfortunate knack for casting suspicion on itself.

The company has also ducked full disclosure of its murky ownership structure. This information is very important in the United States and other Western countries, who fear that Huawei is an instrument of the state that could easily be co-opted in an escalating tech conflict. Huawei's stonewalling has done little to dispel this concern. Its standard response is to stress that nothing in China's national security law requires the company to act on behalf of the state.[59] Similarly, on ownership, Huawei maintains that it is employee owned and independent of state interference. That is a stretch. It is over 95 percent owned by a "trade union committee" whose membership, funding, and relationship with the Chinese government remain unclear.[60]

Transparency has never been a notable characteristic of Chinese businesses. Yet transparency is precisely what Huawei needs to address its serious image problem and dispel American fears. If it has nothing hide, then there is nothing to fear from disclosure. Yet Huawei continues to reject this approach. The company's response is symptomatic of China's broader public image problem, which I will take up in more detail later in this book.

While Donald Trump launched the all-out attack on Huawei, the Biden administration has not eased the pressure. This may have important unintended consequences. Huawei's initial response to US sanctions was to reorient its supply chain away from the United States toward Taiwan and Japan.[61] But it has also moved aggressively to push for self-sufficiency, in line with the Chinese government's strategic top-down focus. Huawei has redoubled its efforts in semiconductor development, focusing on its HiSilicon subsidiary, with support from Taiwan's MediaTek. The new smartphone model it released in September 2019, the Mate 30, was produced without any US components.

Blacklisting the company could backfire for the United States. The immediate impacts of US sanctions have taken a severe toll on Huawei's once dominant smartphone business, prompting a nearly 30 percent plunge in the company's overall revenues in 2021.[62] But, over time, this pressure will only encourage Huawei to accelerate its push for self-sufficiency, meaning that the United States will lose its leverage as a source of demand and as a potential choke point in its supply chain. By fixating on the false narrative of Huawei as a modern-day Trojan Horse, a savings-short United States risks ignoring far more serious challenges at home. The mythical Helen of Troy would have quickly looked for a different horse. Another lesson lost.

6

Winning Cold Wars

THE WORLD TILTED WHEN THE BERLIN WALL came down in late 1989. The Cold War was about to end without ever turning hot and the long-awaited peace dividend was at hand. Now, some thirty-three years later, with war in Ukraine, the world may be tilting back again. The Russian Federation, the like-minded successor state to the former Soviet Union, has shattered the post–Cold War peace, risking unthinkable carnage in Europe and the world.

This shock comes amid the seemingly inexorable escalation of another cold war on a different front—the mounting conflict between the United States and China. The frictions of a trade war have morphed quickly into a tech war, and now there are visible manifestations of a twentieth-century-style cold war. As US-China tensions mount in the context of the Russo-Ukrainian War, there is a naïve presumption that the situation is manageable. Never mind the waste and perils of such a clash—economic inefficiencies, geopolitical tensions, and growing risks of a broader world war. America, China, and now Russia all insist they are on the right side of history.

The possibility of another cold war deserves special attention in our assessment of the false narratives underpinning conflict between the United States and China. While history is filled with examples of belligerent relationships between nations, only one precedent really matters today—the forty-four-year Cold War between the United States and the Soviet Union, from 1947 to 1991.[1] Yet the lessons of that earlier period seem lost. As the victor in the Cold War, the United States apparently thinks that what worked against the Soviet Union will work against China. But China, as an ally to the USSR in the early days of that conflict, also believes it has a clear understanding of what is at risk. Confident and forewarned, neither the United States nor China senses any urgency for de-escalation.

This complacency is both dangerous and, in a sense, surprising. Each side recognizes that it is engaged in a power struggle for global hegemony. Defeat is not an option. Not only would it shatter the aspirational promises of the loser's national dream, it would inject a new and worrisome instability into the global balance of power and the world economy. It is disturbing that great powers dismiss such risks.

The history of the first cold war sheds considerable light on how to think about a second one. The United States and the USSR were both heavily burdened by rapidly rising military expenditures. They were peer competitors in weapons technology, but not as economic rivals. The US economy dwarfed that of the Soviet Union; at the onset of the Cold War, in 1947, the Soviet economy was slightly less than 30 percent the size of America's.[2] US economic growth was in a sweet spot during the 1950s and 1960s before encountering difficulties in the 1970s and early 1980s. The smaller Soviet economy, while seemingly strong on the surface, always struggled. In the end, America's economic strength prevailed while the Soviet economy, hugely inefficient and overburdened with keeping pace militarily, eventually imploded.

Can the United States count on a similar outcome in a second cold war with China? As I stressed in Part I, the US economy is facing formidable challenges. There has already been a major slowing of underlying economic growth, and prospects for a spontaneous reversal are dim. The Chinese economy has also slowed from its blistering pace in the thirty years since the Deng Xiaoping takeoff, but it is still expanding nearly four times as fast as the US economy. And the scale comparison between the United States and China—with by one measure the GDP of the two nations having reached parity in 2016—is far different from what it was in the first cold war, when the Soviet economy was considerably smaller than America's.[3] This underscores a profound contrast between the two periods. Today, scale differentials and relative growth trajectories are both the opposite of what prevailed in the first cold war. America is lacking the most decisive advantage it had against the USSR.[4]

China, of course, could always stumble, but the argument in Part I of this book suggests that such an outcome is unlikely. Much of China's recent economic slowing is traceable to a deliberate rebalancing strategy, reflecting a shift to more slowly growing private consumption and services, as well as temporary headwinds from Covid-19 containment and a conscious deleveraging campaign aimed at weaning its economy from more than a decade of debt-intensive growth. Still, a Chinese growth accident can hardly be ruled out, and much Western thinking has long favored such a possibility. While Chinese resilience has confounded the pessimists time and again, past performance is no guarantee of future results. If the Chinese economy encounters serious trouble, it could easily lose a second cold war.

The past offers a grim reminder of the dark side of great power struggles. Much has been written about the history of military conflict between rising and ruling powers—the so-called Thucydides Trap.[5] More often than not, and by a fairly wide margin, such clashes culminated in outright war. Notwithstanding the nuclear belligerence that Vladimir Putin has injected into the war in Ukraine, today most still dismiss this possibility as unthinkable in an era of nuclear deterrence. Yet accidents can happen. The Cuban missile crisis of 1962 is a high-risk example of how close the first cold war came to turning hot. Today, a possible spark in the Taiwan Straits or the South China Sea raises similar risks, as does China's dramatic expansion in naval power along with its stunning recent advances in weapons technologies. It would be smug to think that such a conflict would inevitably go America's way.

Henry Kissinger remarked a few years ago that the United States and China were already in the "foothills of a new cold war." He went on to warn that further conflict escalation between the world's two largest economies could lead to an outcome "even worse than it was in Europe" during World War II.[6] The endgame of conflict escalation is always unknown. The only certainties are that cold wars are not easy to win, and that a protracted battle between two great powers is likely to take a heavy toll on both and cause significant collateral damage to the rest of the world.

Kissinger's warning is spot on. As Herman Kahn presciently warned at the height of Cold War 1.0, cavalier dismissal of a hot war as unthinkable in an era of nuclear deterrence risks a dangerous complacency that could result in an accidental war.[7] There is no excuse for avoiding a careful assessment of the risks of a new cold war. That is even more true with the shocking outbreak of military conflict in Eastern Europe.

Two Telegrams

There is no precise definition of a cold war. In its simplest sense, it is a deep, broad-based state of protracted conflict between nations that stops short of direct, widespread military action. Such a conflict can take many forms, from sharp rhetorical exchanges to restrictions on cross-border activity of people, finance, and commerce. The trade and tech wars between the United States and China are obvious and important examples of such nonmilitary conflict. A cold war is all that and more. It is a clash on multiple fronts that brings constant worry over what could happen if the temperature gets raised.

George Kennan's famous "Long Telegram," written on the occasion of his departure from Moscow as the US embassy's chargé d'affaires (senior foreign service officer), provided the first comprehensive assessment of what a cold war meant to America.[8] Written on February 22, 1946, in the immediate aftermath of World War II, it was addressed to Secretary of State James Byrnes, in response to an official query as to why the USSR had refused to join the newly created International Monetary Fund and World Bank. At the time it was sent, the Long Telegram was the lengthiest diplomatic dispatch in State Department history.[9] In keeping with Kennan's analytical approach to foreign policy strategy, it was organized as a five-part assessment of a political speech delivered by Joseph Stalin thirteen days earlier. Kennan used that occasion to warn Washington of what was likely to come from the Soviet Union.

The Long Telegram provided a systemic assessment of the Soviet threat. It stressed the internal contradictions of the Stalinist regime—the imposition of an intensive military industrialization on a largely rural and agricultural society; the economic strains arising from recent territorial expansions;

and "continued secretiveness about internal affairs, designed to conceal weakness." Kennan underscored the tensions between those contradictions and the Soviet need to restrain its adversary, the United States. Over time, he argued, these tensions would create a string of failures that would lead the Soviet system to collapse of its own weight.

Until that happened, however, the USSR posed major risks to what was then the very fragile stability of the early postwar world. The Long Telegram stressed that the Kremlin had a "neurotic view of global affairs that was aimed at setting Western powers against each other." The exercise of Soviet power was highly strategic, he cautioned, making it a formidable adversary for the West. He saw the Soviet regime as "impervious to logic of reason, and . . . highly sensitive to logic of force."[10] Seventy-six years later, Kennan's words could have just as easily been describing Vladimir Putin.

The concluding section of the Long Telegram made the critical point that the United States, as the Soviet Union's primary adversary, could not afford to take the risks of escalation lightly. Conflict "should be approached with same thoroughness and care as [a] solution of major strategic problem[s] in war, and if necessary, with no smaller outlay in planning effort." Outright war, however, was not needed for successful implementation of this strategy. It would take, instead, "long-term, patient, but firm and vigilant containment." The United States would ultimately prevail, Kennan concluded, if it had the "courage and self-confidence to cling to our own methods and conceptions of human society."[11]

The case for containment became George Kennan's legacy. It assured him a prominent place in the history of US foreign policy.[12] There would, of course, be no instant validation of this strategy. That finally came with the dissolution of the Soviet Union in 1991, forty-five years after the Long Telegram was sent to Washington. The subsequent breakup of the USSR and the eventual reemergence of the Russian Federation as a new global adversary for the United States was well beyond the scope of his observations back in 1946. Nor did he have much to say about other potential adversaries. Other than a nod to the possibility of support of Chinese communists and other unfriendly governments to the Soviet cause, Kennan made no mention of a looming strategic threat from China. That was understandable—in 1946, China was in the throes of a revolution whose outcome was still unknown.

Seventy-five years after Kennan's missive, a new telegram surfaced. Published by the Atlantic Council and once again written anonymously (an edited version of Kennan's dispatch ultimately appeared in *Foreign Affairs* under the pseudonym "X"), "The Longer Telegram" purports to offer an updated view of US cold war strategy—this time with China as the antagonist.[13] The name of the new effort is apt. At thirty thousand words, it makes Kennan's five-thousand-word effort look *de minimis* by comparison.[14]

Unlike the Long Telegram of 1946, which focused on the structural weaknesses of the Soviet system, the Longer Telegram framed America's China problem in personal rather than analytical terms, focusing almost exclusively on the role and character of its leader, Xi Jinping. It urges that "all US political and policy responses to China . . . should be focused through the principal lens of Xi himself."

The Longer Telegram argues that Xi Jinping is very different from his immediate predecessors, Hu Jintao and Jiang Zemin: "Xi is a man in a hurry; his predecessors were not." This is true on one important level. The pace of reforms and economic rebalancing had slowed in the years preceding Xi's tenure in office. But the Longer Telegram misses a key point. The slowing not only raised concerns of "reform fatigue" but caused many to fear that China could be trapped in an incomplete transition, leaving its economy and its people vulnerable to external shocks such as the Global Financial Crisis of 2008–9 that now tend to arise with great regularity.[15] Speedier reforms are not necessarily a bad thing—they could well boost a lagging rebalancing and provide China with greater resilience to cope with such shocks.

Yes, as we have seen, Xi has been far more assertive than his predecessors in a number of ways, from an early focus on anti-corruption and comprehensive Third Plenum reforms to the Belt and Road Initiative and a "dual circulation" strategy of structural rebalancing, and now to a more recent focus on "common prosperity."[16] The same can be said for his focus on ideology. But the Longer Telegram conflates these efforts with China's human rights violations and muscular actions in the South China Sea and the Taiwan Straits. By characterizing Xi's China as the greatest threat of the post–World War II era, the new telegram at times sounds like former USTR Robert Lighthizer. And like Lighthizer's Section 301 complaint, it renders most of its verdicts through a combination of unsubstantiated assertions and circumstantial evidence.

The Longer Telegram is laced with some fifteen staccato-like action lists and numerous unsubstantiated chest-thumping assertions, such as that the dollar should never be allowed to fall. Its initial assertion is entirely correct—the United States lacks a fundamental China strategy—but its bottom line basically boils down to a character assassination of Xi Jinping.

That the United States lacks a strategy, while important, is hardly a new critique. George H. W. Bush famously said in the 1988 presidential campaign that he wasn't good at the "vision thing"; neither, apparently, is the United States.[17] That wasn't always the case—look no further than Kennan's successful containment strategy—but in recent years, America seems to have become more impulsive in its foreign policy and has lost patience for longer-term thinking. In both Afghanistan and Iraq, the United States was quick to rush into military conflict but slow to grasp the consequences of those missteps. Strategy became reactive, supposedly underpinned by core American values rather than a deliberate well-thought-out framework better suited to address the complex challenges faced by many nations around the world. It is far too soon to judge if that is now changing in response to the Russo-Ukrainian War.

The China debate is obviously of great importance for the United States. Yet it is tough to debate the anonymous author of the Longer Telegram, who is identified only as "a former senior government official with deep expertise and experience dealing with China." The Atlantic Council puts its imprimatur on this approach "for reasons we consider legitimate but that will remain confidential."[18] All this is cloaked in the same secrecy that Soviet experts like Kennan, as well as most of China's critics, have long found particularly distasteful.

While the two telegrams strike a common note in warning of the perils of cold war, there is an important twist. As Kennan put it in 1946, America would succeed against the Soviet Union if it focused on strengthening from within. The Longer Telegram seems to acknowledge this on one level but then, unlike Kennan, enters the vortex of personal blame and paranoia—a perfect example of the biased mindset that now grips the American political class. This is a classic symptom of the conflict phase of codependency, from which there is no easy exit. America's willingness to engage in a cold war with China favors blame over self-renewal.

Cold War 1.0

The first cold war was a four-decade period of political and ideological conflict between the two dominant military victors of World War II.[19] When they were united in combatting Germany's Third Reich, the United States and the USSR were, in Cold War historian John Lewis Gaddis's words, two nations in "pursuit of compatible objectives by incompatible systems."[20] This disconnect, which was evident throughout the war, became glaringly apparent as soon as Germany surrendered.

The most obvious distinction in the taxonomy of wars is the contrast between cold and hot. The Cold War featured an arms race, military posturing and frictions, and several close calls like the Cuban missile crisis. But while they engaged in constant proxy wars, most notably in Korea, Vietnam, Afghanistan, and Angola, the two superpowers avoided a direct confrontation between their militaries. The threat of nuclear destruction forced them to restrain themselves. The conflict stayed frosty and contentious, but the antagonists avoided catastrophe.

The circumstances surrounding the end of the Cold War in 1991 exposed the sharp economic divergence between the two incompatible systems. On the surface, Soviet economic performance over the broad span of the Cold War appeared impressive—4 percent average growth in per capita GDP from 1947 to 1991, versus 2.1 percent in the United States over the same period. But Soviet strength was front-loaded, with average gains of 5.5 percent over the three decades from 1947 to 1976 giving way to just 0.9 percent between 1977 and 1991. In the last two years before the dissolution of the USSR, per capita output shrank by 4.3 percent on average, presaging a collapse for the successor state, the Russian Federation, that eventually totaled 36 percent over the first eight years of its existence, from 1991 to 1999.[21]

Despite the formidable challenges the United States faced in the 1970s and 1980s, its economic foundation was solid by comparison. In the fourteen-year period from 1977 to 1991, when the Soviet economy started to slow dramatically, US per capita growth held steady at 2.1 percent, little different from the pace in the first thirty years of the Cold War.[22] In the end, a rela-tively strong and resilient US economy prevailed over a weak and crumbling Soviet economy. The strength of the Soviet military establishment, the basis of its clout in the first cold war, had far outstripped the nation's ca-pacity to support it. The same can be said of the heavy burden on the USSR of supporting its satellite nations. The demise of the Soviet Union was a classic manifestation of what historian Paul Kennedy has called imperial overreach.[23]

This difference in economic performance provides a useful template to assess the potential ramifications of a second cold war between the United States and China. The faltering Soviet economy was critical in bringing the first cold war to an end. But the juxtaposition of this collapse against the resilience of a much larger US economy is of great importance in drawing out comparisons with the Chinese economy in a subsequent cold war.

The strength of the US economy between 1947 and 1991 involved far more than scale and growth. The economy was balanced, with especially strong underlying support from the twin pillars of saving and productivity. The net national saving rate, which as I argued earlier, is the best measure of an economy's capacity-enhancing investment potential, averaged 8.8 per-cent of national income. Reflecting this ample cushion of saving, the cur-rent account was basically in balance over the entire span of the Cold War. Significantly, America saved enough during Cold War 1.0 not only to sup-port business fixed investment but to fund the large defense buildup needed to counter the Soviet Union.

Moreover, underpinned by an ample reservoir of domestic saving and a balanced current account, the United States was free of major trade fric-tions for the first three decades of the Cold War. America's foreign trade position, the single most important component of the current account, was in fractional surplus at 0.8 percent of GDP from 1947 to 1975 but then slipped into deficit in the mid-1970s, averaging 1.6 percent of GDP from 1976 to 1991. During that latter period, trade tensions with Japan were a major source of international economic conflict. That development, how-ever, was unconnected to relationship tensions between the United States and the Soviet Union.

US productivity growth was solid throughout the first cold war, expanding at a 2.2 percent annual rate over the 1947–91 period. Long considered vital to economic prosperity, productivity is synonymous with improved efficiency and innovation as an outgrowth of new technologies embodied in investment-led growth.[24] America's impressive productivity performance in the decades following World War II was key to its competitive prowess. Moreover, with baby boomers entering the labor market at a record rate, the civilian labor force expanded at a 1.7 percent pace during the Cold War era.[25] The combination of solid productivity and labor force growth underscored the strong underlying growth potential of the US economy.

But the vigor did not last. As noted earlier, America encountered economic difficulties in the 1970s and 1980s. Yet despite the painful stagflation described in Chapter 2—slowing growth, rising unemployment and inflation—the comparative resilience of the US economy remained impressive. With the Soviet Union under increasing economic pressure, America prevailed on the basis of the size and relative health of its economy.

Cold War 2.0

Henry Kissinger's 2019 comment describing the United States and China as already "in the foothills of another cold war" was hardly a casual quip.[26] As the quintessential cold warrior and the architect of America's modern policy framework with China, Kissinger spoke from experience.

Still, many observers in the United States resist putting the cold war label on the current US-China conflict.[27] China seems to lack the territorial ambitions that underlaid the Soviet appetite for satellite states. Notwithstanding the ascendancy of Xi Jinping Thought, the current conflict does not feature the stark ideological competition the earlier cold war did. And the linkages between the two codependent economies contrast sharply with the absence of meaningful ties between the US and Soviet economies.

But recent developments offer a far chillier comparison. The combination of a trade war, a tech war, venomous charges over the origins of Covid-19, and the bipartisan anti-China sentiment stance of the US Congress all underscore the breadth and depth of America's concerns over Chinese actions. Well supported by public opinion polls, America's increasingly strident anti-China mindset constantly articulated by senior US government officials speaks to something well beyond a conventional geopolitical spat.

The same can be said for the territorial disputes in the South China Sea, to say nothing of the long-simmering human rights and political concerns in Tibet, Hong Kong, and Taiwan, along with increasingly contentious allegations over China's treatment of ethnic Uyghur minorities in Xinjiang Province. Moreover, AUKUS, a new trilateral security pact between Australia, the United Kingdom, and the United States, is clearly aimed at China and has cold war written all over it. Perhaps the strongest case arises from China's new unlimited partnership with Russia—forged on the brink of a devastating war in Ukraine that has split the world more than at any point since World War II. All in all, the circumstantial evidence is compelling. For the sake of argument, call it Cold War 2.0.

But will it end the same way? The economic comparison, which was decisive in the outcome of the first cold war, points to a very different conclusion for Cold War 2.0. The prospects for the Chinese economy look far brighter than those of the faltering Soviet Union at any point in the first cold war—provided, of course, that China stays the course of rebalancing and reform. The problem is with the United States. By virtually all measures, the US economy is in worse shape today than it was during Cold War 1.0.

If we take America's economic performance over the most recent decade as an indication of the country's ability to withstand the emerging pressures of a new cold war with China, the results are especially worrisome. As can be seen in Table 2, over the past ten years, from 2012 to 2021, real GDP growth in the United States averaged just 2.1 percent, far short of the 3.5 percent pace hit in the first cold war. Labor productivity growth has slowed accordingly, from a solid 2.2 percent pace during Cold War 1.0 to just 1.3 percent in the decade ending in 2021. In fact, the recent productivity slowdown marks the second weakest performance of any decade of the entire post–World War II era.[28]

The saving underpinnings of today's US economy are even more problematic. The net domestic saving rate averaged just 3.2 percent from 2012 to 2021, well less than half the 8.8 percent average from 1947 to 1991. Reflecting this shortfall, the current account and trade balance moved into sharp

Table 2. America's Diminished Capacity to Wage a Cold War

US economy	Then: 1947–91	Now: 2012–21
Real GDP growth	3.5%	2.1%
Productivity growth	2.2	1.3
Net domestic saving rate	8.8	3.2
Current account balance	–0.1	–2.4
Foreign trade balance	–0.1	–4.4

Note: Saving rate is % of national income; current account and trade balances as % of GDP. Productivity average starts in 1948 and trade balance is for goods. Source: US Department of Commerce (Bureau of Economic Analysis) and US Bureau of Labor Statistics.

deficit over the decade ending in 2021—in striking contrast with near balance prevailing in both measures during Cold War 1.0.

The picture that emerges from this comparison is disturbing. The US economy was in excellent shape to wage battle with the former Soviet Union during Cold War 1.0. But it heads into Cold War 2.0 battered by a succession of crises—the Global Financial Crisis of 2008–9 as well as the Covid shock of 2020—and afflicted with weaker economic fundamentals that point to a worrisome vulnerability that was not evident in the first cold war. As we will see in Chapter 12, that has not escaped the attention of China.

Based on its long history, many believe that American exceptionalism will somehow prevail under any and all circumstances—whether in conflict with China or anyone else. Yet with the US economy in considerably worse shape than it was fifty years ago, such resilience could be an especially tall order. With outsize post-Covid budget deficits likely to put sustained additional pressure on domestic saving, as well as on current account and trade deficits, America risks engaging China in a new cold war with one hand tied behind its back.

Finally, there are the economic scale comparisons between the two nations. As measured by purchasing-power parity metrics, the US economy, which dwarfed the Soviet economy at the onset of the first cold war, is smaller than the Chinese economy at the start of the second cold war. All in all, the strategy of economic dominance that so effectively brought victory in Cold War 1.0 could turn against a weaker America in Cold War 2.0.

Thucydides and Kissinger

Rhetorical escalation is a prominent feature of the cold war mindset. Nikita Khrushchev's famous 1956 threat, "We will bury you," left little doubt of what he thought was at stake.[29] In the 1950s and early '60s, American schoolchildren went through regular nuclear drills.[30] And there was a real sense of fear during the Cuban missile crisis of 1962. Mao Zedong was equally well-practiced in the art of belligerent cold-war posturing, at one point urging defeat of "United States aggressors and all their running dogs."[31]

Strident rhetoric plays a central role in the conflict phase of codependency, and it didn't come solely from the leaders of the former Soviet Union and China. The United States has also played an active role in rhetorical combat. Wisconsin Senator Joe McCarthy engaged in notorious red-baiting in the early 1950s, and wild accusations against China sadly became accepted behavior among members of the Trump administration in 2020.

In a succession of carefully orchestrated speeches delivered in the summer of 2020, cold-war-like tirades were unleashed at China by four of America's most senior officials: National Security Advisor Robert O'Brien, who focused on China as an ideological threat; FBI Director Christopher Wray, who addressed Chinese espionage; Attorney General William Barr, who spoke about the economic competition; and Secretary of State Mike Pompeo, who pulled it all together in a full frontal attack delivered at the Nixon Library in California.[32]

Coming from America's senior foreign policy official and the person fourth in the line of succession to the US presidency, Mike Pompeo's words had special meaning. Among his many memorable lines were references to "China's virulent strain of Communism"; the assertion that "Xi Jinping is a true believer in a bankrupt, totalitarian ideology"; and the vow that, in the end, "the free world must triumph over this tyranny." The speech was given at the Nixon Library to provide an uncomfortable contrast to the opening of US-China relations that President Nixon initiated with his historic visit to China in 1972. Pompeo's strident language and unsubstantiated allegations could have come right out of the McCarthy playbook of the 1950s.[33]

Combative rhetoric, while nothing new in cold war clashes, need not result in escalation. But the vitriolic charges and counter charges undermine trust and energize confrontation, setting the stage for an accidental conflict to escalate into something far worse. With tensions high in both the South China Sea and the Taiwan Straits, to say nothing of war-torn Ukraine, the danger of accidental escalation should not be taken lightly. History is filled with examples of mishaps sparking military skirmishes that then escalated into full-blown war.[34]

Graham Allison has offered a rich historical context to conflicts between rising and incumbent leading powers.[35] The "Thucydides Trap," as he called it in deference to Thucydides's history of the Peloponnesian War between Athens (the ruling power) and Sparta (the rising power) in the fifth century BC, underscores the significant chances of a rivalry turning into outright military conflict. That, of course, is the ultimate and most worrisome risk of a cold war.

On the surface, the implications of Allison's hypothesis are frightening. Looking at sixteen cases of major power conflicts back to the sixteenth century, he finds that twelve of them led to war. Does that mean there is a 75 percent chance of military conflict between the United States and China? Probably not. Most importantly, the continuum of conflict history looks very different today from how it looked prior to the nuclear weapons era. From the Ottoman Empire's repeated challenges to the ruling Hapsburgs in the sixteenth and seventeenth centuries to the devastating conflicts of World Wars I and II, it was pretty much a certainty that great power conflicts would lead to war. But as conventional warfare has given way to potential nuclear confrontation, the odds of a full-blown hot war have dropped almost to zero—or at least so we thought until Vladimir Putin said otherwise in the early days of his war against Ukraine. In the last three examples that Allison studied—all major power conflicts in the twentieth century— military conflict did not occur precisely because of the threat of nuclear destruction.

Does that mean that cold wars in an era of nuclear deterrence are ultimately just a geostrategic bluffing game, or the subject of fanciful fiction wrapped around frighteningly realistic narratives?[36] That is not the feel-good conclusion that follows from our assessment of relationship conflict. The cold war represents the most contentious aspects of the conflict phase of codependency—the rupture of what had once been a deep economic interdependence. Nuclear deterrence hardly prevents a costly arms buildup. Nor is there an automatic brake on conflict escalation, as Vladimir Putin's nuclear saber-rattling underscores in 2022.

China's military buildup and PLA force modernization have long been a major priority for Xi Jinping.[37] While US defense spending is still about three times China's, I will argue in Chapter 11 that there is good reason to expect that gap to be eliminated by the early 2030s. Several years ago, the US defense establishment sounded the alarm over the extraordinary expansion of the Chinese navy, which is now the largest maritime force in the world.[38] Although China has a relatively small arsenal of nuclear weapons, a major expansion of its nuclear missile silos in Gansu Province became evident in the summer of 2021.[39] That was quickly followed by the testing of a nuclear-capable hypersonic weapon that has shocked the US defense community.[40]

America's top military official, General Mark Milley, chairman of the Joint Chiefs of Staff, has compared the hypersonic weapon to Sputnik, the 1957 Soviet satellite whose launch presaged a major surge of defense spending by both sides in Cold War 1.0.[41] Many believe that that development led to the demise of the Soviet Union for precisely the reasons Paul Kennedy described—a defense overreach that outstripped the capacity of a weakening economy to support it.[42] China's relative economic strength points to the opposite conclusion—that its stunning military buildup is well within its means.[43]

If the aim of any arms race is to preserve the balance of power, China's rapid military modernization may alter the burden of maintaining that balance. If so, the contrast between the economic underpinnings of the two cold wars bears noting again. Ultimately, the weakening Soviet economy was incapable of sustaining an arms race with the United States and its much stronger economy. But the far more powerful Chinese economy is better positioned today to support a sustained military buildup—not only when compared with the Soviet Union but also compared with a decidedly weaker US economy. As Kissinger warned, just because a hot war is un-likely in an era of nuclear deterrence, Cold War 2.0 should not be dismissed as meaningless geostrategic posturing. Like its predecessor, this cold war could also have profound and lasting effects on the global balance of power. But unlike its predecessor, it may not permit the lessons of Thucydides to be dismissed out of hand.

Sino-Russian Cold War Triangulation

Fast-moving events often turn history inside out. The ancient lessons of Thucydides and their modern-day translation by Henry Kissinger have re-cently taken on new meaning. In one of the great and potentially tragic ironies of modern history, the Russian Federation, as the successor state to the defeated combatant in the first cold war, now poses grave risks to world peace and stability in a second cold war. This not only complicates America's false narratives on the new challenges it faces from China, it also raises the possibility of a strategic miscalculation by China.

These new risks stem from two major developments: China's newfound partnership with Russia and Russia's shocking aggression in prosecuting its war with Ukraine. On February 4, 2022, on the eve of the opening of the Beijing Winter Olympics, Xi Jinping and Russian President Vladimir Putin signed a comprehensive partnership agreement.[44] It covered several key areas of mutual interest, from climate change and health security to sus-tainable development and poverty reduction. But those issues were window dressing for a seismic breakthrough on geostrategic power sharing: the key line in the five-thousand-word-plus document read, "Friendship between the two States has no limits."

In an effort to underscore the importance of the new agreement, Chi-nese Foreign Minister Wang Yi subsequently characterized it as going well beyond a normal alliance, stressing that Russia is now China's "chief" stra-tegic partner, "no matter how perilous the international landscape."[45] Twenty days after the agreement was signed—and, conveniently for China, four days after the conclusion of the Beijing Winter Olympics—Russia invaded Ukraine, in an act of unilateral aggression that shocked the world.

On one level, this action borrowed a page from the first cold war. One of

the turning points in that earlier conflict was the Sino-American rapprochement of the early 1970s. As an outgrowth of US President Richard Nixon's
historic visit to China in 1972, America and China joined together in isolat-
ing the former Soviet Union at a time when its economic foundations were
starting to weaken. In geostrategic terms, this was a classic triangulation
gambit, two unlikely partners joining forces to put pressure on an adversary. As Henry Kissinger, Nixon's national security advisor and architect of
the trip to China, later put it, "The Sino-US rapprochement started out as a
tactical aspect of the Cold War; it evolved to where it became central to the
evolution of the new global order."[46] It took seventeen years for the Berlin
Wall to fall, but the Soviet Union eventually imploded under the weight of
triangulation pressures.

That painful lesson was not lost on Vladimir Putin, who has long described the demise of the USSR as the greatest catastrophe of the twentieth
century.[47] Putin apparently views a deepening, unlimited relationship with
China as an important step in Russia's campaign to redress this unfair loss
of power. America should have seen it coming. The first foreign trip that
Xi Jinping took as China's president was to Moscow, in early 2013. He and
Putin have since met thirty-seven times, more than any other pair of leaders in the world.[48]

But this is not just about Xi. In 2001, former Chinese president Jiang
Zemin and Vladimir Putin had signed the "Treaty of Good-Neighborliness
and Friendly Cooperation" as a commitment to their shared strategic values.[49] For China, that was a time of harmony and growing global connect-
edness. Later that year, China would enter the World Trade Organization
with great fanfare. Russia was also embracing growing partnerships with
the West, having just ascended to great nation status by joining the so-called
Group of Seven (G-7), turning it into the G-8.

Twenty-one years later, as their leaders met in Beijing in February 2022,
the world looked very different for both nations. Russia had been tossed out
of the G-8 for invading and annexing Crimea in 2014,[50] and China was involved in an escalating conflict with the United States. Meanwhile, America, convinced it could prevail over China through an aggressive strategy of
bilateral trade and technology pressures, was unprepared for the strategic
challenge of the new Russo-Sino partnership. Just as the United States and

China successfully triangulated the Soviet Union in the first cold war, America was now on the receiving end of the same strategy.

The war in Ukraine casts this new triangulation in an entirely different light. It is at best an uncomfortable development for China. Long committed to the "Five Principles of Peaceful Coexistence" first enunciated by Premier Zhou Enlai in the mid-1950s, China frames its core values in international relations in terms of respect for territorial sovereignty, non-aggression, and non-interference in other countries' internal affairs.[51] Yet Russia's invasion and subsequent brutal attacks on Ukraine and its people are diametrically opposed to these core Chinese principles. That leaves China struggling with the inconsistency between its beliefs and the actions of its unlimited partner.

But China has more at risk than the supposed morality of its principles. Questions have already been raised about Chinese support for its Russian partner's brutal Ukrainian military campaign. If China gives just the slightest nod in that direction, either by providing military assistance or by cushioning the blow of the financial sanctions the West has imposed on Russia, it risks being judged guilty by association.

The United States seems convinced that it should seize on this threat and put pressure on China to unwind the new triangulation gambit.[52] After all, China has its own history of falling out with the former Soviet Union, in the late 1950s and early 1960s. And over the longer sweep of time, there has been no love lost between the two nations.[53]

Yet this borders on wishful thinking. China views its new, unlimited partnership with Russia as a strategic response to an American containment strategy that was first prosecuted through a trade war, then a tech war, and now through the ideological rhetoric of a cold war. While the war in Ukraine undoubtedly makes China uncomfortable with its Russian partner, the Chinese leadership is predictably taking the long view, looking beyond the immediate war to its bid for great power status by 2049. China's rejuvenation strategy remains unwavering, even in the face of this horrific conflict. The Ukrainian war, however atrocious, is apparently a small price to pay for the Russian partnership's potential to help realize the key objectives of Xi Jinping's cherished Chinese Dream. I will take up the wisdom of this calculus in Chapter 11.

That raises an equally important strategic question for the United States. Looking past the war in Ukraine—obviously a difficult thing to do in the heat of the conflict—how well is America prepared to face this new twist in its coming cold war with China? The combination of Sino-Russian triangulation and America's considerably weaker economic position, compared with that in the first cold war, are important reasons to believe that US victory in a second cold war is far from assured. Operating under the erroneous presumption that what worked last time is applicable today, America risks embracing yet another false narrative in managing its conflict with China.

Sun Tzu on Winning

As tensions mount, the cold war framework takes on added importance as a tool for assessing many of the risks and potential ramifications of a conflicted US-China relationship. But as in military conflict, success in a cold war rarely comes from brute force. Strategy is what ultimately separates winning from losing. That should worry the United States, which, as the Longer Telegram correctly underscored, currently has no long-term strategic framework for dealing with China. On the other hand, the Chinese have long been steeped in strategic thinking. As the Chinese military strategist Sun Tzu wrote in the fifth century BC in *The Art of War:* "When your strategy is deep and far-reaching . . . you can win before you even fight."[54] There was a time when the United States valued strategy more highly. George Kennan's emphasis on patient containment in the Long Telegram was very much in keeping with the spirit of Sun Tzu. Unfortunately, the United States now suffers from a seemingly chronic strategy deficit.

But what does a win in a cold war actually look like? The demise of the Soviet Union after Cold War 1.0 is one possibility: the loser suffers a systemic failure. A cease-fire and disarmament offer another option, allowing both combatants the opportunity for healing and renewal. I will explore a path to that possibility in Part IV of this book. But another potential outcome to a cold war is an enduring standoff that destroys the relationship between former partners. This entails some form of "decoupling"—a breakdown of the cross-border linkages of trade, technology, financial capital, labor, and even information flows. All of these possibilities are currently in play in Cold War 2.0.

The risks of decoupling, with its reduced trade and capital flows, have received much attention as the United States and China now move apart after years of coming together.[55] Yet after declining in 2019–20 due to the combined impacts of Trump's tariffs and Covid, trade between the two nations has since bounced back sharply. The total of merchandise exports and imports between the United States and China hit $658 billion in 2021, down only fractionally from the record high of $662 billion set in 2018 and about $100 billion above the 2010–17 average. The United States and China continue to have the largest bilateral trade of goods and services between any two countries in the world.[56] Chinese holdings of US Treasury securities fell to $1.1 trillion in late 2021; while that is down 10 percent from its peak holdings in 2017, China remains the second largest foreign owner of US debt, only slightly behind the $1.3 trillion held by Japan.[57]

Similar trends are evident in people-to-people exchange. Pre-Covid issuance of US visas to Chinese nationals fell to 27,541 in 2019. While that is down 35 percent from the record set in 2018, China remained in first place, ahead of India, in visa issuance at foreign service posts. Despite the effect of Covid-related travel restrictions on overall visa issuance in 2020, China held its number one position throughout the pandemic.[58]

Unfortunately, the new cold war, as well as an outbreak of anti-Asian racial bias in the United States, has taken a toll on the issuance of visas to Chinese nationals studying in the United States. The growth rate of student visas for Chinese enrolled in US colleges and universities slowed to 1.2 percent during 2019 and 2020, the weakest two years since 2005 and 2006. Yet there are still over 370,000 students from China studying in the United States, nearly three times the number a decade earlier, and China remains by far the largest source of foreign students in American educational institutions.[59] The recent easing of student and academic visa restrictions by the Biden administration is a hopeful sign of improvement in this key aspect of the person-to-person exchange.[60]

The sharp reduction in cross-border transfer of technology products and services, along with the reduced flow of non-tech trade, capital, and people, is a hint of what we might see in a more protracted cold-war decoupling. In a codependent relationship, the impacts of these actions are felt by both nations. For example, lost opportunities for Chinese students and immigrants, as well as tariff-related reductions in US demand for Chinese exports, have been reinforced by impacts on the United States stemming from trade diversion to higher-cost foreign suppliers, and from the loss of foreign student purchasing power in the United States. The damage has so far been minimal, but it would only grow in a protracted cold war.

A recent study by the Rhodium Group and the China Center of the US Chamber of Commerce offers a more comprehensive assessment of decoupling's implications.[61] They estimate four channels of potential macro impacts: trade, investment, person-to-person exchange, and knowledge flows. In all four channels, partial decoupling is expected to lead to large losses for the United States, with especially acute impacts in four key industries—aviation, semiconductors, chemicals, and medical devices. The study makes clear that a full-blown decoupling, which goes well beyond the partial version the researchers modeled, will have far worse impacts on China-centric global supply chains, with potentially important national-security spillovers on a supply-chain-dependent United States.

In an interdependent world, bilateral decoupling of the world's largest trading relationship will also have global impacts. The greater level of trade today compared with that during Cold War 1.0 underscores this possibility. Despite a long slowdown in the aftermath of the 2008–9 Global Financial Crisis, trade still stands at around 28 percent of world GDP.[62] That's essentially double the 13.5 percent average share in the 1947–91 period of the first cold war. The more tightly trade is woven into the fabric of global commerce, the tougher it will be to disentangle those linkages. That lowers the odds of a pervasive and disruptive global decoupling like the worldwide trade war of the early 1930s.

The complexity of these linkages makes a full-blown global decoupling all the more unlikely. As I noted earlier, goods that used to be produced entirely in individual countries have been increasingly unbundled to many countries. Most goods now are produced piecemeal, assembled through fragmented trade in components and parts that are manufactured in a vast network of multi-country global value chains.[63] This diffusion of bilateral trade through multi-country supply chains dampens the effects of a bilateral decoupling of any two economies, no matter how large.

These considerations bear critically on the impacts of a US-China trade conflict. While bilateral decoupling need not lead to global decoupling, it can result in trade diversion that is amplified by global value chains.[64] The shift in the structure of trade, from traditional exchange of finished goods produced in individual countries to GVC-driven trade from multiple production platforms, also reflects important shifts in the structure of an increasingly integrated pan-Asian factory. Researchers from the World Bank and World Trade Organization recently found that the massive widening of the US-China merchandise trade deficit since China joined the WTO in 2001 stems mainly from the offshoring of production and assembly to China from other developed countries (especially Japan, Korea, and Taiwan).[65] That is very different from viewing the bilateral problem exclusively as Chinese-initiated import penetration into US markets, as portrayed by most Washington politicians and some leading academics.[66]

Significantly, increased GVC connectivity also means that tariffs imposed on shipments of finished goods from China to the United States will be felt not only by Chinese exporters but by third-party countries that are linked to China-centered supply chains. The recent US tariffs have had an impact not just on China but on trade-sensitive economies throughout East Asia. Supply-chain linkages have spread America's so-called China fix throughout the region.[67]

None of this implies that we might not see a further decoupling of the US-China relationship—in real terms through trade flows, in financial terms through capital flows, and with further reductions in technology and labor flows. That poses an even thornier political problem. The trade diversion arising from bilateral decoupling would mean that US sourcing would migrate from low-cost Chinese production platforms to a constellation of higher-cost foreign producers. As I pointed out earlier, that would impose the equivalent of a tax hike on US companies, workers, and households.

Taken to its extreme, decoupling would not only damage the nations directly in conflict—the United States and China—but also pose risks for the world. A thought experiment illustrates this point. Using the International

Monetary Fund's *World Economic Outlook* database, it is possible to "excise" China statistically from the global economy. This is basically an exercise in global growth arithmetic—subtracting China's impacts from the overall growth of the world economy to see what a complete decoupling would mean.

In one sense, this statistical exercise would replicate the supposed autarky, or self-sufficiency, of the Soviet Union during Cold War 1.0. Under a protracted, increasingly contentious cold war scenario, the United States and its allies could be thought of as aiming to sever China's economic links to the rest of the world. While this is unlikely to happen, the thought experiment provides a benchmark to illustrate how a complete Chinese decoupling might affect the rest of the world economy.

Unsurprisingly, a full-blown Chinese decoupling would be a big deal for the rest of the world. Over the period from 1980 to 2020, a rising China accounted for 23 percent of the total increase in global economic growth. Total world GDP growth averaged 3.3 percent over that forty-year period, and without China, whose share of world GDP rose from 2.5 percent in 1980 to 18 percent in 2020, the global economy would have grown by just 2.5 percent a year.[68]

That is a very worrisome result. Most experts on the global business cycle put the recession threshold of the world economy at approximately 2.5 percent global GDP growth.[69] The world is a big place, and global recessions rarely bring down all two-hundred-plus economies at the same time; in a typical global recession, contractions occur in just under 50 percent of nations.[70] The 2.5 percent threshold captures that dispersion in the incidence of contraction quite well. What these results mean is that absent China, the post-1980 world economy would have been hovering near the global recession threshold more often than not.

The experiment becomes even more interesting when China is hypothetically excised from the global growth record in the years immediately after the Global Financial Crisis of 2008–9. The result shows that the Chinese economy's resilience over the 2012–16 period was literally the only thing that stood between a subpar recovery and a recessionary relapse in the world economy. During those five years, while world GDP expanded by 3.5 percent a year, China accounted for 35 percent of that gain. Absent China, world

GDP growth would have averaged just 2.3 percent, slightly below the 2.5 percent global recession threshold.

These calculations are only a thought exercise, and not to be taken literally. An actual world economy with no China would look very different from what you get by simple subtraction. But the exercise underscores the major role China has played as an engine of global growth—especially in the aftermath of the Global Financial Crisis. Since its takeoff in 1980, the export-led Chinese economy has relied heavily on demand from the rest of the world to sustain its growth strategy. But at the same time, the world economy would have been in much tougher shape were it not for Chinese growth. That means no one will be spared if a protracted cold war takes the decoupling of China to the limit.

This tale of two cold wars sheds considerable light on the future course of the US-China conflict. Most importantly, the outcome of the first cold war with the USSR is unlikely to be a good predictor of a second one with China. Cold War 1.0 underscored the advantage that came from America's economic strength and resilience. Cold War 2.0 hints at a potential role reversal, with the United States, today, enjoying nothing like the economic advantage it once had over the Soviet Union.

Sun Tzu counseled that a well-conceived strategy was everything—it offered the tantalizing possibility of winning without fighting. Notwithstanding several proxy wars, George Kennan's containment strategy brought that approach to the first cold war with the USSR because the United States had the economic leverage it needed to sustain that effort over several decades. It lacks that leverage today. The United States is operating under the dangerous illusion of another false narrative if it presumes that what worked in the first cold war will be just as effective today. As Sun Tzu also said, "if you know yourself, you will not be imperiled."

7
From Trump to Biden—
The Plot Thickens

DONALD TRUMP, WHO FAMOUSLY DECLARED that trade wars are "easy to win," left little doubt as to the future course of conflict escalation. He saw another cold war with China as all but inevitable. Nor did his defeat in November 2020 foreclose this possibility. Will President Biden add another chapter to the conflict scripted by Trump?

The Trump view of China was laced with false narratives. From trade deficits and the hollowing out of a once proud US manufacturing sector, to vulnerable technologies and America's underinvestment in human capital, China was repeatedly disparaged as the source of the problem. Yet the case against it was political, lacking in analytical coherence, built on dubious evidence, and at odds with basic macroeconomic principles. But it resonated with the American public and their elected representatives. It was much easier to point the finger elsewhere than take a hard look in the mirror, as Sun Tzu admonished.

Repetition breeds acceptance. Look no further than Trump's own record as forty-fifth president. It didn't matter that fact-checkers caught him in over thirty thousand lies during his four years in office.[1] Support from his base only solidified. That support never broadened throughout his presidency, but anti-China sentiment did. Irrespective of demographic and political cohort, opinion polling showed that the American public saw China in an ever-darker light.[2] Like Japan in the 1980s, blaming China has widespread appeal.

US public opinion about China was not changed by the election of Joe Biden. If anything, the negative perceptions of China may have hardened as the debate over the origins of Covid-19 was rekindled in early 2021. On his first day in office, January 20, 2021, President Biden reversed many of Trump's most controversial policies—from rejoining the Paris Agreement on climate change and the World Health Organization to ending the Muslim travel ban and stopping construction of the Mexico border wall. But fearful of adverse polling data and acutely sensitive to his party's tenuous hold on Congress, he held firm on Trump's China policy.

While domestic political considerations figured prominently in this decision, the Biden administration may have something else in mind. For most of the post–World War II era, America's Asia policy has been more tactical than strategic. Initially, the highest priority was balancing the rebuilding of war-ravaged Japan against conflict on the Korean peninsula. Focus on China, especially during the tumultuous days of Mao Zedong, was an afterthought. As George Kennan put it in the Long Telegram of the first cold war, "America's China strategy" was an oxymoron.

That started to change with the Nixon-Kissinger rapprochement of the 1970s, and it gathered steam during the Deng Xiaoping era. But even then, America's China strategy remained unfocused, characterized by a conscious effort of "strategic ambiguity" in dealing with tough issues like Taiwan.[3] Purposeful vagueness in international relations is a recipe for trouble. It only works when there is deep mutual trust. When trust breaks down, as it has today, conflict inevitably follows.

The United States and China had entered the conflict phase of codependency well before Donald Trump took office. But the trade and tech wars that his administration sparked both shredded any vestiges of mutual trust and underscored the lack of a coherent US strategy toward China. Trump's transactional "art of the deal" framework was antithetical to a strategic approach. What was America seeking to achieve from this conflict? Was the goal simply to punish China, or was Trump in search of another scapegoat to assuage his base? Or was the United States truly aiming for a more fundamental shift in the Chinese model?

To craft a more robust policy toward China, the Biden administration must first come to grips with the flawed approach of the Trump administration. There is no bilateral remedy for America's multilateral trade problems, which stem from its macroeconomic saving imbalances. Unless the Biden team faces up to the incoherence of the approach it has inherited, any effort at a well-intentioned strategic reassessment is doomed to failure. But that works both ways. Just as it does for China, a strategic reassessment also forces America to face some of its toughest domestic economic challenges. In the best case, this could set up a creative tension between the United States and China that might provide a key to conflict resolution.

A Legacy of Failure

Donald Trump is out of office, but Trumpism endures. That is particularly true of US trade policy. Long viewed through the Ricardian lens of mutual benefits, trade under Trump instead became a means to achieve unilateral gains, the linchpin of his nationalistic emphasis on "America First."[4] This rethinking of trade policy took dead aim at China and rocked the foundations of the US-China relationship.

Trade had been the ballast in the two countries' partnership since the 1980s. The idea that the cross-border exchange of goods and services would help to set the rules of economic engagement between them was the basic premise of America's willingness to support China's accession to the World Trade Organization in 2001. At the time, US leaders hoped that Chinese WTO membership would ensure its convergence on Western norms. As China traded by our rules, went the argument, it would become more like us.

In retrospect, this was a naïve assessment. The painful memories of China's century of humiliation made its leaders determined never again to succumb to the will of others. China would join the WTO and make other international commitments on the basis of its own priorities, not the West's. Its global engagement would reflect the special "Chinese characteristics" of its own system, history, and aspirations.

America's adversarial naïveté has not just been evident in its engagement with China. It is also a striking characteristic of a similar pattern of US responses to Russia.[5] Time and again over the past twenty years, the United States and its European NATO allies have been forced to confront the paranoia of Vladimir Putin's alleged security concerns. Fearful of territorial encroachment on his western flank and deeply resentful of the implosion and subsequent dismemberment of the former Soviet Union, Putin has repeatedly sparked conflict over these concerns—from Chechnya in 1999 and Georgia in 2008 to Crimea in 2014 and now Ukraine. The West's strategic response not only bordered on appeasement by shying away from military conflict but sought to engage with the Russian Federation on terms compatible with Western values. Russia had been welcomed with open arms into the G-7 family of elite powers in 1997 for precisely that reason. Like China, as Russia grew closer, went the now familiar argument, it would become more like us.

Maybe not. As subsequent events have unfolded, it has become clear that both China and Russia had no such intentions. In the case of Russia, the West's miscalculation had grave military consequences. Fortunately, that has not been the case with China, at least not yet. But China's independent streak was nevertheless an especially difficult affront to many in the United States who were hoping for assimilation in accordance with "Western characteristics." When they concluded that those hopes were premised on a false narrative, the US-China trust deficit deepened. China's WTO credibility gap became the basis of many of the alleged violations featured in the Section 301 complaint. America had been swindled, went the argument, into going to bat for China's WTO accession.

Trump's trade war jettisoned the ballast that came from a strong bilateral trading relationship. Trade with China was no longer viewed as the means to secure mutual benefits but as a threat to American prosperity. Allegations of unfair trading practices put China in the crosshairs of US protectionism. Tariffs, sanctions, and the blacklisting of the "entity list" set American trade policy on a course it had not traveled since the 1930s.

For Trump, this was all a big tactical gamble that only a well-practiced dealmaker could successfully execute.[6] US negotiating strategy was aimed at squeezing China, exacting concessions so tough that it would ultimately flinch and change its behavior, putting an end to the unfair trading practices that Trump claimed were standing in the way of making America great again. After successive rounds of escalating tariffs and intense negotiations, the United States and China signed a "Phase I" trade deal on January 15, 2020.[7] Trump believed this was confirmation that the Art of the Deal worked just as he had promised it would—forcing China to finally give ground on its unfair trading practices. Ironically, Biden is following the same basic approach by imposing severe sanctions on Russia for prosecuting a devastating war in Ukraine. As this book goes to press, prospects of a sanctions-driven peace deal seem remote.

Yet the Phase I trade deal with China was doomed from the start. Most importantly, it purported to offer a bilateral fix for a multilateral problem. Taking aim at one of America's 102 bilateral trade deficits (the official count in 2018, when the trade war commenced, which has since increased to 106 in 2021) to ease the pressures on middle-class US workers would accomplish next to nothing.[8] As long as domestic saving remained inadequate, any narrowing of America's outsize trade deficit with China would be diverted to other nations. And, as I showed in Chapter 4, that's exactly what happened: the narrowing of the Chinese piece of the US trade deficit has been more than offset by sharply widening imbalances with Mexico, Vietnam, Taiwan, Singapore, South Korea, India, and others. The overall trade deficit has expanded—not contracted—since the onset of the trade war. Predictably, the China-centric fix backfired.

Still, the Phase I accord was greeted with great fanfare by both sides. The main feature of the deal was a commitment by China to increase its purchases of US products by at least $200 billion by the end of 2021. There were other aspects of the deal, which paid lip service to the broad structural issues emphasized by the Section 301 report of March 2018. Yet contrary to the Trump administration's vehement claims, the Phase I deal contained no meaningful breakthroughs on forced technology transfer, intellectual property rights protection, state-owned enterprise subsidies, or cybersecurity.[9] There was a meaningless clause on currency manipulation, which threatened to penalize China if it pushed the renminbi lower; the only problem with this stipulation was that China's currency was rising, not falling. And there was some language on agriculture primarily meant to please a political constituency that was especially important to President Trump.

There were many other reasons Phase I didn't work, not least the fact that the goal of increasing Chinese purchases of US products by $200 billion in two years was unrealistic from the start. The agreement was framed relative to the 2017 level of US merchandise exports to China, which totaled

$132 billion. A $200 billion increase off that base would have meant aver-age gains in excess of 50 percent per year in both 2020 and 2021—a virtual impossibility. The vigorous 18 percent average annual growth rate recorded from 2000 to 2013 would have had to nearly triple.

Unsurprisingly, and exacerbated by Covid-related disruptions in global trade, the bilateral trade commitments of the Phase I trade deal never had a chance. While US exports to China did increase by an average of 18 per-cent in 2020–21, identical to the earlier growth spurt, this was far below the agreed-upon trajectory. According to Peterson Institute economist Chad Bown's detailed tabulation of Phase I compliance, the shortfall was wide-spread. Chinese purchases came in well below target for motor vehicles and parts, aircraft engines and components, and a broad range of miscella-neous manufactured items; the only Chinese purchases of US products that came in above target were for semiconductors and medical equipment.[10] By the end of 2021, Chinese purchases of US-made merchandise remained close to 40 percent below the stipulated Phase I trajectory.[11] Not only was this bilateral agreement the wrong solution for America's broader multi-lateral problem, it missed its own target by precisely the same $200 billion margin it was expected to hit.

That result is in keeping with the Trump administration's history of bad trade math. The Phase I accord, in Trump's view, was testament to the pow-erful leverage of tariffs. He insisted for years that he loved tariffs and that they would impose a steep tax on China that would force compliance with tough US demands.[12] They were depicted as the ultimate stick in his "Art of the Deal" negotiating tactics. But they only reflected Trump's basic mis-understanding of whose pockets tariff payments come from. Contrary to his repeated assertions, the fees are not collected from China but from US importers at the port of entry into the United States. The president was cor-rect in one sense—tariff collections did in fact surge, from $38.5 billion in 2017 to $77.8 billion in 2019.[13] Yet this was not a penalty on China. It was the equivalent of a steep tax increase on US companies, and ultimately on American consumers.[14]

Despite these profound shortcomings, the Biden administration has em-braced the Trump administration's Phase I bilateral framework as a pillar of its trade policy with China. Even though the two-year agreement was effectively concluded at the end of 2021, Katherine Tai, the new US trade representative, has argued repeatedly that China should be held accountable for its failure to hit the $200 billion incremental purchase trajectory required by the January 2020 deal.[15]

This is a disappointing outcome, especially coming after Tai's long and arduous nine-month review of US trade policy toward China. As initially conceived by the Trump administration, Phase I was a political effort that was doomed to failure. It accomplished next to nothing in resolving the conflicted trade relationship between the United States and China. Negotiating it wasted time and diplomatic energy. In the end, it led to a progressive escalation of animosity between the two nations. All this appears to have escaped the scrutiny of the new USTR.

Trump's Phase I deal was an unfortunate combination of political theater and bad economics. Under Biden there is less theatrics, but the basic analytical flaw endures: an attempt to solve a multilateral saving problem with a bilateral, China-centric fix. Phase I was based on a foundation of false narratives, unworkable from the start. Biden, the anti-Trump Democrat, appears unwilling or unable to see this problem any differently from his predecessor.

The Biden Pivot

It wasn't just the weather that was cold when American and Chinese officials convened in March 2021 in Anchorage, Alaska. The Biden administration's first high-level meeting with Chinese counterparts was far from the classic light-touch diplomatic encounter that first meetings between governments usually are. It was icily reminiscent of Cold War 1.0.

The US negotiators, Secretary of State Antony Blinken and National Security Advisor Jake Sullivan, were aggressive and blunt in laying out the Biden administration's China stance.[16] They went well beyond the trade conflict and the Phase I deal that had been signed fourteen months earlier. The Biden team broadened the focus to embrace human rights and security concerns, justifying this shift with allusions to China's mistreatment of ethnic Uyghur minorities in Xinjiang Province and territorial adventurism in the South China Sea. Blinken and Sullivan apparently preferred the confrontational trappings of the art of the deal over the more traditional, delicate art of US diplomacy that would have been expected in this initial meeting with senior Chinese officials.

Predictably, this evoked a furious response from the Chinese team, Foreign Affairs Director Yang Jiechi and Foreign Minister Wang Yi. In keeping with the "wolf warrior" mindset that had been increasingly evident since 2020, the Chinese officials objected in unusually strong terms.[17] Empowered by the rise of their now rejuvenated nation, China's diplomats have become hypersensitive to virtually any critical comment from the West, and Wang and Yang unleashed a defensive tirade in response. On the US side, the discussion was all about the red lines of universal values. The Chinese side was not just irritated over what they considered condescending treatment from their US counterparts but indignant at the hypocrisy coming from the so-called bastion of democracy, which Wang argued had been compromised by systemic racism and, on January 6, 2021, by an attempted political insurrection.

This very public exchange was viewed in the West with shock and horror.[18] A censored version, aligned with the Chinese case for American human rights abuses, was celebrated in China.[19] Far from calming relations after four contentious years of escalating conflict, the Biden administration, with full support of the US Congress and American public opinion, had upped the ante.[20] And China responded in kind. There was no backing off from the trade war, no new proposals for reversing the tariffs and sanctions that had been initiated by both sides.

The two teams had dug in their heels, with each side apparently viewing reconciliation as a sign of weakness. The Biden administration was boxed in by politicized anti-China aftershocks triggered by the Trump administration.[21] And a nationalistic China and its wolf warriors left little doubt that there had been a major rethinking of its earlier passive approach to foreign policy. The low-profile "hide and bide" stance of Deng Xiaoping had been discarded. The Anchorage summit had cold war written all over it. The opening exchange, laced with charges and countercharges in full view of the media, offered no path for de-escalation.

But the real puzzle of Anchorage is why both nations held firm to the

Phase I framework of engagement. Why hang on to a flawed, unworkable agreement? This is where the plot thickens.

The story line leads to Kurt Campbell, currently the Biden administration's National Security Council coordinator for the Indo-Pacific. In an earlier incarnation at the State Department, Campbell played a key role in developing one of the Obama administration's signature foreign policy initiatives—the "pivot to Asia." The basic idea was that US foreign policy needed to start focusing on what was to follow a decades-long commitment to the Middle East. There was hope that as US engagements in Iraq and Afghanistan wound down, there would be new capacity to refocus American assets—military and financial—on East Asia, which was falling under the rapidly expanding shadow of a rising China.

Initially, the pivot featured an important policy initiative, the Trans-Pacific Partnership (TPP). The United States led long and arduous negotiations with eleven other countries—mostly in East Asia but also Canada, Mexico, and Peru—to establish what would have been the largest trade agreement in the world. But there was an obvious and important catch: as initially conceived, the TPP was to exclude China, the largest economy in the region and the largest trading nation in the world. This exclusion was a blatant attempt at China containment. Despite strenuous but unconvincing arguments to the contrary from the United States and its partners, the TPP was clearly aimed at pushing back against China's growing influence in the region and the world.[22] By offering American leadership as an alternative, the pivot was also meant as a direct affront to Beijing's "peaceful rise" narrative.[23]

The genesis of the idea lay in America's revisionist statecraft with China. A long-simmering complaint had been brewing in US economic and foreign policy circles over China's failure to comply with the terms of its 2001 accession to the World Trade Organization. Because China was not playing by Western rules, went the argument, it should be denied the growth dividends that have come from a surge of pan-regional trade. The TPP aspect of the pivot was intended to provide a counterweight to the economic might that China had acquired unfairly through its alleged noncompliance with WTO protocols.

Starting in 2009, the Obama administration threw the full weight of its diplomatic power into TPP negotiations. Secretary of State Hillary Clinton was quick to embrace the notion of an Asian rebalancing to US foreign policy.[24] It fell to Kurt Campbell, then the assistant secretary of state for East Asian and Pacific affairs, to flesh out the details. He not only was an active participant in the tough debate and negotiations over TPP but also went on to champion the pivot as one of Hillary Clinton's major foreign policy proposals during the 2016 US presidential election campaign.[25]

Had Clinton won the 2016 presidential election, Campbell undoubtedly would have played a key role in executing a China containment strategy under the TPP umbrella. But that never happened. Instead, President Trump, on his first day in office, pulled the United States out of the TPP agreement as an anti-trade protest. The remaining eleven nations eventually signed a modified version in 2018 now dubbed the CPTPP (Comprehensive and Progressive Agreement for Trans-Pacific Partnership). But the basic thrust endures: since its inception, the TPP, with or without the United States, has stood for one thing above all—an Asia without China.

Curiously, China has since responded to its exclusion from this framework by applying for membership.[26] It remains to be seen if China will meet the standards required for acceptance by all eleven CPTPP members— especially those pertaining to market access, labor rights, and government procurement.[27] Winning unanimous approval could be problematic given that Australia and Canada, both of which have recently locked horns with China, would have to vote to admit it.[28] If China, however, were to succeed in sidestepping their objections and become a full CPTPP member, it would be one of the great ironies of modern trade policy: a pan-regional agreement forged by the United States and intended to exclude China that would end up being broadened to include China while America remained on the outside looking in.

The pivot didn't die with Hillary Clinton's loss in 2016. Campbell went on the speaking circuit as a consultant, think-tank leader, and author of the definitive book on the Asian pivot.[29] Now, as the senior Asia point person in the Biden White House, he has joined forces with Jake Sullivan, Joe Biden's national security advisor and the junior member of the Anchorage negotiating team, in framing the pivot as a new lever to address America's China problem.[30] What started as Obama's pivot has now become Biden's.[31]

Unsurprisingly, the pivot resurfaced with a vengeance in the fall of 2021 with a major new foreign policy initiative: a trilateral security agreement between Australia, the United Kingdom, and the United States.[32] The so-called AUKUS framework builds on earlier Western intentions of China containment. Its signature initiative is to equip Australia with advanced nuclear-powered submarine technologies jointly developed by the United States and the United Kingdom as a direct counter to China's growing naval strength in the Asia Pacific region.[33] As per Kissinger's imagery, AUKUS makes the foothills of a new cold war now look higher and steeper.

Conflicted Coexistence

It continues to be unclear what America is pivoting toward. Trump's defeat in the 2020 presidential election was widely thought to signal a turning point for the US-China relationship.[34] Despite the March 2021 disaster in Anchorage, that may still be the case in the Biden regime. But while turning points signal a new direction, it remains to be seen which path comes next.

That was the essence of Antony Blinken's opening statement in Anchorage. He offered three possibilities for the future of the US-China relationship— adversarial, competitive, and collaborative. The adversarial path leads to Cold War 2.0. As I argued in the last chapter, this could be a serious strategic blunder for the United States. Not only is China considerably stronger than America's first cold war adversary, the Soviet Union, the US economy is a good deal weaker than it was then. Cold War 2.0 would be a pivot to nowhere.

In Anchorage, both sides strenuously dismissed the possibility of a new cold war. But the Biden administration was explicit in expanding the conflict from trade to human rights and geopolitical security, while also escalating the rhetoric of confrontation. The cold-war-like indignation of the Chinese response only compounded the animosity. While no one wants a cold war, neither side seems to want to avoid one.

Breaking the chain of conflict escalation is far from easy, especially with the stakes as high as they are between the United States and China. As I will argue in Part IV of this book, collaborative efforts to address common problems—such as climate change, global health, and cybersecurity—are critical for a restoration of mutual trust, without which it will be impossible to tackle the more contentious issues. The Biden administration's early actions to rejoin the Paris Agreement on climate change, as well as to reinstate US membership in the World Health Organization, are hopeful if tentative steps toward collaboration.

Competition, the middle ground between conflict and collaboration, is the stumbling block, largely because competition has different meanings for different systems. The United States likes to think of competition within the framework of a market-based free enterprise system. For China, it is viewed through the lens of market-based socialism. Yet both nations frequently overstep the boundaries of their respective competitive paradigms. That is especially true of China, with its highly subsidized state-owned enterprises, but also of the United States, where the heavy hand of government intervention is glaringly evident during all-too-frequent crises. As evidenced by the now-contested terms of China's WTO accession, the desire for fair competition is often expressed in terms of reciprocity or equal treatment, but the differences between systems make this hard to define, let alone pull off.[35] Clashing values and priorities have long been key sticking points in the debate over China's WTO compliance.

The Biden pivot is hardly a well-defined path for relationship healing; it is more a statement of emphasis. Curiously, the US administration now frames the blend between collaboration, conflict, and competition in the murky Cold War vernacular of coexistence, effectively a standoff between two powerful nations with two very different systems.[36] Using a label to define its strategy is in keeping with one of the long-standing practices of America's diplomatic approach to China.[37] Unfortunately, the term *coexistence* speaks more to the generic nature of transnational relationships than to the specifics of the China challenge.

What does coexistence mean for two nations embroiled in a conflicted codependency? At face value, it seems like a diplomatic shrug of the shoulders akin to the earlier construct of "strategic ambiguity," a determination to allow each system reasonable latitude to shape its own trajectory, and then figure out some noncontentious coping mechanism. The problem arises when one nation's latitude encroaches on the other's. Therein lies the challenge of a sustainable coexistence—establishing tripwires, or "red lines," of unacceptable encroachment, with penalties for noncompliance. The more serious problem, of course, comes in the enforcement of red lines—and the consequences of a breach.

In theory, that is what trade agreements are all about. The same can be said of broader compacts between nations—especially agreement on a market-opening bilateral investment treaty that was almost concluded by the United States and China in 2016 before being abandoned by the Trump administration in 2017. Whether the focus is trade in goods and services, cross-border investments, or defense and security, carefully negotiated, verifiable, enforceable agreements are essential for sustainable coexistence. As I will detail in the final part of this book, that is the ultimate means to conflict resolution.

To be effective, a negotiated treaty must address the core issues of dysfunctional relationships. Phase I was an abject failure because it followed the continuum of a misdirected trade war. It was ineffective because it squandered the opportunity to shift US-China engagement from conflict escalation to competitive tension. Ultimately, the resolution of that tension is essential to bring coexistence to life as a meaningful antidote to the conflict phase of codependency. That has yet to happen for the United States and China.

Bidenomics

A troubled relationship with China is, of course, only one of the many major issues on the plate of America's forty-sixth president. Gun violence, voting rights, immigration, systemic racism, a crumbling infrastructure, mounting inequality, post-Covid healing, and now a treacherous geostrategic confrontation with Russia—the list goes on and on.

America's China problem can't just be added to this list, however, without recognition of how it fits into America's fundamental economic challenges. While China has a high priority on the US foreign policy agenda, it can't be tackled in isolation from the other forces buffeting the United States and its economy.

A key problem for Bidenomics is a tough starting point. When Joe Biden came into office in early 2021, domestic saving, the federal budget deficit, and the current account deficit were all in exceedingly precarious positions. The enactment of urgently needed Covid relief, infrastructure support, and new social programs pushed the US federal budget deficit to an unprecedented peacetime average of nearly 13 percent of GDP over 2020 and 2021; while the deficit is expected to recede to 4 percent over the following five years (2022–26), that remains more than a percentage point above its long-term average.[38] And unfortunately, optimistic long-term US budget deficit projections don't have the greatest track record.[39] Outsize deficits are likely to be an enduring hallmark of Bidenomics.

Therein lies one of the Biden administration's key macroeconomic challenges. Embarking on massive deficit spending when the net domestic saving rate is historically low—just 3.2 percent of national income when Biden entered office in 2021—will only exacerbate one of the most politically contentious aspects of the China problem: the enormous trade deficit. With large budget deficits likely to cause a further shortfall of already depressed domestic saving, the US current account deficit, which hit a thirteen-year high of 3.6 percent of GDP in 2021, could widen even more.[40] Such an outcome would put further pressure on America's already massive multilateral trade deficit.

That's where China compounds the problems for Bidenomics. While the Chinese piece of the overall trade deficit has come down somewhat due to Trump's tariffs, it remains by far the largest share of America's multilateral trade imbalance. With domestic saving falling and the current account deficit rising, one of two things should happen: either the US-China bilateral trade deficit will widen sharply further or continued high tariffs on Chinese products will force additional trade diversion to America's higher-cost trading partners, resulting in the functional equivalent of further tax hikes on US companies and consumers. That outcome could prove especially difficult for a US economy now being threatened by its first upsurge of inflation in a generation.

All this is another way of saying that the macroeconomic underpinnings of America's China problem are looking increasingly problematic, at least through 2025. Because of low interest rates, deficit spending under Bidenomics is not likely to have a major impact on federal government debt servicing obligations; that could eventually change, of course, as the Federal Reserve now starts to raise interest rates to fight inflation. In the meantime, the fiscal stimulus will still lead to an increase in the trade deficit in general, and the deficit with China in particular; that, in fact, was precisely what happened in 2021, as both the multilateral and the bilateral China trade deficits widened sharply. Earlier, I argued that bilateral trade deficits should not be addressed as an actionable policy target by a savings-short nation like the United States. But it seems safe to presume that the politics of China bashing will continue to take precedence over the next few years irrespective of the macroeconomic consequences of such actions.

Bidenomics could also affect the value of the US dollar. The broad dollar index fell 9 percent in inflation-adjusted terms over the final eight months of 2020 before rebounding by about 6 percent over the course of 2021.[41] With the US current account deficit going from bad to worse and the Federal Reserve likely to be restrained in boosting its benchmark policy interest rate even in the face of a vigorous recovery and accelerating inflation, dollar weakness in 2020 could be a warning of more to come.[42]

With war raging in Ukraine the dollar has gone the other way in early 2022, strengthening as a safe haven as it normally does during periods of global turmoil and tension. But as the world stabilizes, fundamentals should come back into play. The US dollar has experienced three major corrections in the past fifty years—in the 1970s, the mid-1980s, and the first decade of the 2000s. The declines averaged a little more than 30 percent, or three times the magnitude of the drop that occurred during 2020. With the shortfall in domestic saving and the current account deficit more extended today than during the dollar's earlier corrections, there is a compelling case for another sharp correction in the US dollar. So far, there has only been a hint of that. More could be on the way.

A decline in the US dollar, in turn, is likely to put further upward pressure on the Chinese currency, the renminbi, which has risen about 45 percent in inflation-adjusted terms since early 2000.[43] To the extent that Chinese authorities attempt to resist currency appreciation out of fear that it will damage their economy or destabilize their financial system, the Washington politics of China bashing will only intensify. US politicians, who have long been critical of any renminbi depreciation—whether market-driven or a policy-driven "manipulation"—would likely be further inflamed.

At the same time, a renewed decline in the dollar would undoubtedly raise questions about the demise of the greenback as the world's reserve currency and the possibility that the renminbi might inherit the role. While such a regime change cannot be ruled out at some point in the future, this is neither the time nor the circumstances under which that outcome is likely to play out. A still embryonic Chinese financial system is far from deserving reserve currency status. And despite the fiscal profligacy of Bidenomics, the long dominant US dollar is unlikely to surrender its "exorbitant privilege" any time soon.[44]

Even with a powerful post-Covid rebound, the Biden era is likely to prove surprisingly challenging for a savings-short, deficit-prone US economy. And that outcome will undoubtedly have important implications for the US-China conflict. Political pressures to address the China problem are likely to build, as a result, raising big questions for both nations: Does the United States have the political will to address its saving problem, or will it continue to blame China for its trade deficits? Will China seize the opportunity presented by America's economic challenges by attempting to increase its economic and geostrategic power?

America's Narratives of Denial

America's false narratives on China—especially those pertaining to trade, technology, and geostrategic conflict—have one important thing in common: they are deeply rooted in a social and political critique of a one-party authoritarian state that appears antithetical to the core values of American democracy. Never mind that that democracy is currently under attack from within.[45] The vehemence of America's false narratives on China leaves no room for the "whataboutism" of a polarized nation.[46]

Perhaps that is the greatest irony of all. With the United States in the grips of historic self-doubt, it may well need a scapegoat as a way of convincing itself that all is okay, that its leadership as the bastion of democracy is intact.[47] Is it a coincidence that America's false narratives on China have reached a fever pitch in such a climate of insecurity?

Earlier, I stressed the potential for viral dissemination of politically driven false narratives, including the allegations of unfair Chinese trading practices, the so-called Huawei threat, and America's hubris in presuming it can win another cold war. The enduring persistence of the false narrative, even if corrected by careful analysis and fact-checking, suggests that these impressions will continue to shape US public opinion for many years.

This raises even bigger questions: Why have false narratives of China become such an important element of America's sense of self? Is it because of a deep moral conviction in the superior value of democracy—respect, dignity, freedom of expression, and opportunity—and the related altruistic desire to share those values with others? Is it because of America's time-worn instincts to engage China in noble conflict, conflating the struggles with China with the "good war" of World War II rather than with the more corrosive possibility of another "forever" war, such as those in Vietnam, Iraq, and Afghanistan?[48] Or is something else at work, stemming from what psychologists have long identified as one of the strongest human emotions—denial?[49]

We should take this last possibility seriously. When it comes to the current state and future prospects of the US economy, the case for American denial is unfortunately quite compelling. The confluence of sharply rising inequality—income, gender, and racial—slowing productivity, mounting federal deficits and debt, subpar domestic saving, and ever widening current account and trade deficits paints a distressing picture of America. Yet the US body politic is pre-programmed to ignore these problems, sensing that to do otherwise would be an unfathomable admission of failure. That all but ducks what is perhaps the most intractable economic dilemma in the United States: it has lived well beyond its means since the late 1970s and is finding it ever more difficult to continue doing so.

Historically, those means have been defined by the economy's self-generated income. This measure, in turn, largely reflects the returns accruing to labor in the form of wage compensation—underpinning the fundamentals of a nation living off what it earns from current production. Therein lies a key aspect of the problem. In the United States, labor earnings, in the form of total wages and salaries (private industry and the public sector, combined) peaked at 51.4 percent of gross domestic product in 1970 before falling to 42.2 percent in 2013. While it rebounded to 44.9 percent by 2021, it remains well below the peak.[50]

As James Truslow Adams hinted, this shortfall of internally generated labor income poses a major challenge for a nation steeped in the aspirational promises of the American Dream. Without the prosperity that comes from the fair and just rewards of hard work, Americans have turned to alternative sources of purchasing power—namely, appreciation in the value of their asset holdings, from investments in homes and financial instruments. This seemed to work well for a long time. In the heady atmosphere of the 1980s and '90s, American consumers eagerly reaped the windfalls of psychological wealth effects from their investment portfolios and, courtesy of financial innovation, used home equity credit lines and second mortgages to extract capital gains directly from their largest investment, the home.[51] No reason to worry.

But relying too heavily on those supplementary sources of purchasing power ultimately had tough consequences. The new forms of wealth-based saving encouraged households to draw down traditional saving that used to be set aside from labor income—reducing the income-based personal saving rate from a peak of 13.5 percent in 1971 to a low of 3.1 percent in 2005.[52] Why save the old-fashioned way out of work-related earnings, if asset markets could make more money for you much faster? This development, in conjunction with increasingly chronic federal budget deficits, squeezed overall domestic saving; that, in turn, forced the United States to borrow surplus saving from abroad and run large current account and foreign trade deficits in order to attract foreign capital. It all seemed so easy.

In the end, the confluence of an asset-dependent economy and ever-widening foreign trade deficits is not a sustainable solution for an income- and savings-short nation. Asset and credit bubbles have too frequently gone to excess, bursting and triggering 1990s-style Japanese balance sheet recessions that are typically followed by anemic recoveries.[53] That happened in the United States in the early 2000s, in the aftermath of the dotcom and equity bubbles, and again a few years later after the bursting of property and credit bubbles. Bubbles, themselves, are one of the most seductive manifestations of denial, fueled by speculative belief that lofty asset prices can only go higher. Only when they burst does the true cost of denial become apparent.

The perils faced by an asset-dependent US economy bear special mention in the context of the US-China relationship. China, with its vast reservoir of surplus saving, has become one of the largest sources of foreign capital for a savings-short US economy. Due in large part to Covid, America's federal budget deficits exploded in 2020 and 2021, and while the usual array of optimistic forecasts call for budget gaps to recede in the coming years, these deficits are likely to remain historically large for years, if not decades, to come.[54] That will leave domestic saving under constant pressure, forcing the United States to keep drawing on surplus foreign saving to fund domestic investment and economic growth. As one of America's largest foreign lenders, China will undoubtedly play a large part in filling that void. Yet the mounting conflict with the United States draws into question the willingness of Chinese lenders to play that role.

America's denial is deep. The public is highly uncomfortable with even the slightest hint that the United States may have to stop living beyond its means. It is unwilling to face the possibility that China might no longer want to fund an overextended American lifestyle. It is equally unwilling to believe a correction in asset or debt cycles could come about through a reversion to the mean, or through a decline in the US dollar. And, so, denial sets in as a classic defense mechanism—not just as a myopic rationale to "keep dancing as long as the music is playing" but also out of a sense of entitlement that comes with America's self-image as "the last, best hope of man on Earth."[55]

Denial is not only rooted in this Reaganesque version of American culture but at the heart of many of the nation's false narratives of China. The bilateral bluster over the trade deficit, the fear of Huawei as a Trojan Horse, and the tough cold-war rhetoric are all signs of America's unwillingness to accept responsibility for self-inflicted problems. Saving, which may well be the ultimate act of economic responsibility, has a pejorative connotation for many. It is invariably associated with the "paradox of thrift," in which saving is considered a threat to economic growth because it diverts income away from the consumer demand that typically supports the economy.[56] This is a short-sighted view. Without saving, foundational investments in people, infrastructure, and innovation are hard to sustain. Unless the denial over saving imperatives cracks, America's long-term growth challenges will only intensify.

But denial can also lead to conflict. In ducking the saving challenge, the American public would rather pin the blame for the nation's economic difficulties on others. That was true thirty years ago with Japan and it is true today with China. Depending on the nature of the clash and the perception of the threat, conflict escalation can go well beyond economics—not so much with Japan in the 1980s but increasingly with China today. In cold wars, the risks of denial are even more worrisome as a potential source of accidental conflict.

The dirty little secret of America's penchant for living beyond its means is that the price of denial is cheap, underwritten by the confluence of exceptionally low interest rates and frothy asset markets, both of which have been underpinned by low inflation. As long as those unusual conditions endure, American denial will undoubtedly persist. The day will come, however, when these circumstances, namely inflation and interest rates, start to revert to their more normal state. At that point, which may well be approaching, the price of denial will start to increase, putting pressure on the United States to accept the urgent need for self-renewal and for living within its means. The longer it avoids doing so, the tougher the reckoning will be.

Until denial cracks and that moment of reckoning arrives, America will undoubtedly remain short of saving, plagued by trade deficits, and unwilling or unable to resolve its conflict with China. Sun Tzu's counsel of avoiding peril by knowing yourself has never been more apt. Of course, his words apply not only to the United States but also to China. China, steeped in its own set of false narratives, is faced with an equally daunting strain of denial, to which we now turn.

PART THREE

CHINA'S FALSE NARRATIVES OF AMERICA

THE UNITED STATES HARDLY OWNS a monopoly on false narratives. China is just as susceptible, if not more so. The conflict between the two nations has been exacerbated by an unfortunate collision of false narratives from both sides. Information distortion—promulgated by social networks in America and state censorship in China—plays a key role in perpetuating this confluence of falsehoods.

Yet the two systems distort information in very different ways. In the United States, the constitutional privileges of free speech have been amplified into unrestricted expression of polarized opinions on vast open-architecture social media platforms. Baseless conspiracy theories, such as the Big Lie of a rigged 2020 US presidential election, are an obvious example. The same can be said of many of America's false narratives directed at China—from trade and technology to Covid origins and geostrategic threats.

Chinese censorship entails a very different strain of information distortion. It comes not from the polarization of social and political anxiety as in America, but from the fears and repressive actions of an insecure authoritarian state. Censorship has a long history in the propaganda apparatus of the People's Republic of China, but it has taken on heightened importance under Xi Jinping. Beyond the Internet scrubbing of the Great Firewall of China, a stylized nationalist narrative that is devoid of debate and focused on the goals, power, and control of the Party has become an increasingly vital objective of the state.

By blurring the distinction between true and false narratives, Chinese censorship distorts the nation's sense of self. The false narrative, as a result, has become tightly woven into the fabric of the Chinese Dream. The United States faces the opposite challenge, as false narratives born of political and social polarization threaten the core national values embedded in the American Dream. Ultimately, the paths implied by both nations' dreams will be fact-checked by history. Censorship and other forms of information distortion can't rewrite that history—they can only distort it, and only for a while. The question is for how long.

Censorship enables a profusion of false narratives that distort China's impressions of the United States. Three bear critically on conflict escalation with America.

Consumerism is at the top of the list. For fifteen years, China has understood the need to rebalance its economic growth model. Its development takeoff, which was initially powered by the producer, has long needed to draw more support from China's vast population of consumers. Chinese leaders incorrectly presumed that this would be easy to pull off. If America could do it, why not China? Yet despite all the fanfare, it hasn't happened. To a significant extent, this reflects China's unfamiliarity and misunderstanding of consumer societies. Replicating America's model of the world's dominant consumer hasn't been easy for China—and could be further compromised by new regulatory and "common prosperity" initiatives that create uncertainly and inhibit the "animal spirits" of households and entrepreneurs. Without more progress on consumerism, China's rebalancing will be stymied, leaving its economy vulnerable and ripe for conflict.

Second, China has long sought to emulate America's economic and geo-strategic clout. Unsurprisingly, Chinese GDP will soon exceed that of the United States. The race for scale, however, is just one aspect of the contest. Fixated on speed, China has neglected the quality of the economic growth experience, and that needs to change. Shifting the focus from quantity to quality won't be easy, especially for China's "blended economy." Chinese strategy has been aimed at combining elements from two systems, US-style capitalism and state-directed, market-based socialism. The resulting hybrid system—allowing markets to play a so-called decisive role in partnership with state control—reflects the delicate balance of China's "mixed-ownership model." Yet that attempted balancing act misreads the malleability of US-style capitalism, presupposing that state-directed intervention can effectively override market-based resource allocation. Does China's steadfast commitment to a blended approach undermine the efficiency and sustainability of economic development, creating false premises for conflict?

Last, China's development trajectory has a deeper meaning. It is the means, not the endpoint, of the Chinese Dream. Xi Jinping frequently underscores the lofty goal of reaching the pinnacle as a "great modern socialist country" by 2049, the centenary anniversary of the founding of the People's Republic of China. Consistent with this great-power aspiration, the Party has expended considerable energy in developing what it calls a "new model of major country relations." This power sharing arrangement, initially envisioned by Xi Jinping to put China on a par with the United States, has since been supplanted by the "unlimited partnership" agreement signed by Xi and Russia's president Vladimir Putin in February 2022 on the brink of the Russo-Ukrainian War. Both efforts were misdirected. The risk for China is that it may be focusing prematurely on its future as a great power while neglecting geostrategic conflict with the West and without doing the hard work required for its own internal transformation. History offers countless examples of overstretch that arise from a presumptive extrapolation of past performance. A conflict-prone China ignores that lesson at great peril.

Why do nations cling to false narratives? Two sharply contrasting systems, the United States and China, share that unfortunate tendency. The reasons are different, but the implications are the same in one critical respect: dueling false narratives are a recipe for relationship conflict. For both the United States and China, conflict resolution hinges on abandoning these deeply entrenched illusions. What will it take to achieve that outcome?

8

Censorship as Conflict

NUMBER 5 WEST CHANG'AN AVENUE in Beijing is where the headquarters of the Chinese Communist Party's Propaganda (or Publicity) Department (CCPPD) is located—next door to the Ministry of Industry and Information Technology and within walking distance of China's leadership compound, *Zhongnanhai*. The CCPPD's proximity to power goes well beyond locational geography. In the 1920s, before the People's Republic was founded, the CCPPD became tightly aligned with the Communist Party's revolutionary campaign for political control of the country. The partnership has flourished ever since. With the exception of an eleven-year suspension of activities during the Cultural Revolution, from 1966 to 1976, the CCPPD has played a key role in virtually all aspects of Chinese governance.

The Propaganda Department oversees a sprawling network of information control that permeates all aspects of expression in Chinese society.[1] Its efforts to monitor information dissemination are estimated to involve at least two million "public opinion analysts" situated in a vast network of offices across the country.[2] That is the tip of a much larger iceberg. In addition to the CCPPD, many other agencies actively participate in information control. They include Party efforts such as the United Work Front Department and the External Propaganda Office, as well as State Council (government) bodies such as the National Press and Publication Administration and the Office of the Central Leading Group for Cyberspace Affairs. Add to that a multiplicity of information control activities embedded in the People's

Liberation Army, and there can be little doubt of the Chinese government's ability to see, hear, and influence all aspects of the country's discourse.[3]

In any society, censorship is the petri dish of false narratives. It distorts reality, ideas, and values, inhibits the exchange of views, stifles discovery, and enables an ever-expanding web of fiction to stand as official statements of fact. Taken to an extreme, censorship can hollow out a country's soul, leave it without a true sense of self, and create a false and ultimately fragile national identity.

The heavy hand of information control smothers Chinese expression. Censorship, from state- to self-directed, means that China sorely lacks the give and take of a free and open exchange of information, ideas, and opinions. That is true of internally generated content, but it also applies to information to and from abroad. Chinese people are fed the news—produced, directed, written, and curated by the state—and are fearful of public debate over the veracity of its content.

It is not just that the state controls the conversation. It is that Chinese censors effectively define the discourse. The Party line is literally that—a top-down insistence that the information flow be tightly aligned with CCP-centric dictates of the state. Information isn't just filtered; it is altered to conform with official views of Party doctrine. Growing numbers of sensitive issues are quickly expunged from public discourse. In China, censorship dominates the inside debate and injects state-sponsored spin into the outside debate. It is one of the most corrosive characteristics of the single-party authoritarian Chinese state.

Propaganda with Chinese Characteristics

Chinese censorship is directed at all forms of media—newspapers, television, film, literature, music, education. The multimedia Internet platform gets special attention, with stringent keyword filtering through the infamous Great Firewall of China.[4] Major US outlets such as *The New York Times, The Wall Street Journal,* and *Bloomberg* are completely blocked; similar restrictions have recently been placed on India's newspapers.[5] More latitude, albeit within tightly defined content limits, is allowed for some major international platforms headquartered in the United Kingdom (such as the *Financial Times*),

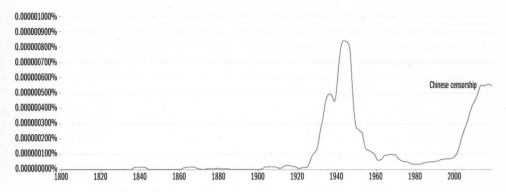

Figure 3. "Chinese Censorship"; Google Ngram Book Search from 1800 to 2019.
Google Books Ngram Viewer, http://books.google.com/ngrams.

Japan (*Yomiuri Shimbun*), Germany (*Bild*), and Singapore (*The Straits Times*).
But these outsiders are often chastised and warned when they get too close
to the subtle tripwires of censorship sensitivity.[6]

In keeping with these efforts, Freedom House, a US-based democracy
and human rights advocacy organization, consistently ranks China near the
bottom in its annual assessment of global freedom. In 2021, China scored
only 9 out of 100 on the global freedom index; that placed it in the bottom
10 percent among all 210 countries and territories and was the lowest ranking given to any major country. On Freedom House's Internet freedom
index, which includes a smaller sample of seventy countries, China scored
just 10 out of 100—the lowest score of any nation.[7]

Rarely a day goes by without a shocking new revelation about the reach
of Chinese censorship. This has not escaped the attention of others around
the world. A Google Ngram search on the term *Chinese censorship* (Figure 3)
underscores the surge of attention it has received since the ascendancy of
Xi Jinping in late 2012. While recent mentions of the phrase fall short of
what occurred during China's revolutionary period of the 1950s, the recent
surge of citations far outstrips trends since then. Nor can there be any
doubt as to what accounts for the upsurge. Following decades of economic
opening-up in the 1980s, 1990s, and early 2000s, which saw renewed vigor
of free and open personal expression, the pendulum of information control

has swung decisively the other way under Xi Jinping's leadership—toward discipline, ideology, and increased Party oversight.[8]

Xi telegraphed this move early in his administration. In 2013, he turned the focus back to the ideological roots of the People's Republic of China and to the Party's role in reinforcing them. He stressed a "mass-line" reeducation campaign, which was linked to the most sweeping anti-corruption campaign since the Cultural Revolution. The goal was to reestablish a tight connection between the people (the masses) and the Party. The problem, as Xi saw it, was not only that the people had lost sight of the ideological underpinnings of their nation's success but that the Party itself had become ossified and corrupt, out of step with the basic needs of the Chinese people. A trusted connection, he thought, could be reestablished only if both the masses and the Party recommitted to a strict interpretation of their original vision.[9]

Accordingly, the propaganda machine went into high gear in 2013 as an instrument of mass-line reeducation, reversing the trend toward liberalization begun in the early 1990s. Attention was first drawn to "four bad habits" that Xi felt were putting China at risk—formalism, bureaucracy, hedonism, and extravagance.[10] *Formalism* referred to the redundancies of superficial management procedures, including excessive office meetings, unnecessary seminars, and superfluous award celebrations. The bad habits of *bureaucracy* were couched in terms of the excesses of a process-driven culture, such as unnecessary paper flow and meaningless flowcharts. *Hedonism* meant the decadence of overly luxurious lifestyle habits such as golf. And *extravagance* was a critique of the Chinese people's lifestyle, which Xi thought had grown overly materialistic.

The nomenclature is both arbitrary and redundant in places—what, really, is the difference between formalism and bureaucracy, between hedonism and extravagance? Certainly, all modern societies are prone to these and other bad habits.[11] The difference for China is that from the start of his presidency in 2013, Xi Jinping was determined to do something about it. With some urgency, the mass-line campaign hinted at crisis if the ideological reawakening and recommitment did not occur quickly. This message dovetailed with Xi's subsequent warnings about China's unresolved "principal contradiction" that, according to the dialectic of Marxian ideology, could bring revolution and collapse if ideology became untethered from the real needs of the people. Xi's subsequent reworking of the principal contraction as a foundational pillar of Xi Jinping Thought in 2017 reflected his new emphasis on ideological commitment.

The mass-line campaign provided an added justification for increased censorship and information spin. Without the persuasive powers of the state and its leaders, went the argument, China's masses would veer from Party teachings, and the danger of crisis would only grow. Censorship was essential to preserve the "true line" of a socialist nation. Observers in the West see it very differently—as a Xi Jinping power play aimed at stifling dissent, eliminating opposition views and personalities, and narrowing the space within which any discourse is allowed to occur.[12]

There is, of course, a great deal of complexity in the motives of any leader. Different systems, with different values and goals, often diverge in how they identify problems and propose solutions. This is a classic manifestation of the dueling narratives that will be addressed in Part IV of this book. The problem becomes even more acute when the duel is based on conflict-prone false narratives.

But that is getting ahead of the story. At this point, one thing is certain: as the Google Ngram word search shows, the dramatic increase in the awareness of Chinese censorship over the past decade coincides with an equally dramatic move toward greater ideological purity under Xi Jinping Thought. This is hardly a coincidence, and it raises important questions: What is the Party afraid of? Why isn't China's new ideological thrust strong enough to stand on its own, without increased censorship and other forms of information control?

Discourse Power: BRI and Daryl Morey

Important hints to the answers to these questions can be found in the tensions inherent in the Chinese Dream—an aspirational narrative framed around a nationalistic longing for rejuvenation. The problem is that this rejuvenation is rooted in a dark period of Chinese history when a powerful and proud nation was subjected to the humiliation of foreign occupation. Rejuvenation is less about the enduring strengths of the Chinese nation and its people than about overcoming the inherent vulnerability of a fragile system that may still be healing from the painful wounds of its past.

This point is far from easy for China to accept. While the Party and its leadership are attempting to send a nationalistic message of pride and renewal, the actual messaging can be seen as something closer to denial: instilling a false sense of security in a chronically insecure nation. The Chinese Dream has become the rationale for information control, aligned with that denial, in providing the organizing principles for censorship in Xi Jinping's China. A more uplifting vision of national purpose would require a new approach to promote buy-in and offset counter-messaging that reinforces insecurity.

China's increased reliance on "discourse power"—controlling the narrative abroad to conform with the messaging at home—puts censorship in context. Unsurprisingly, Xi has been at the center of a growing emphasis on discourse power. Since 2016 he has explicitly urged Chinese officials to "tell a good China story" about the nation's accomplishments—emphasizing its goals, dreams, and aspirations.[13] Discourse power, in this context, refers to the constant reinforcement by senior Chinese leaders of the thematic aspects of the China brand that project a positive story inward to its people and outward to the world.

Discourse power relies on the full range of tools in the Chinese propaganda arsenal, from subtle information distortion to aggressive censorship. The CCPPD is very frank about its role in discourse governance, stating on its website that "an ideal discourse system should be a systematic and practical one that seeks to communicate the 'political ideas, political demands, and national interests' of China to international audiences."[14]

There are many historical examples of modern China's use of discourse power and the propaganda machine's important role in shaping and reinforcing popular narratives. Slogans have always played an important role in shaping the organizing principles of Chinese censorship. Under Deng Xiaoping, development strategy was messaged through the slogan "reforms and opening up," which in turn rested on the foundation of the "four modernizations"—science, technology, agriculture, and industry. Later it was Jiang Zemin's "peaceful rise," followed by Hu Jintao's "scientific development"—

all wrapped around the unifying structure of "socialism with Chinese characteristics" or, eventually, "market-based socialism."[15]

These themes turned into mantra-like statements that were repeated constantly in official pronouncements, legislative actions approved by the CCP and enacted by the National People's Congress, and in the strategies of China's five-year plans. The themes were regularly parroted by media outlets, at cultural events, and on educational platforms. It was an exercise in branding, supported at every step by a multiplicity of CCPPD censorship tools directed at multiple communications platforms.

But that was in the pre-digital era. In retrospect, those earlier fragmented efforts at discourse power were primitive and inefficient by comparison with what exists today on large-scale social media platforms, slick websites, bot-based messaging, and other forms of digitized communication.[16] The new technologies of rumor spread underscored in Chapter 3 leave little doubt that the leverage behind China's discourse power has been amplified dramatically.

The Belt and Road Initiative (BRI) provides an important example. As Xi Jinping's signature foreign policy effort, the BRI was designed to put China at the center of an extraordinary $30 trillion infrastructure network linking Asia together and connecting the region to the rest of the world. It is billed by many, especially the Chinese, as the most ambitious global policy initiative since the US-led Marshall Plan of the early 1950s, which was focused on rebuilding a war-ravaged Europe.

While this claim is highly debatable, as are claims of Chinese originality in conceptualizing and designing this pan-regional infrastructure program, that is beside the point.[17] The CCPPD has been very persuasive in attempting to shape discourse on the BRI, especially in its efforts to spin a positive response to it on European media platforms following Xi's highly personal rollout. According to a Czech research team, from 2013 to 2017, Chinese-authored narratives on the BRI far outnumbered those produced by European media counterparts.[18] A separate quantitative assessment of European BRI discourse stressed sharp increases in online media feedback from the United Kingdom, France, and Germany.[19]

The US impression of the BRI has been very different from that of Europe.[20] In keeping with the conflicted state of the US-China relationship, the BRI has been couched in extremely negative terms by a wide range of critics, from politicians and academics to research organizations and business executives.[21] Depicted variously as a geostrategic power play, a debt trap for loan recipients, an environmental threat, and a Trojan Horse for technology dominance similar to the Huawei narrative, the BRI has been widely billed as one of America's most formidable global strategic challenges.[22] As a consequence, US discourse power has been aimed more at criticizing the BRI than crediting China for providing an alternative solution to Asia's infrastructure problems.[23]

The Chinese propaganda response, while swift to counter the negative US view of the BRI with its own massive messaging campaign, has been unable to dislodge this critical sentiment.[24] But its efforts to do so are emblematic of a new and important dimension of Chinese information control and censorship—a willingness to take the discourse battle directly onto offshore media platforms.[25] This occurs not only through aggressive counter-messaging but also by overt pressures on Chinese-dependent foreign businesses—the functional equivalent of exported censorship.

One of the more notorious recent examples of this development was controversy that arose after Daryl Morey, the general manager of the Houston Rockets basketball team, tweeted his support for pro-democracy activists in Hong Kong during the city's massive protest demonstrations in October 2019. For China, this was unacceptable foreign interference in sensitive internal matters. Chinese authorities were quick to respond by cutting ties initially with the Rockets and then with the entire National Basketball Association. Basketball is China's favorite spectator sport, with close to 800 million Chinese reported to have watched the 2019 NBA playoff games.[26] Threatened with large financial losses if its games were no longer televised in China, the NBA caved under Chinese pressures and immediately went into aggressive damage control.

NBA executives called Morey's action "regrettable," and Morey, who had never been to Hong Kong or even expressed public views on any topic outside of basketball, soon deleted the offending tweet. US politicians then jumped in, claiming foul, further inflaming public backlash in America. One thing led to another, including intervention by NBA superstar LeBron

James, who criticized Morey for tweeting his support to Hong Kong pro-testers.[27] That, in turn, sparked anti-Lebron jersey-burning protests in Hong Kong. Eventually the furor subsided—but not before the NBA suffered an estimated $400 billion in financial losses from forgone Chinese television and sponsorship revenues.[28] A year later, Daryl Morey resigned as general manager of the Houston Rockets.

Exported censorship is a key element of China's ever-changing system of propaganda and information control. What began as strict controls over domestic discourse in print media and then television, followed by restrictions on Chinese social media platforms such as WeChat, Sina Weibo, and Douyin, has now moved directly into the arena of commercial retaliation. The silencing of the NBA is a classic example of how China now converts its considerable economic clout into external censorship, putting pressure on foreign actors and public opinion makers who dare to challenge the up-lifting "China stories" of Xi Jinping.[29]

Nor is the NBA-China conflict an isolated case of China's increased penchant for exported censorship. There have been countless examples in recent years of foreign companies bending to Chinese will by altering their messaging in their own home markets. In 2017, for example, Cambridge University Press removed academic articles that referenced "sensitive" topics in its highly regarded journal *China Quarterly*.[30] In 2018, the US clothing retailer the Gap was forced to apologize for selling a T-shirt with an image of China that did not include Taiwan.[31] During the height of the Daryl Morey controversy in October 2019, ESPN, the leading US sports cable TV network, instituted a ban on any commentary about China-related political issues.[32] The following month, DC Comics removed a Batman promotional poster that appeared to sympathize with Hong Kong protestors.[33] In April 2020, the European Union agreed to censor references to China in a report on the origins of Covid-19.[34] In early 2021, H&M, Nike, and Burberry all faced boycotts and other intimidation in China after they announced they would stop sourcing fabric from Xinjiang Province to protest human rights violations.[35] And in late 2021, Walmart and Intel, two of America's most iconic companies, also felt the heat over their pro-US stance on Xinjiang.[36]

China's efforts at global information control are supported by an increasingly sophisticated array of Internet-focused tools, including organized online trolling via "astroturfing" (fake-persona Twitter and other social media accounts), manually administered PLA-established Twitter "sock puppets," and automated robot, or machine-driven, messaging ("bots")—all aimed at manipulating foreign public opinion.[37] This expansion of discourse power is the outgrowth of a hypersensitive, insecure leadership that is more than willing to throw its considerable economic weight behind its long-standing propaganda culture in order to perpetuate the good stories of China that Xi Jinping prefers. Anything that strays from the Party line is seen as a threat to be countered aggressively.

The outbreak of the Covid-19 pandemic elicited an especially furious response by Chinese censors. With the novel coronavirus apparently originating in the Huanan Seafood Wholesale Market in Wuhan, the capital of China's Hubei Province, concerns were immediately raised in the United States, especially by President Trump and Senator Tom Cotton, that Covid was spawned by the suspicious activity of a lab accident at the nearby Wuhan Institute of Virology.[38] The destruction of all physical evidence, including live-animal specimens from the Wuhan market, heightened suspicions of a Chinese cover-up. This suggested that there may have been more to the outbreak than official accounts of a zoonotic, or natural, jump from a wild animal host (direct or intermediary) to a human. That explanation, which was initially favored by many leading epidemiologists (both in China and the West) as well as by preliminary investigative reports from a team of international experts assembled by the World Health Organization, suddenly became difficult for China to defend.

Apoplectic over allegations that it was responsible for the worst pandemic in a century, China's propaganda machine went into high gear to counter this claim. Official statements of indignant denial, along with counter accusations of US culpability, were fueled by a massive Chinese Twitter campaign directed at spinning a very different version of the Covid-origins narrative.

That wasn't easy to do, as Twitter cannot be accessed inside of China. But that didn't stop China from turning up the heat on exported censorship to an unprecedented degree. According to a ProPublica investigation, over ten thousand fake individual Twitter accounts traceable to the Chinese government were established in the early days of Covid.[39] The Atlantic Council's Digital Forensic Research Lab (DFRLab) found that a large network of Chinese embassies created at least thirty additional new Twitter accounts in the first seven months of 2020.[40] A detailed empirical study by the Oxford Internet Institute revealed comparable, rapidly expanding actions on both Twitter and Facebook into early 2021.[41] And these efforts were augmented by an aggressive campaign to "like" and retweet the fake messaging that cast China's Covid response in a positive light.[42] As noted above, this messaging-based crisis response strategy reflects long-standing practices of the Chinese government to engage and pay foreign actors to churn the discourse via "astroturfing" on global social media platforms.[43]

Further amplification of social media chatter went into high gear in the early days of Covid as China scrambled to align its discourse power with the good stories of Xi Jinping. Outside of China, very few were fooled by the profusion of fraudulent messaging. But that didn't stop the CCPPD. Curiously, this is somewhat at odds with the quantitative assessment of narrative traction that was discussed in Chapter 3, notably the MIT Media Lab's assessment of Twitter-based messaging in the United States, which found that bot-based dissemination of false narratives was relatively ineffective in shaping public opinion. Apparently, China's digitized leveraging of Covid-related discourse power was designed more as a play to the home crowd and to ethnic Chinese living abroad than to foreign nationals outside of China.

The US-China conflict is being waged on many fronts: tariffs, sanctions, and diplomatic animosity have all come into play. Moreover, as in Cold War 1.0, censorship and information distortion have increased the animosity between the two sides. But the current cold war is very different in one key respect—not just because the economic gap between the two antagonists has been reversed, but also because the soft conflicts of the discourse war are playing a much larger role in reinforcing the hard conflicts over trade and technology. This points to an increasingly dangerous weaponization of the propaganda conflict between the United States and China.

The Disinformation War

Chinese censorship has become an increasingly important instrument of information-based conflict. Xi Jinping drove that point home on July 1, 2021, when he delivered an important and disturbing address marking the

Whataboutism and False Equivalency

China is hardly alone in waging conflict through information distortion. Most nations, including free societies like the United States, are also afflicted by varying degrees of information distortion—the whataboutism retort. In assessing the mounting tensions between the United States and China, we need to think carefully about how the gradations of this tendency impact conflict escalation. Certainly, there is an element of false equivalency in this comparison. Censorship, such as that practiced by China, occupies one end of the spectrum as direct government action to prevent speech or expression of views by all members of society. Information distortion in the United States, a country which Freedom House metrics place slightly above midrange in its scoring of free societies, comes not from official government edict but from polarized political segments within American society.[1]

The significance of this difference does not negate a comparison of the implications that these two strains of information distortion have on fomenting conflict between the two nations. The fact that China practices the extremes of state-directed censorship that America abhors does not let the United States off the hook for condoning the twisting of logic and facts to make the case against China. While this twist, or distortion, is not censorship in the strict sense, its impact on public discourse and opinion has important consequences in shaping policy actions and economic impacts that are comparable to those of censored societies. For example, Chinese discourse portrays America's China strategy as one of containment. While the US vehemently denies that allegation as an example of distorted propaganda, the Trump administration's bilateral bluster did, indeed, hold China accountable for a multilateral trade deficit that it alleged had ruined the lives of American workers and decimated a once-proud manufacturing sector. Both arguments, while operating at different points on the distortion scale, have played important roles in sparking conflict.

While information campaigns have a long history in the conflicts between nations, there is an important difference today. An open-architecture Internet, combined with costless information dissemination and the amplification of social networks, has forever transformed public discourse. Biased messaging, either coming from the state in the case of China or from polarizing politicians in the case of the United States, has enabled social media platforms to become vessels of information distortion. Like-minded netizens tend to stick together, rarely opting for opinion crossover.

Such self-selection of content results in a confirmation bias that tends to magnify strongly expressed opinions, leading both censored and distorted information to become polarizing and divisive.

The Internet has redefined the full spectrum of information dissemination. Like earlier communication platforms—the printing press, radio, and TV—it not only brings people together but changes society.[2] In free societies like the United States, information controls have been put in place in an attempt to safeguard and protect otherwise undefended citizens. But this hasn't always worked out very well. Content moderation by fact-checking or in-house control systems has become almost meaningless, as the extremes of discourse find deep conviction and acceptance in polarized pockets of society. While none of this comes as a big surprise to the American public, many US political leaders, including former President Barack Obama, share a growing recognition that something needs to be done about it.[3] Slowly but surely, US public authorities are swinging into action. In the same vein as the revelation that the CEOs of major tobacco companies had testified to Congress in the 1990s that their product was not addictive while knowing full well that it was, Facebook, the world's leading social network, may now be facing its own "Big Tobacco" moment.[4]

That spells not only greater regulatory oversight but increased content intervention, opening the door to a wide range of possibilities from voluntary monitoring, including age-specific parental oversight, to outright bans on dangerous netizens like Donald Trump.[5] Triggered by keyword filtering, such intervention risks turning content moderation into an editing function that in one sense is little different than censorship. From that perspective, neither strain of information distortion, that practiced in either China or the United States, is worse than the other. Both play equally destructive roles instigating relationship conflicts. Information distortion in either form encourages false narratives, manipulates public opinion, and enables vengeful policies to be aimed from one nation toward another. A blurring of the distinction between subtle information distortion and explicit state-directed censorship starts to occur.

The West views Chinese censorship as morally repugnant and politically repressive. China has expressed similar views about information distortion in the United States.[6] Each nation believes that the other's practices inflame biases and stoke tensions. On one level, this is an obvious false equivalency. There is a critical difference between state-directed censorship as an official act of a repressive government and the information distortion that arises from private actors stoking social and political tensions within a nation. Of course, should groups embracing the extremes of information distortion seize control of a democratically elected government and convert fact distortion, or "alternative facts" as it became known in the Trump administration, into official government policy, then the equivalency would no longer be false.[7] Notwithstanding the Republican Party's enduring conviction in the Big Lie of a rigged 2020 US presidential election, fortunately, that has been the exception rather than the rule in the United States. Meanwhile, the Chinese censorship regime remains in a league of its own.

The important distinction between China's state-directed censorship and America's group-sponsored information distortion should not be minimized. Yet what matters most in our assessment of conflict escalation is the interplay between these two tendencies. The intersection of these different strains of information distortion plays a critical catalytic role in the dynamic of conflict escalation between the United States and China.

1. According to Freedom House, the United States received a "Global Freedom" score of 83 out of 100 points in 2021, down 10 points from its score of 93 in 2013; in 2021, the "political rights" component of the total US index reading had a score of 32, which was slightly above the midpoint of the 18- to 40-point range for all free countries, while its "civil liberties" score of 51 was slightly below the upper quartile of the 26- to 60-point range for all free countries. See Sarah Repucci and Amy Slipowitz, "Democracy under Siege," *Freedom in the World 2021* (New York: Freedom House, 2021).
2. See Clay Shirky, "The Political Power of Social Media: Technology, the Public Sphere, and Political Change," *Foreign Affairs*, January/February 2011.
3. According to a recent public opinion poll conducted in September 2021 and released in October 2021, fully 95 percent of American adults believe that the spread of misinformation is a serious problem in the United States traceable to social media and its user community, as well as to US politicians; see Pearson Institute and AP-NORC, "The American Public Views the Spread of Misinformation as a Major Problem," October 8, 2021. In an April 2022 speech at Stanford University, President Barack Obama underscored his concerns over the increasingly worrisome threats that online disinformation poses to American democracy; see Steven Lee Myers, "Obama Calls for More Regulatory Oversight of Social Media Giants," *New York Times*, April 21, 2022.
4. The original Big Tobacco moment dates to 1994 when a whistleblower, Jeffrey Wigand, leaked internal tobacco industry documents that validated the health risks of nicotine contained in cigarettes, which led to severe legal actions against major US tobacco companies. See Barnaby J. Feder, "Former Tobacco Official Begins Giving Deposition," *New York Times*, November 30, 1995; and Michael L. Stern, "Henry Waxman and the Tobacco Industry: A Case Study in Congressional Oversight," The Constitution Project, May 2017. Today, the comparison is being made to the whistleblower and former Facebook employee Frances Haugen, who has disclosed massive internal documentation attesting to the knowledge that Facebook and its Instagram subsidiary possessed about hazardous,

fear-stoking content on their social networks. See Cat Zakrzewski, "Facebook Whistle-blower's Revelations Could Usher In Tech's 'Big Tobacco Moment,' Lawmakers Say," *Washington Post*, October 6, 2021.

5. Trump's ban from Twitter (permanent) and Facebook (time-bound to two years followed by further review) was tied to his central role in the January 6, 2021, political insurrection. Twitter's statement made explicit reference to "the risk of further incitement of violence"; the Facebook Oversight Board cited Trump's violation of Facebook's Community Standards and Instagram's Community Guidelines as "maintaining an unfounded narrative of election fraud and persistent calls to action [that] created an environment where serious risk of violence was possible."

6. See GT staff reporters, "Revealing Four-Step Misinformation Campaign against China on Virus Origins Tracing," *Global Times* (China), August 25, 2021; also see Zheping Huang, "Global Times Editor Hu Xijin on US-China relations, Press Freedom in China, and the June 4 Protests," *Quartz*, August 9, 2016.

7. The "alternative facts" oxymoron was made famous by former Trump administration senior advisor Kellyanne Conway; see Aaron Blake, "Kellyanne Conway's Legacy: The 'Alternative Facts'-ification of the GOP," *Washington Post*, August 24, 2020.

hundredth anniversary of the founding of the Chinese Communist Party.[44] It was a predictable speech in many respects—not only celebrating the extraordinary rise of modern China but underscoring the important role the Party played in that unparalleled development.

But Xi went well beyond those widely anticipated celebratory remarks and drew attention to three controversial aspects of Party strategy—the role of free expression, the imperatives of CCP control, and the adversarial threat. His emphasis on these issues sharpens our focus on Chinese censorship and discourse power and adds to our understanding of the interplay between conflict escalation and the disinformation war.

Free expression. In the July 2021 speech, Xi emphasized one of modern China's most prominent self-proclaimed virtues—that the nation and its ideological underpinnings rest firmly on the notion of "freeing the mind" of Chinese people. His stress on independent and enlightened thinking had a direct antecedent in Deng Xiaoping's historic speech of December 1978, which set China on a path of reform, opening up, and growth. Deng argued that after ten tumultuous years of the Cultural Revolution, which had the effect of "closing people's minds," it was urgent to reverse course and "emancipate the mind, use the brain, seek truth from facts, and unite to look forward."[45] For many, this was a startling breath of fresh air that allowed a spirited reawakening of Chinese society—hopeful signs of a more enlightened governance and freer expression in arts, literature, music, and academic pursuits.[46]

That hope was short-lived, especially after the tragic events in Tiananmen Square in June 1989. Party leadership has allowed citizens' thinking to be anything but emancipated in the decades since Deng spoke. The Propaganda Department has not only defined the parameters of "truth seeking" but distorted the facts of which its version of the truth is presumably comprised. Public discourse is forbidden on a wide range of topics that are judged to challenge the nation's social and political stability. Censorship imprisons the mind—the opposite of the freedom of expression that Deng espoused and Xi celebrated. Nor is it constant—it feeds on itself and grows over time.

Until the late 1990s, modern Chinese censorship usually was thought of in terms of the "Three T's"—Tiananmen Square, Tibet, and Taiwan.[47] Later, discussion was also forbidden on topics like religion and cults (such as Falun Gong), pollution, personal experiences during the Cultural Revolution, and LGBTQ issues. Now, the sensitive-topics list encompasses virtually anything that might be at odds with CCP policy or, more recently, cast doubt on the good stories put forward by Xi Jinping. That not only includes criticism of the Party and its leaders, it also pertains to any references to increasingly sensitive developments: the Hong Kong democracy movement, Taiwanese independence, the conditions of ethnic Uyghurs in Xinjiang, the Covid origins debate, military activity in the South China Sea, recent Russian atrocities in Ukraine, and so on.[48] Today the forbidden list is almost endless.

Porous filtering, even in a highly restrictive censorship regime like China's, compromises information control. While VPNs (virtual private networks) allow citizens to circumvent state-administered Internet controls, the Chinese government has recently tightened up those workarounds.[49] Voluntary self-censorship, by individuals, businesses, and web-based information platforms, has become an increasingly important aspect of information control in China.[50] Fearful of legal recriminations and motivated by a sense of patriotism and Party-directed national purpose, Chinese citizens maintain a flourishing culture of voluntary discourse control.

In short, today's China, even if it wanted to, is utterly incapable of seeking truth from facts, as Deng Xiaoping urged in 1978 and as Xi Jinping reiterated in 2021. The only thing the Chinese public knows about fact discovery comes from the Party. Seeking truth from a fact-based discovery process, despite having been stressed endlessly by a long string of Chinese leaders, has become a shibboleth, a vacuous phrase devoid of meaning. Xi's stress on free thinking stood in direct contradiction to the practices of censorship and information control that he and other Party leaders have long supported.

Party control. A second disturbing aspect of Xi's July 2021 speech touches on the issue of Party control. The CCP's greatest fear is to be toppled from power.[51] Based on China's long history of political instability, this is understandable. While the Chinese Communist Party is, indeed, the largest political organization in the world today, as Xi likes to stress (and did so in the July 2021 speech), its membership of 95 million represents less than 7 percent of China's population. The Party may have the trust of that elite 7 percent, but what about the rest of the Chinese population?[52]

Support from this broader population is not preordained. It requires the "convincing mechanism" of a massive projection of internally focused discourse power and an equally firm threat of consequences for those who dare to challenge the message. That could be a key reason behind the leadership's dread of an open debate over fact-based truth seeking. And it could explain one of the most insidious aspects of China's information control campaign: it needs a strict censorship regime to maintain control over the 93 percent of the population who are not CCP members. Quashing dissent, rather than encouraging free expression, has become the *sine qua non* of CCP control. That is a sign of insecurity and weakness, not strength.

Xi Jinping's Party-centric celebratory remarks of July 2021 were clearly directed at the 7 percent card-carrying cadres. After paying lip service to the political involvement of the broader population of Chinese people, he said that "China's success hinges on the Party. We must uphold the firm leadership of the Party." He came across as intolerant of any slippage in support and threatened dire consequences should the populace lose faith: "Any attempt to divide the Party from the Chinese people or to set the People against the Party is bound to fail." It was the ultimate in authoritarian math: $7 + x = 100$, with censorship and other forms of discourse control the "x-factor" in China's political power equation.

The threat. Finally, the July 2021 speech has important implications for relationship conflict. As China has risen, the decibel level of CCP discourse power has increased commensurately. In Xi's words, "We will not, however, accept sanctimonious preaching from those who feel they have the right to lecture us." That explains the confrontation in Anchorage earlier that year. It was hardly a spontaneous outburst when China's senior foreign policy official, Yang Jiechi, unleashed his wolf-warrior response at Secretary Blinken. Blinken's accusations on human rights and territorial aggression sparked a carefully scripted Chinese counterattack on issues like systemic racism and the frailty of democracy that Yang knew full well are of great sensitivity to the United States. As a Party leader, when confronted about his country's conduct—especially accusations that counter "the good stories of China"—he apparently felt compelled to retaliate in kind.

But the smoking gun came from the lips of Xi Jinping. In that memorable speech of July 2021, the information spin underpinning Party leadership took the form of an unmistakable threat: "We will never allow any foreign force to bully, oppress, or subjugate us. Anyone who would attempt to do so will find themselves on a collision course with a great wall of steel forged by over 1.4 billion Chinese people . . . Having the courage to fight and the fortitude to win is what has made our Party invincible."

That statement ties the knot between censorship and relationship conflict. Whenever political power is too concentrated in leadership regimes, conditions are ripe for information distortion. Disinformation becomes the critical means of keeping control. That is not only true of an authoritarian China, with its state-directed censorship regime, it also bears on the struggle for political power in a polarized United States. Yet there is a critical difference: In freely elected democracies, elections offer the people at least a chance to mediate the outcome. In single-party authoritarian states, no such opportunity exists. Alas, when democracies are under attack from within by would-be authoritarians, the contrast becomes tougher to make.[53]

When information distortion is combined with the viral spread of false narratives on social media platforms, it is especially dangerous. This interplay is different in the two political systems governing the United States and China. Heavily censored information control in China's single-party state has prompted concerns that China now practices a unique strain of "digital authoritarianism."[54] That term has an ominous, almost Orwellian ring, evoking the ultimate dystopian application of technology toward political and social control.[55]

But that is hardly good reason to ignore the "digital polarization" that now afflicts the United States with a worrisome, if not corrosive, impact on American public discourse.[56] There is no American analogue of the Great Firewall of China, but the United States does have a Facebook business model tightly aligned with AI-enabled economic incentives that fuel anger, divisiveness, and political repression.[57] It speaks to the potential of psychological manipulation that is closer to Huxley than to Orwell.[58]

Apples and oranges? Only to a point: From the standpoint of conflict escalation, I have repeatedly stressed that the objective assessment of impacts matters more than the morality of causal equivalency. Both the digitization of authoritarianism and polarization amplify the extremes of political posturing, leaving the two nations, with their penchants for false narratives, ripe for conflict. China's wolf warriors and America's MAGA crowd are instruments of that amplification. Fierce nationalism, in both instances, overrides humility and self-awareness and results in blaming others for self-inflicted problems. False narratives arise from this lethal combination of information distortion and the inclination to blame. It becomes increasingly difficult to arrest the interplay, to stop the conflict from escalating.

These dark forces are at work today in the increasingly worrisome clash between China and the United States. China's use of censorship and discourse power to defend its "invincible Party" is on a collision course with the false narratives that are undermining America's suddenly shaky democracy. Conflicts over trade and technology are bad enough. The disinformation war between the United States and China compounds the problem. The interplay between conflict escalation and information distortion turns the question back to accountability. As Xi Jinping concluded in his celebratory remarks on the occasion of the CCP's centenary, "The people are the true heroes, for it is they who create history." Apparently, he is not above giving them a helping hand.

9

Consumerism and Animal Spirits

WEN JIABAO PLAYED A PIVOTAL ROLE in China's modern economic history. We have seen how, as premier in 2007, he drew attention to an important paradox in the nation's economic growth model. It seemed all-powerful, Wen warned, but problems were brewing beneath the surface. The Chinese economy was becoming increasingly unstable, unbalanced, uncoordinated, and unsustainable. This paradox of the "Four Uns" was a call for change. Yet in the fifteen years that have followed, China has struggled to answer that call.

In one sense, Wen was stating the obvious. Over the 1980 to 2006 period, from the Deng Xiaoping takeoff up to Wen's warning, top-line GDP growth averaged 10 percent. That was a stunning accomplishment by any standard. But 84 percent of the cumulative increase over that period was driven by the combined impacts of surging exports and massive increases in fixed capital investment.[1] This left the economy out of kilter, with outsize balance-of-payments and foreign trade surpluses, excess demand for energy and other natural resources, severe pollution, and worrisome increases in income and wealth inequality. Wen was only saying that the rapidly growing but lopsided Chinese economy had hit its limits—the formula had to change. Yet he offered few hints as to how.

After a vigorous internal debate, a new solution came into focus. It was framed around the imperatives of what can be called structural rebalancing, in this case a major shift in the sources of economic growth from production to consumption. On one level, that made great sense: the Chinese middle class would create a natural constituency for consumerism. But it wasn't as simple as pushing a button.

The production mindset, which had consistently delivered such powerful growth dividends, had become deeply engrained in the culture and institutions of the modern Chinese economy. Growth was addictive and the nation clamored for more. Unsurprisingly, the seduction of extrapolation weighed heavily against change. Who wanted to abandon an approach that had kept China on an extraordinary 10 percent growth trajectory for decades, growing faster for longer than any large developing economy in modern history?

But circumstances have an uncanny knack of confounding extrapolation. At the very moment that Wen Jiabao spoke of the paradox of the Four Uns, in March 2007, the US subprime mortgage bubble was starting to deflate, setting in motion a chain of events that would culminate in a wrenching global financial crisis and worldwide recession. For China, that shock sent a clear message that a growth strategy dependent on global demand had outlived its usefulness. If that hint wasn't enough, protectionist moves toward deglobalization sealed the verdict. Structural change in the Chinese economy suddenly became a high priority.

The embrace of consumerism was not just a defensive shift away from overreliance on an increasingly precarious state of global demand. An equally compelling motive came from the longing of China's vast population to raise household living standards and grab a greater share of the nation's economic growth bonanza.

This is where China has been stymied. The leadership mistakenly believed it would be relatively straightforward to develop a structural rebalancing strategy. "All" it would take would be three key efforts—uncovering new sources of job creation, boosting worker pay, and putting surplus saving to work in supporting discretionary consumption. If America could do it, why not China?

There was great logic to this approach. Services-led growth and urbanization would drive employment and worker wages, boosting labor income, which could then underpin the expansion of consumer purchasing power. Excess saving was the pivotal variable in the equation, a largely untapped reservoir of spendable household income that could turbo-charge personal consumption. Put that to work and presto—a shift in the sources of economic growth away from excess reliance on exports and investment to an increasingly consumer-led growth model. Just like America.

While the economic case for consumerism is well understood, bringing it to life is a different matter. There is a critical behavioral aspect to household decision making that has long confounded economic theory. People save for a reason—they do not simply redeploy their income on a whim to stop saving and start spending. This decision touches on one of the biggest imponderables of China's consumer-led transformation: for a society that historically has placed a high priority on saving, what would it take to tip the balance toward greater spending? Chinese policymakers have struggled with the answer.

That struggle hints at a weak link in China's growth strategy. Well versed in solving the engineering-like problems of central planning—infrastructure, urbanization, logistics, and other aspects of the production model—Chinese technocrats may not be well equipped to address the behavioral complexities of a dynamic market economy. That is not only the case for an incomplete consumerism, it also shows up in China's stunning recent reversal of long-standing support for business decision making, especially for risk-taking entrepreneurs.

Business operators who dare to take a chance on an idea—a new technology, product, or service, or a vision of a new market—do so for a variety of reasons. Over the past fifteen years, Chinese policymakers have enthusiastically supported such entrepreneurial activity. Now, under the guise of ideological purity, they are suddenly addressing what they see as undesirable consequences of this new source of dynamism. These concerns have led the government to impose regulatory constraints on Internet platform companies and fiscal constraints on the financial rewards of such activity. Some think China's entrepreneurial support to its "new economy" is suddenly at risk.

Was it all easier said than done? Chinese policymakers were tantalizingly close to the Promised Land of rebalancing and structural transformation. But they couldn't figure out how to take the final steps, the actions that drive behavioral commitments to economic dynamism required of consumers and businesspeople alike. The false narratives masking this struggle with economic transformation could have unexpectedly important implications for conflict with the United States.

The Missing Chinese Consumer

China's stunning success on the production side of its economy following its development takeoff in 1980 was not accompanied by a commensurate growth of consumer demand. This was surprising in one sense. Household incomes were well supported by the boost in employment and wages spawned by increased production. By 2010, China's overall output (or GDP) per capita had increased thirtyfold from the extremely low level of 1980.[2] This was strong enough to take China from a low-income, impoverished society into the middle-income strata of nations in a single generation.[3]

But this vigor was largely dependent on the government's promotion of an aggressive investment program aimed at boosting the nation's export capacity. By contrast, there was no organic surge of internal private consumption. Consumers, while certainly benefiting from the job creation supported by the externally oriented push for economic growth, were not the drivers of the Chinese economy that they were in the United States. Consumption was more on the trailing edge, pulled along by the Chinese production model.

This shows up as a sharp decline in household consumption as a share of GDP during the economic takeoff and early stages of development. After peaking at 53.5 percent in 1985, the consumption portion of the economy fell steadily for the next twenty-five years, hitting a low of 34.3 percent in 2010, from which it has barely inched up to just 38.1 percent in 2020.[4] To a certain extent this steep decline exaggerates the weakness of Chinese consumer demand. When other components of the economy are rising briskly, as was the case for exports and investment, that vigor takes share away from lagging sectors like personal consumption, where growth invariably is relatively more subdued.

Still, there can be no mistaking the underperformance of the Chinese consumer, particularly in comparison to the US consumer. During the same thirty-year period, 1980 to 2010, when the consumption share of the Chinese economy was declining sharply, American consumers went the other way. The US consumption share of GDP rose by more than 7 percentage points, from 61 percent in 1980 to 68.5 percent in 2011.[5] Total spending by American consumers in 2019 was 2.7 times the level of expenditures by Chinese consumers; in per capita terms, the comparison is far more dramatic—the average American consumes nearly twelve times what the average Chinese citizen does.[6] China is now the largest economy in the world, measured on a purchasing-power parity basis, but its household spending remains far below the American counterpart.

This comparison encapsulates the two extremes of consumer cultures. The excesses of the American consumer, as well as the restraint of the Chinese consumer, both reflect a unique interplay of economic fundamentals, demography, culture, and confidence. As the engine of the US economy, the American consumer benefits from powerful support with respect to all these factors. The Chinese consumer, more the caboose on the growth train, faces stiff headwinds on all counts.

Economic research has long pointed to labor income, the largest source of household purchasing power, as the main driver of consumer demand.[7] Total worker compensation, which reflects the combination of employment and pay rates, is tied closely to the growth in overall economic activity. In the past ten years, Chinese labor income was generally well supported by its high-growth economy. These gains came mostly in the earlier portion of that interval. Overall labor compensation went from 46 percent of GDP in 2011 to 52 percent by 2015 but has remained stuck there ever since.[8]

Significantly, the improvement since 2011 only brings China's labor income share back to its earlier post-1992 average. In 2019, China's labor share of GDP was basically in line with that of other large developing economies and slightly below the portion of more advanced nations.[9] China needed to do far better to bring its consumer culture to life.

But labor income, while necessary, is not sufficient to spark consumer-led growth in China. As in America, other sources of purchasing power are typically needed. In the United States, labor income has been augmented by the purchasing power extracted from rising asset values, especially homes. For the most part, China has not indulged in such activity. While some citizens have made money in its highly volatile residential property markets, strict regulatory oversight has limited the growth of home equity credit lines and second mortgages that have played such an important role in driving home wealth extraction in more advanced economies like the United States.[10]

But the most important difference for China is the behavioral impediment, a strong preference for saving over consumption. Disposable, or after-tax, personal income must either be spent or saved. When households earmark large portions of their income for saving, less remains for current consumption. In China since 2005, household saving has fluctuated between 36 percent and 43 percent of disposable personal income.[11] The most recent reading, 35 percent in 2019, is at the lower end of the fifteen-year range and well below the nearly 43 percent peak reached in 2010. This downtrend does little to dispel the notion of excess Chinese household saving; at 35 percent in 2019, the personal saving rate was still above the 31 percent average that prevailed from 1992 to 2004.

There is, of course, nothing wrong with saving. As I stressed in Part I of this book, saving is the seed corn of investment and economic growth. But there can be too much of a good thing. As Wen Jiabao counseled in 2007, the persistence of imbalances in the Chinese economy—the first of his Four Uns—underscored the dark side of excess saving. Overly cautious Chinese households and outsize balance-of-payments surpluses, if left unaddressed, will ultimately endanger the sustainability of economic growth.

Chinese households' excess saving is more of a curse than a blessing at this point. It poses a major challenge for a consumer-led rebalancing of China's economy. If it continues, a significant portion of newfound growth in labor income will not be channeled into discretionary purchases such as cars, furniture, appliances, travel, or entertainment. Without an active culture of discretionary consumer demand, the structural changes required of Chinese rebalancing will be incomplete. That won't be resolved until, or unless, China tackles its saving problem.

The Rebalancing Strategy

China's Twelfth Five-Year Plan, which spanned the years 2011 to 2015, was framed around a strategy broadly consistent with Wen Jiabao's 2007 concerns over the Four Uns. It was a pro-consumption plan that offered foundational support for a structural rebalancing of the Chinese economy based on three key building blocks—expansion of the services sector to boost job creation, ongoing urbanization to raise real wages, and social safety net reforms to reduce fear-driven precautionary saving.

This template was later refined in the Thirteenth and Fourteenth Five-Year Plans of 2016–20 and 2021–25, respectively. China's leadership was committed to the strategy and had the wherewithal to pull it off. There was good reason to think it would work.

But it wasn't enough. The services-led impetus to employment growth has been impressive, and this is important for several reasons. First, after all the attention on manufacturing as the spark to early-stage development, China's services sector was woefully underdeveloped. When Wen Jiabao introduced the Four Uns in 2007, the so-called tertiary sector (largely services) totaled just 43 percent of Chinese GDP—by far the lowest such portion of any major economy in the world. Second, services are a luxury that poorer nations can't initially afford. As development progresses, services support nascent consumer lifestyles—wholesale and retail trade and their distribution channels, telecommunications platforms of connectivity, and public utilities required of modern urban life. For well-off nations, services also entail a broad array of personal and professional support activities—from doctors and lawyers to travel, entertainment, and leisure. For the most affluent societies, the possibilities in services are endless.

But for China in 2007, services played a special role as the engine of job creation. Unlike manufacturing activity, where time-honored productivity recipes call for replacing workers with machines, services are inherently labor-intensive. It still takes people to offer and provide services. This means that when compared to manufacturing activity, most services typically generate more jobs per unit of output. When Wen Jiabao spoke of the Four Uns in 2007, China's tertiary sector generated 30 percent more jobs per unit of output than the manufacturing-dominated secondary sector.[12] That provided critically important leverage to China's rebalancing strategy. As China shifted the composition of its overall output into services, it boosted gains in the most labor-intensive, job-creating sector of its economy.

China's employment trends since 2007 bear this out. As the tertiary sector rose from 42.9 percent of GDP in 2007 to 54.5 percent in 2020—an impressive structural shift by any measure—trend growth in real GDP slowed sharply, from nearly 12 percent in the five years ending in 2007 to a little under 6 percent over the 2016–20 period. Yet at the same time, urban employment growth averaged 11.9 million per year from 2007 to 2020, a marked pickup from the 10.3 million annual pace of job creation recorded from 2000 to 2006.[13] That increase produced a stunning result: rebalancing away from labor-saving manufacturing activity toward labor-intensive services was a net plus for Chinese employment—even in the face of a more slowly growing economy. The shift to services provided a powerful assist for the consumer-led rebalancing strategy.

Urbanization appeared to be the icing on the cake. The Chinese urbanization story is unprecedented in the history of economic development. The urban share of the nation's population has risen from less than 20 percent in 1980 to nearly 65 percent in 2021.[14] This shift, which amounted to nearly 20 percentage points alone since Wen Jiabao's pronouncement in 2007, has been a major source of labor income growth. The key reason is that since 2000, China's urban workers have earned between two and a half to three times as much as their rural counterparts. That means the shift of workers from rural to urban areas has continually raised average wages and spendable income for the Chinese workforce.[15] Like the shift to labor-intensive services-led growth, the wage and earnings differentials of urbanization provided vigorous support to household income generation.

Urbanization also offers important support to China's services strategy. Newly urbanized areas—the expansion of existing cities as well as the creation of new cities—are a natural source of demand for a variety of infrastructure services. Cities require electricity from public utilities, connectivity from telecommunications providers, security and protection from local police and fire departments, schools and teachers for education, and wholesale and retail trade networks for personal shopping. Senior Chinese policymakers have long understood that the more China urbanizes, the greater its intrinsic demand for core services.[16]

China's rebalancing strategy is tightly aligned with the confluence of these two trends—the shift to labor-intensive services and the transition to a higher-wage urban workforce. This combination provided solid support to labor income generation even as the economy slowed. The only missing piece was the translation of the growth in household incomes into discretionary consumption. That is where China has fallen short.

The Problem

Excess household saving is the culprit. Since 1992, household saving has averaged about 35 percent of Chinese disposable personal income, more than five times the 6.3 percent average personal saving rate of the United States over the same period.[17] America's subpar saving is not what China needs. But the comparison underscores a key point that bears critically on the relationship between the two economies—the United States saves too little, and China saves too much.

China's excess saving is driven more by fear and insecurity than by a multigenerational tradition of frugality, as some have argued.[18] Several factors appear to be at work, especially the rapid aging of the Chinese population and the lack of retirement income security. A recent assessment by researchers from the International Monetary Fund found that about two-thirds of China's unusually high personal saving reflected a combination of these two factors.[19]

In the case of China, there can be little doubt that excess personal saving is a visible manifestation of an insecure and uncertain future. With most Chinese families facing the prospects of aging without the support of robust retirement plans or adequate medical insurance, they have not been translating their newfound labor income into discretionary consumption. Instead, they have diverted much of it into something like a contingency fund—setting aside money they might need to make ends meet when they are no longer working. They are afflicted by what economists call precautionary saving.[20]

Until the Chinese government offers a secure and predictable commitment to a social safety net, the fear-driven preference for precautionary saving can be expected to persist. This response is not irrational, nor is it preordained by Asian culture—it arises out of a perfectly rational, deep-rooted anxiety over financial security that is an important outgrowth of China's serious aging problem.[21]

The aging of the Chinese population is a well-documented consequence of the one-child family planning policy put in place in 1980 to stem what was seen at the time as an unsustainable population explosion.[22] Population growth slowed dramatically in response, creating an ominous skewing in the demographic mix—fewer younger people alongside an aging adult population. This led to what demographers call a rising old-age dependency ratio—an increase in the elderly cohort relative to a shrinking share of the working-age population. There are fewer young people working to support the country's seniors.

China's old-age dependency ratio—defined as the number of people aged sixty-five years and older relative to those in the twenty- to sixty-four-year-old cohort—has already doubled from 9 percent when the one-child policy began in 1980 to 18 percent in 2020. But that increase pales in comparison to what UN demographers have long thought might occur in the future for China—old-age dependency soaring to nearly 60 percent by 2060. However, the future may be arriving sooner than widely expected. Recent data revealed that Chinese population growth actually came to a virtual standstill in 2021, recording the slowest rate of growth since catastrophic declines during the Great Famine years of 1960–61.[23] I have been following the ups and downs of Chinese statistics for a quarter of a century. The population data released in January 2022 were one of the biggest shocks in my experience as a China watcher.

Aging societies have understandable concerns about retirement security. With that aging progressing far more rapidly than expected, there is good reason to believe those concerns are intensifying. Under those circumstances it makes perfect sense for people to err on the side of caution and set aside their own funds for support. In China, where the social safety net is not sufficient to support a rapidly aging population, that caution is especially pronounced. It is the essence of China's strong preference for precautionary saving.

That wasn't always the case. In the early days of the centrally planned economy under Mao Zedong, Chinese workers were employed by the state. Their wages were extremely low, but they enjoyed the benefits of the "iron rice bowl"—cradle-to-grave support for housing, food, medical care, education, and retirement.[24] The benefits were meager, but they offered low-wage

Chinese workers and their families a measure of security commensurate with their modest lifestyles. This arrangement changed abruptly with major reforms in the late 1990s, which included a massive downsizing of the state-owned enterprise sector, steep job losses, and a virtual dismantling of the iron rice bowl.[25]

Aging without financial security is an economic nightmare for any society. In China, this development happened very quickly, instilling deep fear among households. How could aging workers make ends meet for themselves and their families without a state-supported safety net? The Chinese people answered that question with a sharp boost in personal saving to cover the needs that the state once provided. Formerly secure workers, accustomed to what Americans would consider a penurious lifestyle, were willing to forgo new consumption and instead use their rising incomes to compensate for the now dismantled safety net. Precautionary saving became the functional equivalent of a tax, a growing wedge between labor income generation and consumer spending.

None of this was a deep secret to Wen Jiabao and other Chinese leaders as they sat down in 2007 to debate and frame economic strategy for the years ahead. The pro-consumption plan, in its simplest sense, aimed at services development and urbanization to promote labor income generation, while also addressing demographic and safety net issues to tackle the excess saving problem. As noted, labor income generation wasn't the main problem—excess saving was the far bigger issue. Dealing with the saving problem, though a tall order, seemed doable—at least on paper.

There is some progress to report. In 2021, after several earlier efforts to relax the one-child policy, the government finally signaled its intention to relax family planning restrictions by allowing couples to have up to three children in an effort to address the country's skewed demographics.[26] Moreover, the Fourteenth Five-Year Plan, enacted in 2021, features expanded initiatives in China's healthcare and retirement systems. While the approach makes sense, these actions may be too little, too late.

That gets to the tougher news. The end of China's one-child policy will hardly provide an instant solution for the aging problem. Even if a large number of child-bearing women elect multiple births—an iffy proposition, at best—it will take a generation for these newly born children to become active wage earners and begin resolving China's old-age dependency prob-lem.[27] Even under the heroic assumption of an upsurge in the birth rate, an extrapolation of recent and prospective demographic trends suggests that the first visible signs of improvement in the aging problem—a flattening out of the elderly dependency ratio—won't appear until 2040.[28] In the mean-time, the aging burden will continue to mount, leaving Chinese families predisposed toward precautionary saving and reluctant to step up and fuel new discretionary consumption.

But it's not just the lagging impact of a shifting family planning policy regime that will inhibit a reduction in fear-driven precautionary saving. China's safety net reforms have been very slow to arrive. Since the days of Wen Jiabao, plan after plan has promised better safety net security, but im-plementation has lagged.[29] Coverage is not the problem—there is now near-universal enrollment in China's nationwide healthcare plan, especially fol-lowing consolidation of the urban and rural schemes in 2016.[30] But these plans provide extremely low levels of benefits. Payouts from the main urban employee plan are no more than $385 per year, and considerably less on the rural plan, making the notion of healthcare security an oxymoron.[31] Chi-nese workers are forced to supplement covered benefits with the "red en-velopes" of informal cash payments, further strapping households' earned labor income.[32]

A comparable problem is evident with the Chinese retirement system. Like healthcare, there are encouraging signs on coverage—almost 70 per-cent of China's urban workforce is now covered by either the urban or rural pension plan.[33] But also like health insurance, the system is severely under-funded and provides meager benefits. The National Social Security Fund—by far the largest pension fund in China—had only about $445 billion of assets under management in 2020.[34] That works out to a little less than $600 of assets per worker, hardly enough to fund lifetime benefits for a rapidly aging workforce. The bulk of the support for the elderly is left in the hands of their children or other close relatives, absorbing a great deal of household income that might otherwise have gone toward discretionary spending.

China's safety net problem suffers from the drawback that shows up else-where in its economic strategy—an emphasis on quantity over quality. That is what gave rise to Wen Jiabao's critique of the hyper-growth implications of Deng Xiaoping's reforms. But it also applies to recent efforts to address China's safety net deficiencies. Whether it's healthcare or retirement, government policy has focused on increasing the number of people enrolled in government plans rather than on expanding the benefits paid out to each individual under these plans. With the family planning policy reforms likely to take at least several decades before they bring meaningful relief to the aging problem, financial insecurity is likely to remain a serious constraint on Chinese households for many years to come.

All this points to an uncomfortable outcome for Chinese rebalancing. There is good reason to believe that even in the face of rising incomes, fear-driven precautionary saving will continue to inhibit discretionary consumption, meaning that the consumer-led structural transformation of the Chinese economy as modeled after America's template is likely to remain a distant target.

Perhaps because of those difficulties, the government now seems to be placing less emphasis on consumer-led rebalancing than it did in the days of Wen Jiabao. Consumption still shows up as a priority in the premier's heavily watched annual work reports and is still featured as an important objective in the nation's five-year strategy plans. But it has slid lower on the priority list. In Premier Li Keqiang's 2022 Work Report to the National People's Congress, for example, domestic demand was ranked fifth on the agenda of nine major tasks for the year, behind other key objectives such as macroeconomic stability, supporting enterprises and other market entities, streamlining government efficiency, and implementing innovation-driven development; safety net priorities like healthcare and social security were relegated to ninth place, at the bottom of the heap in the premier's 2022 policy focus list.[35]

Has China come full circle? In some respects, its economic strategy now looks more like the production-oriented plans of the 1990s than the consumer-led rebalancing vision of Wen Jiabao's Four Uns. While domestic demand imperatives have not fallen completely out of favor, they are increasingly subsumed under a new "dual circulation" approach that emphasizes the interplay between internal demand and the supply-chain-type efficiencies required of an increasingly challenging external, or global, demand climate.[36] All this raises a key strategic question: is consumerism simply too difficult a problem for China to solve?

The Animal Spirits Deficit

Since early 2007, when Wen Jiabao first publicly urged China to rethink its growth model, the leadership has understood the importance of drawing on the country's vast population to support a shift toward consumer-led economic growth. Its approach has been logical, analytically sound, and well grounded in the long record of success in other consumer-led economies, especially the United States. Why couldn't China follow suit?

The simple answer is that it's not that easy to persuade consumers to consume. Having the wherewithal—the purchasing power of household income—is not the same thing as actually spending. As noted above, China has laid the foundation for sustained growth in household purchasing power by shifting to labor-intensive services and encouraging rural-to-urban migration. The growth of massive new cities has provided a powerful assist to services demand. This broad thrust of China's economic strategy is well supported by historical precedent—it mirrors what the United States and other consumer societies have done.

But at this point China has been stymied. The rise in labor income has not resulted in consumer-led growth of the overall economy, largely because of the persistence of fear-driven precautionary saving. Chinese leaders get this. For the past fifteen years, they have recognized the need to alleviate the insecurities that have given rise to excessive precautionary saving. They understand that the sources of that insecurity—namely, the lack of a robust social safety net—need to be addressed if consumer-led rebalancing is to succeed.[37] But understanding alone is not sufficient.

There are some signs of progress, but not enough to move the needle on household confidence. More revenues from taxes on state-owned enterprises are now earmarked for the National Social Security Fund. The fund's assets under management have grown 13 percent a year since 2010, some 30 percent faster than GDP growth over the same period.[38] But healthcare benefits have lagged, increasing by an average of just 2.6 percent between 2010 and 2018—far short of the 9.3 percent pace of GDP growth.[39] On balance, Chinese households remain unconvinced that their fears for the future are being adequately addressed; household saving remains stubbornly high. Economic restructuring is falling behind in a very tough race against the rapid aging of the Chinese population. As a leading Chinese demographer famously cautioned, "There is now no doubt China will be old before it is rich."[40]

Raising public confidence doesn't come naturally for China's economic policymakers. Well versed in the engineering approach of Soviet-style central planning, they have been more adept at refining and adjusting the structure of production—first shifting from agriculture to manufacturing, and then from manufacturing to services. As macro-engineers, they have excelled at building massive new cities and connecting them with state-of-the-art infrastructure. Chinese planners may be great technocrats, but they are out of their comfort zone when tackling amorphous behavioral considerations like confidence. Yet for households and businesses, confidence may well hold the key to the next, and possibly most critical, stage of rebalancing.

Confidence is a critical underpinning of any dynamic economy. Nobel Prize–winning economists George Akerlof and Robert Shiller view it as the cornerstone of their broader theory of "animal spirits."[41] This notion, widely popularized by John Maynard Keynes in the 1930s, is best thought of as a "spontaneous urge to action" that goes beyond the basic analytics of rational decision making.[42] Akerlof and Shiller argue that traditional economic theory, and the models built from it, is inherently deficient because it overlooks the all-important impacts of animal spirits on economic activity.

China, like any economy, ultimately requires the animal spirits of a confident and successful society. This is the secret sauce of both a dynamic business sector and strong consumerism. It gets to the crux of the issue China faces—to elevate the decision-making confidence of private sector actors to achieve an extra sense of risk-taking and commitment to action. China's record is mixed on unleashing animal spirits—so far, entrepreneurs have benefited more than consumers.[43]

There is no precise formula for igniting animal spirits. Keynes's notion of a spontaneous urge to action is ambiguous at best. He viewed animal spirits as the essence of capitalism. China, with its mixed model of market-based socialism, claims to have its own unique strain of animal spirits. The state plays a far more active role in guiding markets, businesses, and consumers than it does in capitalist systems. Still, at least in theory, there is ample latitude within the framework of state-directed guidance to allow for the spontaneous urge to action by private sector decision makers—entrepreneurs and consumers alike. To achieve that, the Chinese economy, like any other, requires a foundation of trust and the promise of opportunity. Trust resides in the consistency of leadership priorities, in transparent governance, and in wise regulatory oversight. Opportunity comes from the potential rewards of hard work. Supported by output and income growth, human nature, ultimately where confidence resides, hopefully will take over.

Until recently, lack of confidence was not a problem for China's private business sector, where animal spirits sparked a new dynamism. Spectacular growth of AI-enabled platform Internet companies like Alibaba (and its fintech subsidiary, Ant), Tencent, Meituan (food delivery), and Didi Chuxing (ride sharing) couldn't have occurred without a burst of animal spirits. The ecosystem behind this dynamism reflects the combination of creative and hard-working talent, research-based innovation, a supportive start-up culture, and an ample supply of financial risk capital. A new generation of Chinese entrepreneurs drew on the catalytic spark of animal spirits and brought energy and commitment to a new powerful source of economic growth. This was the latest in a succession of Chinese economic miracles, and it offered an important plus—meaningful hope for China's long-awaited shift to home-grown, or indigenous, innovation.[44]

That was then. Unfortunately, there is reason to believe that the pendulum of animal spirits in China's business sector may now be swinging from surplus to deficit.[45] In the summer of 2021, the Chinese government launched two major policy initiatives: regulatory constraints aimed largely at Internet platform companies, and a "common prosperity" campaign focused on the excesses of income generation and wealth creation. This combination runs against the grain of earlier policy reforms that have prompted the spectacular rise of China's "new economy."

Why would the government reverse course just when animal spirits seem about to turbo-charge the burst of indigenous innovation that had become such a high priority in the country's growth strategy? A key reason is purported concerns over data security. As we saw in Chapter 5, Kai-Fu Lee, one of the leading experts on artificial intelligence in China, has argued that big data is the pivotal element in China's push for competitive supremacy in AI-related businesses.[46] Lee stresses that China's leading position in assembling big data is a major competitive advantage. What happens if China loses that edge?

The government now seems to be asking the same question. As we also saw in Chapter 5, senior Chinese leaders increasingly see strict controls over large proprietary databases as crucial to the nation's broad strategy.[47] In one sense, this is understandable: the leadership places extremely high value on its claims over big data as the high-octane fuel of its push into artificial intelligence. Never mind that much of the data has been gathered through the surreptitious gaze of the surveillance state.[48] In keeping with China's August 2021 enactment of the Personal Information Protection Law, which aims to protect "individuals, society, and national security from harms stemming from abuse and mishandling of personal information," the government apparently felt that the time was ripe to act on its concerns over data security.

At the same time, following the public listing of the ride-sharing company Didi Chuxing in June 2021, the Chinese government has imposed new regulatory constraints on the listing of Chinese companies in US capital markets. This was not done merely out of concern for the security of Didi's large trove of mobility and transportation data. It was also a retaliation for similar actions taken by US regulators as part of Trump's trade war. Moreover, the Chinese government has cited anti-monopoly concerns in justifying its latest regulatory actions, especially as they pertain to the high-profile public offering of Ant, China's largest fintech company, that was put on ice in late 2020. All in all, it appears that Chinese authorities are aiming the full force of their regulatory power at the business models and offshore financing capacity of the economy's heretofore most dynamic sector. There is debate over the impacts of these actions but there can be no mistaking the significance of this major shift in policy.[49]

Those actions were tough enough. But in the summer of 2021, the Chinese government doubled down, with President Xi Jinping throwing the full force of his power into a new "common prosperity" campaign aimed at addressing the widening disparities in China's income and wealth distributions.[50] The government has also banished crypto-currencies under the guise of financial stability and, in keeping with the earlier focus of Xi Jinping, has taken aim at a new strain of "bad habits" in the name of social stability. This latter development, with its focus on lifestyle excesses such as video gaming, online music, celebrity fan culture, and private tutoring, along with bans on e-cigarettes and business drinking, reflects an important shift in the strategy of Chinese rebalancing—from structural to social engineering.[51]

This new twin thrust of Chinese policy—reregulation plus redistribution—strikes at the heart of the market-based "reforms and opening up" that have underpinned China's spectacular economic growth since the 1980s.[52] While the common prosperity campaign is consistent with Deng's earlier views on the sequencing of Chinese development from more advanced to backward areas, it also pushes back against the rewards of wealth accumulation that entrepreneurs and risk-takers have come to expect from new-economy endeavors.

These restraints on the scope and rewards of new Chinese businesses are antithetical to the creativity, energy, and hard work that entrepreneurs need to flourish in an intensely competitive environment, and that have been so important in powering China's dynamic private sector. That may have lasting consequences for the next, innovations-driven, phase of Chinese economic development. Without animal spirits, it is difficult to make a compelling case for indigenous innovation. And without indigenous innovation, Chinese development will inevitably hit a wall.

Chinese households have suffered from a more chronic strain of the animal spirits deficit. The excesses of fear-driven precautionary saving speak to a long-standing lack of confidence of Chinese households. Weighed down by deep-seated fears of financial insecurity, they have been unwilling to broaden their horizons as consumers by moving beyond the bare necessities of life to indulge in discretionary activities like home improvement and modern furnishings or entertainment and leisure activities. Their preference for precautionary saving continues to thwart the rebalancing efforts that could make or break consumer-led growth in China.

For any economy, confidence and trust go hand in hand. Households need to be able to trust their leaders' promises, which form the basis of the social contract underpinning consumerism. They not only have to be confident of their own job and wage security, they also have to trust the government's support for retirement and healthcare as critical components of China's social safety net. The same is true of Chinese entrepreneurs—they, too, need to trust that the rules of regulatory oversight and the rewards of their hard work will not be altered by the shifting whims of government oversight.

Modern China lacks this foundation of trust. As I noted in Chapter 8, the math of political distrust is compelling: the 7 percent of Chinese who are CCP members have not instilled confidence in the 93 percent who remain on the outside. But now there is also economic distrust, reflected in China's mounting animal spirits deficit. That could well be the visible manifestation of an enduring impediment to creating a robust Chinese consumerism and a new impediment in stifling the most dynamic part of the business sector. Without a more vibrant and spontaneous unleashing of animal spirits, China's economic dynamism could start to ebb. In the end, it's not that easy to be like America.

From Economic to Ideological Conflict

If the animal spirits deficit inhibits indigenous innovation and stymies the shift to consumer-led growth, it could force the Chinese economy back to its earlier producer orientation. China's leadership seems to be preparing for this possibility. As noted above, it has made consumerism a lower priority in the government's recent annual work reports and five-year plans and has also announced a new focus on "dual circulation."[53]

Dual circulation is a hybrid strategy that promotes a combined emphasis on both internal and external demand. It was first proposed by Xi Jinping in May 2020 in an attempt to marry the ideological thrust of Xi Jinping Thought with the global pressures arising from the Covid shock and the ongoing trade war with the United States. Like many Chinese policy pronouncements, dual circulation is laced with ambiguity. Xi stresses that it does not mean the strategic pillar of internal demand and consumerism has been abandoned, but that there is a need to add an extra dimension of efficient external circulation to China's development strategy.[54]

This could be a real stretch. If we take official explanations at face value, the Chinese economy still faces the same issues that have frustrated its consumer-led rebalancing—especially the wedge between labor income generation and discretionary consumption traceable to excess saving and an inadequate social safety net. Dual circulation thus looks like a hedge—a return to relying on external support in the event the impetus to internal demand stalls out.

This could prove problematic for the US-China conflict. Rebalancing, as a macroeconomic strategy, would lessen the pressures of a conflicted codependency and so help ease tensions on both sides. By allowing, even encouraging, a reduced reliance on external demand, a consumer-led rebalancing would diminish China's multilateral trade surpluses, including the outsize imbalance with the United States, and lower China's trade frictions with other nations. The United States, meanwhile, would do well to pursue the opposite strategy: rebalancing by boosting domestic saving would reduce its multilateral trade deficit, including its outsize bilateral imbalance with China.

Of the two, China has been the more likely candidate for rebalancing. It has enormous incentives to change, while the United States has been more content to stay the course with its time-tested but ultimately unsustainable approach. As I hinted in Part I of this book, the odds were always in favor of an asymmetrical rebalancing—an effective consumer-led transformation of the Chinese economy accompanied by persistent savings-short growth in the US economy.[55] China would have benefited significantly from this divergence. It would have emerged in a much stronger position as an engine of global growth and a moderating influence on global imbalances and trade tensions. The United States, heavily reliant on surplus saving from the rest of the world to fund its economic growth, would have grown progressively weaker.

But now, with an explosion of post-Covid federal budget deficits in the United States and with Chinese consumers unable to gain traction, the odds of rebalancing are receding for both nations. The macroeconomic pressures of a conflicted codependency could intensify as a result, bringing a renewed widening of saving disparities between the two economies. China's surplus saving could stay large or even rise, while the US deficit saving position seems likely to endure and possibly deepen further, exacerbating America's multilateral current account and trade imbalances.

A flourishing Chinese consumerism could have prevented one aspect of this outcome. From the standpoint of sustainable economic development, it was in China's best interest to push ahead with the heavy lifting of consumer-led rebalancing. That once seemed like China's most likely course, but no longer. Instead, its focus has shifted to ideological rebalancing. While the leadership still recognizes the imperatives of structural change, its highest priority now is the ideological purity of Xi Jinping Thought and the iron grip of Party control. New regulatory actions and the common prosperity campaign underscore this shift in priorities.

The reemergence and emphasis of the ideological debate are of enormous importance to China. Just as the pendulum once swung from Mao to Deng, it is now swinging back the other way. Xi's laser-like fixation on socialist principles, together with the ascendancy of the CCP's ideological champion, Wang Huning, to China's top leadership team, point to a conservative backlash to the liberalization that occurred under Jiang Zemin and Hu Jintao.[56] This tug-of-war between the extremes of the ideological spectrum is, of course, not unique to China. In Western societies it is expressed through cross-party election politics, whereas in China it takes the form of factional power shifts within the Party.

Xi's new ideological thrust is likely to have important unintended consequences. Under the guise of common prosperity, the animal spirits deficit that was rooted in a weak social safety net is now spreading into China's dynamic "new economy." At the same time, the social engineering implications of common prosperity appear increasingly aligned with Wang Huning's scathing critique of American society. Wang, as Xi Jinping's ideological alter ego, paints an especially bleak picture of the United States as a money-focused collection of "hollowed out" families in the grips of an oppressive system, which "ensures that the capitalists exploit the workers."[57] China's false narratives of America apparently are just as grounded in ideology as in economics.

All this leaves the US-China conflict on an ominous trajectory. It started with the economics of saving and trade disparities. Absent rebalancing, those problems will persist and most likely worsen, leaving both nations unwittingly opting for vulnerability over resilience. Now, ideology exacerbates the conflict, with the steady drumbeat of Cold War 2.0 reinforced by the ascendancy of Xi Jinping Thought.

This is a potentially lethal combination. China's state-directed censorship and America's polarized information distortion amplifies the false narratives that arise all too frequently from the toxic interplay of economic vulnerability and ideology. America and China have descended to the low road of conflict escalation. What will it take to avoid the grim endgame of an increasingly hostile codependency?

10

China with American Characteristics

CHINESE LEADERS HAVE LONG FINESSED the debate between different systems. Since the days of Jiang Zemin in the early 1990s, they have coalesced around the notion of a socialist market economy.[1] As this term suggests, it is a blended approach, drawing on US-style market capitalism while preserving the socialist principles of state ownership and government control of the economy. Over the years, the balance between these two approaches has tipped back and forth. Market-driven reforms were increasingly favored between 1980 and 2010 before the Party and the socialist state reasserted control during the Xi Jinping era.

This blended approach sounds good in theory. It is an attempt to choose the best ideas of two very different systems and apply them to operational practices of economic activity and engagement with other nations. But the actual task of bringing these systems together raises profound questions about the organizing principles of the Chinese economy. What is the nature of the interplay? How does one avoid the inherent conflicts of two incompatible systems? Or does it all fit together seamlessly?

These pragmatic questions of implementation cannot be answered by the purity of ideological assertions or the rigor of economic analysis. The answers, instead, hinge on the ability of China's senior leaders to select an optimal mixture of the best features of each system.

Hybrid economic models are loaded with inconsistencies. The great paradox of the Xi Jinping era—the "mixed-ownership model" that emphasizes the decisive role of markets alongside state control of assets—remains un-resolved. China wants American-style market structures, but without the volatility and risks that are endemic to market-based systems. Yet capital markets without risk or volatility are, of course, a contradiction in terms.

The concept of the socialist market economy raises an even deeper issue. What is China attempting to accomplish by injecting market-based capital-ism into its socialist model? Do its socialist technocrats have a clear under-standing of how the American model works?

China's codependent relationship with the United States hints at the an-swers to these questions. As is the case in human relationships, the early stages of an economic codependency often feature an aspirational transfer-ence, in essence, taking on some of the characteristics of a partner. The United States became infatuated with Japanese quality circles in the late 1980s, and China has shown a similar infatuation with the United States. It wants to grow, urbanize, and innovate like America and project the same level of military power. American characteristics are an unspoken part of the Chinese Dream.

China also suffers from scale envy. In my decades of travel to China, one of the questions I get asked most frequently is, "When do you think Chinese GDP will surpass that of the United States?" Most people are asking about the absolute size of nominal GDP, where convergence is close at hand, rather than per capita GDP, where convergence is more a distant hope. Rightly or wrongly, the Chinese people and their leaders associate scale with prosperity and power. In many respects, this reflects a recurring theme in China: viewing quantity rather than quality as the arbiter of a successful economy.

It's not as if China considers the United States the perfect role model, especially now. Still, something about the American journey holds a deep, almost heroic fascination for the Chinese. It's as if the imperfections of the American experience reveal the risks as well as the opportunities that China might encounter as it musters the courage and determination to push ahead on its own epic adventure.

In the end, China's blended strategy overlooks one of the most important aspects of the US experience—learning from mistakes. The false pride of China's tightly constrained censorship and discourse power closes off this feedback loop. As a result, the image of a China with American characteristics often falls wide of the mark, based more on state-directed self-assessment than reality. These distorted perceptions are a recipe for false narratives that push China further into conflict with the United States.

The Mixed-Ownership Paradox

China's state-owned enterprises (SOEs) are the most important and highly visible manifestation of the blended socialist market economy. Initially created by a series of actions spearheaded by Deng Xiaoping in the late 1970s and early 1980s, SOEs have been a work in progress ever since. Deng's goal was to create world-class companies from entities historically embedded in the bureaucracy of the centrally planned economy. The first wave of SOE reforms, which focused on management autonomy, were followed by reforms to procurement practices, the introduction of shareholding structures, and a transition from state to bank funding. Production was no longer set by government quotas but instead aligned with nascent competitive pressures.[2]

A turning point came in 1993, when the Party issued a "Decision on Issues Related to the Establishment of a Socialist Market Economy System"— the first official endorsement of China's blended system.[3] The goal in this round of reforms was to align SOEs with a Chinese version of the market economy by separating management from the government and empowering a targeted group of SOEs with property rights and operational autonomy. While these early "marketization reforms" succeeded in reducing the SOE share in the overall Chinese economy, job losses associated with the resulting efficiency enhancements elicited considerable controversy and pushback from conservative political forces.[4]

To its great credit, the government persevered, and in 1997 it enacted a more sweeping program of SOE reforms, guided by the principle of "grasping the big, letting go of the small" that was popularized by President Jiang Zemin and Premier Zhu Rongji.[5] "Big" and "small" referred to SOE scale; this was China's attempt at "creative destruction"—the market-driven purging of inefficient companies in order to make way for new ones.[6] While the state was encouraged to preserve control over large and powerful SOEs, the smaller and, by inference, weaker ones could be "let go" through closures or consolidation. In this emphasis on scale, classic for modern China, size was viewed as a sign of strength, while smaller SOEs were considered weak and relatively expendable.

While impressive in terms of consolidation and efficiency enhancement, these first efforts at SOE reforms lacked a critical ingredient—a corporate governance structure that empowered active shareholder participation in enterprise operations. As the majority shareholder, the state had the last word on management selection and decision making.[7] This theoretically came to an end in 2008 during the Hu Jintao administration with the enactment of new reforms aimed at providing operational autonomy for SOEs, officially terminating direct intervention by the Party and the state government, while also providing incentives for the growth of private enterprises to compete with SOEs.[8] In practice, however, the heavy hand of state guidance was still evident at key times—especially when the Chinese economy was threatened by domestic pressures stemming from global crises.

Under Xi Jinping, it quickly became apparent that the Party thought Hu Jintao's "autonomy reforms" of 2008 had gone too far. In his signature "Third Plenum Reform" initiatives of late 2013, Xi pushed for a different strain of SOE restructuring under the guise of a so-called comprehensive deepening of Chinese reforms—a key premise of what would become known as Xi Jinping Thought. This gave rise to a "mixed-ownership reform model" for SOEs that was in keeping with the overarching paradox of the Third Plenum—namely, reforms that purportedly encouraged a decisive role for markets while underscoring "unswerving support" for state ownership and control of strategic assets. The government's efforts to "vigorously develop a mixed [ownership] economy" meant essentially that it wanted to have it both ways—a Chinese model of state control overlaying an American market-based system.[9]

According to Premier Li Keqiang's explanation of this initiative in the 2014 Work Report to the National People's Congress, mixed-ownership SOE reforms (MOSOERs) preserved China's long-standing balance between state control and market-based mechanisms.[10] As such, Premier Li urged, they should be viewed less as a new initiative and more as a continuation of earlier efforts aimed at enhancing corporate efficiency and improving international competitiveness. Still, something different was in the air. After decades of increasing Western-style marketization and privatization, the very mention of MOSOERs suggested that the pendulum was swinging back toward increased state control.

China watchers were disappointed. Economist Nicholas Lardy of the Peterson Institute had a typical response. In 2014 he had published a book, *Markets over Mao*, celebrating the emerging vibrancy of China's dynamic private sector; just five years later he came out with a very different take, *The State Strikes Back*.[11] Western observers like Lardy recognized that the Chinese government's backtracking had important implications for SOE reform as well as for the efficiency and vitality of the entire Chinese system. In the vernacular of Jiang Zemin and Zhu Rongji, "grasping the big" had apparently overtaken "letting go."

The 2017 reform of China Unicom was emblematic of the MOSOER wave. Founded as a state-owned enterprise in 1994, China Unicom is the nation's third leading telecom service provider (behind China Mobile and China Telecom), with the sixth largest mobile subscription base in the world.[12] In search of new capital as well as technical expertise, China Unicom announced an $11.7 billion capital injection in August 2017, to be used primarily for 4G and 5G platform upgrades.[13] The new funding, which amounted to 35 percent of the company's outstanding equity, was promoted as an example of a broadening of the SOE's private investor base. And with four large Chinese Internet groups—Tencent, Baidu, JD.com, and Alibaba—accounting for 37 percent of the capital injection, the reform had the added benefit of drawing on the capital and expertise of some of China's most high-profile dynamic technology companies.

But the China Unicom reform broke very little new ground in one important area. Prior to the August 2017 capital injection, the state held a 63 percent stake of the company's outstanding shares. Following the new injection, press reports suggested that the state share would be slashed to 37 percent.[14] This was misleading—it pertained only to the stake of China Unicom's SOE parent company. A significant portion of the new capital came from other SOEs, such as China Life Insurance, and from government-sponsored funds like the China Structural Reform Fund, Huaihai Fangzhou

Fund, and Xinquan Fund.[15] On a fully consolidated basis, the state owner-ship share was reduced only from 63 percent to 58 percent. The govern-ment, in effect, was raising new money from itself.

This mixing of ownership, more on paper than in substance, brought to mind the profusion of equity share crossholdings of Japan's fabled *keiret-sus*, which had proved so problematic during that nation's lost decades.[16] During the final stages of its equity market bubble in the late 1980s, Japan's large companies inflated their earnings by investing in each other's rising shares. When the bubble burst in the early 1990s, sharp losses in the value of these crossholdings took a severe toll on the investor base of interlocking *keiretsus*, helping to create a generation of insolvent zombie corporations.[17]

As in Japan, China Unicom's mixed-ownership "reforms" are more like financial engineering than true efficiency enhancement. Conflating the eco-nomic gains of restructuring strategies with monetary returns from finan-cial engineering is a common practice elsewhere in the world. Yet research on a wide range of economies, including the United States, Japan, and Ger-many, shows that there is little connection between such balance-sheet ma-neuvers and lasting improvements in productivity.[18] China is unlikely to be an exception. But that hasn't stopped Chinese SOEs and policymakers from embracing the failed practices of financial engineering that have proved equally disappointing elsewhere. Meanwhile, with senior officials like Pre-mier Li Keqiang openly admitting that China has its own zombie problem, the Japan comparison was hardly idle conjecture.[19]

Zombies and debt overhangs go hand in hand. By mid-2020, Chinese nonfinancial corporate debt had risen to 163 percent of GDP, a dramatic increase from 94 percent at the end of 2008. While China's corporate debt ratio edged a bit lower in late 2020 and early 2021, it is still above the peak level of Japanese corporate indebtedness, 145 percent of GDP, which was reached in late 1993 when Japan's zombie problem was at its worst.[20] China's companies had set a record for debt-intensive growth.

The Chinese government rationalized this debt binge as necessary to protect its businesses from the unprecedented shock of the 2008–9 Global Financial Crisis. This was reminiscent of Japan's rationale in the early '90s, which held that "evergreen lending" to its zombies was needed to keep its banks intact in accordance with Basel international risk standards and avoid systemic risk in an already weakened financial system.[21] Neither explanation was satisfactory. Japan's excuse turned out to be an egregious miscalculation that kept its zombies on life support and, as a result, helped perpetuate its lost-decade syndrome. China's more recent build-up of corporate debt, concentrated in its state-owned enterprise sector, has prompted concerns over the prospects of zombie SOEs.[22] The lessons of Japan became an active topic of debate in senior Chinese policy circles.

In a widely noted May 2016 interview in *People's Daily*, China's official state newspaper, an "authoritative person"—rumored to be a high-ranking senior official very close to Xi Jinping—famously warned of the potential Japanization of China. With a stagnant Japanese economy now having experienced at least three "lost decades," the front-page commentary prompted great consternation in Chinese markets and policy circles.[23] The authoritative person explicitly mentioned the mounting risks of increased leverage, asset bubbles, potential crises, and the deadweight of excess capacity and zombies. The interview gave near-official credence to the lessons of Japan as a warning to China and ultimately set the stage for many subsequent Chinese policy actions such as supply-side structural reforms, deleveraging, and a clampdown on the Chinese property sector.

The emphasis on mixed-ownership SOE reform since 2017 does little to temper the concerns of a Japanization with Chinese characteristics. If these reforms continue to encourage financial engineering rather than sustained productivity enhancement and more meaningful corporate restructuring, the risks of a debt-intensive Japanization may grow. Nothing in the current blended system can inoculate China from these mounting risks.

Incomplete Capital Market Reforms

Financial markets are the circulatory system of economies.[24] They intermediate flows between borrowers and lenders, between savers and investors, between consumers and businesses, and in the case of China, between the state and the private sector. Financial markets also provide the conduit for government policy actions to influence the real economy. Regulatory oversight of the intermediation process reflects government awareness of markets' tendency to misprice risk and overshoot the tolerable limits of financial stability.

Credit intermediation takes place through either banks or capital markets. Both are accident prone, giving rise to periodic cycles of nonperforming bank loans and valuation stress in equity and bond markets. Regulatory oversight aims at avoiding, or at least limiting, the impacts of bank lending crises; policy interventions by monetary authorities are meant to do the same in tempering capital-markets distress. That is the case both in free-market capitalist systems as well as in blended systems like China's. As the all-too-frequent occurrence of financial crises suggests, this oversight hasn't always worked out well, especially in free-market systems like the United States.[25]

China's bias toward control in managing the real side of the socialist market economy is mirrored in its tight regulatory oversight of all aspects of its financial system. As reforms have moved the country toward greater marketization, the government has relaxed its oversight of the state-dominated financial system. But mindful of the systemic risks of financial instability, it has moved more slowly on financial marketization than on economic liberalization.

Chinese financialization is accordingly at the low end of the spectrum for large economies; China is ranked #10 in the Financial Development Index of the International Monetary Fund, behind the United States, the United Kingdom, and Japan.[26] Moreover, despite its inherent wariness of marketization, China's financial sector is not well insulated from systemic risks. This is borne out by comparative metrics of financial stability. According to the 2021 *Global Financial Stability Report* of the International Monetary Fund (IMF), Chinese financial vulnerability is particularly worrisome for households, nonfinancial firms, the banking sector, and asset managers; less concern is evident for insurance companies, shadow banking, and sovereign (i.e., government) borrowers.[27]

The structure of China's financial system is heavily bank-centric, with bank lending accounting for 63 percent of total credit intermediation, compared to 35 percent in the United States.[28] And there is a worrisome Japanese-like precedent in this concentration: just as Japan boasted the eight largest banks in the world in 1989, on the eve of its first lost decade, China currently has the world's four largest banks.[29] Japan's overreliance on its poorly managed big banks was a well-known feature of its bubble economy. As the "authoritative person" implied in 2016, bank-centric China should not take that comparison lightly.

By contrast, Chinese equity financing makes up less than 20 percent of total credit flows, and the corporate bond market share of credit intermediation remains less than 10 percent. The balance is spread out between the government bond market and nonbank intermediaries, popularly known as shadow banking.[30] A US-style structure of credit intermediation would imply a major shift in Chinese credit flows away from bank lending toward capital markets. That transition has barely begun.

The greater emphasis on capital markets in more advanced economies reflects the more active role of "risk capital" in fueling new sources of growth and innovation. That is particularly relevant for China, where bank lending practices are steeped in the central planning legacy of fiscal transfers to the state agencies that later became state-owned enterprises. While banks have broadened out their role to provide funding to a much larger swath of the Chinese economy, the state retains control over the bank lending spigot by influencing both the volume of loan growth and the selection of borrowers, as well as the magnitude of credit lines.

The contribution of capital market activity has recently taken on greater importance in China, but only partly because of reforms. Also at work are the impacts of a government-directed deleveraging campaign aimed at reducing the steadily increasing debt intensity of the Chinese economy that occurred in the decade after the Global Financial Crisis. Like bank concentration risk, deleveraging is also very much in keeping with the concerns of a debt-intensive Japanization that were conveyed by the "authoritative person" in 2016. With China's deleveraging campaign aimed at traditional banks and shadow-bank lenders, capital markets were pressured to fill the void.

Deleveraging has drawn special attention to China's shadow banking activities, where individuals have invested heavily in a profusion of unregulated, high-yielding wealth management products and entrusted loans in search of better yields.[31] Shadow banking has recently been one of the most rapidly growing sources of Chinese credit intermediation. By the end of 2018, China's nonbank credit intermediation accounted for 10 percent of all shadow banking activity worldwide, five times its share in 2012.[32] The recent deleveraging campaign has made considerable progress in limiting shadow banking activity in an effort to contain systemic risks that could spill over into other segments of Chinese financial markets.[33] The vulnerability assessment of the IMF's latest *Global Financial Stability Report,* noted above, places China's shadow-banking-dominated "Other Financial Institutions" sector in the top quintile on its resilience scale, a sharp contrast to the relatively poor rankings it assigns to Chinese banks, corporations, and households.

Given China's sharp upsurge in debt, it would be foolish to think that the deleveraging campaign would not have serious consequences. That became painfully evident in the summer of 2021 with the high-profile demise of Evergrande, China's second-largest property developer. Given the company's debt overhang of some $300 billion, Evergrande's problems pose broader risks to the Chinese financial system, with potential knock-on effects in global markets.[34] Even so, the magnitude of those ripple effects is likely to be far less than anticipated by those who loudly proclaim that Evergrande is China's Lehman Brothers.[35]

Three considerations argue to the contrary. First, the Chinese government has ample resources to backstop Evergrande loan defaults and contain any spillovers to other assets and markets. With some $7.5 trillion in domestic saving and another $3-trillion-plus in foreign exchange reserves, China has more than enough financial capacity to absorb a worst-case Evergrande implosion. Large liquidity injections by the People's Bank of China in the fall of 2021 underscored that point.[36]

Second, Evergrande is not a classic shock—the "black swan" crisis—but a deliberate consequence of a Chinese policy aimed at deleveraging, de-risking, and preserving financial stability.[37] China's commendable progress in reducing shadow banking activity has limited the potential for deleveraging contagion to infect other segments of its financial markets. Unlike Lehman's collapse, which caused devastating collateral damage that shocked US and global financial markets, the Evergrande problem has not blindsided Chinese policymakers.

Third, the risks to the real Chinese economy—the greatest peril in a financial crisis—are limited. The demand side of the Chinese property market is well supported by the ongoing migration of rural workers to cities. This is very different from the collapse of speculative housing bubbles in countries like Japan and the United States, where supply overhangs were unsupported by demand. While the urban share of the Chinese population has now risen above 60 percent, there is still plenty of upside until it reaches the 80 to 85 percent threshold typical of more advanced economies.[38] Notwithstanding recent accounts of shrinking cities—reminiscent of earlier false alarms over a profusion of ghost cities—China's underlying demand for urban shelter remains firm, limiting Evergrande's downside risks to the overall economy.[39]

Still, the Evergrande scare should not be taken lightly. Financial stability is of great importance for all modern economies, including China. Its consumer-led rebalancing strategy requires well-developed, stable capital markets. They offer better premiums than low-return bank deposits, which squeeze Chinese savers and put pressure on the investment returns needed to boost household purchasing power. With nonlabor income accounting for only about 13.5 percent of total disposable household income in China in 2019, far short of the 22 percent peak in 2011 and less than half the 29 percent share in the United States, the portfolio diversification potential of expanded capital market activity offers considerable opportunity to augment the growth in labor income and boost household purchasing power and discretionary consumption.[40] While better returns don't fully compensate for the pitfalls of fear-driven precautionary saving, they provide welcome diversification and higher yielding options for income-constrained Chinese consumers.

China's latest capital market reform efforts have focused on what the government has dubbed a "higher level" opening-up.[41] Its multitiered equity markets, long dominated by a "main board" alongside a separate exchange for small and medium-sized companies, have been augmented by the new Shenzhen-based ChiNext market, for science-based and technology companies, and the more recent Shanghai-based STAR board for R&D-intensive companies. Together with the NEEQ board for small ("micro") companies and a variety of regional trading platforms (including the new Beijing Stock

Exchange launched in late 2021 as an offshoot of the NEEQ board focusing on innovative small- and medium-sized enterprises), China's reform agenda has brought its equity markets into closer alignment with its push for scientific development and indigenous innovation.[42] With a robust market infrastructure now in place, the challenge inevitably will shift to the scaling up of equity flows as a share of credit intermediation.

All that gets to the thorniest question of all for Chinese capital market reforms: to what extent is the government willing to let go of control and embrace aggressive capital raising in its most dynamic sectors? Letting go is proving hard to do. Moreover, as I noted in the previous chapter, Beijing's recent regulatory interventions in the initial public offering of Ant, the post-IPO actions taken against Didi Chuxing, and new restraints on initial public offerings in US markets have sent a chill through financial markets, both in China and around the world. Not only do these actions underscore the tradeoff between the imperatives of capital market liberalization and state political control, they also bear critically on China's ability to raise capital in its vital push for indigenous innovation.

This is yet another example of how China struggles with the American characteristics of its development strategy. On one level, the Chinese leadership appreciates what the US approach requires in terms of capital market and enterprise reforms. By listing its companies in international capital markets and taking actions to conform with foreign accounting and governance standards, China appears to be welcoming Western discipline on its corporate structure. Indeed, both China and the Western world have been making the case for capital market integrity since the days of its campaign for WTO accession.[43] But as seen through the lens of Party control, the lax oversight of crisis-prone US capital markets can be viewed as a recipe for instability—especially with its emphasis on risk-taking in both regulated capital markets and unregulated hedge funds and other shadow banking activity. This would not have been as disconcerting in an earlier era of market-based liberalization that was far more permissive of the volatility risks inherent in capital markets activity. But under the ideological constraints of Xi Jinping Thought it is a different matter. China's yet-unfinished capital market reform agenda hangs in the balance.

The Façade

China's blended socialist market economy is trapped between two systems—the command and control of the state and the institutional framework of markets. The management of this hybrid system has proved challenging, especially as the economy and the financial system have continued to grow in both scale and complexity. In the old days of central planning, China relied on an elaborate system of interindustry quotas and subsidies to hit its economic targets. Deng Xiaoping's reforms and opening-up created the need for a new approach.

That approach was aligned with the market-based elements of the hybrid system. Central planning was de-emphasized in favor of a new policy and regulatory framework that drew many of its characteristics from the United States, the quintessential market economy. But the effort to create a Chinese system with American characteristics ran into inherent contradictions that have compromised its operation.

The People's Bank of China (PBC) is a case in point. Until 1978 the PBC was China's only bank, functioning in the dual capacity of a commercial and a central bank.[44] It was an arm of the state that controlled all aspects of the nation's financial system, from currency and credit creation to sovereign bond issuance. But having been designed to manage the finances of a centrally planned economy, the PBC was incompatible with the needs of a socialist market economy. The post-1978 reforms and opening-up forced it to change dramatically.

Between 1979 and 1984, the PBC gradually spun off its commercial functions, leading to the establishment of China's four large banks—Industrial and Commercial Bank of China (ICBC), China Construction Bank (CCB), the Bank of China (BOC), and the Agricultural Bank of China (ABC). While autonomous on paper, in practice the "Big Four" remained arms of the state. Each had its own designated core functionality: ICBC focused on the intermediation of deposit gathering to Chinese businesses; CCB provided financing for China's massive investment boom; BOC was responsible for international finance; and ABC provided financial services to farmers.[45] Significantly, these functions were not determined by market forces but ordained by the state.

From the start of the modern reform era, the four banks had little autonomy to set their own lending policies. Tight control by the state made sense in the early days of the transition from central planning to the socialist market economy. Back then, bank credit officers were mainly bureaucrats operating in the financing conduits of a central plan. Lacking a sound, well-developed lending culture and vulnerable to corruption, they had little understanding of credit risk. Many could hardly distinguish between good and bad loans.[46] There were plenty of the latter in China's investment-led takeoff. This led to a steady buildup of nonperforming loans during the 1980s and 1990s, eventually requiring significant capital injections and a major restructuring of the Chinese banking system.[47]

As that restructuring occurred in the early 2000s, the government realized that it had taken the wrong approach to managing its financial system. But it remained unwilling to give professional managers, policymakers, and regulators the independent authority they needed to put the financial infrastructure on the same basis as the country's blended, increasingly marketized economy. This was a visible manifestation of the control problem that still plagues China today—the push and pull between the Party and the invisible yet often harsh democracy of market forces.

Instead, the government went for a second-best option. It started by designing a financial system that, in outward appearance, drew heavily on the features of the US financial system. But in fact, China had grafted a Western-style policy and regulatory structure onto a state-controlled financial system. As in the American system, the central bank performed an important monitoring function by tracking and analyzing financial flows. Moreover, the People's Bank of China was reconfigured in outward appearance as a clone of America's Federal Reserve. Mirroring the Fed's system of twelve districts, each with its own regional headquarters bank, in 1997 China established nine districts for the PBC, each also with its own regional headquarters. And as in the United States, where the New York district plays a special role given its proximity to Wall Street as the historic center of the American financial system, the Shanghai district of the PBC was granted a comparable role in China's reformed central bank.[48]

But there was an important catch. Premier Zhu Rongji was named the first governor of the newly reorganized central bank in 1997, making him the Chinese equivalent of the Fed Chair at the time, Alan Greenspan.[49] Zhu was analytical, tough-mined, disciplined, and uncorruptible—ideal qualities in an independent central banker. But he was also the head of China's State Council and a senior leader of the Communist Party. He made key decisions on monetary and regulatory policy in his capacity as premier and Party leader, not as a politically independent PBC governor. This left the PBC as a policy authority in name only.

The same happened with regulatory oversight of China's financial system. Unlike the US Fed, which had the dual responsibility for monetary and regulatory policies, China wisely separated these functions. It left the *analysis* of monetary policy—very different from the *decisions* on monetary policy—to the PBC and gave additional monitoring authority to newly established regulators of banks (the China Banking and Regulatory Commission, or CBRC), insurance companies (the China Insurance Regulatory Commission, or CIRC), and securities markets (China Securities Regulatory Commission, or CSRC).[50] On paper, it once again looked very much like America—or even better. But in practice, as with monetary policy, the ultimate decision-making authority on Chinese regulatory matters rested with the state and the Party.

This might have made sense as a transitional approach, a way of guiding the transformation from complete government control of a centrally planned system to a market-driven system. The hope was that as the socialist market economy evolved, the emphasis would increasingly shift toward the market piece of the system, with the ideological strictures of socialism receding in importance. That direction could, in fact, be inferred from actions taken by the successive administrations of Deng Xiaoping, Jiang Zemin, and Hu Jintao. As markets grew in importance, a concomitant shift toward independent policy authority and regulatory oversight appeared increasingly likely. China seemed to be converging on the American model.

This turned out to be an overly generous assessment. Realistically, there was little hope that the state and the Party would let go of their ultimate decision-making authority. But there was reason to think that a succession of small steps in that direction would be both desirable and conceivable in an era of reforms and opening-up. That was especially the case for the establishment of an independent monetary authority; academic research has long supported the effectiveness of politically independent central banks in hitting their mandated targets of price stability.[51] It made little sense to outsource inflation targeting to the political calculus of the Party or the State Council.

Yet that is precisely what China has done. The PBC never achieved independent policy functionality. Zhou Xiaochuan, its longest serving and most widely renowned governor, was especially candid in publicly admitting this.[52] Decisions on monetary policy, from changes in bank reserve requirements to adjustments in benchmark lending rates, were left to the State Council and CCP leadership. In the end, China's financial system only had a superficial resemblance to Western systems.

In the new era of Xi Jinping Thought, any hope of policymaking autonomy has been all but dashed. The blended economy is being remixed. The hand of the Party and the state has been strengthened while the democratization implied by markets has been weakened. A vast bureaucracy of Western-looking institutions—from the People's Bank of China to a large family of financial regulators—presents the façade of a China with American characteristics. But behind it, the system operates more through Party-centric control than by the invisible hand of capitalism.

Scale Fixation

As its development has unfolded over the past forty years, China has grown fixated on scale. Economic development is deemed to be successful when a nation achieves alignment between the size of its population and the scale of its economy. A large population should have a large economy, and as the country with the largest population, China feels it must have the world's largest economy as well.

That date is now rapidly coming into focus. China's economy is within sight of passing the US economy as the world's largest. Barely a week goes by without some breathless account of the coming convergence. The math behind it is straightforward. China's population of 1.4 billion is more than four times that of the United States, and its economy is growing considerably faster. Based on a reasonable extrapolation of recent trends in both economies, that magical moment should occur sometime between 2029 and 2031—possibly sooner, if the pace of Chinese currency appreciation picks up.[53]

While convergence gets headlines, it is hardly an earth-shattering development. For China, the real surprise is that its economy has taken so long to reach its present size—and the more interesting questions pertain to the implications of scale, not just for China but for the United States and the rest of the world.

While nations understandably take pride in being ranked first, there is more to prosperity than aggregate GDP. Absolute size matters far less to average citizens, who measure economic well-being on a per capita basis. Each concept—absolute size and per capita GDP—reveals different aspects of the growth race between nations. While China may be close to convergence with the United States in aggregate GDP—it has already achieved that on a purchasing-power parity basis—it is several decades away from even contemplating that possibility in per capita terms.[54] In 2021, its per capita GDP, as expressed in US dollars, was only 17 percent of that in the United States. Extrapolating off this basis by applying average per capita growth for the two economies from 1981 to 2020—9.7 percent for China and 4.2 percent for the United States—gives us 2055 as a rough date for per capita GDP convergence.[55] This calculation, of course, is highly conjectural and sensitive to shifts in currencies, inflation, economic cycles, and possible shocks. But it is useful in framing the broad parameters of the per capita convergence race.

Yet China remains fixated on the scale convergence of aggregate GDP. It enjoys the attention it draws as the world's leader in sales of automobiles, oil, steel, lumber, cement, and a broad array of luxury goods; in natural resource demand, including now the largest carbon trading market; and in e-commerce traffic—to say nothing of having the largest Internet community in the world. With the largest population in the world, China finally appears to be punching at its weight.

But the punch is more about raw mass than a material improvement in its population's quality of life. That apparently matters a good deal for the Chinese leadership. In his CCP centenary speech of July 1, 2021, Xi Jinping spoke of the power that comes with scale as "a great wall of steel forged by over 1.4 billion Chinese people." How does that fit with his earlier description of the Chinese Dream as a great renewal that "must incessantly bring benefits to the people"? The image of a great wall of steel speaks more to a conflict-prone nationalism than to people-centric aspirations of a good life.

This same disconnect shows up in a critical assessment of the modern Chinese growth experience. As we have seen, from Deng Xiaoping's time to now, the Party has emphasized the quantity dimension of growth rather than its quality. That was true of the three decades of 10 percent hyper growth that began in 1980, which Wen Jiabao ultimately criticized as unstable, unbalanced, uncoordinated, and unsustainable. It was true of the SOE reforms aimed at "grasping the big." And it is true of China's financial sector, now dominated by the four largest banks in the world.

China certainly is big, and its scale is a visible manifestation of that size as an outgrowth of its fixation on high-speed growth. Quantity drives the egotistical race for number one. The United States also has a history of fixating on scale. That was the case, for instance, in response to the earlier supposed threat from Japan. In his best-selling 1979 book *Japan as Number One*, Ezra Vogel offered a compelling warning about America's looming competitive nemesis.[56] The Japan threat was couched in terms of the genius of its economic model, as a new and powerful industrial engine of prosperity. The China threat, by contrast, is viewed as less about the brilliance of a new model and more about a ruthless economic behemoth.

A major difference between the threat posed by Japan then and China today is where the two nations started the race. In 1980, the year after Vogel's book was published, Japan's per capita GDP was 77 percent of that in the United States; today, China's is just 17 percent of the United States'.[57] Forty years ago, the possibility of convergence with the United States on per capita GDP terms was clearly in Japan's sights. Vogel and many others warned that the United States was up against the wall (even though a drop in the world rankings would not have been felt by even one US citizen).[58] Needless to say, the story took a very different twist when Japan tumbled into its lost-decades trap, a detour that was not lost on the Japanization warnings of China's "authoritative person" in 2016. Even so, the China-Japan comparison is important—not just in assessing China's risk of following in Japan's footsteps but in shedding light on the conflicts that can arise from the convergence race between powerful nations.

Relative to Japan, today's China threat is far more distant on a per capita basis but closer at hand in absolute scale. But here as well, it is important to distinguish between quantity and quality. China's power projection draws increasingly on the extrapolation of scale. As it closes in on the United States in aggregate GDP, a muscular China is throwing the weight of its scale into the great dream of global rejuvenation. And the United States is falling victim to that possibility, buying into scale-related fears, and sounding the alarm on China as the new great existential threat.[59] The convergence sweepstakes is rife with its own strain of false narratives.

The Perils of Self-Delusion

Self-delusion and denial go hand in hand. As China has struggled to become the blended system promised by the phrase *socialist market economy*, it has been moved by both necessity and aspiration to embrace many American characteristics. The necessity stems from the failure of central planning and the related perception that some form of marketization was the remedy. The aspiration was aimed initially at poverty reduction and eventually, through the imagery of the Chinese Dream, at the rejuvenation of China's standing among nations. By remaking their nation with some American trappings, modern Chinese leaders believed they could turn the blended system into a recipe for harmony, sustained prosperity, and national pride.

That belief was a stretch, at times bordering on delusion. The transition from the liberalization of the Deng Xiaoping era to the ideological discipline of Xi Jinping Thought has turned the notion of the blended system inside out. The balance between markets and socialism, which had been tilting in favor of markets, is now favoring more orthodox socialist answers to China's wide range of challenges and problems. Steeped in denial, Chinese leaders fall back on slogans and ideology rather than face up to the inherent inconsistencies of their hybrid system.

This is a problematic outcome for China. From the financial engineering of mixed-ownership SOE reforms and incomplete capital market liberalization to the façade of US-style financial markets and a fixation on scale, China's American characteristics are laced with contradictions. To some extent, this is a predictable outgrowth of the transference of codependency noted earlier. Just as this classic aspect of relationship pathology tends to undermine a sense of self in humans, transference weakens a sense of national purpose in economic relationships. The inherent contradictions of a China with American characteristics are very much at odds with the aspirations of the Chinese Dream.

The United States sees things differently. It is understandably uncomfortable with China's ideological backtracking. It wanted to believe that China would become more like America. Unlike its attitude forty years ago, when it admired and eventually adopted many characteristics of Japan's so-called industrial miracle—especially just-in-time inventory management, quality circles, and even some aspects of industrial policy—today's United States has no desire to embrace characteristics of the Chinese system.[60] Chinese attributes, unlike Japan's, are nowhere on America's wish list. That is especially true today as China's ideological and economic mix pivots away from America's comfort zone.

All this further complicates the US-China conflict. China's newfound ideological discipline, as espoused by Xi Jinping and Wang Huning, means that it has lost an important element of flexibility that a more blended system might have provided. Unfortunately, the same can be said of America's increasingly vitriolic, bipartisan China bashing. The continuity of anti-China policies from Donald Trump to Joe Biden points to an equally worrisome lack of flexibility on the US side.

Resolution of a conflicted codependency requires flexibility from both partners if they are serious about rebuilding trust. Self-delusion and denial work the other way, as a lethal combination that exaggerates threats, magnifies conflict, and undermines trust. With the US-China trade war having already sparked a tech war and the early skirmishes of a cold war, self-delusion and denial have led to a cascade of false narratives in both countries. This corrosive outcome works at cross-purposes with resolution, making it that much harder to arrest an increasingly accident-prone escalation of conflict.

11

A New Model of Major
Country Relationships

CHINESE CULTURE REGARDS THE SNAKE as an auspicious symbol of luck and prosperity.[1] It was certainly auspicious for Xi Jinping, who began his tenure as China's fifth-generation leader in 2013, the year of the snake by the Chinese lunar calendar. The year not only marked his formal election as president of the Chinese government but also saw the enactment of the sweeping reforms of the Party's Third Plenum, the rollout of the Belt and Road Initiative, the launching of a major anti-corruption campaign, and the Sunnylands Summit with US President Barack Obama.

The year of the snake was auspicious as well for the rejuvenation spin of the Chinese Dream, which the new leader first stressed in late 2012. As a prideful, nationalistic promise to the Chinese people, the dream envisioned a new global role for China after a century of humiliation. But it was long on aspiration and short on clarity as to how that goal might be achieved. That started to come into focus at the Sunnylands Summit, held on June 7–8, 2013, in Rancho Mirage, California. For Xi, the meeting was an opportunity to draw President Obama into China's ambitions of global leadership, framed around what he called "a new model of major country relationships."[2]

The imagery of shared partnership with other major countries, especially the United States, fit well with the aspirations of the Chinese Dream. In the months and years following the Sunnylands Summit of 2013, China's senior foreign policy team, notably State Councilor Yang Jiechi and Foreign

Minister Wang Yi, elaborated on the new model in a series of high-profile speeches and articles.[3] It became a part of the standard discourse in high-level CCP meetings, policy statements, and conferences.

In one respect, Xi's proposal was an important break from the past. The concept of a new major power relationship stood in sharp contrast with the accepted wisdom of Deng Xiaoping, who preferred that China keep a low profile—what he called hiding strength and biding time. For Xi, the days of biding time were over. Power aspirations could now be expressed openly, rather than whispered among a tight circle of cadres.

Nor would China any longer hide its strength. Just as Xi's economic strategy and ideological focus moved China away from the liberalized features of the socialist market economy, his new approach to global leadership took dead aim on another key aspect of Deng's long-standing norms—the outward projection of national power. Xi not only rejected Deng's approach but also broke with the ancient wisdom of the Chinese military strategist Sun Tzu, who counseled military leaders to "appear weak when you are strong, and strong when you are weak."[4] Against the accepted wisdom of ancient and modern China, Xi opted for a decidedly muscular translation of his patriotic articulation of the Chinese Dream.

The rhetoric was not well grounded in reality. Apart from all but ignoring the role of the world's other major powers, the notion of a new relationship model between China and the United States faced three key problems. First, China was positioning itself for leadership before its own internal strength suggested it was ready to assume that role; as most recently exemplified by the demise of the Soviet Union, history does not reward premature power projection. Second, the Chinese leadership had misread America's willingness to share global leadership with China; they ignored or underestimated the growing bipartisan anti-China sentiment of the US body politic. Third, China did not live up to many of the relationship promises Xi made at Sunnylands—especially regarding its military posture in the South China Sea and its commitment to cybersecurity; the broken promises of Beijing's subsequent actions spoke louder than Xi's words, and very differently.

Failed promises sow distrust in any relationship. For the United States and China, Xi Jinping's bold proclamation of a new model of major country relationships has become a gigantic false narrative. It compounds the blame and suspicion that have tainted an already conflicted codependency, fuels conflict escalation, and makes resolution all the more difficult.

The subsequent escalation of conflict between the United States and China has been an unmistakable repudiation of Xi's new model of major country relationships. But that hasn't stopped him from trying a similar approach with another major power. China's February 2022 unlimited partnership agreement with the Russian Federation is not exactly a new model for two nations that previously had been tightly aligned in the 1950s. But it comes at a new and precarious juncture in a divided world, split between ideology and governance, between democracy and autocracy, between war and peace. The new model of major country relationships could well devolve into a new model of a world in conflict.

A New Model?

What was this new model of major country relations? Was it a brash attempt at a new framework of power sharing, a proposal of engagement and partnership between two great nations? Was it an effort to counter the thinly veiled China containment strategy implicit in the Obama administration's "pivot to Asia"? Or was it a ploy of the Thucydides Trap—a rising power seizing an opportunity to elbow its way into a coequal position of global leadership?

From China's perspective, the model was an attempt to put a distinct Chinese stamp on the basic principles of global strategic engagement. After Xi Jinping expressed that view at Sunnylands, then State Councilor Yang Jiechi elaborated, stating that the principles covered "cooperation in political, economic, security, and cultural terms" and were meant to "replace confrontation with cooperation, zero-sum game with win-win results."[5] Yang later added that the new relationship framework rested on four strategic building blocks—"upholding mutual respect and equality, the pursuit of mutual benefit and common development, to help one another through thick and thin, and to step up exchanges and mutual learning in an open and inclusive spirit." He boasted that this new model of major country relationships was "a major breakthrough in the established theories of international relations."[6]

This is the classic language of diplomacy—sweeping, principled statements invoking lofty and inarguable concepts like mutual understanding, strategic trust, and respect for core interests, while, of course, seeking opportunities for coordination and cooperation. As typically happens in diplomacy, these generalizations offered much leeway for interpretation. That is nothing new for the US-China relationship. It is in keeping with the time-honored "strategic ambiguity" that both the United States and China have relied on to avoid open conflict over Taiwanese sovereignty for the past fifty years.[7] But it left the new relationship proposal lacking in clarity, with no concrete actionable path to implementation.

President Obama contributed to this ambiguity by stressing in a press conference at Sunnylands that both he and President Xi recognized the "unique opportunity to take the US-China relationship to a new level."[8] This was a far cry from Xi's expansive endorsement of the concept. But the mere mention by the American president of a "new level" was enough for the Chinese press, as well as some seasoned US and Chinese security experts, to conclude that the two leaders both supported a different, if not unique, approach to bilateral diplomacy that had the potential to be of enormous historic importance.[9] Xi went further, repeatedly trying to put more words of tacit approval in Obama's mouth than the US president was willing to utter. But the impression of mutual endorsement—despite subtle distinctions between the two leaders—was not lost in global policy circles.

Converting the artform of diplomatic language into actionable results is challenging in the best of circumstances. For a conflicted US-China co-dependency, it was all but impossible. High-level exchanges between Xi and Obama, as well as between senior foreign policy leaders from both nations, were long on verbiage but short on specific proposals for putting the new model into practice. There were plenty of lofty statements on what it would take to make a new great power relationship great. And many ideas percolated up from lower levels about producing a more detailed agenda and a timetable of deliverables.[10] But little was accomplished in bringing the new relationship to life.

In many respects, the back-and-forth was simply the latest installment in a long history of diplomatic kabuki between the United States and China. Since the days of the Nixon-Kissinger breakthroughs with Mao and Zhou Enlai in the early 1970s, there has always been joint recognition of the two nations' special relationship. That relationship has repeatedly been rebranded in efforts to alter and, at times, sharpen the focus—from strategic partnership (Nixon/Kissinger) to strategic competition (George W. Bush) to "co-opetition" (Fu Ying).[11] In recent years the United States has depicted China variously as a responsible stakeholder (Robert Zoellick), a revisionist power (Trump), and, ultimately, an existential threat (Mike Pompeo). Labels are cheap—the costs are in the fine print.[12]

Unfortunately, so much effort has been wasted on branding and labeling that the hard work of relationship building has been neglected. In large part, that is because a label is not a plan. Xi compounded the problem at Sunnylands by adding the word "model" to the proposed new relationship structure. For economists, that usually means math.[13] But models can be theoretical or empirical, abstract or simple, broad or detailed. The concept of a model implies something else: a coherent, internally consistent structure that frames a specific set of questions. To do that, models must be transparent in conveying the assumptions that underpin their structures. The so-called new model of major country relationships fell short on all those counts. At best it was a wish, and at worst, a slogan.

Ultimately, however, the new model failed for a more important reason—it didn't pass the most basic reality check. For policymakers and political leaders, the bottom line is accountability—using a model-based framework as a check on compliance with a specific agreement.[14] What good is a model if it doesn't conform to reality? That was the key problem with Xi Jinping's new model of major country relations. The crux of his approach was the laudable desire to replace confrontation with cooperation—turning zero-sum outcomes into positive-sum breakthroughs. But as conflict deepened between the United States and China in the years after Sunnylands, the lack of cooperation led some to propose yet another extreme on the branding continuum, arguing that an emerging global leadership vacuum was, in effect, leading to the standoff of a "G-Zero" world.[15]

China as a Premature Leader

China is most assuredly a major country. But is it truly ready for global leadership, as its new model of major country relationships seems to presume?

To an important extent, the answer to this question goes back to China's scale fixation that I stressed in the previous chapter. In making the case for a new relationship, China's senior leaders seem to be conflating the absolute size of their economy with leadership clout. This makes sense on one level: the larger the economy, the greater its capacity for outlays on military expenditures, foreign direct investment, foreign aid, import demand, consumer spending, and other forms of global power projection. But there is more to clout than scale alone.

As a proxy for the power projection associated with global leadership, military spending is obviously of special significance. In 2020, China's defense budget was reported to be just 1.7 percent of GDP, far short of the United States' 3.7 percent share.[16] But with dollar-based estimates of Chinese GDP on a trajectory to converge with the United States around 2030, the defense spending gap is expected to narrow even if the disparity in the GDP shares of military spending remains wide. This is exactly what has happened over the past fifteen years. China's defense outlays, despite consistently being a much smaller share of its GDP, rose in US dollar terms from nearly 8 percent of America's total in 2005 to 33 percent by 2020.[17]

In purchasing-power parity (PPP) terms, a more meaningful metric in many respects, the convergence has been even more dramatic. As we have seen, in large part this is because PPP-based Chinese GDP actually surpassed that of the United States in 2016. As a result, by 2020, despite the significant disparity in the defense spending shares of US and Chinese nominal GDP, the dollar volume of China's military budget had risen to 54 percent of that in the United States in PPP terms—fully 1.7 times the current-dollar differential of 33 percent.[18]

With China's defense spending second only to that of the United States and greater in US dollar terms than the combined defense expenditures of India, Russia, Japan, South Korea, and Taiwan, there can be little doubt of its ascendancy as a global military power.[19] In a break from the quantity emphasis that dominates most aspects of China's ascendancy, here its leaders have also focused on quality. Xi Jinping has long emphasized an information-based modernization of the People's Liberation Army, drawing heavily on China's growing AI capabilities. The PLA's stunning recent progress in the new technologies of modern warfare, from stealth aircraft and laser targeting to breakthroughs in space exploration and, according to recent reports, hypersonic weaponry, dovetails with Xi's focus on improving the quality of China's defense capabilities.[20]

Moreover, there is a consensus that official statistics on Chinese military outlays significantly understate the full extent of the nation's defense spending. Among other things, they leave out paramilitary forces charged with internal security, the coast guard, and the increasingly impressive Chinese space program.[21] Even without these adjustments, the Chinese military budget could exceed that of the United States in US dollar terms as soon as 2032–3; making allowance for the understatement, convergence could be expected well before then.[22]

This defense buildup has raised deep questions in geostrategic circles. What will happen when China's military spending equals, and then exceeds, that of the United States? How will China deploy what would then be a growing abundance of its military assets? With tensions mounting in the Taiwan Straits and in the South China Sea, those questions have grown urgent. They frame today's cold war comparisons in an ominous light. Unlike Cold War 1.0, when the Soviet threat was military and ideological but not economic, Cold War 2.0 entails both military and economic threats. Is that seemingly intimidating comparison enough to give China the major country status it seeks in its new relationship model with the United States? Or is this just a replay of the ill-fated arms race that ultimately defeated the last great-power pretender?

The contrast between China's economic strength in absolute terms versus its strength on a per capita basis sheds important light on these questions. China scores high in absolute comparisons, both in nominal GDP and in its military clout. But, as noted in the previous chapter, it scores much worse on a per capita basis, which is a far more relevant gauge of economic prosperity.[23] China may be closing in on the United States in dollar-based GDP, but in 2021 it was still ranked number 100 out of 225 nations in PPP-based per capita GDP.[24]

This disparity raises an important point regarding military power projection as China's means to a new relationship with the United States. The historian Paul Kennedy, in his seminal study of the rise and fall of great powers, concluded that "all of the major shifts in the world's *military-power* balances have followed alterations in the *productive* balances."[25] To the extent that China's power and leadership projection is driven more by its nominal GDP than by its per capita output, it could be a manifestation of what Kennedy called "imperial overstretch." This time-honored tendency of great powers to expand their military reach beyond the foundational support of their domestic economies underscores Kennedy's famous conclusion that such "strategical overextension" is what ultimately causes great powers to decline.[26] Could China be guilty of premature overreach—seeking geostrategic power before it is firmly established as an economic power? The same question applies even more so to Russia as a far weaker economy now facing the possibility of protracted conflict in Ukraine.

China's incomplete rebalancing and restructuring agenda reinforces the case for overreach. Even the Soviet economy, with a consumption share of GDP just below 60 percent in the latter half of the 1980s, was better balanced than China's today, with its sub–40 percent consumption share.[27] Scale does not compensate for persistent macroeconomic imbalances, nor does it insulate the Chinese economy from financial crises, debt implosions, and other shocks those imbalances might render even more destabilizing. The persistent disparity between absolute and per capita growth, alongside disappointing progress on structural rebalancing, suggests that it may well be premature for China to equate its scale and military might with the global leadership envisioned in Xi's new model.

America Doesn't Share Well

US pushback on China's relationship gambit at Sunnylands began almost immediately after the Obama-Xi joint press conference of June 8, 2013. While several pundits lauded the new global partnership as a possible breakthrough, the official view in Washington was far less enthusiastic. Susan Rice, US national security advisor, was an exception, stressing the need to "operationalize a new model of major power relations."[28] But her immediate predecessor, Tom Donilon, framed the idea as a "new model of relations between an existing power and an emerging one."[29] This underscored the contrast between a rich country and a relatively poor one, a reminder that the United States and China were hardly coequal major country partners.

But the strategic justification of the pushback can be traced back to the Asian pivot, initially championed by former Secretary of State Hillary Clinton, who had long favored a more assertive stance toward China.[30] As I argued in Chapter 7, the pivot was a thinly veiled China containment strategy. Clinton and her senior Asia deputy, Kurt Campbell, denied this intent, but the US-led proposal for a Trans-Pacific Partnership said otherwise: TPP was a monumental, high-standard pan-regional trade agreement that specifically excluded China. How could Barack Obama throw the full weight of his presidency into a TPP-led pivot as his signature foreign policy initiative while also endorsing a new major-country power sharing arrangement with China?

The inherent contradiction of these two interpretations was a constant source of tension during Obama's second term. The containment of China, the focus of America's pivot, was a zero-sum strategy.[31] Yet according to Chinese rhetoric, the new model of major country relationships was about the positive sum of win-win power sharing. The ongoing tension between these two perspectives did not lend itself easily to détente, or as some have suggested, the grand bargain of appeasement in the South China Sea.[32] As the war-prone history of the twentieth century cautions us, that is all too often the language of tragic failure.[33]

As soon as Xi and Obama departed Sunnylands, the hopes for a new relationship began to fade. Rice's desire to operationalize the model never materialized. There were a series of follow-up exchanges between the United States and China, including the annual Strategic and Economic Dialogue (S&ED) in July 2013 as well as subsequent S&ED efforts in 2014, 2015, and 2016. There were also three more head-to-head meetings between Obama and Xi, including a full state visit by Xi to Washington in September 2015. On that occasion, Obama brought the increasingly contentious cybersecurity issue to a head by confronting Xi with top-secret evidence of Chinese cyberhacking. The meeting resulted in the bilateral Cyber Agreement, a one-off breakthrough forged mainly by confrontation and threat rather than any new spirit of cooperation.[34] Still, the new model of major power relations lacked a comprehensive framework for implementation and action. Sunnylands was becoming a distant memory, more of a successful event-planning exercise than a meaningful breakthrough for a new and lasting relationship.

Meanwhile, challenging economic conditions in both nations offered little support for an encouraging turn in the relationship. The US economy remained in an anemic postcrisis recovery—expanding at only a 2.3 percent average rate during Obama's second term in office, from 2013 to 2016, well short of the norms of earlier economic recoveries.[35] Chinese economic growth was also slowing, having settled into a 7.3 percent growth trajectory over the same period, well below the heady 10 percent pace of the prior three decades.[36] Absent the tailwinds of vigorous economic growth, political support for bold relationship gambits waned in both countries.

America's headaches were especially problematic. The US merchandise trade deficit widened from $700 billion in 2013 to $750 billion by 2016. More than half of that erosion was traceable to a deterioration of bilateral trade with China, which went from a $318 billion deficit in 2013 to $347 billion in 2016.[37] It didn't matter that the trade imbalance was an outgrowth of subpar domestic saving that gave rise to a US current account deficit that averaged 2.1 percent of GDP over the same period.[38] The American public, never known for self-reflection or a grasp of macroeconomic accounting identities, wanted to point the finger elsewhere. US political sentiment shifted increasingly toward the bilateral bluster of China bashing.

Meanwhile, the ongoing angst of America's middle class from a combination of real wage stagnation and mounting inequality provided fertile ground for a new nationalism.[39] Like China, which was caught up in rejuvenation after its century of humiliation, the American public embraced its own sense of victimization. Blue-collar American workers felt crushed with the disappearance of manufacturing industries. Communities and families were reeling from economic and social hardship. Into that mindset of growing despair entered an inexperienced politician playing to the fears of a troubled electorate with a boisterous promise to make America great again. China became the lightning rod of his strident protectionism. The blame game was on with a vengeance, and the new model never had a chance.

Broken Promises

But it wasn't just political backlash in the United States and incomplete rebalancing in China that undermined the possibility of a new major country relationship. Despite Xi Jinping's lofty promises at the Sunnylands Summit, China never lived to up to its part in the proposed bargain. Its militarization of disputed territory in the South China Sea was only the most blatant of its broken promises.

While public commentary by both leaders in June 2013 avoided any explicit references to the South China Sea, there could be no mistaking Washington's growing sense of unease over Chinese intentions in this long-disputed area. The issue came to a head during Xi Jinping's state visit to the United States in September 2015. In response to media questioning, he stated unequivocally that "there is no intention to militarize" the Nansha Islands—the Chinese name for the Spratly archipelago west of the Philippines. China was within its rights, he maintained, to engage in construction activity "to uphold our own territorial sovereignty."[40]

Xi was not being truthful. His statement was decisively refuted by the subsequent release of satellite imagery that gave clear evidence of Chinese militarization in several contested areas of the South China Sea. Construction activity went far beyond hum-drum offices and housing and included point-defense fortifications, anti-aircraft weaponry, expanded runways, radar installations, and command-and-control facilities.[41] Nor were the military bases confined to just one island, shoal, or reclaimed reef. China had built similar installations at most of its outposts in the disputed territories, including the Fiery Cross, Mischief, and Subi Reefs, activity that appeared to replicate its earlier construction of smaller military facilities on the Gaven, Hughes, Johnson, and Cuarteron Reefs.[42] When confronted with this incontrovertible evidence, a senior spokesperson for China's Ministry of Defense first shrugged his shoulders and then conceded that these are "necessary military facilities."[43]

The Chinese leadership dug in its heels, arguing that it was defending its national sovereignty. Yet its concept of sovereignty was a considerable stretch. For years, China has insisted that a "nine-dash line," first sketched on an Asian map in 1947 by leaders of the Republic of China and later redrawn in the early 1950s by PRC Premier Zhou Enlai, defined an inviolable national boundary.[44] The dashed perimeter, which covers 1.4 million square miles of the South China Sea, stretches north-to-south from China's Hainan Island to Malaysia, and east-to-west from the Philippines to Vietnam. Xi

Jinping argued that China had the right under international law to protect its sovereignty in this vast expanse of territory.

The problem is not only that Xi was duplicitous when he denied militarization, but also China's hyperbolic concept of its sovereignty. Its exaggerated territorial claims have been challenged repeatedly by its neighbors and the United States. Earlier in 2013, China was embroiled in a similar clash with Japan over the Senkaku/Diaoyu Islands in the East China Sea.[45] But the dispute in the east pales by comparison with what is at stake in the South China Sea. This vast southern expanse is an area of great strategic importance in terms of natural resources, fishing rights, and shipping lanes. And the dispute involved ASEAN (Association of Southeast Asian Nations) allies whose support is vital for America's geostrategic pivot to Asia.

In 2016, the Hague Arbitration Tribunal issued a landmark ruling against China in favor of the Philippines in a fishing rights dispute in waters close to the Scarborough Shoal, a triangular landform of reefs and rocks well within the nine-dash perimeter.[46] More important than the contested fishing grounds, the tribunal found that China's claims related to the nine-dash line had no historical or legal basis.[47]

China categorically rejected the tribunal's finding despite its earlier ratification of the United Nations Convention on the Law of the Sea (UNCLOS), which binds it to accept Hague tribunal rulings whether it likes them or not. With its direct violation of international law, China came across not just as a bully to its neighbors but as a provocative threat to the freedom of navigation that UNCLOS is meant to guarantee. By challenging the security of international shipping lanes long used by major nations, China was not exactly enhancing its image as a credible and trustworthy advocate of a new model of major country relationships. That only added to concerns that China's unchecked actions in the South China Sea could be a precursor of more ambitious territorial encroachment outside the nine-dash line.[48]

Nor did China step up to the role of responsible partnership with the United States on other key issues of mutual concern, from cybersecurity and human rights, to denuclearization of the Korean peninsula, to Middle East security. From the Chinese perspective, these were not broken promises, just different approaches by a different system.[49] Unsurprisingly, the US perspective was different. The American political establishment was united in its strenuous objections to China's positions in all these crucial areas.[50]

The point is not who is right or wrong on individual matters of dispute but whether both sides are willing to settle their differences within the structure of a new major country relationship. Wasn't that the purpose of the model in the first place—a framework for win-win reconciliation rather than zero-sum confrontation? The ongoing dispute in the South China Sea is only the most glaring example of the consequences of distrust—the opposite of what should happen in a responsible trust-based partnership.

The United States has its own tendency to break promises that has also undermined any hope for a new model for major country relationships. Donald Trump's 2018 declaration of a trade war with China is the most obvious example. Based on weak evidence and amateurish analytics, allegations of unfair Chinese trading practices were driven more by Trump's political agenda than by the rule-based norms of international trade and finance. Nor could Obama's Asia pivot, the containment policy embedded in the TPP, or Biden's endorsement of the trilateral AUKUS security agreement be seen as friendly and constructive approaches to bilateral engagement.

Just as the United States defends those actions under the democracy-seeking guise of the American Dream, whose values it considers universal, China justifies its position through the rejuvenation-focused Chinese Dream. The history of geopolitics offers a litany of broken promises. The new model of major country relationships has failed that history's most basic stress test.

The New Model of Denial

The new model of major country relationships was a Chinese false narrative that the United States initially condoned. For China, it was a global leadership gambit, aligned with an increasingly muscular power projection, that fit well with Xi Jinping's political priorities. For the United States, the Obama administration's passive response was a squandered opportunity to hold China accountable for the leadership responsibilities it was trying to claim.

But the possibility of an enlightened new relationship model faced bigger problems. It was at odds with a codependency that saw conflicts arising from unsustainable growth models. China's economic rebalancing remains incomplete, leaving it overly dependent on external demand from the United States to support its growth. The United States remains woefully short of saving, leaving it heavily reliant on surplus savers like China to fund investment and economic growth. Conflicts over trade imbalances are an inevitable outgrowth of pressures faced by both the deficit saver and the surplus saver. And that has led to an insidious escalation of conflict. The new model of major country relationships completely ignored this economic context.

This disconnect is an outgrowth of political expediency, the quicksand of denial. To this day, leaders in both the United States and China remain in deep denial over the pressures that a conflicted codependency creates. Codependency is a construct they prefer to ignore. Politicians view it as a sign of weakness, symptomatic of needy nations that lack the wherewithal to stand on their own and have no choice but to turn elsewhere for economic support.

Codependency, in that sense, is thought to be incompatible with the patriotic expression of strength that resonates with the public in both America and China. The false bravura of self-promotion and nationalistic pride has more popular appeal than an honest discourse over economic challenges, risks, and pitfalls. Politicians in multiparty systems like the United States, or even in one-party systems like China, all depend on public approval to maintain their grip on power. Unlike the low-profile admonition of Deng Xiaoping, the projection of power has enormous political appeal—especially for nations most afflicted by self-doubt. That includes China.

I know this from personal experience, having lectured and spoken to a broad cross-section of leaders in both the United States and China about the economics of relationship challenges over the past twenty-five years. Most, on both sides, squirm at the mere mention of codependency. For Americans, the relationship is thought to be largely one-sided—China is viewed as far more dependent on the United States than vice versa.[51] This mindset was one of the major justifications of Trump's trade war, which was initiated under the false presumption that the conflict would only damage China, leaving America unscathed.

For China, the mere mention of codependency runs against the grain of the prideful Chinese Dream. Denial hardly even describes China's distaste of the notion that, as a proud and strong nation, it might be beholden to any other country for anything. For some in China, any suggestion of dependence rubs the raw nerves of an earlier, painful humiliation. Most prefer to ignore the concept altogether. The cover of the Chinese version of my 2014 book, *Unbalanced: The Codependency of America and China,* made literally no reference to the US-China relationship, let alone the concept of codependency, in the supposed translation of the title.[52]

Denial is a classic symptom of codependency, according to professional diagnostic conventions of American psychiatrists and psychologists.[53] Lacking a sense of self, codependent partners tend to be hypersensitive to criticism or negative feedback, preferring instead to deflect it onto others. The resulting denial fuels an escalating cycle of blame and conflict that drives codependent partners apart.

Unfortunately, this progressively dysfunctional pathology applies all too well to the conflict between the United States and China. The United States sees its trade deficit as China's fault, as if its own lack of saving had nothing to do with it. China sees its surplus saving and its related current account and trade surpluses as benevolent support for deficit-prone America, as if its own underfunded social safety net and the resulting suppression of personal consumption were not its own doing. Both economies are steeped in denial over the effects of their self-inflicted saving imbalances. Each then turns that denial into blame directed at the other.

The grand scheme for a new model of major country relationships boiled down to an exercise in politically expedient sloganeering. It was devoid of economic context—not just of each nation individually but of the relationship between them. That's not to say that economics is the sole basis of relations between nations. But without the ballast that economic linkages provide, partnership commitments become tenuous because they are not bound by the incentives and hard targets of shared prosperity. Political linkages can compensate to some degree—as has been the case for the European Monetary Union—but only for like-minded systems. The United States and China are not like-minded in their views of economic relationships.[54]

This ill-fated relationship gambit may have a deeper meaning. For China, the new relationship model was more about geostrategic power than anything else. It was trying to execute a power play much like its hyper-growth gambit of the past forty years—in effect, using its size and the speed of its ascendancy to leapfrog over other, more economically advanced nations. Xi Jinping, who had promised great power status for China in 2049 as a centennial celebration of achievement for the People's Republic of China, apparently lacked the patience to stay within his own timetable. He was, indeed, the "man in a hurry" depicted in the inflammatory Longer Telegram of 2021.[55] For him, the major power relationship model was an opportunistic shortcut.

America, skeptical from the start, ultimately rejected the premise of this power-sharing arrangement. It opted, instead, to confront China rather than engage it. The trade war, which quickly morphed into a tech conflict with mounting risks of a new cold war, is highly visible evidence of that confrontation. This is consistent with the long history of great power struggles: hegemons never give up easily.

In the end, the new model of major country relationships failed to improve on the old model—it did not temper the pressures of a conflicted co-dependency. Nor was it framed in a spirit of trust and commitment. As the US-China conflict escalated, the new model quickly became one of China's most audacious false narratives.

Enter Russia

Xi Jinping's failed relationship gambit with the United States is now a distant memory. He was a relative neophyte in 2013, his first year as Party leader, when he proposed this seemingly ambitious idea. Since then, he has come to believe that the United States was dead set on Chinese containment. With Obama's Asia pivot quickly followed by Trump's trade and tech wars, a new partnership with an adversarial America ultimately made little sense for China.

That was all the more evident as Wang Huning's dystopian views of America gained traction in Chinese leadership circles.[56] Beset by recurring financial crises, a struggling economy, and a broad constellation of adverse social, ethnic, and political circumstances, the United States was increasingly seen as a great power in decline.[57] There was a growing view that these circumstances presented a rising China with the ideal opportunity to seize the advantage.[58]

Consistent with China's long-established hierarchy of diplomatic partnerships, Xi viewed relationship building as increasingly vital to the great power aspirations of the Chinese Dream.[59] That is where Russia fit into China's grand strategy calculus. In Russia, China would find a like-minded partner. The two autocracies wouldn't challenge each other in sensitive areas like human rights, inequality, and censorship. By embracing Vladimir Putin as an "unlimited partner" in February 2022, Xi was convinced that what didn't work with the United States would be far more successful with Russia.

The attraction was not ideological: Russia's strain of socialism had long dissipated. For China, it was more about the complementarity of resources—Russia's energy and other raw materials—and a geographic proximity that aligned with Xi's signature foreign policy gambit, the Belt and Road Initiative. China would be the dominant partner, since its economy was six times the size of Russia's and on its way to seven times by 2024, according to IMF forecasts[60]—and its producers would benefit from Russian demand.

The partnership importantly reflected the two nations' shared distaste for US-centric global leadership, and an appreciation of the benefits of collective strength as a counterweight to the weakened hegemon. They could stand together, united in resisting their shared existential fears of US containment. For Vladimir Putin and his paranoia over NATO expansion, partnership was almost a matter of survival for the Russian Federation. If that meant Xi had to put up with Putin's military ambitions as a price for partnership, he was more than willing to acquiesce.[61] For Xi Jinping it was a grand strategy with Chinese characteristics—the ultimate triumph of rejuvenation.

Then came the war in Ukraine. There is no lack of speculation over what Putin told Xi in February 2022 about the carnage that was to commence just twenty days after they announced their unlimited partnership agreement.[62] While it seems likely that Putin revealed his plan to invade, it seems equally reasonable to presume that he assured Xi (and genuinely believed) it would be a short war leading to quick capitulation by Ukrainian leadership and installation of a pro-Russia puppet government. Both leaders probably shared the view that like memories of Russia's earlier, short wars—in Georgia, Chechnya, and Crimea—the impact of a "special operation" in Ukraine would fade quickly, leaving the new unlimited partners free to get back to their shared geostrategic power and leadership agenda.

Needless to say, that view was wrong. Both nations not only underestimated the capacity of the Ukrainian military and the strength and character of the Ukrainian people, but perhaps most importantly, they failed to anticipate how the war would become a transformative force of Western unity in standing against Russian aggression. Putin, convinced that war would fragment the Western alliance, got the opposite response—not just unprecedented sanctions but humanitarian assistance and joint military commitments on a scale not seen since World War II. Germany, the most powerful economy in Europe with its understandably difficult history of conflict, has led the way with a stunning turnaround in its defense and military posture.[63] Far from fragmenting, the Western alliance of values, assets, and policies became tighter, more unified, and more steadfast.

This show of strength raises the distinct possibility that Vladimir Putin may have set a diabolical trap for Xi Jinping. Putin may not have appreciated the flaws in his plan for a short military campaign, but he must have known what he would do if that plan didn't work out and the war dragged on. When the quick strike bogged down amid poor planning, a dishonest command structure, and unexpected resistance by the Ukrainian military, the Russian Army resorted to unrelenting carnage focused on unprotected Ukrainian civilians and their cities. The Chinese partnership with Russia quickly became something very different from what Xi Jinping might have imagined.

That is where China may be trapped. The subtext of the February 2022 agreement is unmistakable: unlimited partnership means support. Yet if China offers Russia either direct military assistance or financial arrangements that cushion Western sanctions, it will find itself judged guilty by association and secondary sanctions will undoubtedly follow. Reinforced by the "friend-shoring" of weaponized networks of supply chains and dollar-based cross-border financial flows noted in Chapter 5, China and Russia will find themselves quickly joined in a partnership of isolation. For the world's second largest economy, which remains deeply integrated with the rest of the world, the trap would turn into a quagmire.

This could be a make-or-break decision for Xi Jinping, China's most ambitious leader since Mao and one who is tireless in his search for great power status. But there is nothing great about being trapped. As Vladimir Putin's only serious partner, Xi has the leverage to escape that trap by forcing Russia to the peace table.[64] And as a leader who claims to be steeped in a deeply principled ideology, he need look no further than China's "Five Principles of Peaceful Coexistence" to find moral justification to act.

So far, Russia's new unlimited partner has held firm, trapped in the embarrassment of a relationship that is at growing risk of backfiring. Sensing the dire consequences of direct military assistance, both China and Russia predictably have dismissed speculation about such assistance as "disinformation."[65] While there has been some waffling by senior Chinese officials claiming neutrality—including by abstaining on UN Security Council votes to condemn Russia's invasion of Ukraine[66]—there has been no backing away from the core commitment of the new Sino-Russian partnership and China's related insistence that unchecked NATO expansion caused the conflict.[67] As the war continued and evidence of Russian atrocities mounted, Foreign Minister Wang Yi, the wolf warrior of Anchorage, dug in his heels and repeatedly insisted that this new special relationship goes well beyond the garden-variety alliance and will endure long after the war in Ukraine subsides.[68]

Hard as it appears for a nation to reverse a brand-new unlimited partnership, in one sense this is a very easy choice for Xi Jinping.[69] Abandoning the partnership would incur Putin's displeasure, to put it mildly. Xi would also have to swallow some false pride, never easy for an authoritarian. But this may be Xi Jinping's singular opportunity to gain immense stature as a global statesman, worthy of the great power status he has long envisioned. Conflict resolution with the United States would undoubtedly follow. It would be hard to ask for more.

Alas, there is a compelling counterargument, which I pointed out in Chapter 6. If Xi Jinping elects to take the long view and look beyond the war in Ukraine in search of the partnership he believes is essential to counter

US containment, then all bets could be off. For Xi, it boils down to risk assessment—weighing the benefits of supporting an unlimited partnership with Russia against the costs of global isolation. Even "sitting on the fence" as US Treasury Secretary Janet Yellen has cautioned, could have dire consequences for a Chinese economy so heavily dependent on the rest of the world.[70] By siding with Russia, Xi would deal himself and his nation a stunning setback. Not only would that choice represent a second and far more glaring failure to establish a new model of major power relations, it could be China's ultimate, most tragic false narrative.

The Slippery Slope

Why do nations embrace false narratives? Sometimes it is out of ignorance—the failure to understand a tough problem. But often it is by design. Both the United States and China suffer this unfortunate tendency in large part because they are not willing to face problems of their own making. America wants to blame its massive trade imbalances and threats to its technological supremacy on others rather than accept that they arise because of its own shortfall of domestic saving. China blames others for a loss of global status and power that was at least partially self-inflicted.

Both nations find it easier to embrace false narratives than to take on the heavy lifting of structural change required to sustain longer-term economic prosperity. But false narratives are not just politically expedient; they are also seductive in promising simple solutions to complex and difficult problems. Donald Trump argued that America could make itself great again simply by "getting tough" with China. China believes that its massive size is a sure-fire recipe for rejuvenation and prosperity.

False narratives are dishonest by definition: they misrepresent issues and problems that bear critically on nations. Yet they frame persuasive arguments to gullible citizens who are often not in a position to understand why they're false. They lead to policy mistakes that can exacerbate the very problems they are trying to deflect. Trump's tariffs, as an outgrowth of his misdirected bilateral trade deficit bluster, imposed the equivalent of taxes on American businesses and consumers by forcing them (not China) to pay import duties and by limiting the availability of some products, requiring substitution with more expensive alternatives. China's mixed-ownership state-owned enterprise reforms, while reaffirming state control of a blended economy, constrained Chinese productivity growth and heightened the risk of a debt-intensive "Japanization"—leaving China susceptible to Japan's dreaded economic disease.

False narratives are particularly treacherous for nations in conflict. Not only do they promote erroneous premises of blame, they also justify destabilizing actions to compensate for vulnerability at home. America's trade and tech wars with China, along with cold-war-like saber-rattling, are visible manifestations of that tendency. The same is true of China's animal spirits deficit, which undermines private entrepreneurialism, and its unsupported claims of sovereignty in the South China Sea.

False narratives deflect attention from serious attempts to resolve difficult problems. Yet when enabled by the insidious practices of information distortion, they gain acceptance in national discourse. Whether it is strict censorship in China or polarized Big Lies in America, the implications are the same in one important respect—false narratives are not self-correcting. Instead, to keep the charade alive, one false narrative invariably begets another. Viral spread through social media injects a dangerous accelerant. That leaves both nations increasingly accident prone, careening recklessly down the path of conflict escalation.

PART FOUR

DUELING NARRATIVES

A PROFUSION OF FALSE NARRATIVES has led to the outbreak and escalation of an accidental conflict—one that didn't have to happen but is now exceedingly difficult to de-escalate. The clash between the world's two major powers would not have occurred but for the mounting divisiveness of their codependency. It will take a new spirit of trust to neutralize the false narratives, repair the damage, and rebuild a more constructive and sustainable relationship.

The false narratives featured in this book speak to the fears and insecurities that both America and China project on each other. But there is a deeper message in the sum of the parts. Both nations share common struggles with structural economic imbalances, state intervention in markets, innovation, and information distortion. But each approaches these issues from different perspectives—China with its blended, market-based socialism and America with its open-ended capitalism. This duality of their false narratives—the contrasts between shared challenges—is at the core of conflict escalation and may well hold the key to de-escalation.

As with individuals, the resolution of conflict between nations starts with the restoration of trust, a long and arduous process under the best of circumstances. The trust problem does not exist at the person-to-person level in either the United States or China. Even though US public opinion polls report the most unfavorable view of China on record, Americans' negative perceptions are largely focused on the Chinese government, especially the Communist Party's stances on issues like human rights, intellectual property protection, trade policy, and the origins of Covid-19. The target of Chinese distrust is similar, focused on US government actions aimed at punishing China, containing its rise.

It would be easy to personalize the distrust by focusing on the top leaders of both nations. America, with its election cycle, presents China with a moving target. Hoping for relief after the defeat of Donald Trump, the Chinese have been disappointed by President Biden's continuation of anti-China policies. For America, a one-party China presents more of a fixed target, especially with Xi Jinping now in place indefinitely. America's distrust of Xi stems importantly from the power consolidation that has occurred under his leadership—including the elimination of presidential term limits and the purging of opponents under the guise of an anti-corruption campaign. Of added concern to the United States is the renewed emphasis on ideology manifested by Xi Jinping Thought and a more muscular approach to Chinese foreign policy.

A successful path of conflict resolution must be goal oriented. It must include rebuilding trust, codifying fair, sustainable, and enforceable rules, and embracing a healthy interdependency as a new relationship paradigm. That would allow both the United States and China to focus on strengthening from within rather than playing the victim and falsely blaming each other. The shift from codependency to interdependency would give both nations a chance to draw on a collaborative and trusting appreciation of mutual opportunities.

Only confident and secure leaders can muster the combination of political will and courage to rebuild trust. Such a shift won't be easy, especially with distrust having been compounded by information distortion on both sides. It starts with a conversation, followed by a commitment to address important areas of mutual interest such as climate change, global health, and cybersecurity. With collaboration comes the opportunity for a more far-reaching constructive relationship.

Sustained conflict resolution can't occur until both nations shift the focus of their trade dispute from a misdirected bilateral focus to the multilateral reality of modern globalization. That means coming up with a new and enforceable framework for addressing structural conflicts over technology and trade while also establishing a new, robust structure of bilateral consultation, engagement, and accountability. This book concludes with a plan that is aligned with these considerations.

Conflict resolution ultimately requires both sides to recognize the pitfalls of codependency. In many respects, the relationship was destined for trouble from the start. When frictions inevitably crept in, a cacophony of false narratives raised blame and scorn beyond what either side could tolerate. As bad as it is today, the inevitable next accident will undoubtedly make the situation worse. China's new unlimited partnership with Russia brings that possibility into sharper focus. Shifting the relationship paradigm to a healthier interdependency is the only way out. Neither nation can afford to squander the opportunity.

12

Accidental Conflict

THE US-CHINA CONFLICT IS AN ACCIDENT that didn't have to happen. Conflict escalation is an inherent risk of codependency, but there was also an
opportunity to forestall and possibly even avoid collision. That didn't occur
for a variety of reasons, especially those traceable to a destructive confluence of false narratives that undermined both nations' perceptions of their
economic security.

Our story began with a surprising tale of vulnerability. America's shortfall of domestic saving and China's incomplete structural rebalancing raise
genuine concerns about their longer-term economic prospects. Deep fears
of looming threats from their codependent partner compound that shared
anxiety. China has a dark view of the United States as being on a trajectory
of decline while aiming to contain a rising power. The United States fears
that a rising China threatens the emerging advanced industries that will
shape its future. This injects a worrisome fragility into the lofty aspirations
of both the American Dream and the Chinese Dream.

The policy community of each nation is steeped in denial over such possibilities.[1] That is a classic symptom of codependency, as is an unwillingness to accept responsibility for self-inflicted vulnerability. Rather than look
in the mirror, as Sun Tzu might have counseled, both sides are inclined to
point the finger elsewhere. The result is economic paranoia, with both nations consumed by fears of the threat that each poses to the other.[2]

The progression of conflict escalation has an ominous historical ring. Not only is history filled with examples of war between rising and incumbent powers, but there is a special vulnerability evident today. I stressed earlier that the United States, as the incumbent hegemon, currently has a much weaker economy than it did in 1947–91, when it successfully prosecuted the first cold war. By contrast, China and its relatively strong economy pose a far greater adversarial challenge than did the Soviet Union, with its massively inefficient, declining economy. For America, this raises the unthinkable possibility of being on the losing side of a new cold war, thereby increasing the danger of preemptive actions to forestall such an outcome.

Standing down from a cold war in the face of escalating trade and tech conflicts will require nothing less than a new framework of engagement—economic and political—to mitigate an increasingly treacherous conflict. Coming to terms on technology and innovation, long key to enhanced development and prosperity, must be central to any such resolution.

Absent a new approach, resolution by immaculate conception is sheer fantasy, and the conflict will only intensify. With conflict escalation comes heightened vulnerability to unexpected sparks. History does not treat that possibility kindly. We need look no further than the assassination of Archduke Franz Ferdinand of Austria-Hungary as the spark to World War I.[3] But while one flash point is bad enough, the odds of a consequential accident increase sharply as flash points multiply. Heightened tensions in Asia—the Taiwan Straits, the South China Sea, and Hong Kong—are all cause for worry, but so is the more immediate conflict in Ukraine.

Without the economic ballast provided by the cross-border trade of goods, services, and financial capital, there are no built-in safeguards against conflict escalation. A decoupling of the US-China relationship has amounted to an effort to jettison that ballast, creating an even more ominous strain of conflict. The longer resolution is deferred, the more powerful the gravity of conflict escalation and the greater the risks of a tragic endgame.

The Duality of False Narratives

I have stressed from the outset that China and the United States are a study in contrasts, in their economies, social values, and systems of governance. But like two slices from the same pie, these contrasts can be viewed holistically. Comparisons between the two nations reveal a striking duality—in effect, "contrasts between two related concepts."[4] The classic example of duality in economics is the juxtaposition between a developing economy's impoverished agricultural sector and its more prosperous manufacturing sector; the two sectors are linked pieces of the same puzzle.[5] For China and the United States, the false narratives that underpin each nation's assessment of the other offer different perspectives on problems the two countries have in common. Understanding this duality is crucial in tying together our assessment of the false narratives on both sides of the US-China conflict. It may also point the way toward conflict resolution. The clash of false narratives is an inevitable outcome of this duality.

The two economic models are an important case in point. In many respects, the US and Chinese economies are mirror images of each other. The United States consumes to excess while China's consumption share is the lowest of any major economy in the world. Conversely, China produces to excess, with an investment share of GDP that is over twice that of the United States and has a large foreign trade surplus that contrasts sharply with America's chronic deficits. Trade between the two nations brings their duality to life—China as the ultimate low-cost producer supports America as the ultimate high-spending consumer. Yet without US demand, the Chinese producer would have floundered.

The prospective implications of this symmetry are reflected in the duality of the countries' economic narratives. China views its consumption prospects through the American lens, understanding that job creation and real wage increases support labor income, the dominant source of household purchasing power. Yet the two economies view their labor income challenges from very different perspectives. Chinese employment is driven by the structural shift to services, and its real wage increases are an outgrowth of China's rural-to-urban migration. At work in both instances are "convergence narratives," with China aspiring to emulate the characteristics of a more mature, advanced US economy with its much larger services sector and higher real wages. There is considerable irony to this duality of consumerism: China aspires to what America has taken to excess.

The duality of saving that emerges from the US-China consumption comparison has an especially important bearing on the economic conflict between the two nations. I argued earlier that the fear-driven precautionary saving of the Chinese people is largely an outgrowth of a rapidly aging population combined with a deficient social safety net. The American experience points to a remedy: a combination of more secure safety net funding and increased sources of nonlabor income generation through a broader portfolio of household investment choices. China's consumerism would strengthen if its government drew on the lessons of duality that are evident in America's saving experience.

This duality, of course, becomes more problematic when saving disparities are translated into bilateral trade imbalances. As should by now be obvious, nations with chronic shortfalls of saving, like the United States, tend to run trade deficits in order to attract the surplus saving they need to fund investment and economic growth. Conversely, nations with chronic saving surpluses, like China, are inclined to run trade surpluses in order to deploy their excess capital into higher-return foreign assets and also to prevent their currencies from rising and impeding economic growth. It is at this point that the dual saving narratives get ensnared in codependency.

America, the deficit saver, looks past its trade deficits with some 106 countries (as of 2021) and falsely blames China for its massive overall trade gap. China's large piece of that multilateral trade deficit reflects a lack of US domestic saving, supply chain measurement distortions, and China's own excess saving and comparative advantage as a low-cost producer—all of which are far more telling and important than America's allegations of unfair Chinese trading practices. Bilateral blame for a multilateral problem simply doesn't compute, and the China-focused "fix" arising from Trump's tariffs has already backfired, prompting trade diversion to America's other (higher cost) foreign suppliers.[6] US consumers have paid a steep price for this false narrative. That the Biden administration doesn't get this is worrisome.

On the other side of the equation, China's surplus saving has spawned equally pernicious false narratives. For starters, China has been more than willing to draw on the excesses of US consumer demand to underpin its export-led impetus to economic growth. Yet this was a serious misreading by China's leaders: what they saw as stable and sustainable external support for their country's exports has, over the past two and a half decades, been drawn into sharp question by a series of asset bubbles and related global crises.[7] China's approach also reflected its mistaken belief that it could get away with a mercantilist economic growth model that repressed the demand of its own consumers and led to multilateral trade surpluses (with 157 countries in 2019).[8] These imbalances, first highlighted in China by Wen Jiabao in 2007, have led to major, as yet uncorrected distortions in China's macroeconomic structure. Like the United States, China has paid a steep price for its false saving narrative.

America's and China's false economic narratives are different sides of the same coin. The duality of saving—as both a reflection of internal balance and a driver of external linkages—ties their two unbalanced economies together. It spawns one false narrative that leads to another, as America blames China for the trade implications of its saving problem and China interprets that reaction as a threat of containment. Yet from a relationship perspective, China, as the surplus saver, supports America as the deficit saver—very much in keeping with the enabling pathology of codependency.[9]

Left unaddressed, the duality of these false narratives can take a conflict-prone codependency to the breaking point. That is very much the risk today. But there may be an important silver lining. False saving narratives provoke conflict, but they also offer important clues to conflict resolution—a point I will take up in the final chapter of this book.

The Duality of State Control

The duality of state control offers a different lens with which to examine the contrasts and tensions between the two economic systems. For China and its blended economy, the mixed-ownership model underscores the balancing act between state-owned enterprises and a quasi-market-driven private sector; as noted earlier, the recent push toward mixed-ownership SOE reform reinforces the crossholdings of state assets, which complicates this balancing act by deepening the Chinese government's control.

For the United States and its private enterprise system, the balance is more subtle, with the state's role largely confined to regulatory oversight and crisis intervention, overlain by policy-mandated actions of fiscal and monetary authorities. Both nations embrace the activism of industrial policy aimed at targeted support of key industries; the main difference is that China admits it and the United States does not. There can be no mistaking the role of the state in Chinese initiatives like "Made in China 2025." The United States denies that it engages in such practices, philosophically viewing industrial policy as an illegitimate intervention in free markets.[10] Yet as we saw in Chapter 4, supports such as the Pentagon's DARPA-sponsored R&D programs, frequent "Buy American" campaigns, long-standing farm price subsidies, and recent efforts to assist the US semiconductor industry as part of a broad package of measures intended to counter China's competitive threat to US industry all say otherwise.[11]

In neither case is the state's role set in stone. After three decades of market-driven liberalization, the pendulum in China has swung back. The Xi Jinping era has been notable for an increasingly assertive role for the state.[12] And in the aftermath of a series of crises, the US government has been forced to take a more activist role in managing an increasingly unfettered, deregulated, and unstable system.[13]

In both cases, tough circumstances got in the way. In America, repeated crises exposed the combined risks of balance-sheet carnage, liquidity strains, and, ultimately, solvency—first in the equity bubble in the early 2000s, then in the Global Financial Crisis of 2008–9, and finally in the Covid shock of 2020. Each time, the US government had to act as a lender-of-last-resort to rescue a battered system.[14] The Federal Reserve has played a special role in America's newfound activism, not only providing the lifelines of crisis-related lending programs but also running an overly accommodative monetary policy long after the crises ended. This had the effect of holding interest rates extremely low to support demand and enable outsize federal budget deficits as well as inject excess liquidity into financial markets through a massive expansion of the Fed's balance sheet.[15] The US central bank, in effect, was subsidizing the cost of capital, distorting investment decisions, and thereby underwriting a de facto industrial policy, the American way.

These tough circumstances were not lost on Chinese leaders. Consistent with Wang Huning's dark image of America, there was a gathering sense that America was entering an era of decline. The combination of frequent crises, social turmoil, and political polarization was thought to be finally taking a lasting toll on the hegemon. For an increasingly assertive and ambitious China, this was viewed by many in its leadership circles as a defining moment in the inevitable great power race.[16]

That's not to say that China didn't have its plate full during this period as well. Amid fears of the perils that might arise from an ossified and corrupt Communist Party, Xi Jinping's anti-corruption and ideological campaigns took on new meaning. China drew an especially important lesson from the Global Financial Crisis: the high volatility of market-based alternatives in the West was not an acceptable option for a nation fixated on stability.[17] Instead, the Chinese government seized on the opportunity piece of its dual meaning for crisis, *wēijī* (危机), and used the turmoil in the West during the early twenty-first century as the occasion to consolidate its control, through both ideology and governance, as the guardian of socialist principles.

The United States and China share one important implication of this shift to government activism: the distortion of organic market-based outcomes by the increasingly heavy hand of the state. In America, this was an outgrowth of unprecedented fiscal and monetary stimulus spawned by a continuum of crises. In China, it was more a conscious exercise of CCP strategy and power, reflecting a key Chinese presumption that any so-called wisdom of the markets is less trustworthy than strict, ideologically conforming guidance by the state. This presumption was repeatedly reinforced by the extreme dislocations in Western financial markets during the increasingly frequent crises of the past two and a half decades. In this case, unlike in the case of consumerism, China had no desire to emulate what it perceived as an America in decline.

For China, state-directed intervention in distressed markets in times of crisis and turmoil was also seen as an opportunity to demonstrate the advantages of state power as an instrument of Chinese rejuvenation. The United States saw intervention very differently. It was more that the state rose to tough occasions, defending the American Dream when it was in peril. By inference, this meant that the United States all but condoned reckless behavior, dismissing the possibility of "moral hazard" and thereby providing an excuse for government intervention during times of distress.[18] China, meanwhile, considers socialist ideology sufficient moral and political justification for increased CCP control.

China's new campaign for common prosperity, noted in Chapter 9, frames its long-standing debate over state control in a different light.[19] As unveiled in the summer of 2021, this effort appears to be largely focused on reducing growing inequalities in Chinese society, with wealth inequality singled out for special attention. That turned a spotlight on the vast riches accumulated by the entrepreneurs who founded China's vibrant Internet platform companies, including Alibaba, Didi Chuxing, Tencent, Pinduoduo, and Meituan. The result was a full-throttle assault on the animal spirits that had been driving one of China's most dynamic sectors.[20] Global stock markets initially reacted violently, wiping some $1.5 trillion off the equity market value of Chinese Internet platform companies in a few months.[21]

But the common prosperity campaign was directed at more than the new platform companies. It also included government efforts to purge the Chinese system of the allegedly corrosive social effects these platforms spawned: addictive activities such as video gaming, inappropriate and unpatriotic music, and extreme sexual attitudes, all of which appealed to the younger generation, as well as the pressures that a private tutoring culture were thought to impose on stressed-out Chinese students and their families. These actions didn't come out of the blue but were foreshadowed by Xi Jinping's 2013 efforts to address the "four bad habits" of formalism, bureaucracy, hedonism, and extravagance as part of a "mass line" education campaign.

It is hard to know where China is headed on the road to common prosperity. In one respect, this is a classic Marxist narrative aimed at what is alleged to be the inevitable and corrupt excesses of capitalist-driven economic development.[22] Of course, progress for poor nations, irrespective of their ideological leanings, does not come with a guarantee of synchronous improvement in living standards for all strata of society. Chapter 9 noted that for China, there has long been hope that gains accruing to early-stage beneficiaries would eventually spread to others. In fact, this sequencing of development dividends was anticipated by Deng Xiaoping's 1986 suggestion "to let some people and some areas get rich first" and then later "have the duty to help the backward areas."[23] From that perspective, the push for common prosperity can be seen as an effort to fulfill the second part of

Deng's statement. While this concept has a long shelf-life in the modern history of the PRC, there can be no mistaking the important signaling effect of its renewed emphasis in 2021.[24]

Curiously, in the aftermath of the August 2021 announcement of the common prosperity campaign, the CCP has tried to play down its impact. Given all the controversy that this campaign has unleashed, perhaps they doth protest too much. But the post-announcement discourse spin has been unmistakable: Chinese officials offer compelling arguments for addressing the stresses on young students, then make an entirely different case against inequality. They also warn of the need to protect proprietary data and then make an anti-monopoly argument—rather ironically for a government that has long supported the inherent monopolies of massive state-owned enterprises. All this raises questions of segmentation bias, a myopic focus on the small pieces of a much bigger puzzle. Ultimately, what matters most for the Chinese economy is how these pieces fit together. Rationalizing policy actions on a case-by-case basis overlooks the combined impacts of these measures.

The confluence of this emphasis on common prosperity with restraints on China's dynamic Internet platform companies raises the possibility of a profound change in Chinese growth and development strategy. In many respects, the new campaign is the social engineering corollary to the anti-corruption campaign of 2013–15—now purging the system of bad habits after the bad (or corrupt) actors have been eliminated.[25] While it is premature to render a verdict on this initiative, there is no mistaking the key message: the wide umbrella of common prosperity may change the rules of engagement between the state, the economy, and Chinese society.

Social and economic inequities have long been a major issue in the United States as well, one that many believe propelled Donald Trump to the presidency.[26] But there is an important difference. While US debate over inequality and Internet-enabled social and political polarization has intensified sharply, so far, the body politic has been ambivalent about how to address it. The debate, of course, remains fluid, with congressional focus recently shifting to the destabilizing role of social media, a point I will return to shortly. But egalitarianism has long been more of an elusive aspirational goal for the United States rather than a tactical focus for policy strategy and design. President Biden is attempting to change this with new progressive tax proposals, but as I write this, the fate of those proposals is uncertain.

Here, the US-China duality is particularly striking. China is focusing on the *immediacy* of a strategy to address the very problems that the United States knows full well it must *eventually* resolve. This should not be surprising. Two very different political systems have come to strikingly different conclusions about the role of the state in coping with the inherent contradictions of their ownership and reward narratives.

China, by focusing on common prosperity, is attempting to use state intervention to improve the quality dimension of its growth experience, the long neglect of which became glaringly apparent during an extraordinary period of rapid economic growth. While the United States may share that inclination to focus on the quality of economic growth, it is far more reluctant to promote it through direct government action. Washington has essentially abdicated this problem to free markets and to the freedom of choice long cherished by open, liberal societies. The Biden administration's "Build Back Better" proposal was a possible exception that, in the end, failed to win congressional approval.

This shared agenda has important implications for a conflicted relationship. Both nations want to improve the quality of their economic growth experience but are taking entirely different approaches to do that. In an era characterized by the here and now of climate change, social tensions arising from increased inequality, and a devastating pandemic, it is far from clear that either system has a good answer.

The Duality of Innovation and Information Distortion

The interplay between indigenous innovation and productivity enhancement is the Holy Grail of sustained economic growth and development.[27] That has long been true of advanced economies and developing nations alike. But the current context adds a new dimension to this interplay. The innovation potential has shifted from hardware to software, from products to applications.

Earlier, we saw that data-driven artificial intelligence has played a key role in raising the stakes in the US-China relationship conflict. Astonishing breakthroughs in AI-enabled applications in activities ranging from transportation and manufacturing, life sciences and fintech, to weapons development have fundamentally altered both the innovation calculus and the path to the frontier of global technology leadership. At the same time, this progress reflects the duality of a double-edged sword—spectacular payback potential for individual nations but problematic implications for the conflicts of codependency.

The escalating technology battle between the United States and China is a textbook example of dueling false narratives. With its chronic deficiency of domestic saving, America lacks the wherewithal to invest in the critical building blocks of innovation—especially in key areas that China has recently emphasized the most, like R&D spending and STEM-based higher education.[28] Yet rather than increase national saving to address this shortfall, US politicians embrace the false narrative that vilifies China as a tech predator and as a dire challenge to America's leadership in new technologies and advanced industries.

America's fixation on Huawei as the lightning rod in the conflict adds to this false narrative. Not only is China's leading technology company widely portrayed as the mythically threatening Trojan Horse that can exploit a new 5G global telecommunications platform, it also provides a focus for American fears that the Chinese will snatch away US technology leadership through devious means. Rounding out America's tech conflict with China are allegations of forced technology transfer, cyberhacking, and unfair industrial policies, all of which supposedly undermine support for the industries of the future as charged in the USTR's March 2018 Section 301 complaint. For US politicians, China's rapid progress in global innovation is America's competitive nightmare as well as a major national security risk. Largely for these reasons, Democrats and Republicans alike have cast China as an existential threat to America's prosperity.[29]

As I argued in Chapter 5, most of these allegations of Chinese innovation and technology threats are not just a reflection of shortcomings at home; they are also misdirected, exaggerated, and outdated. But China is far from innocent in this battle of false narratives. Like most nations that ascended as industrial powers in earlier years, China is undoubtedly guilty of transgressions in the rough and tumble arena of global combat for new technologies.[30] Its size and the speed of its ascent compound the pressures on the United States and the rest of the advanced world. But China's biggest problem in the technology race is the opacity of its actions and intentions—specifically, a culture of nondisclosure and obfuscation that only adds to the impression that the Chinese government has something to hide. That's not only true of Huawei, where ownership transparency and arrogance are long-standing issues.[31] It is also a problem with China's response to allegations over the origins of Covid, its military intentions in the South China Sea, and its deeply entrenched censorship regime. One of the great contradictions of modern China is its combination of an open economy and a closed culture of discourse.

Opacity has obvious and important relationship implications. With the United States in denial of its own shortcomings on innovation, vulnerability easily turns into suspicion. Chinese opacity amplifies that suspicion, giving more credence to the Section 301 allegations the Trump administration offered as justification for its trade war in 2018. It didn't matter how weak the evidence was. China's unwillingness to speak directly to the substance of America's charges, and thereby temper suspicion by increased transparency and disclosure, has further inflamed US paranoia and America's related penchant for false narratives of the China threat. Chinese opacity is a breeding ground for false narratives; its censorship regime not only leads to information distortion at home but encourages outsiders to be equally duplicitous in their characterizations of China.[32]

Information distortion has exacerbated both sides of the US-China conflict. In China, censorship not only speaks to an undercurrent of distrust between the CCP and the Chinese people, it also corrodes trust with other nations. In both China and the United States, information distortion has been amplified by AI-enabled manipulation of big data, giving enormous scale to the divisive false narratives that create anxiety on both sides. Record levels of anti-China sentiment in the United States are a highly visible manifestation of the power of this amplification mechanism; irrespective of demographic cohort or political allegiance, fears of the threat from China are now in a league of their own.[33] Similar results show up in the limited polling in China, where the United States receives by far the most negative views of any major country in the world; that's hardly surprising for an increasingly nationalistic and rejuvenation-fixated Chinese society facing what it believes are dire threats of US-led containment.[34]

There can be no mistaking the increasingly powerful duality of information distortion—censorship in the case of China and polarized discourse in America. It has not only compounded the relationship conflict between the two nations but made conflict resolution more problematic.

The special problems of social networks show how hard it is to reconcile the two countries' approaches. Under the rubric of its new push for "common prosperity," China is trying to address what it considers the "bad habits" encouraged by AI-enabled social networks. For America, as the world's quintessential free and open society, concerns over polarization and privacy lead to a different set of social network problems, which it has been either unwilling or unable to get a grip on. For both the United States and China, the arguments of Chapter 3 lead to the conclusion that the viral dissemination of dueling false narratives makes social networks all the more toxic as a catalyst to conflict escalation. All this raises one of the hardest governance questions of all: should seemingly innovative social networks be harnessed before or after they do irreparable damage? More realistically, given the damage already done, what options do free and open societies now have in addressing this contentious issue? That was the very question posed by Facebook whistleblower Frances Haugen in her stunning testimony in front of the US Congress in October 2021—a point that was echoed by Barack Obama in a stirring speech at Stanford University in April 2022.[35]

The Missing Piece

Duality goes only so far toward linking together the false narratives driving the US-China conflict. It is especially useful for pairing the two countries' narratives about three important legs of the economic stool—saving, the role of the state, and innovation. Duality reveals how each nation is positioned against the other, and how that positioning reinforces the conflict that has arisen between them. It enables us to reduce the tension to its essence—two unbalanced, surprisingly vulnerable economies, each view-ing the other as a threat to sustainable growth and prosperity. Conflict has emerged from their moves to neutralize these threats.

But an important piece is missing from this assessment—the character of the relationship itself. I have argued from the start that the conflict is a predictable outgrowth of the intrinsic tensions of an economic codependency. But the tensions of codependency have a duality in their own right.[36] Whatever frictions arise when nations change the terms of engagement, as the United States and China both have been doing, the far bigger risk comes with the ultimate breakup. That culminating event instills a deep sense of loss, with devastating consequences for both partners. Balancing frictional conflict creep against the consequences of a full-blown breakup is the toughest operational challenge of sustaining a hyperreactive codependency between powerful nations.

That balancing act has become increasingly precarious. The decoupling of the trade and technology linkages between the United States and China—a destabilizing outcome in its own right—is well under way. Both economies are experiencing the early signs of damage—trade diversion and increased costs in the United States, and diminished external demand for export-dependent China. And we have seen how this is only the beginning, ac-cording to the consensus of public opinion.[37]

Where this is headed is anyone's guess. The final chapter of this book proposes an action plan aimed at forestalling the worst-case outcome by repurposing a mutually destructive codependency as a mutually beneficial relationship. The conflict between the United States and China has inten-sified because of the duality of saving, state control, and innovation, but it has been exacerbated by the most treacherous aspect of the relationship dynamic—a power struggle between two dominant nations. And power has always been where the rubber meets the road in the long history of relation-ship conflict.

Unsurprisingly, the two nations have different perspectives on how this ultimately decisive aspect of the conflict is likely to play out. The United States, as the incumbent hegemon, is mindful of the historical tendency for great-power conflicts to ensnare leading nations in hot wars—the "Thucy-dides Trap."[38] China views its power projection as a forward-looking manifestation of the Chinese Dream. Xi Jinping's fanciful fixation on a "new model of major country relationships" was framed around the belief that China needs partnership support to achieve great power status by 2049, the centennial anniversary of the founding of the People's Republic of China. From China's perspective, that destiny of greatness need not mean war.

That is wishful thinking. Historical precedents like the Thucydides Trap need to be taken seriously in assessing the duality of US-China power projections. While the existence of weapons of mass destruction makes it tempting to rule out full-scale military conflict, neither country can afford to ignore that possibility, especially given the ongoing tensions in the Taiwan Straits and South China Sea, to say nothing of recent thinly veiled threats of nuclear aggression by Russian President Vladimir Putin.[39] These frictions underscore the now very real risk that accidental sparks may trigger a broad military clash. China's recent flexing of muscular military power, especially with its advances in weaponry and force projection, could well trap America as the modern-day Athens—borrowing a page right out of Thucydides's script.[40] There is a certain irony in the latest incarnation of Xi's relationship gambit—the unlimited partnership with Russia that was consummated on the eve of a devastating war in Ukraine. The ominous implications of the Thucydides Trap have been framed in a different, but even more troubling, light.

Nor can the United States afford to be complacent if military conflict is avoided but a cold war persists. It is worth stressing again that the US economy is far weaker today than it was when America successfully waged the first cold war against the former Soviet Union from 1947 to 1991. As Paul Kennedy wrote of great power conflicts, nations have a much better chance of prevailing if their power projection rests on a foundation of economic strength.[41] America's slow productivity growth, diminished saving capacity, and chronic current account and foreign trade deficits mean that its fears of a rising China may well be appropriate. China shares this view. Its recent assertiveness as a rising power appears increasingly aligned with America's vulnerability.

History also tells us that power struggles tend to be personal. Xi Jinping is an impatient leader, a paradox in a nation known for deliberative, long-term strategic thinking. His audacious power sharing proposal—the new model of major country relationships of Chapter 11—was presented as a fait accompli to US President Barack Obama at the Sunnylands Summit in 2013. It is an understatement to call that proposal premature. While the Chinese economy was on the cusp of becoming the world's largest when Xi put this idea on the table, there is still much to accomplish on reforms, rebalancing, and overall living standards before it attains coequal status with the United States. Nor is a deeply suspicious US body politic, with its mounting bipartisan surge of anti-China sentiment, willing to embrace the rising power on Xi's terms. Both the Obama and Trump administrations preferred China containment as a more politically palatable national security strategy. Joe Biden appears to be following the same course. Xi's new relationship model was the wrong model at the wrong time.

The personal aspect of power struggles injects an added layer of complexity into this relationship. Political leaders have outsize influence on public opinion, but they also convey a sense of social identity and aspirational buy-in that shape a nation's ethos. Both the United States and China use the metaphor of a dream to express that vision to their people. The clash between the Chinese Dream and the American Dream—China's push for rejuvenation versus America's focus on domestic security and prosperity—arises in large part because the two countries are at distinctly different points in their histories. The American Dream was conceived as a source of solace and hope during the Great Depression, while the Chinese Dream, although it draws on a painful legacy of national humiliation, was framed by Xi Jinping in 2012, at a celebratory moment of national ascendancy.

How much of this conflict, then, is truly personal—traceable to the views of individual leaders rather than to the unique characteristics of two different systems? The Chinese Dream was first articulated as a powerful national mantra only about ten years ago. The more seasoned American Dream has been espoused by some fifteen American presidents, from Franklin Roosevelt to Joe Biden, over a ninety-year span. As the Longer Telegram of the Atlantic Council hinted, the clash with the United States may indeed be more about Xi Jinping than about China.

The sharp contrast between two very different systems of governance further complicates the conflict. In a one-party authoritarian state, the lack of electoral accountability means that personalization of power and conflict is a much bigger risk than is the case in a freely elected democracy with the built-in corrective mechanism of regular elections and periodic changes in leadership. That's not to say that conflict can't be personalized in the United States, as the sad legacy of Donald Trump shows us—a temporary aberration, one hopes, in the great American experiment. By contrast, the now open-ended tenure of President Xi underscores the more enduring personalization of conflict-prone perceptions of China.

The Gravity of Accidental Conflict

In retrospect, accidental conflict between America and China was bound to happen. It is an inevitable outgrowth of the false narratives that both nations have embraced about each other. Lacking in credible fact-based support, the false narrative typically arises out of a political or ideological campaign. While many of the narratives of US-China codependency are false, that hasn't prevented them from gaining acceptance and sparking conflict. Irrespective of their veracity or lack of it, they have become the rationale for contentious policy actions that have taken the conflict into the open. That is especially true of the tariffs and sanctions of 2018 and 2019, and of the increasingly bellicose rhetorical exchanges that evoke an earlier cold war.

The false narratives are not random expressions of displeasure. In human relationships, as codependency undermines each partner's sense of self, the reactions of the partner start to take on exaggerated importance in shaping self-esteem.[42] There is a comparable condition in codependent economic relationships. Both the United States and China act as if they are deeply troubled about their own sense of economic self, lashing out at the other to defend the vulnerable and fragile façades of their national dreams. Blaming the partner when the real focus should be on self-improvement is also a classic symptom of codependency.[43]

That gets us to the essence of the conundrum. Neither country disputes the other's objective of sustained economic growth and prosperity. Yet each has fallen far short of what is required to realize its goals and blames the other for that shortcoming. Savings-short America has underinvested in the very innovation that it blames China for compromising. And an increasingly state-dominated China cannot bring itself to support consumerism and freedom of choice, both necessary ingredients of the sustained economic growth it is convinced America wants to contain. Beneath the façade of scale and strength, the two largest economies in the world are gripped by deep and troubling insecurity.

The false narrative is a defense mechanism that masks these insecurities. It arises out of the universal political inclination to deny and blame, deflecting attention away from self-generated problems. Leaders who own up to vulnerability are seen as weak and ripe for replacement. Just ask Jimmy Carter, an honest, self-effacing US president who admonished the American public during an energy crisis in 1979 that it was suffering from "a crisis of confidence . . . that strikes at the very heart and soul of our national will."[44] That kind of candor was a major factor in costing him his job in 1980, when he lost his bid for reelection to Ronald Reagan.

The politics of blame are far more expedient. For the United States, Japan was the problem thirty years ago, and now it is China; America's false narratives on trade deficits were virtually identical in both instances.[45] For China too, blame makes good politics, as shown by its obsession over humiliation at the hands of others. The nationalistic appeal of the Chinese Dream and China's related fear of a US containment strategy are no less political than America's blame game. While China's one-party authoritarian governance system adheres to a mechanism of leadership accountability very different from that of a regular electoral system, Xi Jinping's grip on power is at the top of his own political agenda.[46]

Politically inspired false narratives have a long and rich history. And as I noted earlier, once a false narrative gets imbedded into the national discourse, it is very hard to dislodge. That's even more so the case today with new technologies of narrative dissemination turning viral spread by social networks into another instrument of mass destruction. Given the extremes of negative sentiment now affecting both sides of the US-China relationship, reversing that deeply ingrained sentiment could prove even more difficult than rectifying the false narratives that initially created the ill will.

The escalating conflict between the United States and China is almost Newtonian in its gravitational pull. This is less a reflection of individual actions by either nation and more a function of the destabilizing interplay between them. The biases and distortions of codependency have fed on each other—leading to the accidental consequences of misguided policy actions. Normal relationship frictions have been amplified into a dangerous state of conflict. The momentum of escalation has become exceedingly powerful. As one battle has cascaded into the next—the trade war, the tech war, the early skirmishes of a new cold war—one question looms especially large: how can the United States and China overcome the gravity of accidental conflict?

13

From Distrust to Trust

THERE IS NO EASY ANSWER TO THAT QUESTION. But time is running short. With the risks of a serious accident now rising, a strategy of conflict resolution has become an urgent priority. Urgency is not just a time frame—it also means there isn't much margin for error. A resolution strategy will work only if it is responsive to both the severity and the scope of the threat. The remainder of this book is offered in that spirit.

Resolution of the US-China conflict must be framed with two key considerations in mind: the level of trust between the two countries and the character of their relationship. Right now, distrust is pervasive, and the relationship is dysfunctional. An effective strategy of conflict resolution therefore requires both a transition from distrust to trust and a different framework of engagement.

Sequencing is important. Rebuilding trust must commence *before* the two nations tackle the weightier challenge of shifting the relationship paradigm. That is the lesson from the long sweep of history, including the *glasnost* that set the stage for the end of the first cold war.[1] It is also the lesson that applies to disputes that have arisen over China's compliance with its WTO accession protocols. And it was glaringly apparent in the acrimonious exchange between the two countries' senior foreign policy officials in Anchorage in March 2021. The proliferation of false narratives we have looked at are all visible manifestations of blame arising out of insecurity and distrust. There is no point in attempting to execute a more comprehensive strategy of conflict resolution until some semblance of trust is restored.

Distrust has been brewing between the United States and China for decades. It almost seemed as if Chinese leaders knew trouble was coming in the months before Xi Jinping assumed office, in November 2012. Earlier that year, as vice president and heir apparent, he had embarked on a five-day "getting to know you" tour of the United States. On the eve of the visit, Vice Foreign Minister Cui Tiankai said, "There is certainly a trust deficit between China and the United States."[2] Cui, who later became China's longest-serving ambassador to the United States, had a deep understanding of America, but even he may not have suspected the full range of trust problems that were to come.[3]

Distrust has human and historical roots. Japan then, China now, with earlier wars in Korea and Vietnam—does America have an Asia problem? If so, have identity politics played an especially corrosive role in undermining the American piece of the trust equation? From the US perspective, China was both a thief of intellectual property and a cheat on trade. Of course, from China's perspective, the United States was turning out to be like other hostile foreigners, aggressively set on containing Chinese growth and development. Have the identity politics of distrust cut both ways?

The problem was not just words but the association of those words with important shifts in both countries' core values. The year 2017 was pivotal in that respect. In January, Donald Trump, as America's newly inaugurated forty-fifth president, vowed to deliver on his campaign promise to "Make America Great Again" and reverse what he believed was a long trajectory of national decline. Later in 2017, Xi Jinping proposed a critical rethinking of the "principal contradiction," that, as we noted earlier, upgraded China's self-assessment from a backward to a relatively well-off society. This became a linchpin of Xi Jinping Thought and the ideological foundation of an intensified nationalism.

These shifting narratives sealed the fate of a conflicted relationship. The two nations were at odds both rhetorically and philosophically, and in a manner that threatened the deeply ingrained aspirations of their national dreams. The determination of a rising China was pitted against the fears of a vulnerable America. The trust deficit was more than just words—it was validated by the dueling narratives of two powerful leaders. Escalating clashes fueled by the identity politics of both nations soon followed.

It will be extremely challenging for the United States and China to rise above today's toxic climate of distrust and reestablish a mutual commitment to engagement. But conflict resolution cannot occur until that happens. What might break the ice?

The low-hanging fruit of mutual interests is the best place to start. I will consider three areas that are particularly ripe for picking—climate change, world health, and cybersecurity. These are all critical global issues that afford both nations the opportunity to demonstrate their capacity for shared understanding, for joint leadership. A collective sense of accomplishment would be an important first step on the road from distrust to trust.

Historical Biases

Trust between nations is not the same as trust between individuals. The concept of national trust has a tortured history of misunderstanding between countries and their leaders, much of it stemming from the unfortunate human tendency to translate unfamiliarity and discomfort with foreign behavior into a sense of threat. These biases, which when politicized are virtually indistinguishable from identity politics, are the historical antecedents of many of the false narratives that continue to shape Western perceptions of China.

Yale historian Jonathan Spence detailed this pattern of bias in a remarkable forensic assessment of more than eight hundred years of Western impressions of China, from Marco Polo's thirteenth-century journals to Richard Nixon's twentieth-century conversations with Mao Zedong.[4] In the nearly fifty cases Spence examined, Westerners consistently misunderstood Chinese lifestyles, traditions, and values, not perceiving China objectively but more as a distorted mirror image of their own experiences.[5]

Marco Polo, for example, wrote the first serious foreign account of China, based on his seventeen years of living there, and provided an enduring characterization of the Chinese system that remained definitive in the West for centuries. While he got China's colossal scale and trading propensity right, he failed to mention one of the most distinctive characteristics of Chinese women—the binding of their feet that made walking all but impossible; nor did he make any reference to Chinese calligraphy, either as an artform or a means of written communication. His descriptions of China's two-thousand-kilometer Grand Canal, an intra-city waterway that linked its five main river basins, seemed remarkably like the intricate network of inner-city canals in his native Venice. The China in Polo's writing seemed to have more in common with his native Italy than it did with the reality of China at the time. As Spence mused, "Is this really China? Or is it a reverse image of Venice?"[6]

Similar biases were evident, Spence writes, in Nixon's and Kissinger's speeches and writings during their historic breakthrough missions to China in the early 1970s. Nixon suggested that he and Mao shared comparable values because of their equally humble backgrounds—Nixon having been raised in the small community of Yorba Linda, California, and Mao in Shaoshan village in Hunan Province. Kissinger saw parallels between Western and Chinese uses of power. Mao's projection of raw power, he thought, was strikingly similar to the willpower of Charles de Gaulle, as well as to the pre–World War I power projections of Britain and Germany.[7] But Nixon's and Kissinger's perceptions were more closely aligned with American culture and politics than with anything evident in China at the time.

Spence makes the same argument about the impressions of China conveyed by two notable American authors—Mark Twain and John Steinbeck. Twain conflated the mores of America's Chinatowns with those prevailing in mainland China, while Steinbeck made racist allusions to a "yellow peril" during the 1930s. Both writers' accounts struck a chord of deep concern in the United States—the squalor of Chinese-Americans' living conditions and the threat Chinese immigrants allegedly posed to a nation in the midst of a historic collapse of its economic system. Yet these American experiences had little in common with conditions in China or what those conditions might have implied for the United States. Even more troubling, the imagery of Twain and Steinbeck touched on an undercurrent of prejudice and racism that continues to plague American identity politics. The racial profiling of the so-called China Initiative of the Trump administration, which Joe Biden thankfully brought to an end in early 2022, was an especially worrisome example of that.[8] Remember Vincent Chin?

The Western tendency to see the Chinese experience mirrored in its own history shapes the current US-China debate. It has an impact, for example, on macroeconomic risk assessment of the saving and investment overhangs in China today. Because the United States went into crisis following the bursting of its property bubble in 2006–7, the view is often expressed in the West that China, with its ongoing property-market excesses, will suffer the same outcome. Many in the West also predict that the troubles afflicting Evergrande, China's second-largest property developer, portend a Western-style housing crisis, or a so-called Lehman Brothers moment, that could topple the broader Chinese economy.[9] But as I argued in Chapter 10, this assessment conflates Chinese housing issues with an American precedent that is entirely different. The same applies to China's debt problem—widely viewed in the West, as well as by an "authoritative person" inside China, as a precursor to a Japanese-like debt-deflation scenario.[10]

China is hardly immune to Western-style problems. But Spence's idea of perspective bias underscores how the West fails to take note of China's unique characteristics in assessing macro risk—for instance, the support to housing demand that comes from rural-to-urban migration and the concentration of debt intensity in China's government-supported state-owned enterprises.[11] The broad consensus of Western analysts is that the Chinese economy should perform just like their own economies—driven by risks and vulnerabilities endemic to wealthier, more advanced, market-based systems. Yet China's resilience over the past fifty years says otherwise. Its problems need to be assessed in the context of its own system—not by how they might play out in America or Greece.

This Western bias has an impact on the trust deficit between China and the United States. Earlier I emphasized how most analysts in Washington mistakenly believed that WTO accession provided a rules-based guarantee that China would conform to Western norms. When the Chinese economy failed to converge on America's economic template, the outcome was interpreted as a broken promise, a violation of the so-called Modernization Theory, which claimed that as nations developed they would become more like us.[12] Yet the disconnect between expectations and reality was an outgrowth of the false narrative linking WTO membership to Chinese conformity with Western norms. China, in fact, never made the convergence promise of replicating the American system that US politicians embraced to rationalize their push for Chinese WTO membership. The rise of China contradicts the essence of the sacrosanct Modernization Theory.

Historical biases are like false narratives. They help perpetuate the corrosion of mutual trust by setting us up for an "expectations shock" when nations don't conform with preconceived notions. They instill an unrealistic belief in a course of events—for example, America's conviction that China, once it learned the value of markets, would mold its economy and legal system in accordance with US standards, or China's belief that the United States would respect its exaggerated claims of territorial sovereignty in the South China Sea. One nation's rejection of another's deeply held expectations is often seen as a lack of respect, undermining the essence of trust. As Wang Yi's March 2021 tirade in Anchorage underscores, this also leads to the quick-trigger name-calling of the Chinese strain of identity politics.

While the trust deficit between the United States and China has grown severe in the past decade, it has been building for a long time. When China embraced the United States as a strategic partner in the 1980s and 1990s, there was an optimistic sense that a new history was being written. But as codependency morphed into conflict, the old histories of bias and false narratives quickly came back into play. It wasn't long before both nations were mired in the quicksand of mutual distrust, making it more and more difficult to arrest an increasingly corrosive discourse.

Institutionalized Trust

Trust building is a relatively new experience for the United States and China. Until the historic 1972 visit by President Nixon, China was an enigma to the West, a largely inaccessible land of mystery and intrigue. Television images of Air Force One taxiing on the tarmac of Beijing's airport, and of Nixon shaking hands with Mao and then visiting the Great Wall, brought snippets of China into American living rooms for the first time ever.[13] It was as much a cultural shock to the American public as a wake-up call for US foreign policy. The fascinating imagery belied the challenges both nations faced. China was still in the midst of its violent Cultural Revolution and the United States was engaged in a cold war with the Soviet Union. Despite

Nixon's visit, each nation remained tentative in its appraisal of the other, far from ready to embrace an open, trusting relationship.

Trust building takes time, especially when it involves nations as unfamiliar to each other as the United States and China were back then. There is a standard playbook. Leader-to-leader initiatives like Nixon and Mao's 1972 meeting provide the spark. Then, piece by piece, a network is assembled— first by diplomats, then regulators, policymakers, military leaders, corporate executives and their underlings, educators, and finally people-to-people exchanges among tourists and students. At the same time, an institutional overlay is created, providing structure and continuity that transcend the roles of individual participants and political leaders.

From the start, much time and effort were put into US-China relationship building. The Shanghai Communiqué, signed by both governments at the end of Nixon's visit, envisioned the eventual establishment of formal diplomatic relations.[14] It finessed the toughest issue between the two nations—the Taiwan problem—through a creative exercise in diplomatic ambiguity that became known as the "one China" policy.[15] The United States recognized Taiwan as an "inalienable part of China," though the agreement did not stipulate a time frame for formal reunification.[16] Seven years later, spanning a period that included the death of Mao in 1976, two more US presidents (Gerald Ford and Jimmy Carter), and continued efforts at relationship building conducted through embassy-like liaison offices in both countries, full diplomatic relations were established in early 1979 on the occasion of Deng Xiaoping's official visit to Washington.[17]

Just as Deng's push for reform and opening-up turbo-charged the Chinese economy, his diplomacy energized the institutional efforts at relationship and trust building. Particularly noteworthy were the establishment of critical bilateral mechanisms aimed at enhancing cross-border trade and economic engagement. These efforts were aligned with a key element of Deng's broader economic strategy—to attain Chinese membership in the World Trade Organization as a pivotal support to export-led growth.

It took over a decade of arduous negotiations between the United States and China to reach agreement on Chinese WTO accession in late 2001. For China, it was worth the wait. Global trade had been on an upswing in the nineties, but it took off immediately after China joined the WTO. Global exports surged to a record 31 percent of world GDP by 2008, up dramatically from 23 percent in 2001. Rapidly expanding Chinese exports accounted for a large share of that increase. At the time of its WTO accession in 2001, China accounted for just 3.5 percent of global exports. But by 2008 its share had grown nearly threefold to 10 percent.[18]

Whether through luck or brilliant foresight, China had timed its push for WTO membership perfectly. It was the major beneficiary of the record upswing in the global trade cycle, and it was able to parlay that surge into powerful export-led growth. All this fit perfectly with Deng Xiaoping's hyper-growth gambit. But such a remarkable achievement didn't come easily. Pulling it off required much effort at institutionalized relationship building.

This phase of relationship building was also an exercise in political theater. WTO accession required US congressional approval of "permanent normal trade relations (PNTR)," which granted China lasting "most-favored nation" status with the United States.[19] According to the WTO's level playing field stipulations, this put China on a par with America's other trading partners.[20] Aside from some special and ultimately contentious exemptions that China received as a developing economy—mainly delayed phase-in periods for tariff reductions, services liberalization, and technology transfer—America's political case for PNTR approval rested on the presumption that WTO accession would eventually lock China into a rules-based framework for trade. Supposedly, that would codify the WTO's core principles of nondiscrimination and reciprocity and thereby institutionalize the United States' trust in China as a responsible participant in the global trading system.

Trust building was the subtext of the US political campaign for Chinese WTO membership. First, the effort was seen as tightly aligned with American interests. As President Bill Clinton argued at the time, "The W.T.O. agreement will move China in the right direction," by which he meant in America's direction.[21] Free and open Chinese markets would be a lucrative target for American exporters. And refusal carried dangers: as Clinton warned, "If we don't sell our products to China, someone else will step into the breach."[22]

This was not just a false narrative that failed to take account of China's adherence to its own system. It was also a direct threat—distrust would

have consequences for the United States. The US Congress, and by inference the American people, were led to believe that support for Chinese
WTO accession was in the best interest of US companies and workers.
Trust was not only a political promise but presented as a legally binding
guarantee of compliance with China's WTO accession protocols, based on
what Clinton claimed would be "the largest enforcement effort ever given
for a trade agreement."[23] That was a convincing argument that effectively
sealed the deal with Congress.

Yet it didn't take long before those promises gave way to allegations that
China had broken its WTO accession commitments. In 2004, just three
years after accession, the first of the forty-nine complaints brought so far
(as of this writing) were filed against China through the WTO dispute mechanism. While this number fell far short of the number of complaints that
over the years have been leveled against the United States (178) and Europe
(101), China's image as a good citizen of the WTO had been tainted.[24]

Attacks on China's reputation were reinforced by the annual WTO compliance updates prepared by the US trade representative, which grew steadily
more forceful and accusatory. The USTR's 2020 assessment gave China
especially poor marks for not conforming to "open, market-oriented policies
endorsed by the WTO."[25] Never mind that this vague stipulation was never
clarified in the original accession protocols. The USTR criticized specific
nonmarket transgressions, such as industrial policies, which it alleged to
be broadly consistent with a state-led mercantilist approach.[26] It is hardly
surprising that the 2020 USTR assessment reads just like the Section 301
complaint against China filed in March 2018. They were both written by
the same person, Robert Lighthizer. Both documents politicized WTO compliance and accountability. They were *prima facie* evidence in America's case
for distrusting China.

As the anchor to the US-China economic relationship, trade became the
focal point for many other institutional efforts at trust building, some of
which predated China's WTO membership. In 1983, the United States and
China established the Joint Commission on Commerce and Trade (JCCT),
co-chaired by the US secretary of commerce (and, starting in 2004, the US
trade representative) and a vice premier in China, to manage US-China trade
normalization.[27] The JCCT met annually, twenty-seven times from 1983 to

November 2016. It had sixteen active working groups that addressed issues ranging from agriculture and pharmaceuticals to intellectual property and the environment. It was a robust and effective mechanism of engagement and institutionalized trust building. It was terminated by the Trump administration in 2017.

Over time, both nations recognized that engagement needed to broaden beyond trade. In 2006, US President George W. Bush and Chinese President Hu Jintao initiated a biannual Strategic Economic Dialogue (SED) to provide wider perspectives on key economic issues such as trade, currencies, and bilateral imbalances. The SED was effectively an overlay on the JCCT effort, and it quickly took on greater importance as a high-profile venue for airing grievances and exploring opportunities for future engagement. Led by the US treasury secretary and China's vice premier in charge of trade, it elevated attention to the bilateral relationship.

The SED framework was apparently too narrow for the Obama administration, which in 2009 added an ampersand to the format by including the US State Department and, by inference, China's Ministry of Foreign Affairs. The S&ED, as it then became known, was an even broader forum of engagement, led on the US side by the secretaries of treasury and state and by their counterparts from Chinese leadership.[28] The frequency of the meetings declined from twice to once a year, and the effort came to resemble a full-blown, well-choreographed, G-2-like summit. The communiqués, laced with the platitudes and ambiguities of diplomacy, seemingly elevated the relationship dialogue to a new level, a point not lost on Xi Jinping when he proposed a new model of major country relations at the Sunnylands Summit with Barack Obama in 2013.

Unfortunately, neither the SED nor the successor S&ED could temper the mounting frictions between the United States and China. The two nations increasingly talked past one another rather than seizing collective opportunities for active engagement. The Trump administration made a feeble effort to continue the talks, convening one meeting of what it called a "Comprehensive Economic Dialogue" in June 2017 before terminating the arrangement.[29]

Other institutionalized efforts at relationship building were developed over the years, but many of them worked at cross-purposes. The US-China

Economic and Security Review Commission (USCESRC), purportedly an independent arm of the US Congress, was established in 2000 as the debate intensified over China's WTO accession and the potential effects of a rising Chinese economy on the United States.[30] While the USCESRC, which also reports directly to the president, was created to provide objective, nonpartisan advice on key economic and security issues, over the past twenty years it has taken on a distinctly anti-China bias, both in Congress's choices of its twelve members and in the expert testimony that it selectively gathers from multiple hearings each year.[31]

The 2020 USCESRC annual report, for example, recommended that Congress consider a wide range of actions against China, from retaliation against Chinese censorship and alleged human rights violations to severing linkages with Chinese supply chains and elevating the diplomatic status of the director of the American Institute in Taiwan. There was no assessment of the shared responsibilities for conflict resolution between codependent partners. The focus was entirely on Chinese culpability.[32] Nor was the 2020 report an outlier. I testified three times before the commission, the last time in 2015, and each time I faced aggressive questioning laced with anti-China bias.[33] As the US-China conflict has intensified, the bias of this purportedly objective committee has become glaringly evident. Today the USCESRC is a high-profile forum for America's leading China bashers that fuels animosity and distrust toward China and does little to address meaningful options for rebuilding trust.

Personalization of Trust

Government actions are important for setting the parameters of trust building. In some cases, like WTO accession, they lay out the rules of engagement intended to establish trust and identify the tripwires that, if breached, set off the alarm bells of distrust. But there is far more to trust building than government-to-government exchanges and negotiations. Personal interactions, through conferences, academic exchanges, speeches, business meetings, and other channels of engagement, are just as important. The personal dimension of trust building is vital to lasting relationships. It can also, of course, spark conflict.

China probably holds more conferences each year than any other nation. No one is actually keeping count, but if my inbox is any barometer, China stands alone. Rarely a week goes by when I don't get invited to speak or attend (physically or, now, virtually) a major conference in China. Because I can't possibly attend them all, I turn down over 90 percent of the invitations.

But I do make exceptions, and one of them is the China Development Forum. The CDF was begun by Premier Zhu Rongji in 2000 as a relatively intimate gathering between the Chinese government leaders and a small group of foreign experts that was timed to occur immediately after the annual meeting of China's National People's Congress every March.[34] Zhu held the provocative belief that senior Chinese officials should debate with "outsiders" on newly approved policies and reforms. He viewed the CDF as a kind of stress test for senior officials, and he encouraged free thinking and vigorous exchanges between Chinese insiders and foreign experts.[35]

Before going virtual due to Covid public health protocols, the CDF had grown to Davos-like proportions. It lost the early intimacy of active engagement but gained considerably in participation and notoriety through extensive Chinese and international media coverage. The CDF's strength has always been the frank and open format of debate, discussion, and lively exchange of views. For a high-profile conference based in China, it is unique in that respect. It imparts conviction and character to the relationship building exercise between China, the United States, and the rest of the world.

China has many other platforms that allow for relationship building opportunities with the United States and other countries. They include the annual Boao Forum for Asia, the China Summer Davos, a Global Think Tank Conference, the Understanding China Conference, the China Finance 40 Forum, and on and on.[36] And, of course, there are numerous counterparts on the US side, including events hosted by the National Committee on US-China Relations, the Committee of 100, the Asia Society's Task Force on US-China Policy, and the US-China Business Council. In both the United States and China, these activities, most of which I have participated in over the years, have promoted a shared sense of partnership, engagement, and passionate expression of views, fostering a mutual understanding at the personal level that stands in sharp contrast to the friction and conflict between the two governments.

So-called Track II dialogues have also long been part of the institutionalized exchange of views between the United States and China. The principals in these dialogues are typically former senior government officials, academics, or other experts. The exchanges cover a range of issues, from trade, health, and climate change to cyber, defense, and maritime affairs. A typical meeting involves several days of intense discussions, followed by efforts to craft a consensus document of shared views and policy recommendations that are then reported to the "Track I" of sitting government officials. While Track II dialogues offer a great opportunity for relationship building and fulsome discussions of contentious topics, they have had little influence on public policy in either the United States or China.[37]

This personal commitment to mutual engagement between Americans and Chinese over the past forty years exists alongside an increasingly antagonistic US political system. Historically, pro-China Republicans—traditionally pro-business and pro-trade—have been at odds with anti-China Democrats who are pro-worker, pro–human rights, and anti–trade deficits. But America's bipartisan outbreak of anti-China sentiment has brought the two political parties together in a rare spirit of agreement. To an important extent, this reflects widespread acceptance of the false narratives discussed earlier. Very few issues today garner bipartisan political support in the United States. China bashing is an unfortunate exception.

While China does not suffer from a US-style political polarization, there are many political struggles at the top of the Party structure that bear critically on the relationship with America. One such instance came to light in a 2012 Yale University symposium focused on Henry Kissinger's then just-published book, *On China*.[38] After Nixon's 1972 trip and the breakthrough Shanghai Communiqué, Kissinger had never understood why he was unable to make further progress in moving the countries toward formal diplomatic relations. In the closing session of the Yale conference, he unexpectedly got the answer.

Cornell historian Chen Jian traced the lack of progress in the follow-up negotiations between the United States and China to a rift between Mao

Zedong and Zhou Enlai in 1973 over a proposal to install a "hot line" between Beijing and Washington to avoid nuclear war. The Chinese leadership, aware of a similar arrangement with the Kremlin, asked to be treated with the same respect, and Kissinger, who considered it a low priority request, quickly agreed. But Mao surprisingly rejected the hot line.[39]

Kissinger never understood why, nor did he grasp the significance of this seemingly mundane development. Professor Chen presented newly available Chinese archival information that explained the circumstances. Apparently, in a rage of paranoia, Mao saw the hot-line proposal as evidence that Zhou and Kissinger were setting up a private communication link in order to plot against him; Mao feared that when trouble arose, the first call would go directly to Zhou, not him. An angered Mao turned on Zhou, resulting in a falling out that had enormous consequences for the US-China relationship. Mao quashed the follow-up agreements that Kissinger and Zhou had carefully worked out, and his relationship with Zhou suffered lasting damage.

For Kissinger, this was quite a revelation. Chen Jian had finally explained, nearly forty years later, why his painstaking negotiations with Zhou Enlai had come to a sudden, mystifying stop in 1973.[40] Upon hearing the Chinese perspective for the first time at Yale in 2012, Kissinger's startled response said it all: "I never knew that!"[41]

That underscores one of the most important aspects of trust building. Institutional mechanisms are necessary but not sufficient to safeguard trust between nations. In the end, trust is a highly personal commitment that can be withdrawn as quickly as it is offered. As the Mao-Zhou incident illustrates, the shift from trust to suspicion can be capricious, almost random. Forty-five years later, an unprincipled Donald Trump did not hesitate to shift the US-China relationship from a commitment of trust to the conflict of distrust—all as a play to his "base" for short-term political gain.

Low-Hanging Fruit

Once trust has been broken, however, it is exceedingly difficult to put back together. For the United States and China, the escalating conflict of the past four years makes this especially hard. The United States feels that China has broken the trust in three ways—through unfair trading practices, including technology and intellectual property theft; through military aggression in the South China Sea and Taiwan Straits; and through human rights violations in Xinjiang Province, Hong Kong, and Tibet. China feels that the United States has broken the trust by orchestrating a containment strategy against it, initially personified by America's Asia pivot and the TPP trade initiative, and more recently amplified by Trump's trade and tech wars. The animus of Anchorage, the Biden administration's failure to revoke the Trump tariffs, and the recent AUKUS security agreement make it clear to China that containment is now the official policy of three consecutive US presidential administrations.

These are not trivial threats for either nation. Each feels it is under attack by the other. While the hostilities have so far been largely confined to the economic arena, there is growing concern on both sides that the conflict could grow into something far worse. Thucydides-like concerns over the perils of outright war have been openly discussed by leaders in both countries.[42] Vladimir Putin's nuclear saber-rattling over the war in Ukraine has only heightened concerns of a long unthinkable great power war. Recapturing trust in the midst of such anxious and intense escalation at times almost seems hopeless.

Yet it can be done. The lessons of military conflicts show what it takes to resolve economic tensions between two countries. The sequencing is relatively straightforward: A cease-fire or truce comes first; withdrawing from the front line comes next; then arms reduction. A negotiated agreement, to codify a sustainable truce, is followed by the establishment of guardrails and carefully monitored compliance. With time comes healing and, hopefully, the security and trust of a lasting peace.

Adapting the military model to resolve an increasingly conflicted economic codependency is challenging but possible. Specific actions can be taken by both sides that have the potential to restore a sense of partnership to the severely damaged US-China relationship. I will come to those in the final chapter of this book. But trust comes first: the military model is useless if it doesn't rest on a verifiable foundation of trust. Otherwise, the first sign of renewed tension—an inevitable occurrence—will take on exaggerated significance as a cataclysmic setback and promptly lead to the return of insidious distrust. The delicate truce—to say nothing of hopes for tranquil prosperity—will then quickly unravel.

This is where the personal dimensions of trust building come into play. Relationship trust, between nations as between individuals, rests on a foundation of common interests. It takes true leadership to identify those interests and put them on the negotiating table as an appeal to domestic constituencies and adversarial counterparts alike. The issues should offer compelling opportunities for mutual benefits. They should also be important enough to underscore the risk of failure if they are not taken up with unbiased urgency.

The United States and China do not lack low-hanging fruits of common interest. Three critical issues loom as especially prominent—climate change, global health, and cybersecurity. The first two pose grave threats to humanity, and the third issue, cybersecurity, poses grave risks to global platforms of commerce as well as to the delicate equilibria of social, political, and military stability in each nation. These three issues stand out as urgent challenges facing both the United States and China. And they pass the second test by underscoring the consequences of failure—climatic disaster, recurring pandemics, and commercial and state-sponsored cyberwarfare.

At present, the scales are tipping toward failure on all three counts. First are the imminent threats of climate change. The August 2021 report of the Intergovernmental Panel on Climate Change dispels any doubt of the devastating impact of human actions in boosting greenhouse gas emissions.[43] Some 234 scientists from around the world have concluded that global temperatures have already climbed one degree relative to averages prevailing from 1850 to 1900, and, depending on mitigation measures, will rise by another 1.5 to 2 degrees by 2060. While the IPCC documents the devastating impacts on polar ice and sea levels that would result from such warming, the extreme weather events of 2021 and early 2022—an unprecedented confluence of storms, fires, and floods—tell us that climate change is already here and demands urgent global action. For the United States and China, leadership moments like this rarely occur with such clarity.

Second are the lingering perils of the Covid-19 pandemic. Even in the United States, where scientific breakthroughs have led to miraculously quick development and distribution of vaccines, the mutation of new variants has

collided with political backlash against widely accepted public health protocols. And vaccine nationalism remains rampant around the world, with the
high-income nations having inoculated about 75 percent of their populations, compared with just 14 percent of the populations in low-income nations.[44] In today's interconnected world, it is virtually impossible to arrest
pandemics without a global cure. Approaching the problem narrowly as a
national threat is a recipe for failure—especially with the high likelihood
of a steady stream of variants, to say nothing of the distinct possibility of
another pandemic at some point in the not-so-distant future.[45] Again, this is
a clear opportunity for the United States and China to share leadership on
a global issue of historic importance.

Third is the unprecedented global outbreak of ransomware—hackers holding institutions and individuals hostage over cyber access—which leaves little doubt that the threat to cybersecurity has now reached the danger zone.[46]
Business activity already has been crippled in key segments of the US economy, including energy, food supply, travel services, higher education, Internet services, and water. Similar incidents have been reported in the United
Kingdom, in Continental Europe, and throughout Asia. Even China, with
its supposedly airtight control over the Internet, has seen several instances
of reported ransomware in areas such as shipping and online services platforms.[47] China has been accused as a perpetrator and identified as a victim
in the outbreak of criminal ransomware activity. Ransomware is only one
aspect of the many issues that could compromise cyber connectivity around
the world—including allegations of stolen trade secrets, intellectual property
theft, piracy, and destabilizing social and political turmoil amplified through
social networks. An urgent global solution is needed to address these threats,
and US-China leadership could be decisive in leading the way.

A Long and Arduous Process

The good news is that the United States and China are now engaged in
dialogue in the first area—climate change. As the world's two largest sources
of greenhouse gas emissions, both nations recognize the urgency to act. On
his first day in office, President Biden signed an executive order reinstating
US membership in the Paris Agreement on climate change.[48] He also hosted

a virtual summit on climate for forty global leaders on Earth Day in April 2021, at which both he and Xi Jinping underscored their shared commitment to addressing environmental perils. They reiterated this commitment at the COP26 UN climate change conference, held in Glasgow in November 2021.[49] China's rollout of a nationwide emissions trading system that July—the largest carbon-pricing network in the world—demonstrates its willingness to act boldly.[50] And John Kerry, the Biden administration's climate czar, who played a key role as Obama's secretary of state in the negotiations that led to the Paris agreement in 2015, was eager to engage the Chinese on environmental issues in a mission to Shanghai in early 2021.[51] While short of full collaboration, the United States and China are at least committed to moving in the same direction on climate change, hopefully with the same urgency. Soaring energy prices, as an outgrowth of the Russo-Ukrainian War in 2022, are an unfortunate complication, shifting demand temporarily (one hopes) from oil and natural gas back toward carbon-intensive coal.[52]

The news is less encouraging in the other two areas of mutual interest. The US-China Covid-19 debate is bogged down in an ongoing dispute over controversial circumstances at the Wuhan Institute of Virology during the initial stages of the outbreak. As a new president, Joe Biden had a great opportunity to shift the debate. But he chose not to do so, instead ordering a ninety-day review of Covid origins by the five leading US intelligence agencies.[53] The problem with this approach is that the Covid origins debate is more about blame than about problem-solving. And there is the added critical complication of a dead end, since the US intelligence review, together with two noteworthy collaborative studies of some forty-seven scientists published in early 2022, concluded that there is little persuasive evidence to pin the blame on a lab accident at the Wuhan Institute of Virology.[54] Yet the Biden administration has been unwilling to let go and move on.[55]

This has become a highly politicized issue that only serves to reinforce America's rhetorical hostilities with China.[56] Meanwhile, the Chinese stiffen at the mere mention of the events in Wuhan in late 2019. Certainly, they did not make matters easy for themselves by stonewalling requests for information on the circumstances surrounding the initial outbreak of Covid-19.[57] Chinese censors were quick to scrub the Internet of commentary and data regarding the early outbreaks. While Chinese officials counter by claiming they have made full disclosure on Covid's origins, this position is at odds with their unwillingness to provide any evidence from infected animal samples from the Huanan Seafood Wholesale Market in Wuhan.[58] At the mere mention of these concerns—by US officials or the World Health Organization—China goes into its wolf-warrior drill, which only inflames suspicion and ill feeling. Even after the intelligence review ordered by President Biden all but dismissed the lab-accident thesis, Chinese officials slammed the investigation in full-on Trumpian style as a "witch hunt" and offered the outlandish possibility that a military lab in Fort Detrick, Maryland, was a more likely source of Covid than the Wuhan Institute of Virology.[59] Like the US government, Chinese officials also have refused to let go and move on.

This misdirected focus on the Covid origins debate deflects attention away from the unfinished business that both nations still face on post-pandemic public health policy. The United States itself is embroiled in a highly politicized debate over masks and vaccine resistance, which has only intensified social and political polarization. Meanwhile, China has struggled with its "zero tolerance" policy in coping with the echo effects of the highly transmissible Omicron variant of Covid-19; with lockdowns having spread to China's largest cities like Shenzhen (March 2022) and Shanghai (April 2022), the Chinese economy was under growing pressure in early 2022. Shifting the Covid debate away from blame toward collaborative progress on public health protocols would benefit both nations.

Nor has there been much good news about US-Chinese collaboration on cybersecurity. The Biden administration has aggressively portrayed China as a key actor in the recent profusion of ransomware attacks, especially the massive hack of Microsoft's Exchange email platform discovered in early 2021.[60] The lack of cyber engagement between the United States and China has compromised any efforts at mediation. Military-to-military consultations on cyber issues, at one time a very constructive data-sharing and troubleshooting effort, have been suspended since 2014 after the United States indicted five Chinese military officers on cyber-espionage charges—an act that, at the time, appeared to be more of a publicity stunt than a serious legal response.[61]

There is an important lesson in these crosscurrents of action and inaction.

US-China joint commitments on climate change, while tentative at best, show that similar collaborative efforts are also possible on pandemics and cybersecurity. The action on climate came after a profusion of weather-related natural disasters in 2021. While it is disappointing that the worst pandemic in a century has not sparked comparable action on global health, the ongoing carnage of variant-prone Covid-19 may yet force some collective response. Joint efforts at addressing cybersecurity issues seem far more remote, despite the severity of the threat. It will probably take a major cross-border cyber failure to bring the United States and China jointly to the table to address risks to the digitized world's precarious infrastructure.

Experience demonstrates that national governments are inclined to act only reluctantly, after the fact, in dealing with transnational problems. But with climate change, global health, and cybersecurity, waiting may no longer be an option. China and the United States have a joint opportunity for a rare demonstration of global leadership. Trust building between two conflicted nations, to say nothing of the fate of the world, may hang in the balance.

Trust Building as an Act of Courage

There is an important catch in all this. It goes back to the human aspect of relationship conflicts between countries. As much as we extol the virtues of institutional- and rules-based foundations of national systems, decision making can never be completely depersonalized. Xi Jinping, clearly miffed by the escalating conflict with the United States on multiple fronts, attended Joe Biden's 2021 Earth Day climate summit only reluctantly, confirming his (virtual) attendance just two days ahead of the event.[62] That he agreed only at the last minute to participate in a global event focused on an issue of great importance to China shows that even the low-hanging fruit may not be that easy to pick.

The trust building that could come from working together on important issues requires a certain uncomfortable element of compartmentalization—the ability of leaders to prevent a hyper-emotional response to one issue from limiting progress on other areas of mutual concern. For the United States, that hot button is human rights. Can America collaborate with China on climate change, pandemics, and cybersecurity without compromising its core values on human rights? A similar question can be asked of China, which has had irrefutable evidence of environmental degradation for at least twenty years.[63] It has every reason to tackle the issue with great urgency— individually and as a leader of a global coalition. But with Xi Jinping's image tied to nationalistic rejuvenation, can the Chinese leader swallow his pride amid the steady stream of American attacks over trade, technology, cyber-security, and human rights in order to partner with the United States on climate change?

The same is true of Joe Biden.[64] With America's Covid-19 death count surpassing the one million threshold in May 2022 and certain to rise con-siderably further even if new variants don't emerge, the case for US-China collaboration is more compelling than ever. Instead, Biden has preferred to prosecute the lab-origins debate and stay the course on US-centric vac-cine nationalism rather than lead global efforts to address a devastating pandemic.[65]

For Biden, the reason is not hard to fathom. He faces a very difficult po-litical balancing act. His razor-thin majority in the US Congress, together with big bets on major legislative initiatives on infrastructure and social programs, compromise his willingness to take major risks on China before the 2022 midterm congressional elections. With US public opinion polling showing all-time lows in American support for China, Biden is just as reluc-tant as Xi to compartmentalize and grasp collaborative opportunities. Mind-ful of the contentious, politically charged concerns over human rights and the false narratives of unfair trading practices, he prefers, instead, to hew the Trump line on China.

There is an equally important caveat on trust for China. It relates to our earlier discussion of censorship and what it implies for the CCP's balance between having the trust of the Chinese people and maintaining control of them. To this point, I have focused on trust between nations, not on trust within each nation. Yet these are two sides of the same coin. Motivated by the preservation of CCP power, China's regime of information control un-derscores its lack of faith in open debate and fact-based truth seeking. Can a system so steeped in a culture of distrust truly be expected to trust any other nation?

While trust may not come naturally to Chinese leaders, as the falling out between Mao and Zhou over a hot line reminds us, conflict resolution won't happen without a resumption of trust building. The success of Nixon's trip to China was due importantly to the trust building that occurred in preparatory meetings between Henry Kissinger and Zhou Enlai. From that perspective, simply sitting down at the same table could be important once again for both the United States and China. The conversation itself would be a gesture of reengagement for two codependent economies that have been trapped in a pernicious cycle of conflict escalation. It has the potential to temper the extremes of both American protectionists and Chinese wolf warriors. Yet the conversation will be effective only if it lowers the temperature of hypersensitive, overly reactive defenses—an essential step in restoring trust in any troubled relationship.

Such a conversation is hardly a quick fix, but it would give the United States and China an opportunity to take a deep breath and nurture the personal efforts that relationship rebuilding requires. It would also offer a platform for sharing concerns on mutual challenges and developing an understanding of their common ground. Any progress, however limited, would instill a sense of collective accomplishment—the functional equivalent of a breakthrough after a long period of mounting animosity.

It pays at this point to ponder how trust building might work in practice—what an important first step might look like for the US-China relationship. Global health, amid a once-in-a-century pandemic, provides an obvious and important example of how such collaboration could take shape. On one hand, there is reason to be encouraged by the Biden administration's quick move to rejoin the World Health Organization, with Anthony Fauci, America's leading expert in infectious diseases, spearheading the reengagement.[66] Yet those hopes continue to be marginalized by contentious issues like the lab origins debate and vaccine nationalism.

This is where leadership matters most, in imagining what US-China engagement on Covid and global health might look like. Consider the possibilities of a new agenda for collaborative global health practices, from joint scientific efforts on Covid vaccine development and therapeutic treatments, to data sharing on Covid incidence by demographic cohort, to exchanges of best practices in contact tracing.[67] There would be grassroots opportunities for collaborative efforts by academics, scientists, and labs as well as innumerable possibilities for institutionalized synergies on all aspects of virological research between the Centers for Disease Control and Prevention (CDC), the National Institutes of Health (NIH), and their counterpart institutions in China.[68] Add in government efforts at the central (federal) as well as provincial (state) and local levels, and the networking effects of collaboration on Covid-related health matters start to grow exponentially. With China struggling mightily to contain another Covid outbreak in the spring of 2022—clinging to the "zero tolerance" approach that worked in the first (Wuhan) wave but that cannot arrest the highly transmissible Omicron variant—collaboration opens up the possibilities of a different approach.

This is only one example—perhaps the easiest. Apart from climate change and cybersecurity, there is a long list of other potential action items that might qualify as easier-to-pick low-hanging fruit, all of which might also prompt reengagement between the United States and China.[69] These include re-opening foreign consulates in both countries (Chengdu in China and Houston in the United States), loosening visa restrictions for students and journalists, and restarting educational exchanges like the US Fulbright Program. Other possibilities might include lifting restrictions on NGO (non-governmental organization) activity in both countries, easing the recent constraints on financial capital flows that are having a serious impact on US listings of new Chinese companies, relaxing the increased Treasury oversight of Chinese direct investment in the United States, and ending the recent weaponization of the US "entity list" as part of the tech war with China.[70]

The list goes on. Suffice it to say that there is ample opportunity to exercise good faith. Trust building—in this case, rebuilding—must start somewhere. Yet as promising as all this sounds, neither country has been willing or able to seize these collaborative opportunities. The reason is not hard to fathom—it can be traced back to the political expediency with which I began this book. Leaders in both the United States and China are boxed in by political contracts of their own making or that they inherited from their predecessors.

From a relationship perspective, the goals of trust building are simple: reengagement in proactive discussions, troubleshooting common problems, and relearning the art of familiarity that comes from working together. While simple in concept, the rebuilding of trust is complex in execution.

Yet without trust, leaders are afraid and reluctant to take risks on conflict resolution. Trust gives them the courage to act. After years of deepening distrust, there can be little hope for the grand kumbaya moment of a spontaneous reversal. Focusing on the big global issues like climate, health, and cybersecurity is an important place to start.

A Path to Interdependency

OUR SAGA OF CONFLICT HAS MANY PARTS, all of which are in play as this book goes to press. That was to be expected. As conflict escalation gathered momentum, the clash, as well as its potential resolution, quickly became a moving target.

The tragic history of conflict between nations reminds us that happy endings are never guaranteed. Rather than compete with the dark tales of China hawks, Internet trolls, and novelists, with their gory details of cold or hot wars, our focus will turn to conflict resolution. This points us less to a happy ending than to the reality of facing up to a relationship in distress.

The news flow is an obvious complication, raising the possibility of event-driven rabbit holes that could marginalize particular lines of reasoning. To guard against this, I will take a diagnostics-focused framework approach to conflict resolution. The goal is twofold—narrowing our focus to the sources of conflict escalation and identifying workable options to create a more constructive and enduring relationship.

In the previous chapter I argued that meaningful resolution is a trust-dependent exercise. Without some modicum of trust between the United States and China, any proposed solutions will not be worth the paper they are printed on. There will be no commitment to implementation, and compliance will be a vacuous exercise. A persistence of distrust means that any cease-fire will only be a brief interlude in an unrelenting, escalating conflict.

The basic idea of a framework approach is to rethink the rules and means of engagement between the two nations—not just in economic terms but in political and geostrategic terms as well. A new framework will need to be institutionally grounded, reflecting binding commitments between the two governments and their constituents, individuals and businesses alike. But it will also need to be flexible and resilient, allowing for stress-testing by the inevitable twists and turns of a chaotic world. Most of all, the framework needs to be imagined on a clean slate. The rapid escalation of the US-China conflict is *prima facie* evidence that the current approach is a failure.

Conflict resolution must begin with a cease-fire. That means arresting a progression of escalation and reestablishing a common ground of mutual engagement. Chapter 13 posited three areas—climate change, global health, and cybersecurity—as potential low-hanging fruit for collective action that may lead to a new spirit of trust between the United States and China. A cease-fire would offer an opportunity to pick that fruit.

Yet it is hardly simple. The imagery of low-hanging fruit does not do justice to the contentiousness of these issues. While the United States and China both recognize what is at stake, they disagree profoundly on what a solution might look like. There is dispute over what tactics are acceptable, or required, in tackling these problems effectively. In a deeply conflicted relationship like the one between the United States and China, straightforward disagreements over methods can easily devolve into finger-pointing over suspicions about motives.

The exceedingly hard challenge of trust building starts at the top, with strong, determined, and courageous leadership. Success is less a result of the innate intelligence of leaders well-practiced in the mechanics of risk assessment and more an outgrowth of their collective wisdom, drawing on the intangible characteristics of vision, honesty, and communicative skills. Rather than the hard-knuckle tactics favored (or proclaimed, anyway) by one former US president, the self-reflective wisdom of compromise is far better suited to conflict resolution. It often requires one of the two leaders to gamble on taking the first step without any reciprocal promise from the other. Yet such a courageous move can be decisive in convincing untrusting skeptics to trust the opposing party. Wisdom is knowing when to take that critical step.

Nationalism, the North Star of both the Chinese and the American Dreams, can make that first move an exceedingly difficult, giant step. To a point, it is more expedient and far easier for leaders to appeal to nationalism than to resolve conflict. But only to a point. That's where leadership wisdom comes into play: knowing when to pull back before the conflict hits a breaking point. Until that happens, escalation may well have to intensify before the political calculus can change. That underscores the high-risk note on which I ended Chapter 12—the ominous, increasingly powerful gravity of accidental conflict.

Trust building is necessary but not sufficient for conflict resolution. It only opens the door to the next and even tougher phase, which requires a fundamental rethinking of the framework of engagement. Ultimately, trust building also opens the door to the heavy lifting of resolution—redefining the character of the relationship.

The relationship perspective I have stressed throughout this book offers some hints about the principles that should underpin a workable framework of conflict resolution. Engagement will have to be open and transparent, rather than clouded by information distortion and censorship. That, in turn, will force both nations to be more honest in accepting responsibility for self-inflicted problems rather than relying on convoluted, antagonistic messaging to blame each other. Both nations will then be better able to address and confront the false narratives that have divided them and to accept that their mutual desire for shared prosperity can be achieved only through collaborative efforts.

I do not mean to suggest that the leaders of the world's two most powerful nations should spend time on a relationship psychologist's couch, helpful as that might be. But to the extent that the clash between the United States and China is the predictable outcome of a conflicted codependency, the relationship perspective has great benefits. It is especially helpful in setting out the parameters, the structure, and the accountability required of conflict resolution. It helps redefine the character that two challenged nations bring to problem-solving. And it certainly beats the existing failed approach.

Abandoning Phase I Thinking

A major theme of this book has been the disconnect between bilateral trade imbalances and the multilateral implications of extreme saving positions. This is not a complex theoretical argument—it is driven by the powerful, yet unavoidable, identities of national income accounting. To repeat: Nations with low domestic saving borrow surplus saving from abroad in order to invest and grow. To attract the foreign capital, they run current account and multilateral trade deficits. America's multilateral trade gap consisted of 106 bilateral deficits in 2021.[1] Unless it raises domestic saving, there can be no targeted bilateral fix to America's pervasive multilateral trade problem.

Yet that was exactly the presumption of the Phase I agreement of January 2020, signed by America and China, that was supposed to be a large step in solving the US trade problem. The Trump administration felt it needed to force an intransigent China to come to the table and sign this accord. Large increases in tariffs were viewed as essential to forcing this outcome. As the label of the approach suggests, additional phases were expected, presumably building on the bilateral effort that was adopted in early 2020.[2]

Unsurprisingly, as we saw in Chapter 7, Phase I didn't work. Not only did the overall US trade deficit get worse, but US trade was diverted from China to other, higher-cost foreign producers. That and the added costs arising from sharply increased tariffs on many Chinese imports made for the functional equivalent of a tax hike on American consumers and businesses. Moreover, the Phase I deal did virtually nothing to address the structural aspects of the US-China conflict. If Phase I is ever followed by a second phase, we can expect more of the same.

This flawed logic can be corrected only when the bilateral mindset is abandoned. Thankfully, the so-called deal expired at the end of 2021. But the bilateral thinking behind this approach hasn't, and significant adjustments in US trade policy should be considered immediately. First, the $200 billion requirement for incremental Chinese purchases of US products, which was supposed to have been reached by the end of 2021, should be dropped as a metric of noncooperation and failed compliance. This purchases commitment, which the new USTR Katherine Tai still appears to be clinging to as an indication of future compliance, was unrealistic from the start. Underscoring our bottom-line assessment of Phase I from Chapter 7, Chinese purchases came in at just 57 percent of stipulated levels, literally missing the incremental purchases target by the full $200 billion target of the deal.[3]

Second, the tariff increases put in place by both sides during 2018 and 2019 should be rolled back to the pre-trade-war levels of January 2018; that means reducing US tariffs on Chinese products from the current 19.3 percent rate back to 3.1 percent, and reducing Chinese tariffs on US products from their current rate of 20.7 percent back to 8 percent.[4] Applying those rollbacks to items covered by the initial imposition of tariffs, as well as to the tit-for-tat retaliation that followed, would give Americans an annualized rebate of about $65 billion in combined tariffs—in effect, reversing the functional equivalent of the tax hike imposed by Trump's tariffs.[5]

Abandoning Phase-I-type thinking and its associated tariffs does not mean the United States should forget about reducing its trade deficit. To the contrary, there needs to be a more effective strategy for achieving this. As I have stressed throughout this book, trade disparities mirror saving imbalances. If any nation wants to solve its macroeconomic trade problem—whether a chronic deficit or a chronic surplus—the best way to do it is by addressing its saving problem.

So, instead of beating each other up in an unwinnable trade war, the United States and China should both commit to policy adjustments aimed at rebalancing their saving disparities. The United States should try to increase domestic saving, and China should reduce it. That would lower America's multilateral trade deficit as well as China's multilateral trade surplus—a far more constructive and cost-effective outcome for both economies than the present bilateral trade war, which has only moved the imbalances around. Rearranging the deck chairs on the *Titanic* wasn't very helpful either.

Truly addressing the problem, of course, is easier said than done—especially for the United States, which faces years of enormous federal budget deficits that will squeeze domestic saving all the more. It is easier for political leaders to focus on trade as a lightning rod issue with clear villains and victims than to address saving as a long-term building block for investment, productivity, and economic growth. The persistence of low interest rates is an added incentive for deficit spenders to ignore chronic saving shortfalls. If servicing debt is so cheap, why worry?[6]

Other than the now distinct likelihood that interest rates will probably not remain near zero forever, there are plenty of reasons for both the United

States and China to address their saving problems.[7] Without boosting domestic saving, the United States, over time, will be increasingly unable to invest in manufacturing capacity, infrastructure, research and development, and human capital. So far, America has been able to draw on foreign surplus saving to help fund its domestic investment needs. Eventually, however, creditor nations like China will find other avenues for their surplus saving: they may use it to fund their own investment programs, like clean energy, the Belt and Road Initiative, or social safety net programs such as healthcare and retirement. That will make it far more difficult for savings-short America to self-fund the investments it sorely needs. That, in turn, will have a corrosive impact on US productivity and competitiveness, which could draw the cherished American Dream into serious question.

Similarly, if China fails to absorb its surplus saving, it will probably be because Chinese households are still engaging in excessive precautionary saving, too fearful about the future to spend much on consumer goods in the present. This possibility, which looks all the more likely given China's rapidly aging population and worsening "animal spirits deficit," would mean that China has made little progress toward its macroeconomic goal of consumer-led rebalancing.

Phase I was a fig leaf that allowed both the United States and China to fixate on bilateral trade while ducking the need to address the saving imbalances that both nations must ultimately face. It makes no sense to cling to such a misdirected and analytically unsound framework. The sooner the thinking behind this approach is abandoned, the greater the pressure will be on both nations to confront their challenges squarely. That will force the United States and China to be more open, honest, and self-reflective in framing their mutual grievances.

Structural Focus

Then what happens? After all their handwringing and inflammatory rhetoric, neither the United States nor China can be expected just to walk away from such a high-profile dispute. The body politic in both nations will demand something to show for the effort. There must be more to conflict resolution than simply relegating the thinking behind the Phase I agreement and recent tariff actions to the dustbin of failed policy adventures.

The saving agenda is only one possibility. This correctly shifts the focus of the US-China trade dispute from a bilateral to a multilateral perspective. It doesn't dismiss the grievances that each nation has expressed regarding the other's trading practices, but it frames those grievances as an outgrowth of the saving implications of their national economic strategies against the background of an interdependent, globalized world.

For the political crowd, the saving argument typically falls on deaf ears as an academic cop-out and an unacceptable loss of face.[8] The rap on saving is that it is a long-term issue with little short-term relevance.[9] This is myopic at best. But given the increasingly ominous conflict escalation between the United States and China, there is good reason to believe that the American public is unlikely to be persuaded that a macroeconomic pro-saving agenda should replace a misdirected trade accord like Phase I.

Yet there is a better alternative: starting over—the clean-slate approach. The essence of the US-China economic debate is not the bilateral trade imbalance but the structural conflict that divides the two nations. This is where the message of former USTR Robert Lighthizer actually made the most sense. The Trump administration was not exactly known for veracity in justifying its controversial policies.[10] That was an important aspect of what was wrong with Lighthizer's March 2018 complaint. But the Section 301 report did raise critical concerns about deep-rooted structural tensions between the United States and China. In the end, the list of these concerns may well be more important than the validity of the USTR's allegations.

As we saw in Chapter 4, the list is long, ranging from innovation policy, intellectual property rights, and forced technology transfer to cybersecurity and subsidies to state-owned enterprises. On all these counts, I have argued that the allegations leveled against China were built on a profusion of false narratives. But in one important respect, that is beside the point. The issues are important on their own and will need to be addressed, one way or another, if this deep-rooted conflict is ever to be resolved.

Take, for example, forced technology transfer, stressed in Chapter 4 as the high-profile stalking horse for US-China conflict.[11] This issue touches on the self-generated knowledge base of any nation—the stock of human and intellectual capital that drives innovative breakthroughs that will re-define our future—driverless vehicles, alternative energy technologies, 5G telecommunications equipment, robotics, aerospace, and the applications of artificial intelligence to new services in financial technology, life sciences and pharmaceuticals, and e-commerce. It is one thing if these new products and services are an outgrowth of a nation's unique, tenacious efforts at in-digenous innovation. It is another matter altogether if commercial ties be-tween nations somehow compel the transfer of these breakthroughs from one nation to another. Home-grown innovation is the crux of a nation's com-petitiveness and ultimately the key to its future prosperity. I emphasized earlier that the latter approach, a *forcing* of technology transfer, is a clear violation of the sanctity of a nation's proprietary knowledge-based human capital.[12] I concluded that forcing is not the problem that the American pub-lic has been led to believe.

It follows that the challenge for leading nations, like the United States and China, is to reach an enforceable understanding over intellectual prop-erty rights, namely the way in which such rights are embedded in existing and new technologies and the cross-border transfer of those technologies between companies and their subsidiaries as well as between governments, universities, research scientists, and military and defense-related establish-ments. For a fair system of knowledge sharing to work, there must be a codified understanding that both nations are willing to enforce.

That is not where things are headed. America has delegated its oversight of the interplay between tech transfer and national security largely to the Committee on Foreign Investment in the United States (CFIUS), whose powers have been expanded significantly in recent years.[13] China, through enactment of a new Foreign Investment Law in 2020, has made an explicit promise to ban foreign technology transfer and to protect the intellectual property of other nations. It has empowered both its Ministry of Commerce (MOFCOM) and the State Administration for Market Regulation (SAMR) to oversee and enforce the new rules.[14] It remains to be seen if China's new promises will be kept.

And that's precisely the problem. Two nations, with two very different

systems, are trying to tackle a hugely contentious shared issue in very different ways. Even without questioning either one's motives and intent, this
is a classic recipe for conflict. Each nation believes in the merits of its own
carefully crafted approach to dealing with the critically important issue of
technology transfer. And each doubts the integrity of the other's approach.
What authority might credibly adjudicate disputes over technology transfer
and intellectual property rights protection arising from these two very different systems is left as a prominent loose string.

The same question applies up and down the long list of grievances aired
by the USTR's Section 301 complaint, from industrial policy and the treatment of China's state-owned enterprises to cybersecurity and alleged predatory outbound mergers and acquisitions activities occurring under programs
like China's Belt and Road Initiative.[15] Each nation has its own approach to
each of these areas. There is no effective mechanism to monitor compliance
with existing agreements and resolve the disputes that inevitably arise in
the structural aspects of the US-China relationship. A similar critique has
been made about the 2001 agreement that governed China's accession to
the World Trade Organization.[16] Workable relationships need flexible and
workable rules of engagement, and these rules must periodically be updated
to keep up with the emergence of new industries, products, and technologies. Bringing WTO agreements up to speed with digitization is an important example of such a challenge. Structural grievances need their own
framework of adjudication and resolution.

The Bilateral Investment Treaty

The structural agenda is a proxy for far bigger aspirations shared by both
the United States and China. Each wants fair and increased access to the
other's large and expanding markets in order to promote long-term economic growth and prosperity. A bilateral investment treaty (BIT) is a time-
tested approach that many nations have embraced as a means toward that
end.[17] Over the years, the United States has signed forty-seven BITs, of
which thirty-nine are currently in force.[18] The fact that China has 106 BITs
in force, more than any other nation, is directly relevant to the framework

approach for conflict resolution: the United States and China should do a framework swap, trading Phase I and its associated tariffs for a strong, high-standard BIT.

The United States and China began negotiating a BIT in 2008, but these negotiations, like many pre-existing trade agreements, were abandoned by Donald Trump when he entered office in 2017. This was a major opportunity squandered. According to Michael Froman, USTR of the Obama administration from 2013 to 2017 and lead BIT negotiator, discussions stopped at a time when agreement on a US-China BIT was "more than 90 percent complete."[19] Trump's objections were an extension of his campaign rhetoric that all trade and investment deals negotiated by his predecessors were bad by definition—especially those with China.

What is a bilateral investment treaty, and why is it so important? America's BIT program was initiated by President Ronald Reagan in 1981 as an effort to encourage American companies to invest in developing countries. The US trade representative's office views the BIT as a program that "helps to protect private investment, to develop market-oriented policies in partner countries, and to promote U.S. exports."[20] Both the USTR's and the State Department's descriptions put forward a seemingly rigid template of a "model BIT" that requires "fair, equitable, and non-discriminatory treatment" of direct international investment flows.[21] This makes it sound as if the BIT is compatible only with market-based systems, ruling out its application to China. As it turns out, however, nearly seventeen, or half, of the thirty-nine BITs that the United States currently has in place are with non-market or blended economies, from Albania and Azerbaijan to Slovakia and, yes, Ukraine.[22]

China defines the BIT somewhat differently, as "an agreement signed between two countries or regions that sets out terms and regulations for private investors in the partner country."[23] Unlike the USTR version, there is no reference to market-oriented economies. Europe (thirty-six), Asia (thirty-four), and Africa (twenty) collectively account for 85 percent of the 106 BITs China currently has in place. While it has signed BITs with several nonmarket economies, including North Korea and Cuba, its portfolio of investment treaties also includes developed Western economies such as Japan, Germany, Australia, and South Korea.[24]

A BIT, in short, is a broad rules-based framework for cross-border invest-ment between partner countries, whatever their economic structures may be. This flexibility is especially important to its potential as a mechanism to address the US-China structural agenda. BITs provide leeway in designat-ing "negative lists" of industries that the partners agree will *not* be covered, as well as opportunity to focus on innumerable issue-specific side consid-erations (dubbed "non-conforming measures" in the US BIT model tem-plate) that receive considerable attention in drawn-out country-by-country negotiations. These side issues have covered a wide range of special con-cerns, including foreign exchange reserves (Egypt), exemptions for debt-to-equity conversions (Argentina), new developments in intellectual property investment (Poland), local content requirements (Turkey), government pro-curement practices (Uruguay), minority affairs and social services (Rwanda), and on and on.[25] Such case-specific modifications provide the flexibility to create bespoke BITs tailored to the structural characteristics of each of America's partnerships. That is the special attraction of the BIT as a tem-plate for structural arbitrage between the United States and China.

Consider one important possibility in a US-China BIT as an example of how this structural arbitrage might work: mandating the elimination of ownership caps, or limits, on direct investments by multinational corpora-tions in each market. While seemingly technical in description, this actu-ally would be a very big deal in tackling a key issue on the structural agenda. It would encourage the establishment of wholly owned operations of for-eign multinationals, doing away with the need for the joint-venture struc-ture of cross-border investments. That single provision would take the highly contentious issue of forced technology transfer off the table. If there are no JVs, there is no need to transfer anything from one partner to another. Contentious allegations of forcing, the essence of the intellectual property theft argument that so inflames the US political debate, would all but dis-appear.

There are many other examples of structural arbitrage that could be ad-dressed by a US-China BIT. For example, emphasis on nondiscriminatory behavior of state-owned enterprises, as well as the reciprocal role of govern-ment subsidies—both highly contentious provisions of China's WTO ac-cession protocols—could be codified and underscored in a new BIT. That would address head-on many of the allegations about unfair or nonreciprocal applications of industrial policies.

The European-Chinese experience illustrates the BIT's potential as a framework to tackle structural conflicts. In early 2021, after seven years of negotiation, the European Union reached agreement with China on a BIT-like pact that was dubbed the Comprehensive Agreement on Investment (CAI).[26] Like the hypothetical example above, the CAI calls for China to reduce its previously stringent joint venture requirements for European multinationals; it also provides for an equalization of EU and Chinese subsidies for state-owned enterprises and addresses other structural issues, including intellectual property rights, environmental standards, labor rights, and regulatory transparency. These provisions are all aligned with structural objectives long emphasized by the United States, especially when it comes to China. Unfortunately, the CAI's formal ratification is currently delayed by mounting political frictions over China's human rights record in Xinjiang Province.[27]

That underscores an obvious and important political aspect of a US-China BIT. Two-thirds of the US Senate is required for ratification of any treaty. In America's current hyper-charged political climate, that spells trouble for a BIT, especially one with China. This has prompted some to suggest rebranding the effort as an "agreement" rather than push for enactment of a politically impossible treaty.[28] A congressional-executive agreement, like those that framed both NAFTA and its successor, USMCA, would be a BIT in everything but name; but it would "only" require the approval of the president and a congressional majority, avoiding the unrealistic hurdle of two-thirds Senate approval.[29] In an era of unprecedented political polarization and congressional dysfunction, such a compromise deserves serious consideration.

Politics aside, the BIT approach to US-China structural arbitrage is far preferable to clinging to the mindset of the misdirected and unworkable Phase I bilateral trade framework. Shifting the focus from bilateral trade to a BIT-like adjudication of the structural aspects of the conflict gets to the crux of the growth challenges that both the United States and China face. Going back to the bargaining table and putting the finishing touches on a nearly complete BIT deserves the highest priority in a negotiated strategy of conflict resolution.

Yet even that won't be enough. Lasting conflict resolution also needs an implementation mechanism to head off constant, divisive battles like those that have occurred in the past twenty years over China's fulfillment of the terms of its WTO accession. There needs to be an institutional framework to deal with the weighty matters of oversight, compliance, and dispute resolution—all focused on enforcement of an agreement on structural issues. Only then can America and China truly shift their engagement from distrust back to trust.

New Secretariat

The problem, in many respects, can be traced to the current dysfunctional framework of engagement between the United States and China. The once- or twice-yearly economic and strategic summits that date back to 2006, together with the more recent leader-to-leader meetings, are long on glitz but short on substance. They have accomplished very little as the relationship has deteriorated. The two nations have compelling reasons to rethink the way they exchange views. They need a new structure for their dialogue.

A US-China Secretariat could provide that structure. Like the multinational secretariats of organizations like the United Nations, the Organization for Economic Cooperation and Development, the World Trade Organization, and many others, a US-China Secretariat would provide administrative and coordinating cohesion between the United States and China. It would be the first such effort involving just two nations.[30]

But the world's most important bilateral relationship needs more than just a new bureaucracy. A US-China Secretariat would shift the attention on relationship issues from part-time to full-time. The previous periodic dialogues, such as SED and S&ED until they were canceled by the Trump administration, were more like event-planning exercises supported by massive temporary staffs drawn from numerous government ministries and agencies.[31] A secretariat would be housed in a permanent office, located in a neutral jurisdiction, and staffed by a complement of US and Chinese professionals for whom the relationship would be a full-time job. It would serve as a collaborative platform focused on all aspects of US-China relations as well as a compliance and enforcement mechanism for new and existing agreements between the two nations—including the possibility of a new BIT. The new secretariat, organized functionally rather than as two stand-alone, siloed, country-specific efforts, would have four key responsibilities.

Relationship framing. The secretariat would play an important role in framing the US-China relationship, serving as an official evidence- and research-based platform recognized by both sides. This function would feature a collaborative research program, with jointly authored policy background, or "white papers," focused on mutual growth op-portunities as well as on conflict resolution; joint policy recommenda-tions would be channeled directly into the designated congressional committee deliberations of both nations.

Importantly, the research function would also oversee joint database development and management; this would include proprietary data gathering in areas pertinent to the relationship, such as detailed bilat-eral statistics on trade and capital flows, tariff collections, cross-border investments, patents and copyrights, royalty and license fees for tech-nology transfers, educational exchanges, and many of the other relation-ship metrics noted in this book. The data function should also entail quality scrubbing of dual-platform statistics maintained individually by the two countries, as well as protocols for data security. These ac-tivities should all be aimed at providing support for regular meetings between leaders and senior officials of both nations, as well as produc-ing background materials for military-to-military discussions. A public version of the secretariat's database should be updated regularly and made available to registered users.

Convening. The secretariat should also serve as an important hub for convening and integrating the networks of relationship expertise that already exist in both nations, including academics, think tanks, busi-ness and trade associations, and groups engaged in so-called Track II dialogues. The intent would not be to intervene in any of these activities but to serve as a clearinghouse of expert talent that could be drawn on to address issues of mutual interest. The lack of collaborative efforts during the early stages of the Covid-19 pandemic is a good example of how the convening function of an effective secretariat might have made a real difference in crisis management. Had experts from both the United States and China been invited to develop a consensus in understanding the outbreak, its potential ramifications, and the public health and scientific protocols needed for containment and mitigation, a proactive secretariat might have preempted much of the conflict that subsequently endangered the public health of both nations, as well as the rest of the world.[32]

Oversight and compliance. The secretariat would oversee the implementation and monitoring of agreements between the United States and China. The development and use of "dashboards" as a tracking device to assess detailed implementation and compliance requirements of joint agreements would be especially helpful with a new BIT. With conflicts bound to arise over contentious structural issues—especially intellectual property rights, technology transfer, state-supported industrial subsidies, and cybersecurity—the secretariat should be empowered with a transparent conflict resolution screening function. This could provide a first stop for the airing of grievances between the United States and China; BIT-type disputes, for example, could be screened, evaluated, and hopefully resolved by the secretariat prior to formal submission of complaints to the World Trade Organization's dispute process or to the arbitration tribunal mechanism of the World Bank's International Centre for Settlement of Investment Disputes.[33]

Outreach. The secretariat should also have an important outreach function. A transparent, open, uncensored, web-based communications platform is essential, complete with the public version of the US-China database noted above, working papers of the secretariat's staff researchers, and a coauthored quarterly review of US-China relationship issues. The secretariat should sponsor regular public conferences on key relationship issues. Press officers should hold frequent briefings on relationship developments.

The new secretariat should be jointly headed by two apolitical Chinese and American professionals, empowered to act as senior policy advisors to their respective governments. Political independence is essential for these positions, though achieving it in the current climate will be a challenge, to say the least. The two co-heads would oversee their respective staffs but would be urged to integrate them into comingled US-China departments rather than siloed, country-specific teams. Secretariat leadership should consult regularly with an actively engaged outside advisory board with equal representation from the United States and China but also including members from other key nations and regions.

The point of the secretariat is to elevate the bilateral US-China relationship to the importance it deserves in the governance of both nations. This will undoubtedly be the new organization's greatest challenge. Each nation typically approaches the other from its own perspective, with its own insights, biases, objectives, and aspirations. In a climate of deepening distrust, there is no sharing of efforts, no mutual problem-solving capacity, and no collaborative approach to relationship management. That must change.

The establishment of a US-China Secretariat won't immediately bestow a new spirit of mutually constructive engagement. But it would be an important step in that direction. The bilateral relationship needs constant attention—not just now, at the height of conflict, but also during more normal times so as to avoid future conflicts. A new secretariat, in conjunction with a high-standard BIT that addresses the key areas of structural difference, would give conflict resolution a much better chance than it has today. And it would offer the added bonus of a shared workspace to nurture a climate of interpersonal familiarity. Trust building often starts with small steps.

The Character of Relationships

In the end, conflict resolution requires a transformation in the character of the US-China relationship—from an unhealthy codependency to a robust interdependency. Behind the codependency lies a pair of troubled economies—two nations that all too often ignore the imperatives of self-improvement and fixate on perceived threats from others. Inasmuch as those reactions are typically focused on the touchpoints of trade, financial capital, innovation, and information flows, they are the sore spots where conflict risks are invariably most acute. The US-China trade and tech wars, and the rumblings of a new cold war, are classic manifestations of the conflict phase of codependency.

This conflict feeds on itself. Each nation tends to blame the other for problems of its own making—America views its trade deficit as China's fault, and China views US containment as an excuse for the muscular power projection that draws China's neighbors into an encirclement strategy. That's where false narratives come in—deflecting focus away from the need for self-improvement. Just as the United States avoids addressing its chronic shortfall of saving, China resists structural rebalancing. The resulting interplay between blame, denial, imbalances, and frictions fuels progressive conflict escalation. Decoupling, or a breakup, becomes a very real and destructive possibility.

In an interdependent relationship, however, more confident partners continually aspire to self-improvement. This would have America saving more while China saves less. Each nation would better attend to its own needs, making it more responsive to the needs of others. In turn, each would be better able to appreciate the mutual benefits of partnership. Mutual engagement between interdependent nations would be constructive and sustainable.

The approach I have presented here—trust building by picking the low-hanging fruit of common interest while creating a bespoke BIT and a companion US-China Secretariat—was imagined with those considerations in mind. Such a strategy of structural engagement offers an opportunity for the United States and China to repair the world's most important bilateral relationship. It is a prescription for transforming a conflicted codependency into a constructive interdependency.

Certainly, there are other frameworks for addressing trade disputes. But after the last four years, it seems fair to conclude that the myopic bilateral thinking behind the Phase I approach produced a failed framework. It did little to arrest the ominous trajectory of conflict escalation, and it may have made matters worse. There comes a time to cut losses, pick a different strategy, and act.

That different strategy must be carefully aligned with the sources of conflict. At a minimum, this requires a strong and enforceable agreement on key contentious issues. All that and more can come from a high-standard bilateral investment treaty. A new secretariat has the added potential to make this treaty a living document that nurtures a dynamic, productive, and expanding interdependency. Most of all, this combination of formal agreement and institutional support would allow China and the United States to directly address the structural issues that have divided them.

Can the United States and China make the transition from codependency to interdependency? What will it take to achieve that critical transition? Fear is one incentive. The ominous trajectory of conflict escalation has put both nations in the danger zone. With the shocking outbreak of war in Europe, worrisome geostrategic tensions add an exclamation point to that warning.

Political accountability is another incentive. The political economy of expediency could well be the most insidious aspect of this accidental conflict. Both nations have been compromised by the globalization of a polarized interconnected world that has put considerable pressure on workers and their families. When they view their options as voters or as citizens, they tacitly condone the "easy" solutions of the nationalistic blame game that pit China against America. The leap from distrust to renewed trust is as much a political gambit as an economic strategy. Unmasking the false narratives behind a toxic political expediency is central to the honest and transparent accountability required of conflict resolution.

The dark forces of codependency are not easy to contain. There is nothing automatic in any agenda for conflict resolution, including the approach I have suggested. But whatever the option, one thing is certain: focus on both sides needs to shift from finger-pointing to seizing the collective opportunities of mutual collaboration. Without courage and wisdom, leaders in both nations will be stymied, unable to take that critical step.

For the United States, the strength to undertake that rethinking must come from within—not from strategies of adversarial containment. China has an equally urgent need to confront its internal imbalances and dispel fears of its global intentions, now ominously supported by an increasingly muscular power projection. The clash of dueling false narratives has already destabilized the relationship between the world's two great powers. History would be unforgiving of a failure to arrest this ominous escalation of accidental conflict.

Postscript

I KNEW FROM THE START OF THIS PROJECT that I was chasing a moving target. But with the world in flux as never before, the chase has occasionally left me breathless. It's one thing to focus on trade wars, tech conflicts, even a new cold war. But the start of a hot war in Ukraine and yet another twist in the pandemic have created staggering uncertainties.

In one sense the modern world has always been that way. It's like Moore's Law, the sacred creed of Silicon Valley. The pace of change keeps doubling at predictably shorter intervals. Who can know what will happen to the United States, to China, or to the relationship between them after this book goes to press? What is a reader to make of this book if some of the facts and premises it rests on are swept away by the swirl of events?

The future is, of course, unknowable—as are the inevitable shocks that will shape it. But I have no doubt of the profound impacts those unknown events could have on the future of the US-China relationship. This book has ended with an assessment of the leap from conflict escalation to resolution—and what it might take to accomplish that leap. Yet my prescription is, of course, a conditional assessment, dependent on future developments that could be just as destabilizing as those we are living with today.

As I write this, in May 2022, an unthinkable war rages in Europe at the same time that another Covid variant is having particularly destabilizing effects in China. There is no lack of potential shocks to contemplate, and it doesn't take much imagination to create any number of alternative futures—

both good and bad—that seem completely at odds with the possibilities explored in this book.

How do we think about the future of the US-China conflict in this context? The relationship between these two nations is not a scientific experiment that can be isolated and examined in a laboratory. This book, like my previous book, *Unbalanced*, is grounded in the framework of a conflicted economic codependency. To the extent this framework has been effective in illuminating the pressures that have arisen between the United States and China over the past fifteen years, I remain convinced that it will be helpful in shedding light on relationship pressures in the future.

Many books are outgrowths of the *shock du jour*, linear extrapolations of a seemingly catastrophic current trend. As a recovering Wall Street forecaster, I can only warn of the pitfalls of extrapolation. The next shock is almost always different from the last shock. We need to prepare and think about those seemingly unfathomable possibilities.

In this book I have tried to offer a set of organizing principles with which to understand the impacts of these inevitable shocks, to enable you to think usefully about those future unexpected events—about which we can be certain of little other than their unpredictability. One of the few things we do know is that America and China will continue to be key actors in a rapidly changing, shock-prone world. Whether they choose to cling to their false narratives or overcome them—and in so doing perpetuate their conflicts or strive to resolve them—could be the defining question for the world's most important relationship of the twenty-first century.

NOTES

Chapter 1. Shared History

1. See Stephen R. Platt, *Imperial Twilight: The Opium War and the End of China's Last Golden Age* (New York: Alfred A. Knopf, 2018).
2. See Amanda Foreman, *A World on Fire: Britain's Crucial Role in the American Civil War* (New York: Random House, 2010).
3. Platt, *Imperial Twilight*.
4. See "Invasion of Manchuria," Harry S. Truman Library, available at https://www.trumanlibrary.gov/education/presidential-inquiries/invasion-manchuria.
5. See, for example, Chen Jian, *China's Road to the Korean War: The Making of Sino-American Confrontation* (New York: Columbia University Press, 1994); David Halberstam, *The Coldest Winter: America and the Korean War* (New York: Hyperion, 2007); and Russell Spur, *Enter the Dragon: China's Undeclared War Against the U.S. in Korea, 1950–51* (New York: Newmarket Press, 1988).
6. See Odd Arne Westad, *The Cold War: A World History* (New York: Basic Books, 2017).
7. See Jonathan D. Spence, *The Search for Modern China*, 3rd ed. (New York: W. W. Norton and Co., 2012).
8. See Frank Dikötter, *The Cultural Revolution: A People's History, 1962–1976* (London: Bloomsbury Press, 2016).
9. Source: National Bureau of Statistics (China).
10. See Lawrence H. Summers, "U.S. Economic Prospects: Secular Stagnation, Hysteresis, and the Zero Lower Bound," *Business Economics* (National Association for Business Economics) 49, no. 2 (2014).
11. See Shujie Yao, "Economic Development and Poverty Reduction in China over 20 Years of Reforms," *Economic Development and Cultural Change* 48, no. 3 (April 2000).

12. See Spence, *The Search for Modern China.*

13. See Deng Xiaoping, "Emancipate the Mind, Seek Truth from Facts, Unite and Look Forward," speech before the Central Party Work Conference, December 13, 1978; source: Ezra F. Vogel, *Deng Xiaoping and the Transformation of China* (Cambridge, MA: Harvard University Press, 2011), based on Deng Xiaoping, *Selected Works of Deng Xiaoping, 1975–1982* (Beijing: Foreign Language Press, 1984).

14. See Vogel, *Deng Xiaoping.*

15. See Spence, *The Search for Modern China.*

16. See Isabella W. Weber, *How China Escaped Shock Therapy: The Market Reform Debate* (New York: Routledge, 2021).

17. Source: Author's calculations based on data from the National Bureau of Statistics (China).

18. See Spence, *The Search for Modern China.*

19. Source: International Monetary Fund, *World Economic Output* database.

20. See Stephen S. Roach, *The Next Asia: Opportunities and Challenges for a New Globalization* (Hoboken: John Wiley & Sons, Inc., 2009), 229–33.

21. Source: National Bureau of Statistics (China).

22. Source: National Bureau of Statistics (China).

23. Source: International Monetary Fund, *World Economic Outlook* database.

24. Deng Xiaoping is credited with establishing the leadership taxonomy for the People's Republic of China. Mao Zedong was designated as first generation, Deng second, followed by Jiang Zemin (third), Hu Jintao (fourth), and now Xi Jinping (fifth); see Zhengxu Wang and Anastas Vangeli, "The Rules and Norms of Leadership Succession in China: From Deng Xiaoping to Xi Jinping and Beyond," *China Journal* 76 (July 2016).

25. See full text of Xi Jinping's remarks delivered at a press briefing following his installation as CCP general secretary on November 15, 2012, available at https://www.bbc.com/news/world-asia-china-20338586.

26. See Daniel H. Rosen, *Avoiding the Blind Alley: China's Economic Overhaul and Its Global Implications,* An Asia Society Policy Institute Report (New York: Asia Society, October 2014).

27. See Daniel H. Rosen, "The China Dashboard: Tracking China's Economic Reform Program," Asia Society Policy Institute and the Rhodium Group, Winter 2021.

28. Xi's 2017 speech contained some 32,662 Chinese characters, nearly four times the 8,202-character count of Deng's 1978 speech; source: *People's Daily* (China). The first draft of Deng's speech was reported to have totaled only about sixteen hundred characters; see Vogel, *Deng Xiaoping,* 242–43.

29. See full text of Xi Jinping's report at the Nineteenth CCP National Congress on October 18, 2017, available at http://www.xinhuanet.com/english/special/2017-11/03/c_136725942.htm.

30. The concept of "dual circulation" was first proposed by Xi Jinping in May 2020 and subsequently incorporated into China's Fourteenth Five-Year Plan; see Bert

Hofman, "China's Economic Policy of Dual Circulation," Hinrich Foundation: Sustainable Trade, June 8, 2021.

31. See Yuen Yuen Ang, *China's Gilded Age: The Paradox of Economic Boom and Vast Corruption* (London: Cambridge University Press, 2020); and Xi Jinping's report at the Nineteenth CCP National Congress.

32. See Karl Polanyi, *The Great Transformation: The Political and Economic Origins of Our Time* (Boston: Beacon Press, 1944).

33. See Xi Jinping's report at the Nineteenth CCP Congress; for a discussion of the Marxian interpretation of this shift in China's dialectical relationship, *Tao Guang Yang Hui*, see Rush Doshi, *The Long Game: China's Grand Strategy to Displace American Order* (New York: Oxford University Press, 2021), 176–8.

34. See Aaron L. Friedberg, "The Authoritarian Challenge: China, Russia and the Threat to the Liberal International Order," Japan-US Program, Sasakawa Peace Foundation, August 2017; Jude Blanchette, "Xi's Gamble: The Race to Consolidate Power and Stave Off Disaster," *Foreign Affairs*, July/August 2021; and Rana Mitter and Elsbeth Johnson, "What the West Gets Wrong about China," *Harvard Business Review*, May–June 2021.

35. See "Xi Jinping's Thinking Is Ranked Alongside Mao's," A Second Thought, *The Economist*, October 24, 2017; and Bill Chappell, "China's Xi Is Elevated to New Level, with Echoes of Mao," *The Two-Way* (blog), NPR, October 24, 2017.

36. See Chris Buckley, "China's Communist Party Declares Xi Jinping 'Core' Leader," *New York Times*, October 27, 2016.

37. Chinese leadership scholars complain that the West is making too much of this shift, pointing out that this change in the Chinese constitution merely aligns the succession framework of state leaders with comparable (unlimited) terms of Party leaders; see Jeffrey A. Bader, "7 Things You Need to Know about Lifting Term Limits for Xi Jinping," *Order from Chaos* (blog), Brookings Institution, February 2018.

38. "Hide and bide" is shorthand for Deng Xiaoping's famous "24-character strategy" for China's foreign policy that was first articulated in 1990 in the aftermath of the 1989 Tiananmen Square tragedy: "Observe calmly; secure our position; cope with affairs calmly; hide our capacities and bide our time; be good at maintaining a low profile; and never claim leadership." See Vogel, *Deng Xiaoping;* for the Chinese interpretation, see Huang Youyi, "Context, Not History, Matters for Deng's Famous Phrase," *Global Times* (China), June 15, 2011.

39. The recent profusion of authoritarian regimes around the world has sparked intense debate over the possibility of a backlash and reversal of this trend. See Andrea Kendall-Taylor and Eric Frantz, "How Autocracies Fall," *Washington Quarterly* 37, no. 1 (Spring 2014); Thorsten Benner, "An Era of Authoritarian Influence? How Democracies Should Respond," *Foreign Affairs*, September 2017; and Martin Wolf, "The Rise of Populist Authoritarians," *Financial Times*, January 22, 2019.

40. Ironically, the mistaken diagnosis of transitory inflation in the 1970s has an eerie

parallel with the post-Covid resurgence of US inflation in 2021; see Stephen S. Roach, "The Ghost of Arthur Burns," *Project Syndicate*, May 25, 2021.

41. See Robert J. Gordon, "Can the Inflation of the 1970s Be Explained?" *Brookings Papers on Economic Activity* 1977, no. 1 (1977); George L. Perry, "Inflation in Theory and Practice," *Brookings Papers on Economic Activity* 1980, no. 1 (1980); and J. Bradford De Long, "America's Peacetime Inflation: The 1970s," in C. D. Romer and D. Romer, *Reducing Inflation: Motivation and Strategy* (Chicago: University of Chicago Press, 1997).

42. Source: US Bureau of Labor Statistics.

43. Alan Blinder, Princeton professor and former vice chairman of the Federal Reserve Board, has put much of the debate on monetary policy and inflation published over the years in America's leading journal of contemporary economic issues, the *Brookings Papers on Economic Activity (BPEA)*, in perspective; see Alan S. Blinder, "*BPEA* and Monetary Policy over 50 Years," *Brookings Papers on Economic Activity* 2021, no. 1 (2021).

44. The term *stagflation* is widely attributed to Iain Macleod, British chancellor of the exchequer, who in a speech to Parliament in 1965 bemoaned the combination of stagnant production, high unemployment, and rising inflation afflicting the UK economy. See British House of Commons, *Hansard*, November 17, 1965, 1, 165. There is a rich literature on the sources of stagflation; see, for example, Milton Friedman, "Nobel Lecture: Inflation and Unemployment," *Journal of Political Economy* 85, no. 3 (June 1977); Michael Bruno and Jeffrey D. Sachs, *Economics of Worldwide Stagflation* (Cambridge, MA: Harvard University Press, 1985); and Alan S. Blinder and Jeremy B. Rudd, "The Supply-Shock Explanation of the Great Stagflation Revisited," paper presented at the National Bureau of Economic Research conference on the Great Inflation, Woodstock, VT, September 2008.

45. See Jeffrey Frankel, "The Plaza Accord, 30 Years Later," National Bureau of Economic Research (NBER) Working Paper No. 21813, December 2015; and Takatoshi Ito, "The Plaza Agreement and Japan; Reflection on the 30th Year Anniversary," James A. Baker III Institute of Public Policy, Rice University, October 2015.

46. Source: US Department of Commerce (Bureau of Economic Analysis).

47. These estimates are for Chinese holdings of total long-term dollar-denominated US debt, the bulk of which represent $1.1 trillion of Chinese-owned US Treasury securities as of October 2021; see US Treasury International Capital (TIC) System, available at https://home.treasury.gov/data/treasury-international-capital-tic-system.

48. "Morning again in America" was the tagline to one of Ronald Reagan's most popular political campaign ads when he stood for reelection in 1984; see https://www.reaganfoundation.org/programs-events/webcasts-and-podcasts/podcasts/words-to-live-by/morning-again-in-america/.

49. I will confess to having beat the drum more loudly than most on the perils of the asset-dependent, bubble-prone US economy; see, for example, Stephen Roach,

"America's Inflated Asset Prices Must Fall," *Financial Times*, January 7, 2008; Stephen S. Roach, "Double Bubble Trouble," *New York Times*, March 5, 2008; and Stephen Roach, *Unbalanced: The Codependency of America and China* (New Haven, CT: Yale University Press, 2014), especially chapter 3.

50. Source: International Monetary Fund, *World Economic Outlook* database.

51. The "guesstimate" of a 20 to 30 percent net domestic saving rate in China is based on research that puts the nation's depreciation rate somewhere in the range of 5 to 10 percent. There is good reason to believe that actual depreciation may fall at the low end of that range; unlike older economies, China's investment boom is relatively recent, implying that the aging of its relatively "youthful" capital stock will come later rather than sooner. See Richard Herd, "Estimating Capital Formation and Capital Stock by Economic Sector in China: The Implications for Productivity Growth," World Bank Policy Research Paper No. 9317, July 2020.

52. Many believe that US saving has recovered sharply, as panic-stricken Americans rediscovered frugality in the face of a devastating pandemic. While the personal saving rate did, in fact, surge to a high of 26.1 percent in the second quarter of 2020, this was purely a reflection of massive income-support transfers from the government sector that pushed the federal deficit deep into negative territory—in effect, a shift in the sources of domestic saving. Net domestic saving, as the combined sum of depreciation-adjusted personal, business, and government saving, actually fell back to "zero" in the second and third quarters of 2020 before "recovering" to just 2.9 percent during the first three quarters of 2021. Source: US Department of Commerce (Bureau of Economic Analysis).

53. Source: Congressional Budget Office, Historical Budget Data, available at https://www.cbo.gov/data/budget-economic-data#2.

54. See Laura Silver, Kat Devlin, and Christine Huang, "Unfavorable Views of China Reach Historic Highs in Many Countries," Pew Research Center, October 2020.

55. See Dikötter, *The Cultural Revolution*.

56. Source: International Monetary Fund, *World Economic Outlook* database.

57. Source: International Monetary Fund, *World Economic Outlook* database.

58. Source: National Bureau of Statistics (China).

59. See Ben S. Bernanke, "The Global Saving Glut and the U.S. Current Account Deficit," Sandridge Lecture, Virginia Association of Economists, Richmond, VA, March 10, 2005; Brad W. Setser, "The Return of the East Asian Saving Glut," Council on Foreign Relations, October 19, 2016.

60. As will be emphasized in Chapter 4, the United States, which had merchandise trade deficits with 106 nations in 2021, recorded deficits with an average of one hundred nations over the ten-year period, 2012–21; source: US Department of Commerce (Bureau of Economic Analysis). China ran bilateral merchandise trade surpluses with 157 countries in 2019; source: World Bank, World Integrated Trade Solutions (WITS) database.

61. Source: Congressional Budget Office, Historical Budget Data.

62. Source: International Monetary Fund, *World Economic Outlook* database.
63. Source: Author's calculations for 2020 based on data from the International Monetary Fund, *World Economic Outlook* database.

Chapter 2. From Convenience to Codependency

1. David Ricardo, *On the Principles of Political Economy and Taxation* (London: John Murray, 1817). See Deborah K. Elms and Patrick Low, eds., *Global Value Chains in a Changing World* (Geneva: World Trade Organization, 2013); and World Bank and World Trade Organization, *Global Value Chain Development Report 2019: Technological Innovation, Supply Chain Trade, and Workers in a Globalized World* (Washington DC: World Bank Group, 2019). Also see the OECD's Global Value Chain research platform, available at https://www.oecd.org/sti/ind/global-value-chains.htm.
2. The "win-win" framing of mutual gains from economic relationships has been traced as far back as Aristotle (fourth century BC) and Cicero (first century BC); see Richard P. Nielsen, "Varieties of Win-Win Solutions to Problems with Ethical Dimensions," *Journal of Business Ethics* 88, no. 2 (August 2009).
3. See Richard Baldwin, *The Great Convergence: Information Technology and the New Globalization* (Cambridge, MA: Harvard University Press, 2016).
4. Richard Baldwin's unbundling saga ended with the teaser of a forward-looking glimpse into the future. He raised the science-fiction-like possibility of a third unbundling driven by the elimination of the face-to-face constraints of work and idea generation. Breakthroughs in video connectivity and tele-robotics could well make it possible, he suggested, to conceive of the ultimate separation between the delivery of labor services and the actual work effort itself. As farfetched as that may have sounded when it was written in 2016, the Zoom-supported connectivity of remote work in the Covid-19 era may well be bringing the world tantalizingly close to this next hypothetical unbundling. And that would not be without consequences for what is already shaping up to be one of the most contentious issues facing the United States and China in the years ahead—the conflict over artificial intelligence (AI) that will be discussed in Chapter 5. See Baldwin, *Great Convergence,* chapter 10.
5. See Jason Dedrick, Greg Linden, and Kenneth L. Kraemer, "We Estimate China Only Makes $8.46 from an iPhone—and That's Why Trump's Trade War Is Futile," *The Conversation,* July 2018, available at https://theconversation.com/we-estimate-china-only-makes-8-46-from-an-iphone-and-thats-why-trumps-trade-war-is-futile-99258.
6. See Matt Binder, "Trump to China: Make the iPhone in the U.S., Not China," *Mashable,* January 2019, available at https://mashable.com/article/trump-to-apple-iphone-us-china/.
7. US imports from China totaled $506.4 billion on a "customs" basis in 2021 and $541.5 billion on a CIF basis (which includes cost, insurance, and freight); source: US Department of Commerce (Bureau of Economic Analysis).
8. Moreover, it turns out that close to half of all Chinese exports are, in fact, shipped

out by Chinese subsidiaries of Western multinationals. While these subsidiaries do employ Chinese workers, their foreign ownership also draws the China blame accusation into serious question—especially since China is providing offshore efficiency solutions for high-cost Western multinational corporations. See Robert Koopman, Zhi Wang, and Shang-jin Wei, "How Much of Chinese Exports Is Really Made in China?" NBER Working Paper No. 14109, June 2008.

9. The US merchandise trade deficit with China totaled $354.598 billion in 2021 as measured on a balance-of-payments basis; this was 32 percent of the total US goods trade deficit of $922.026 billion as measured on a balance-of-payments basis and 33 percent of the total US goods trade deficit as measured on a "Census" basis. Source: US Department of Commerce (Bureau of Economic Analysis).

10. In a series of papers, research by MIT professor David Autor and his associates has popularized the notion that the United States has been victimized by a "China Shock." Their basic premise is that China's export boom, widely "recognized as transforming China into the world's factory," has taken a significant toll on manufacturing employment and per capita incomes in America's most trade-exposed regions; see, most recently, David Autor, David Dorn, and Gordon Hanson, "On the Persistence of the China Shock," *Brookings Papers on Economic Activity* 2021, no. 2 (2021). In this paper, as well as in earlier efforts, Autor et al. fail to acknowledge the GVC-enabled transformation of the Chinese factory into an assembly line as I have stressed; the detailed product-specific trade data they use to assess the impacts of Chinese import penetration are taken from UN Comtrade based on SITC (Standard International Trade Classification) product codes, which make no distinction between the Chinese and non-Chinese value-added portion of goods that enter the United States. As such, in light of the increased role of China-centric value chains and the associated increases of non-Chinese components and parts, their use of finished-product trade data seriously biases their estimated results. The 2021 paper by Autor and his colleagues appears to be their ninth effort to make the statistical case for the China Shock; all of these research papers are premised on the same accounting metric of finished goods import penetration that makes no adjustment for value chains. For the first in this series of research papers, see David Autor, David Dorn, and Gordon Hanson, "The China Syndrome: Local Labor Effects of Import Competition in the United States," *American Economic Review* 103, no. 6 (October 2013).

11. See OECD, "Trade in Value Added," available at https://www.oecd.org/sti/ind/measuring-trade-in-value-added.htm.

12. See Adam Taylor, "How a 10-Gallon Hat Helped Heal Relations between China and America," *Washington Post*, September 25, 2015.

13. See Samo Burja, "How Deng Xiaoping Solved China's Trade Problem—And What America Can Learn from Him," *National Interest*, October 19, 2020.

14. See Wang Kaihao, "Deng's 1979 US Visit Captured in Film," *China Daily*, September 4, 2014.

15. See Phil Dougherty, "Chinese Vice Premier Deng Xiaoping (or Teng Hsiao-ping)

Arrives in Seattle for a Two-Day Visit on February 3, 1979," HistoryLing.org Essay 8588, posted April 15, 2008.

16. See US Census, "Trade in Goods with China: 1985 to 2021," available at https://www.census.gov/foreign-trade/balance/c5700.html#1989.

17. See Ezra F. Vogel, *Deng Xiaoping and the Transformation of China* (Cambridge, MA: Harvard University Press, 2011).

18. See Marc Humphries, "Rare Earth Elements: The Global Supply Chain," Congressional Research Service, June 8, 2012.

19. Source: National Bureau of Statistics (China).

20. Source: US Department of Commerce (Bureau of Economic Analysis) and US Bureau of Labor Statistics.

21. There has been considerable debate over the relationship between globalization and the worldwide trend of disinflation in the 1980s and 1990s; the research concludes that the impacts have been significant, especially those from China. See International Monetary Fund, "How Has Globalization Affected Inflation?" *World Economic Outlook: April 2006*, chapter 3; Raphael Auer, Claudio Borio, and Andrew Filardo, "The Globalization of Inflation: The Growing Importance of Global Value Chains," Bank for International Settlements, BIS Working Paper No. 602, January 2017; and Kristin Forbes, "Inflation Dynamics: Dead, Dormant, or Determined Abroad?" *Brookings Papers on Economic Activity* 2019, no. 2 (2019).

22. Source: US Department of Commerce (Bureau of Economic Analysis).

23. See Nicholas R. Lardy, "China and the Asian Contagion," *Foreign Affairs*, July/August 1998; James Kynge, "China Was the Real Victor of Asia's Financial Crisis," *Financial Times*, July 3, 2017; and Peter G. Peterson, Morris Goldstein, and Carla A. Hills, *Safeguarding Prosperity in a Global Financial System: The Future International Financial Architecture*, Report of a Council on Foreign Relations Taskforce, October 1999. Note: The author was a member of the CFR taskforce that in 1998–99 examined the Asian financial crisis in considerable detail.

24. See Eswar S. Prasad, *Gaining Currency: The Rise of the Renminbi* (New York: Oxford University Press, 2017).

25. Source: State Administration of Foreign Exchange (China), https://www.safe.gov.cn/en/.

26. In January 2022, Japan held $1.303 trillion of US Treasury securities, whereas China's holdings totaled $1.060 trillion; source: US Department of the Treasury, "Treasury International Capital (TIC) System," available at https://home.treasury.gov/data/treasury-international-capital-tic-system.

27. See Hiro Ito and Robert N. McCauley, "The Currency Composition of Foreign Exchange Reserves," Bank for International Settlements, BIS Working Paper No. 828, December 2019.

28. Source: US Department of Commerce (Bureau of Economic Analysis); data on International Transactions, International Services, and International Investment Position, available at https://apps.bea.gov/iTable/iTable.cfm?ReqID=62&step=1#reqid=62&step=9&isuri=1&6210=4.

29. See Marco Rubio, "To Fight China on Trade, We Need More Than Tariffs," *New York Times*, March 13, 2018; Kamran Rahman, "Lindsey Graham: 'Accept the Pain' of the U.S.-China Trade War," *Politico*, August 25, 2019.

30. See Stephen Roach, *Unbalanced: The Codependency of America and China* (New Haven, CT: Yale University Press, 2014).

31. See Anne Case and Angus Deaton, *Deaths of Despair and the Future of Capitalism* (Princeton, NJ: Princeton University Press, 2020).

32. See John Lewis Gaddis, *The Cold War: A New History* (New York: Penguin Books, 2005).

33. Source: International Monetary Fund, *World Economic Outlook* database and A. Cheremukhin, et al., "The Economy of the People's Republic of China since 1953," NBER Working Paper No. 21397, July 2015.

34. Source: US Department of Commerce (Bureau of Economic Analysis).

35. Following his death in December 2019 at the age of ninety-two, Paul Volcker was widely praised as America's most courageous central banker. See, for example, Martin Wolf, "The Legacy and Lessons of Paul Volcker," *Financial Times*, December 19, 2019; also see Paul A. Volcker with Christine Harper, *Keeping at It: The Quest for Sound Money and Good Government* (New York: Public Affairs, 2018).

36. James P. Morgan Jr., "What Is Codependency?" *Journal of Clinical Psychology* 47, no. 5 (September 1991); Greg E. Dear, Clare M. Roberts, and Lois Lange, "Defining Codependency: A Thematic Analysis of Published Definitions," in S. Shohov, ed., *Advances in Psychology*, vol. 34 (New York: Nova Science Publishers, 2005); and Timmen L. Cermak, *Diagnosing and Treating Co-Dependence* (Minneapolis: Johnson Institute Books, 1986).

37. See Robert J. Shiller, *Narrative Economics: How Stories Go Viral & Drive Major Economic Events* (Princeton, NJ: Princeton University Press, 2019).

38. See Paul M. Romer, "Mathiness in the Theory of Economic Growth," *American Economic Review: Papers and Proceedings* 105, no. 5 (May 2015).

39. See Jonathan Schlefer, *The Assumptions Economists Make* (Cambridge, MA: Harvard University Press, 2012); Jean Tirole, *Economics for the Common Good* (Princeton, NJ: Princeton University Press, 2019); and Jean Tirole, "Assumptions in Economics," working paper prepared for the Society for Progress 2019 conference on Philosophy Reflections on Core Assumptions in Business Research & Education, October 2019.

40. Of the eighty-six Nobel Prizes that have been awarded in economics since 1986 (technically, the Sveriges Riksbank Prize in Economic Sciences in Memory of Alfred Nobel) only five are related to contributions to behavioral economics; the awards to Daniel Kahneman (2002), Robert Shiller (2013), and Richard Thaler (2017) made explicit mention of behavioral economics, whereas two others were recognized for related accomplishments—Herbert Simon (1978) and Gary Becker (1992). See https://www.nobelprize.org/prizes/economic-sciences/.

41. This is consistent with a diagnosis of "asthenic personality disorder" *(DSM* diagnostic code: 301.6); see American Psychiatric Association, *Diagnostic and Statistical*

Manual of Mental Disorders, 4th and 5th eds. (Washington DC: American Psychiatric Publishing, 2003 and 2013). Also see Ingrid Bacon, Elizabeth McKay, Frances Reynolds, and Anne McIntyre, "The Lived Experience of Codependency: an Interpretative Phenomenological Analysis," *International Journal of Mental Health and Addiction* 18 (June 2020): 754–771.

42. See John H. Porcerelli, Rosemary Cogan, Tsveti Markova, et al., "The Diagnostic and Statistical Manual of Mental Health Disorders, Fourth Edition Defensive Functioning Scale: A Validity Study," *Comprehensive Psychiatry* 52, no. 2 (March–April 2011); and Anthony D. G. Marks, Rebecca L. Blore, Donald W. Hine, and Greg E. Dear, "Development and Validation of a Revised Measure of Codependency," *Australian Journal of Psychology* 64, no. 3 (2012).

43. See, for example, Steven Levitsky and Daniel Ziblatt, *How Democracies Die* (New York: Crown, 2018); and Elizabeth C. Economy, *The Third Revolution: Xi Jinping and the New Chinese State* (New York: Oxford University Press, 2018).

44. See Greg Dear, "Blaming the Victim: Domestic Violence and the Codependency Model," 1996; Janice Haaken, "A Critical Analysis of the Co-dependence Construct," *Psychiatry: Interpersonal and Biological Processes* 53, no. 4 (1990).

Chapter 3. Two Dreams

1. See James Truslow Adams, *The Epic of America* (Boston: Little, Brown & Co., 1931).

2. See Wu Gang and Yan Shuang, "Xi Jinping Pledges 'Great Renewal of Chinese Nation,'" Xinhua News Service and *Global Times* (China), November 30, 2012.

3. While the accounts of Adams (1931) and Xi (2012) are of special and lasting significance, historical archives contain records of earlier mentions of the American and Chinese Dreams. See, for example, Benjamin Franklin, "Information for Those Who Would Remove to Europe," republished in *Boston Magazine,* October 1784, and Zheng Sixiao (1241–1318), a poet from the troubled Southern Song dynasty who wrote a poem in which he coined the phrase "Heart full of Chinese Dream" (中国梦); I am indebted to Robert Shiller for pointing out these earlier references to the American and Chinese Dreams. For additional antecedents to the Chinese Dream, see Zheng Wang, "The Chinese Dream: Concept and Context," *Journal of Chinese Political Science* 19, no. 1 (March 2014).

4. As Yale economist Robert Shiller puts it in more scientific terms, the "brain's activity during dreaming resembles the activity of certain damaged brains, in which lesions of the anterior limbic system and its subcortical connections lead to spontaneous confabulation"; see Robert J. Shiller, *Narrative Economics: How Stories Go Viral & Drive Major Economic Events* (Princeton, NJ: Princeton University Press, 2019). Also see Edward F. Pace-Schott, "Dreaming as a Story-Telling Instinct," *Frontiers in Psychology* (2013); G. William Domhoff, *Finding Meaning in Dreams: A Quantitative Approach* (New York: Plenum Press, 1996); and Calvin S. Hall, *The Meaning of Dreams* (Berkeley: University of California Press, 1953).

5. This is an official English-language translation published by China's state news service, Xinhua; see Wu and Yan, "Xi Jinping Pledges 'Great Renewal.'"

6. See "General Secretary Xi Jinping Explicates the 'Chinese Dream,'" *Chinese Law & Government* 48, no. 6 (2016): 477–79.

7. See, for example, James C. Hsiung, *The Xi Jinping Era: His Comprehensive Strategy Toward the China Dream* (New York and Beijing: CN Times Books, Inc., 2015); Winberg Chai and May-lee Chai, "The Meaning of Xi Jinping's Chinese Dream," *American Journal of Chinese Studies* 20, no. 2 (October 2013); Manoranjan Mohanty, "Xi Jinping and the 'Chinese Dream,'" *Economic and Political Weekly* (Mumbai), September 21, 2013; and Zhao Tingyang, "The China Dream in Question," Harvard-Yenching Institute Working Paper Series, Cambridge, MA, 2013.

8. A recent interview-based project of the China Development Research Foundation has compiled more than one hundred case studies of the impact of the Chinese Dream on a broad cross-section of Chinese citizens; see Mai Lu, ed., *The Chinese Dream and Ordinary Chinese People* (Singapore: Springer, 2021). A portion of this chapter ("Rethinking Prosperity") is based on the introduction to this book written by the author.

9. According to the latest assessment of the US Department of Defense (DOD), China is well ahead of its goals for establishing a "world class military" by 2049; the DOD concludes that the PRC is already ahead of the United States in three key areas—shipbuilding, land-based conventional ballistic and cruise missiles, and integrated air defense systems—and has also significantly improved the PLA's overall combat readiness by embracing new operational concepts and expanding its overseas military footprint. See Office of the Secretary of Defense, *Military and Security Developments Involving the People's Republic of China: 2021*, Annual Report to Congress, Washington DC, November 2021.

10. See Asian Development Bank, *Meeting Asia's Infrastructure Needs*, Manila, 2017; World Bank, *Belt and Road Economics: Opportunities and Risks of Transport Corridors*, Washington DC, June 2019; and Jack Nolan and Wendy Leutert, "Signing Up or Standing Aside: Disaggregating Participation in China's Belt and Road Initiative," Global China, Brookings Institution, October 2020.

11. See International Monetary Fund, *World Economic Outlook* database; and Angus Maddison, *Chinese Economic Performance in the Long Run: 960–2030 AD*, OECD Development Centre Study, 2nd ed. (Paris: OECD Publishing, 2007).

12. See Jonathan D. Spence, *The Search for Modern China*, 3rd ed. (New York: W. W. Norton and Co., 2012), chapters 10 and 11.

13. There has been considerable debate over the causes of China's loss of technology leadership since the seventeenth century; see Justin Yifu Lin, "The Needham Puzzle: Why the Industrial Revolution Did Not Originate in China," *Economic Development and Cultural Change* 43, no. 2 (January 1995).

14. See James Truslow Adams, *The Epic of America* (Boston: Little, Brown & Co., 1931). Adams, also a Pulitzer Prize–winning author of *The Founding of New England*

(1921), wrote twenty-one books between 1916 and 1945; see James Truslow Adams papers, 1918–1948, Columbia University Libraries Archival Collections, available at http://www.columbia.edu/cu/lweb/archival/collections/ldpd_4078384/.

15. Source for GDP: US Department of Commerce (Bureau of Economic Analysis). For unemployment, see Stanley Lebergott, "Labor Force, Employment, and Unemployment, 1929–39: Estimating Methods," *Monthly Labor Review,* US Bureau of Labor Statistics, July 1984.

16. See US Government Accountability Office (GAO), "Military Readiness," Report to Congressional Committees, GAO-21-279, April 2021.

17. See Maddison Project, "Maddison Historical Statistics," Groningen Growth and Development Centre, University of Groningen, Netherlands, available at https://www.rug.nl/ggdc/historicaldevelopment/maddison/.

18. See International Monetary Fund, *World Economic Outlook* database, available at https://www.imf.org/en/Publications/SPROLLs/world-economic-outlook-data bases#sort=%40imfdate%20descending.

19. See Amartya Sen, Jean Paul Fitoussi, and Joseph Stiglitz, *Mismeasuring Our Lives: Why GDP Doesn't Add Up* (New York: The New Press, 2010).

20. See Lu Ya'nan, "China Builds Moderately Prosperous Society, Achieves Centenary Goal," *People's Daily* (China) online, July 5, 2021, available at http://en.people.cn/n3/2021/0705/c90000–9868223.html.

21. This calculation is based on data from the US Department of Commerce (Bureau of Economic Analysis), available at https://www.bea.gov/data/gdp/gross-domestic-product.

22. A similar pattern is evident in a broader measure, growth in total factor productivity, which measures the increment that comes from the combination of a more comprehensive measure of factor inputs—not just labor but also physical and human capital; on that basis, US total factor productivity growth slowed from a 0.7 percent trend over 1955 to 2010 to just 0.4 percent from 2011 to 2019. Source: Penn World Tables Version 10.0 (February 2021), available at https://www.rug.nl/ggdc/productivity/pwt/.

23. Source: World Inequality Database, available at https://wid.world/.

24. The latest data on the income and wealth distributions from the World Inequality Database go through 2015 for China and through 2019 for the United States; the wealth share of the upper decile in the United States is estimated to have declined fractionally from 73 percent in 2015 to 71 percent in 2019.

25. As will be stressed in Chapter 12, the antecedent to the 2021 common prosperity campaign can be traced to Deng Xiaoping's views on the sequencing of Chinese economic development from advanced to backward areas that were underscored in remarks delivered in 1986 at the launch of China's Coastal Development Strategy; see Bert Hofman, "China's Common Prosperity Drive," *EAI Commentary,* National University of Singapore, September 3, 2021. Also see Fuh-Wen Tzeng, "The Political Economy of China's Coastal Development Strategy: A Preliminary Analysis," *Asian Survey* 31, no. 3 (March 1991); Dali L. Yang, "China Adjusts to the

World Economy: The Political Economy of China's Coastal Development Strategy," *Pacific Affairs* 64, no. 1 (Spring 1991); and C. Cindy Fan, "Uneven Development and Beyond: Regional Development Theory in Post-Mao China," *International Journal of Urban and Regional Research* 21, no. 4 (1997).

26. Xi Jinping stressed this point at an August 17, 2021, meeting of the Central Committee for Financial and Economic Affairs that he chairs; see "Xi Stresses Promoting Common Prosperity amid High-Quality Development, Forestalling Major Financial Risks," Xinhua News Service (China), August 18, 2021.

27. See Albert Keidel, "Chinese Regional Inequalities in Income and Well-Being," *Review of Income and Wealth* 55, special issue 1 (July 2009).

28. See, for example, "Xi Jinping's Talk of 'Common Prosperity' Spooks the Prosperous," Free Exchange, *The Economist*, August 28, 2021; Kevin Rudd, "Xi Jinping's Pivot to the State," an address to the Asia Society, New York, September 8, 2021; and Ryan Hass, "Assessing China's 'Common Prosperity' Campaign," *Order from Chaos* (blog), Brookings Institution, September 9, 2021.

29. Source: World Inequality Database, https://wid.world/.

30. See, for example, Edward Glaeser, Wei Huang, Yueran Ma, and Andrei Shleifer, "A Real Estate Boom with Chinese Characteristics," *Journal of Economic Perspectives* 31, no. 1 (Winter 2017); Kenneth S. Rogoff and Yuanchen Yang, "Peak China Housing," NBER Working Paper No. 27697, August 2020; and Stella Yifan Xie and Mike Bird, "The $52 Trillion Bubble: China Grapples with Epic Property Boom," *Wall Street Journal*, July 16, 2020.

31. There has been an outpouring of critical commentary in recent years depicting a shattering of the American Dream; see, for example, J. D. Vance, *Hillbilly Elegy* (New York: Harper, 2019); Gene Ludwig, ed., *The Vanishing American Dream* (New York: Disruption Books, 2020); Noam Chomsky, *Requiem for the American Dream* (New York: Seven Stories Press, 2017); Nicholas Lemann, *Transaction Man: The Rise of the Deal and the Decline of the American Dream* (New York: Farrar, Straus and Giroux, 2019); and Robert D. Putman, *Our Kids: The American Dream in Crisis* (New York: Simon & Schuster, 2015).

32. See Dan P. McAdams and Kate C. McLean, "Narrative Identity," *Current Directions in Psychological Science* 22, no. 3 (June 2013); and Kate C. McLean, Monisha Pasupathi, William L. Dunlop, et al., "The Empirical Structure of Narrative Identity: The Initial Big Three," *Journal of Personality and Social Psychology* 119, no. 4 (2020). Also see Julie Beck, "Life's Stories: How Narrative Creates Personality, *The Atlantic*, August 10, 2015.

33. See, for example, John Kenneth Galbraith, *The Great Crash: 1929* (Boston: Houghton Mifflin, 1961); Studs Terkel, *Hard Times: An Oral History of the Great Depression* (New York: Pantheon Books, 1970); and F. Scott Fitzgerald, *The Great Gatsby* (New York: Charles Scribner's Sons, 1925).

34. See Shiller, *Narrative Economics*.

35. This has been formalized by the so-called SIR model of epidemic spread, driven by the interplay of three factors—the susceptible portion of the population (S),

the infected portion of the population (I), and the recovered (or dead) portion of the population that is no longer susceptible to the disease (R). See William O. Kermack and Anderson G. McKendrick, "A Contribution to the Mathematical Theory of Epidemics," *Proceedings of the Royal Society* 115, no. 772 (1927).

36. The Google Ngram filter is based on the results of an online search engine that charts the frequencies of word usage found in scanned sources of Google Books between 1500 and 2019; for a description, see https://books.google.com/ngrams /info. Also see Robert J. Shiller, "The Digital Tool that Helps Robert Shiller Understand the Past," Faculty Viewpoints, *Yale Insights*, February 8, 2022.

37. In a remarkable essay in early 2021, Yale professor Timothy Snyder was the first to equate the "big lie" of the so-called stolen 2020 US presidential election with historical antecedents of earlier big lies that can be found in Hitlerian anti-Semitism in Nazi Germany and in Stalin's warped explanation of self-imposed starvation in Soviet Ukraine in 1932–33; see Timothy Snyder, "The American Abyss," *New York Times Magazine*, January 9, 2021. The MIT study can be found in Soroush Vosoughi, Deb Roy, and Sinan Aral, "The Spread of True and False News Online," *Science* 359, no. 6380 (March 9, 2018).

38. See Chengcheng Shao, Giovanni Luca Ciampaglia, Onur Varol, Kai-Cheng Yang, Alessandro Flammini, and Fillipo Menczer, "The Spread of Low-Credibility Content by Social Bots," *Nature Communications* 9, article no. 4787 (November 20, 2018).

39. This is what Shiller has dubbed Proposition 5 of narrative economics: "Truth is not enough to stop false narratives." See Shiller, *Narrative Economics*.

40. See Glenn Kessler, "Trump's False or Misleading Claims Total 30,573 over 4 Years," *Washington Post*, January 24, 2021.

41. See Geoffrey Skelley, "Most Republicans Still Won't Accept that Biden Won," *FiveThirtyEight*, May 7, 2021.

42. This is based on the 280 stocks that were in the Bloomberg US Internet Index at the time; see David Kleinbard, "The $1.7 Trillion Dot.com Lesson," CNN Money, November 9, 2000.

43. In a speech shortly before the dotcom bubble burst in March 2000, Greenspan argued in a very public forum that the stock market was foreshadowing a new and lasting paradigm of innovation-based prosperity; see Alan Greenspan, "Technology and the Economy," Remarks Before the Economic Club of New York, New York, January 13, 2000.

44. See Robert J. Shiller, *Irrational Exuberance,* 1st ed. (Princeton, NJ: Princeton University Press, 2000).

45. See Ernst Fehr and Simon Gächter, "Fairness and Retaliation: The Economics of Reciprocity," *Journal of Economic Perspectives* 14, no. 3 (Summer 2000).

46. See Laura Silver, Kat Devlin, and Christine Huang, "Large Majorities Say China Does Not Respect the Personal Freedoms of Its People," Pew Research Center Report, June 30, 2021.

Chapter 4. Bilateral Bluster

1. Section 301, an amendment to the US Trade Act of 1974, authorizes the president to take actions against foreign governments accused of unfair discriminatory actions restricting US commerce. It was especially popular during the Reagan administration (1981–88) when forty-nine Section 301 investigations were conducted; prior to the 2018 China investigation, only one new Section 301 investigation had been initiated since 2001. See Chad P. Bown, "Rogue 301: Trump to Dust Off Another Outdated US Trade Law?" *Trade and Investment Policy Watch* (blog), Peterson Institute for International Economics, August 3, 2017.

2. See Office of the US Trade Representative, Executive Office of the President, "Findings of the Investigation into China's Acts, Policies, and Practices Related to Technology Transfer, Intellectual Property, and Innovation Under Section 301 of the Trade Act of 1974," March 22, 2018 (hereafter USTR Section 301 report).

3. George Schultz and Martin Feldstein, two former senior US economic officials, put it best: "If a country consumes more than it produces, it must import more than it exports. That's not a rip-off; that's arithmetic." See George P. Schultz and Martin Feldstein, "Everything You Need to Know about Trade Economics, in 70 Words," *Washington Post*, May 5, 2017. Surprisingly, the current debate over trade policy is largely devoid of references to saving-investment imbalances; for an important exception, see Matthew C. Klein and Michael Pettis, *Trade Wars Are Class Wars* (New Haven, CT: Yale University Press, 2020), especially chapter 3.

4. Source: US Department of Commerce (Bureau of Economic Analysis).

5. On trade diversion, see Pablo Fajgelbaum, Pinelopi K. Goldberg, Patrick J. Kennedy, Amit Khandelwal, and Daria Taglioni, "The US-China Trade War and Global Reallocations," NBER Working Paper No. 29562, December 2021; also note that US trade with Hong Kong largely reflects so-called re-exports of products largely produced and assembled in China. Trade from both destinations is often lumped together as a result.

6. Relative to China, worker compensation in 2020 was considerably more expensive in many of the trade-diversion beneficiaries such as Canada, Taiwan, South Korea, Italy, and France; partially offsetting these costs were considerably cheaper labor compensation rates in Vietnam and, to a much lesser extent, in Mexico. These comparisons are drawn from a cross-country tabulation by WorldData.info of average income per worker based on primary data from the World Bank, the International Monetary Fund, and the OECD and available at https://www.world data.info/average-income.php. The US Bureau of Labor Statistics' program on the international comparison of hourly compensation costs in manufacturing was discontinued in 2011; previously I had used those statistics to estimate that China's manufacturing compensation in 2010 was just 10 percent of the average manufacturing compensation of America's nine next largest trading partners, weighted by their shares of US imports; see Stephen Roach, *Unbalanced: The Co-dependency of America and China* (New Haven, CT: Yale University Press, 2014),

143n31. While that disparity has narrowed over the ensuing twelve years, the basic conclusion endures: trade diversion is shifting US imports away from low-cost Chinese sourcing toward higher-cost foreign producers—the functional equivalent of a tax increase on American companies and consumers.

7. See Congressional Budget Office, "The 2021 Long-Term Budget Outlook," Washington DC, March 4, 2021.

8. The Trump administration economics team apparently had limited impact in framing the China tariff strategy; see, for example, Josh Boak, Jonathan Lemire, and Jill Colvin, "Is Trump's Economic Team Up For a Trade War?" AP News, Associated Press, August 24, 2019; Damian Paletta, "Trump Is Increasingly Relying on Himself—Not His Aides—in Trade War with China," *Washington Post,* August 6, 2019. Kevin Hassett, chairman of Trump's Council of Economic Advisors, appears to have been an exception; see Lizzie O'Leary, "Kevin Hassett Says Trump's Trade War Is Worth the Cost," *The Atlantic,* September 4, 2019.

9. See Henry W. Nichols, "Joint Ventures," *Virginia Law Review* 36, no. 4 (May 1950).

10. Source: National Bureau of Statistics, *China Statistical Yearbook: 2020;* for global JV count, see Refinitiv at https://www.refinitiv.com/en/financial-data/deals-data/joint-venture-deals.

11. This is also at odds with my own experience as an active participant in Morgan Stanley's joint venture with the China Construction Bank (and a few small minority investors) to establish China International Capital Corporation (CICC) in 1995. In joining with partners in creating China's first investment bank, there was a sharing of business practices, proprietary products, and distribution systems. Yet, contrary to the broader assertions of the USTR, Morgan Stanley was hardly forced into these arrangements. It had its own commercial objectives of wanting to build a world-class financial services firm in China. By the time Morgan Stanley sold its stake in 2010, CICC was well on its way to attaining those goals.

12. See USTR Section 301 report, March 2018, 19.

13. See US-China Business Council, "USCBC 2016 Membership Survey: The Business Environment in China," released December 2019.

14. See US-China Business Council, "USCBC 2017 Membership Survey: The Business Environment in China," released December 2018.

15. See Deloitte, "Sino-Foreign Joint Ventures after COVID: What to Expect?" September 2020.

16. See National Bureau of Statistics, *China Statistical Yearbook: 2009 to 2020,* table 11-15.

17. China's new Foreign Investment Law also contained a key provision that explicitly prohibited the forced transfer of foreign technology or disclosure of business secrets; see Nicolas F. Runnels, "Securing Liberalization: China's New Foreign Investment Law," *Journal of International Law and Politics,* December 6, 2020.

18. See Nicholas R. Lardy, "China: Forced Technology Transfer and Theft?" *China Economic Watch* (blog), Peterson Institute for International Economics, April 29, 2018, based on balance-of-payments data from State Administration of Foreign Exchange (China). Global data on 2020 charges for the use of intellectual prop-

erty are from the World Bank and can be found at https://data.worldbank.org/indicator/BM.GSR.ROYL.CD.

19. See Laura Silver, Kat Devlin, and Christine Huang, "Most Americans Support Tough Stance toward China on Human Rights, Economic Issues," Pew Research Center, March 2021.

20. See Sydney J. Freeberg Jr., "Esper Exhorts Allies to Ban Chinese 5G: Britain's Huawei Dilemma," *Breaking Defense*, September 19, 2019.

21. See IP Commission, "The IP Commission Report: The Report of the Commission on the Theft of American Intellectual Property" and "Update to the IP Commission Report," National Bureau of Asian Research, March 2013 and February 2017.

22. See PricewaterhouseCoopers LLP (PwC) and Center for Responsible Enterprise and Trade (CREATE.org), "Economic Impact of Trade Secret Theft: A Framework for Companies to Safeguard Trade Secrets and Mitigate Potential Threats," February 2014.

23. See OECD/EUIPO, *Trade in Counterfeit and Pirated Goods: Mapping the Economic Impact* (Paris: OECD Publishing, 2016).

24. See Business Software Alliance, "Seizing Opportunity through License Compliance: BSA Global Software Survey," May 2016.

25. Source: CNBC interview with Peter Navarro, June 19, 2018; also see White House Office of Trade and Manufacturing Policy, "How China's Economic Aggression Threatens the Technologies and Intellectual Property of the United States and the World," June 2018. For a critique of America's bilateral fixation on China expressed by the since criminally indicted Navarro, see Klein and Pettis, *Trade Wars Are Class Wars*.

26. See USTR Section 301 report, 152.

27. See Dwight D. Eisenhower's Farewell Address to the Nation, "The Military-Industrial Complex," Dwight D. Eisenhower Presidential Library, January 17, 1961; for a comprehensive assessment of America's follow-up industrial policies of the 1970s, see Michael L. Wachter and Susan M. Wachter, eds., *Toward a New US Industrial Policy?* (Philadelphia: University of Pennsylvania Press: 1981).

28. See Aaron Mehta and Joe Gould, "Biden Requests $715B for Pentagon, Hinting at Administration's Future Priorities," *Defense News*, April 9, 2021; and Daniel Cebul, "U.S. Remains Top Military Spender," *Defense News*, May 2, 2018. Funding levels for the Defense Advanced Research Project Agency (DARPA) have remained relatively steady at just under $4 billion in real terms through 2021, holding at a little over 20 percent of the US Defense Department's overall budget for science and technology; see Marcy E. Gallo, "Defense Advanced Research Projects Agency: Overview and Issues for Congress," Congressional Research Service, August 19, 2021.

29. See Department of Defense, "DOD Awards $69.3 Million Contract to CONTINUS Pharmaceuticals to Develop US-Based Continuous Manufacturing Capability for Critical Medicines," press release, January 15, 2021.

30. On June 8, 2021, the Senate passed the $250 billion "US Innovation and Compe-

tition Act" (S.1260), while on February 4, 2022, the House passed the $335 billion "America COMPETES Act of 2022" (H.R. 4521); congressional reconciliation is pending as this book goes to press. Budgetary cost estimates for both pieces of legislation are based on assessments by the Congressional Budget Office, available at https://www.cbo.gov/. Both bills feature $52 billion in targeted support for the US semiconductor industry; see Catie Edmondson, "Democrats Renew Push to Pass Industrial Policy Bill to Counter China," *New York Times,* January 26, 2022. New regulations implementing the Foreign Investment Risk Review Modernization Act of 2018 (FIRRMA) that were aimed at strengthening oversight and jurisdictional reach of CFIUS went into effect in February 2020. For a discussion of recent multilateral US-European industrial policy collaboration see Frances Burwell, "The US-EU Trade and Technology Council: Seven Steps toward Success," Atlantic Council, September 24, 2021.

31. See Chalmers Johnson, *MITI and the Japanese Miracle: The Growth of Industrial Policy, 1925–1975* (Stanford, CA: Stanford University Press, 1982).

32. See Takeshi Yamaguchi and Hiromu Uezato, "Era of New Industrial Policy?" Morgan Stanley MUFG Research Report, June 11, 2021.

33. See Federation of German Industries (BDI), "The Mittelstand: The Heart of the German Economy," available at https://english.bdi.eu/topics/germany/the-mittel stand/; and Asha-Maria Sharma and Claudia Grüne, "Industrie 4.0: From Concept to New Reality," Germany Trade and Investment: Market Report and Outlook, March 2018.

34. See Niles M. Hansen," French Indicative Planning and the New Industrial State," *Journal of Economic Issues* 3, no. 4 (December 1969).

35. See USTR Section 301 report, 65.

36. See American Enterprise Institute and the Heritage Foundation, "Chinese Investment in the US Dataset," available at http://www.aei.org/china-global-investment -tracker/.

37. See Barry Eichengreen, Doughyun Park, and Kwanho Shin, "When Fast Growing Economies Slow Down: International Evidence and Implications for China," NBER Working Paper No. 16919, March 2011; also see Barry Eichengreen, Doughyun Park, and Kwanho Shin, "Growth Slowdowns Redux: New Evidence on the Middle-Income Trap," NBER Working Paper No. 18673, January 2013.

38. The critical linkage between economic growth and indigenous innovation is discussed in Chapter 9; for an assessment of the empirical validity of the middle-income trap, see Lant Pritchett and Lawrence H. Summers, "Asiaphoria Meets Regression to the Mean," NBER Working Paper No. 20573, October 2014.

39. See Fabrizio Zilibotti, "Growing and Slowing Down Like China," *Journal of the European Economic Association* 15, no. 5 (October 2017).

40. A report by Mandiant, a private US cybersecurity company, was apparently highlighted in the Obama-Xi exchange. See Mandiant, "APT 1: Exposing One of China's Cyber Espionage Units," February 2013; also see the discussion in Roach, *Unbalanced,* 157–60.

41. See US Department of Justice, "U.S. Charges Five Chinese Military Hackers for Cyber Espionage against U.S. Corporations and a Labor Organization for Commercial Advantage," press release, May 19, 2014; see Office of the White House Press Secretary, "Remarks by President Obama and President Xi in Joint Press Conference," Washington DC, September 25, 2015.

42. The USTR Section 301 report conceded that there had been an apparent decline in Chinese cyberattacks since the 2015 US-China cyber accord; see USTR Section 301 report, 170. Moreover, in the two years following the accord, China fell to #6 in the cyber-attack global rankings by late 2017, while the United States rose to #1; see Akamai, "[State of the Internet]/Security: Q2 2017 Report," August 22, 2017. More recent research cited by *The Economist,* based on a CSIS tabulation of 160 publicly reported cases of Chinese cyber espionage over the 2000 to 2020 period, suggests that the incidence of such activity was considerably higher in the second of these two decades; however, in light of the sharply increased scale of the Internet in the second of these two decades, that is hardly a shocking revelation. See "After Failing to Dissuade Cyber-Attacks, America Looks to Its Friends for Help," *The Economist,* July 24, 2021; and Center for Strategic and International Studies (CSIS), "Survey of Chinese Espionage in the United States since 2000," available at https://www.csis.org/programs/technology-policy-program/survey-chinese-linked-espionage-united-states-2000.

43. See Mandiant, "APT1," 24.

44. For example, the Mandiant report singles out Chinese cyberhacking of the US transportation industry as an area of strategic importance in China when, in fact, the actual SEI designation in Chinese planning documents refers to electric motor vehicles; this broad overlap makes it very difficult, if not impossible, to assess the validity of the threat. See Roach, *Unbalanced,* 294n43.

45. In January 2022, China's State Council released a "Digital Plan" as part of its broader Fourteenth Five-Year Plan for the nation as a whole; the digital plan called for an increase in "core digital industries" from 7.8 percent of GDP in 2020 to 10 percent of GDP by 2025. This is a narrow estimate of digital ICT activity that only includes telecommunications, Internet, IT services, hardware, and software industries; the broader measure cited in the text includes the narrow concept plus an estimate of "parts of traditional sectors that have been integrated with digital technology." See Longmei Zhang and Sally Chen, "China's Digital Economy: Opportunities and Risks," IMF Working Paper, WP/19/16, January 2019. Also see "The State Council Issued the 14th Five-Year Plan for the Development of Digital Economy," Xinhuanet, January 12, 2022; and "China's Cabinet Says It Will Promote Transformation of Digital Economy," Reuters, January 12, 2022.

46. See William Cline, Kyoji Fukao, Tokuo Iwaisako, Kenneth N. Kuttner, Adam S. Posen, and Jeffrey J. Schott, "Lessons from Decades Lost: Economic Challenges and Opportunities Facing Japan and the United States," Peterson Institute for International Economics, PIIE Briefing 14-4, December 2014.

47. See Stephen Roach, "Is China the Next Japan?" *Project Syndicate,* June 27, 2016.

48. Source: US Department of Commerce (Bureau of Economic Analysis).

49. Source: US Department of Commerce (Bureau of Economic Analysis).

50. Unlike the Section 301 report on China that was requested by President Trump, conforming with the intent of the Trade Act of 1974, the Section 301 actions against Japan in the 1980s were largely self-initiated by an aggressive USTR and its deputy representative, Robert Lighthizer; see Douglas A. Irwin, "The U.S.-Japan Semiconductor Trade Conflict," chapter 1 in Anne O. Krueger, ed., *The Political Economy of Trade Protection* (Chicago: University of Chicago Press, January 1996).

51. As noted in Chapter 2, this comparison is distorted by global supply chains, which basically didn't exist in the 1980s. That means the made-in-China portion of today's US trade deficit is a good deal smaller than the comparable made-in-Japan share of the 1980s; see OECD, "Trade in Value Added," https://www.oecd.org/sti/ind/measuring-trade-in-value-added.htm.

52. See Jacob M. Schlesinger, "Trump Forged His Ideas on Trade in the 1980s and Never Deviated," *Wall Street Journal*, November 15, 2018.

53. See, for example, Paul A. Samuelson, "Evaluating Reaganomics," *Challenge* 30, no. 6 (1987); Paul Krugman, "Debunking the Reagan Myth," *New York Times*, January 21, 2008; and James Surowiecki, "Tax Evasion: The Great Lie of Supply-Side Economics," *New Yorker*, October 22, 2007. For a confession by a former leading supply-sider, see Bruce Bartlett, *The New American Economy: The Failure of Reaganomics and a New Way Forward* (New York: St. Martin's Press, 2009); also see Martin Feldstein, "Supply Side Economics: Old Truths and New Claims," NBER Working Paper No. 1792, January 1986.

54. During the 1980 US presidential primary campaign, candidate George H. W. Bush referred to the aggressive tax-cut proposals of Ronald Reagan as "voodoo economics"; after he became Reagan's vice president, he back-pedaled on that accusation. See Helen Thomas, "Vice President George Bush Was Only 'Kidding' Reporters When . . ." UPI Archives, February 19, 1982. A similar criticism has been made with respect to recent claims of Modern Monetary Theory; see Kenneth Rogoff, "Modern Monetary Nonsense," *Project Syndicate*, March 4, 2019.

55. In 2021, US federal government revenue was 16 percent of GDP, well below the 17.3 percent average of the preceding fifty years (1971 to 2020); see Congressional Budget Office, "The 2021 Long-Term Budget Outlook," March 4, 2021; and CBO Historical Budget Data, February 2021, available at https://www.cbo.gov/data/budget-economic-data#2.

56. See Stephen Roach, "Japan Then, China Now," *Project Syndicate*, May 27, 2019.

Chapter 5. Huawei as a Trojan Horse

1. See Ondrej Burkacky, Stephanie Lingemann, Markus Simon, and Alexander Hoffmann, "The 5G Era: New Horizons for Advanced Electronics and Industrial Companies," McKinsey & Company, January 2020.

2. See Sherisse Pham, "Who Is Huawei Founder Ren Zhengfei?" CNN Business, March 14, 2019.

3. The brainwashing and subsequent re-programming of the "sleeper agent" by Soviet and Chinese communist military scientists was popularized in the Cold War movie thriller *The Manchurian Candidate,* released in 1962 and remade in 2004.

4. See, for example, Sun Tzu, *The Art of War,* trans. Gary Gagliardi (Seattle, WA: Science of Strategy Institute/Clearbridge Publishing, 1999); Carl von Clausewitz, *On War,* rev. ed. (1832; Princeton, NJ: Princeton University Press, 1989); and Niall Ferguson, *The Pity of War: Explaining World War I* (New York: Basic Books, 2008).

5. The Global Innovations Index (GII) is assembled by researchers from Cornell and INSEAD Universities, in conjunction with the World Intellectual Property Organization (WIPO). For the most recent release, see Cornell University, INSEAD, and WIPO, *The Global Innovation Index 2021: Tracking Innovation through the COVID-19 Crisis* (Ithaca, Fontainebleau, and Geneva, 2021).

6. The GII has been ranking the innovative prowess of countries around the world since 2007. The 2021 index is based on rankings of 132 countries that collectively account for 93.5 percent of the world's population and 97 percent of world GDP (measured in purchasing-power parity); the GII is derived from detailed country-by-country rankings of eighty-one individual metrics of innovative prowess.

7. See Cornell, INSEAD, and WIPO, *The Global Innovation Index 2021,* appendix 1.

8. See Brian Christian, *The Alignment Problem: Machine Learning and Human Values* (New York: W. W. Norton & Company, 2020).

9. See Kai-Fu Lee, *AI Super-Powers: China, Silicon Valley, and the New World Order* (Boston: Houghton Mifflin Harcourt, 2018).

10. See Daitian Li, Tony W. Tong, and Yangao Xiao, "Is China Emerging as the Global Leader in AI?" *Harvard Business Review,* February 2021.

11. See Josh Chin and Liza Lin, *Surveillance State: Inside China's Quest to Launch a New Era of Social Control* (New York: St. Martin's Press, September 2022). In early 2021, China had an estimated 989 million Internet users, fully 68 percent of its population of 1.4 billion; this is nearly equal to the combined population of Internet users in Europe (737 million) and the United States (297 million), which amounts to about 88 percent of their respective populations. Source: Internet World Stats, available at https://www.internetworldstats.com/stats.htm.

12. See Stephen S. Roach, "In Search of Productivity," *Harvard Business Review,* September–October 1998.

13. See Stephen S. Roach, "China's Animal Spirits Deficit," *Project Syndicate,* July 27, 2021.

14. See Lindsay Gorman, "China's Data Ambitions: Strategy, Emerging Technologies, and Implications for Democracies," National Bureau of Asian Research, August 14, 2021.

15. See Matt Pottinger and David Feith, "The Most Powerful Data Broker in the World is Winning the War against the U.S.," *New York Times,* November 30, 2021.

16. See "Full Text of Xi Jinping's Report at the 19th CCP Congress," Xinhua News Service (China), October 2017.

17. See "Xi Jinping Chairs Collective Study Session of Politburo on National Big Data Strategy," Xinhua News Service (China), December 9, 2017; and "Xi Stresses Sound Development of Digital Economy," Xinhua News Service (China), October 19, 2021.

18. See China Institute for Science and Technology Policy, *China AI Development Report: 2018*, Tsinghua University, Beijing, July 2018.

19. See Derek Grossman, Christian Curriden, Logan Ma, Lindsey Polley, J. D. Williams, and Cortez Cooper III, "Chinese Views of Big Data Analytics," RAND Corporation, Santa Monica, CA, 2020.

20. See Louise Lucas and Richard Waters, "China and US Compete to Dominate Big Data," The Big Read, *Financial Times*, May 1, 2018; US Senate, "The New Big Brother: China and Digital Authoritarianism," A Democratic Staff Report Prepared for the Use of the Committee on Foreign Relations, July 21, 2020; and Joe Devanesan, "China and the US Are Now in a Battle over Big Data," TECHWIRE Asia, September 11, 2020.

21. See Graham Allison and Eric Schmidt, "Is China Beating the U.S. to AI Supremacy?" *National Interest,* December 2019.

22. Shoshana Zuboff, *The Age of Surveillance Capitalism: The Fight for a Human Future at the New Frontier of Power* (New York: Public Affairs, 2019).

23. See Ryan C. LaBrie, Gerhard H. Steinke, Xiangmin Li, and Joseph A. Cazier, "Big Data Analytics Sentiment: US-China Reaction to Data Collection by Business and Government," *Technological Forecasting and Social Change* 130 (May 2018).

24. The National Security Commission on Artificial Intelligence was an independent commission established by the US Congress in 2018, consisting of fifteen commissioners, twelve of whom were appointed by the US Congress, two by the US Department of Defense, and one by the US Secretary of Commerce. The purpose of the commission was to provide a comprehensive assessment of AI-related national security and defense needs and to draw policy conclusions for the president and congress. After issuing a 756-page final report in March 2021, the commission was disbanded in October 2021. See National Security Commission on Artificial Intelligence, *Final Report,* March 2021, available at https://www.nscai.gov/; also see Allison and Schmidt, "Is China Beating the U.S. to AI Supremacy?"

25. See Christian, *The Alignment Problem;* also see Henry A. Kissinger, Eric Schmidt, and Daniel Huttenlocher, *The Age of AI and Our Human Future* (New York: Little, Brown and Company, 2021).

26. The economist Robert Gordon has famously suggested that the great wave of innovation was a one-off development that will be exceedingly difficult to replicate in the future. The Gordon view is that scientific breakthroughs today don't compare to the seismic changes of that "special century" of innovation from 1870 to 1970: increased speed of travel (from horses to jet planes), stabilizing interior temperatures at 72 degrees, urbanization, the elimination of manual labor, and

the increased participation of women in the workforce. See Robert J. Gordon, *The Rise and Fall of American Growth: The U.S. Living Standard Since the Civil War* (Princeton, NJ: Princeton University Press, 2016).

27. Source: National Science Board, *Science & Engineering Indicators 2020: The State of U.S. Science and Engineering* (Alexandria, VA: National Science Foundation, January 2020).

28. National Science Board, *Science & Engineering Indicators 2020*.

29. Perhaps the most worrisome aspect of the US-China R&D race can be found in the funding for experimental development—projects earmarked toward applications of research and practical experience aimed at producing new products or improving existing ones; in 2014, China surpassed the United States in spending on experimental R&D and by 2017 was spending 23 percent more than the United States on this key category. Source: National Science Board, *Science & Engineering Indicators 2020*.

30. Over the 2010 to 2017 period, China's R&D expenditures rose by an average of 9.2 percent per year, more than double the 3.8 percent pace of the United States over the same period; if China is able to maintain that growth differential, convergence of R&D shares of the two nations could occur as soon as 2023. Source: Author's calculations based on National Science Board, *Science & Engineering Indicators 2020*.

31. See National Development and Reform Commission, *Report on the Implementation of the 2020 Plan for National Economic and Social Development and on the 2021 Draft Plan for National Economic and Social Development*, delivered at the Fourth Session of the Thirteenth National People's Congress, March 5, 2021.

32. See "China's Basic Research Spending Rises to 6.09% of Entire R&D Expenditure in 2021, a Step Closer to 2025 Goal of 8%," *Global Times* (China), February 25, 2022.

33. Source: National Science Board, *Science & Engineering Indicators 2020*.

34. See Chad P. Bown, "The US-China Trade War and Phase One Agreement," Peterson Institute for International Economics, Working Paper 21–2, February 2021.

35. See Jeremy Ney, "United States Entity List: Limits on American Exports," Belfer Center, Harvard Kennedy School, February 2021.

36. See William A. Carter, "Understanding the Entities Listing in the Context of U.S.-China AI Competition," Center for Strategy and International Studies (CSIS), October 2019.

37. See Ian F. Ferguson and Karen M. Sutter, "U.S. Export Control Reforms and China: Issues for Congress," Congressional Research Service, January 2021.

38. See Faezeh Raei, Anna Ignatenko, and Borislava Mircheva, "Global Value Chains: What Are the Benefits and Why Do Countries Participate?" IMF Working Paper 19/18, January 2019.

39. Source: World Bank Development Indicators and International Monetary Fund *World Economic Outlook* database.

40. See Henry Farrell and Abraham L. Newman, "Weaponized Interdependence: How

Global Economic Networks Shape State Coercion," *International Security* 44, no. 1 (Summer 2019); and Henry Farrell and Abraham L. Newman, "Will the Coronavirus End Globalization as We Know It?" *Foreign Affairs*, March 16, 2020.

41. See Raphael Auer, Claudio Borio, and Andrew Filardo, "The Globalization of Inflation: The Growing Importance of Global Value Chains," Bank for International Settlements, BIS Working Paper No. 602, January 2017.

42. The weaponization of global networks as posited by Professors Farrell and Newman has taken on real-time significance in recent years. On supply-chain liberation and reshoring, see Michael Greenwald, "Achieving Supply Chain Independence in a Post-COVID Economy," *New Atlanticist* (blog), Atlantic Council, May 7, 2020. On alliance-building efforts of "friend shoring" in the Russo-Ukrainian War, see "Remarks by Secretary of the Treasury Janet L. Yellen on Way Forward for the Global Economy," speech before the Atlantic Council, April 13, 2022.

43. Tamim Bayoumi, Jelle Barkema, and Diego A. Cedeiro, "The Inflexible Structure of Global Supply Chains," IMF Working Paper 119/193, September 2019.

44. See Elizabeth Lopatto, "Tim Cook's Trick for Making iPhones Is Now at Risk from the Pandemic: The Perils of Just-In-Time Manufacturing," *The Verge*, March 13, 2020.

45. See Stephen Roach, "A Return to 1970s Stagflation Is Only a Broken Supply Chain Away," *Financial Times*, May 6, 2020; and Stephen Roach, "The Sequencing Trap that Risks Stagflation 2.0," *Financial Times*, October 13, 2021.

46. See Ha-Joon Chang, *Bad Samaritans: Rich Nations, Poor Policies, and the Threat to the Developing World* (London: Random House, 2007).

47. The epic Latin poem *The Aeneid*, written by Virgil between 29 and 19 BC, contains the most detailed description of the Trojan Horse; see Virgil, *The Aeneid*, trans. Robert Fagles (New York: Viking Penguin, 2006).

48. See Homer, *The Odyssey*, trans. Robert Fagles (New York: Viking Penguin, 1996).

49. This account can be found in Euripides's ancient Greek tragedy *The Trojan Woman*, trans. James Morwood, Oxford World Classics (Oxford: Oxford University Press, 2000).

50. See Jeffrey D. Sachs, "The War on Huawei," *Project Syndicate*, December 11, 2018.

51. See US Department of Justice, "Huawei CFO Wanzhou Meng Admits to Misleading Global Financial Institution: Meng Enters into Deferred Prosecution Agreement to Resolve Fraud Charges," press release, September 24, 2021.

52. For discussion of a hidden Telnet daemon program, see Daniele Lepido, "Vodafone Found Hidden Backdoors in Huawei Equipment," *Bloomberg*, April 30, 2019; for discussion of a rumored second backdoor in 2012, see Jordan Robertson and Jamie Tarabay, "Chinese Spies Accused of Using Huawei in Secret Australian Telecom Hack," *Bloomberg*, December 16, 2021.

53. See William Lazonick and Edward March, "The Rise and Demise of Lucent Technologies," paper originally presented to the Conference on Innovation and Competition in the Global Communications Technology Industry, INSEAD, Fontainebleau, France, August 23–24, 2007.

54. See Thomas Donahue, "The Worst Possible Day: U.S. Telecommunications and Huawei," *Prism* (National Defense University Press) 8, no. 3 (January 2020).

55. See Chuin-Wei Yap, "State Support Helped Fuel Huawei's Global Rise," *Wall Street Journal*, December 25, 2019.

56. According to Huawei's 2021 annual report, 107,000 employees (or 54.8% of its total workforce of 195,000) worked in the R&D function where spending totaled CNY 142.7 billion in 2021 (or USD 22.4 billion); see Huawei Investment & Holding Co., Ltd., *2021 Annual Report*, March 28, 2022. For comparative metrics on R&D spending of Huawei competitors, see "Respecting and Protecting Intellectual Property: The Foundation of Innovation," Huawei White Paper on Innovation and Intellectual Property (2020); and Justin Fox, "Amazon Spends Billions on R&D. Just Don't Call It That," *Bloomberg*, February 11, 2021.

57. See Lindsay Maizland and Andrew Chatzky, "Huawei: China's Controversial Tech Giant," Council of Foreign Relations Backgrounder, New York, August 2020.

58. See Chuin-Wei Yap and Dan Strumpf, "Huawei's Yearslong Rise Is Littered with Accusations of Theft and Dubious Ethics," *Wall Street Journal*, May 25, 2019.

59. See Zhou Hanhua, "Law Expert: Chinese Government Can't Force Huawei to Make Backdoors," *Wired*, March 4, 2019. The UK National Security Adviser has also found no evidence of Chinese state interference in Huawei cyber security; see Huawei Cyber Security Evaluation Centre Oversight Board, *Annual Report 2020*.

60. See Christopher Blading and Donald Clarke, "Who Owns Huawei?" *ChinaFile*, April 2019.

61. Market Intelligence & Consulting Institute (Taiwan), "Huawei's Supply Chain and Its Future Prospects Amid the US-China Trade War," June 2020.

62. Huawei's 2021 revenues of 636,807 (CNY millions) were down 28.6 percent from record revenues of 891,368 hit in 2020; see Huawei, *2021 Annual Report*.

Chapter 6. Winning Cold Wars

1. See Robert Hunt Sprinkle, "Two Cold Wars and Why They Ended Differently," *Review of International Studies* 25, no. 4 (October 1999); Walter LaFeber, "An End to Which Cold War?" *Diplomatic History* 16, no. 1 (January 1992); and Volker R. Berghahn, *America and the Intellectual Cold Wars in Europe* (Princeton, NJ: Princeton University Press, 2002).

2. These are purchasing-power parity comparisons complied by Angus Maddison; source: Maddison Project, "Maddison Historical Statistics," Groningen Growth and Development Centre, University of Groningen, Netherlands, https://www.rug .nl/ggdc/historicaldevelopment/maddison/. Many have argued that these estimates, and those of America's Central Intelligence Agency, seriously overstated the size of the Soviet economy. See, for example, Daniel Patrick Moynihan, "The Soviet Economy: Boy, Were We Wrong!" *Washington Post*, July 11, 1990; and Marc Trachtenberg, "Assessing Soviet Economic Performance During the Cold War: A

Failure of Intelligence?" *Texas National Security Review* 1, no. 2 (February 2018). For an even deeper critique, see Luis R. Martinez, "How Much Should We Trust the Dictator's GDP Growth Estimates?" Becker Friedman Institute, University of Chicago, Working Paper No. 2021-78, July 2021.

3. The IMF estimates that Chinese GDP as calculated on a purchasing-power parity (PPP) basis exceeded that of the United States in 2016; source: International Monetary Fund, *World Economic Outlook* database.

4. A historian's perspective of this comparison between two cold wars can be found in Melvyn P. Leffler, "China Isn't the Soviet Union. Confusing the Two Is Dangerous," *The Atlantic,* December 2, 2019.

5. See Graham Allison, *Destined for War: Can America and China Escape Thucydides's Trap?* (New York: Mariner Books, 2017).

6. Kissinger made this statement at Bloomberg's New Economy Forum in Beijing in November 2019; see "Kissinger Says U.S. and China in 'Foothills of a Cold War,'" *Bloomberg News,* November 21, 2019.

7. See Herman Kahn, *Thinking About the Unthinkable* (New York: Horizon Press, 1962).

8. See George F. Kennan, "The Long Telegram," Truman Library Institute, February 22, 1946.

9. While Kennan notes an eight-thousand-word length for the Long Telegram in his memoirs, historian John Lewis Gaddis points out that the actual word count was "just over five thousand." See John Lewis Gaddis, *George F. Kennan: An American Life* (New York: Penguin Press, 2011).

10. See Kennan, "The Long Telegram."

11. See Kennan, "The Long Telegram."

12. See Gaddis, *George F. Kennan.*

13. See "X" (aka George F. Kennan), "The Sources of Soviet Conduct," *Foreign Affairs,* July 1947; and Anonymous, "The Longer Telegram: Toward a New American China Strategy," Atlantic Center, Scowcroft Center for Strategy and Security, January 2021.

14. The Longer Telegram has a word count (excluding footnotes) of 30,824, or about six times the five thousand words of Kennan's original telegram, as per Gaddis, *George F. Kennan.*

15. See Minxin Pei, *China's Trapped Transition: The Limits of Developmental Autocracy* (Cambridge, MA: Harvard University Press, 2006).

16. The "common prosperity campaign" that received great attention in the summer of 2021 postdates the January 2021 publication of the Longer Telegram. As noted previously in Chapter 3, and as will be discussed further in Chapter 12, this campaign is not new; a direct antecedent can be found in similar views on the sequencing of economic development espoused by Deng Xiaoping in the mid-1980s.

17. See Damon Wilson, "President George H.W. Bush Had 'The Vision Thing' in Spades," Atlantic Council, December 3, 2018.

18. See Anonymous, "The Longer Telegram."

19. See, for example, Odd Arne Westad, *The Global Cold War: Third World Interventions and the Making of Our Times* (London: Cambridge University Press, 2005); John Lewis Gaddis, *The Cold War: A New History* (New York: Penguin Books, 2005); and Odd Arne Westad, *The Cold War: A World History* (New York: Basic Books, 2017).

20. See Gaddis, *The Cold War,* chapter 1.

21. Source: Maddison Project, "Maddison Historical Statistics."

22. Source: US Department of Commerce (Bureau of Economic Analysis).

23. See Paul Kennedy, *The Rise and Fall of the Great Powers: Economic Change and Military Conflict from 1500 to 2000* (New York: Random House, 1987).

24. See Robert M. Solow, "A Contribution to the Theory of Economic Growth," *Quarterly Journal of Economics* 70, no. 1 (February 1956); and Edward C. Prescott, "Robert M. Solow's Neoclassical Growth Model: An Influential Contribution to Economics," *Scandinavian Journal of Economics* 90, no. 1 (March 1988).

25. Source: US Bureau of Labor Statistics.

26. See "Kissinger Says U.S. and China in 'Foothills of a Cold War.'"

27. See, for example, Thomas J. Christensen, "There Will Not Be a New Cold War: The Limits of U.S.-Chinese Competition," *Foreign Affairs,* March 21, 2021; Ian Bremmer, "No, the U.S. and China are Not Heading towards a New Cold War," *Time,* December 28, 2020; Hunter Marston, "The US-China Cold War Is a Myth," *Foreign Policy,* September 6, 2017; and Paul Gewirtz, "Can the US-China Crisis Be Stabilized?" *Order from Chaos* (blog), Brookings Institution, June 26, 2019.

28. Ten-year growth rates in labor productivity averaged just 1.17 percent over the three-year 2019–21 interval, the worst performance since the 1.14 percent average gains over the stagflationary decade of 1973–82. Source: US Bureau of Labor Statistics.

29. See "Foreign News: We Will Bury You!" *Time,* November 25, 1956.

30. See Clyde Haberman, "'This Is Not a Drill': The Threat of Nuclear Annihilation," *New York Times,* May 13, 2018.

31. See "Text of Mao's Statement Urging World Revolution against U.S.," *New York Times,* May 21, 1970.

32. See Robert O'Brien, "The Chinese Communist Party's Ideology and Global Ambitions," speech delivered in Phoenix, Arizona, June 24, 2020, available at https://china.usc.edu/robert-o%E2%80%99brien-chinese-communist-party%E2%80%99s-ideology-and-global-ambitions-june-24-2020; Christopher Wray, "The Threat Posed by the Chinese Government and the Chinese Communist Party to the Economic and National Security of the United States," speech delivered to the Hudson Institute, Washington DC, July 7, 2020, available at https://www.fbi.gov/news/speeches/the-threat-posed-by-the-chinese-government-and-the-chinese-communist-party-to-the-economic-and-national-security-of-the-united-states; William P. Barr, "Remarks on China Policy," speech delivered at the Gerald R. Ford Presidential Museum, Grand Rapids, Michigan, July 16, 2020, available at https://www.justice.gov/opa/speech/attorney-general-william-p-barr-delivers-remarks-china-policy-gerald-r-ford-presidential; and Mike Pompeo, "Communist

China and the Free World's Future," speech delivered at the Nixon Library, Yorba Linda, California, July 24, 2020, available at https://www.rev.com/blog/transcripts /mike-pompeo-china-speech-transcript-july-23-at-nixon-library.

33. See Stephen Roach, "America's Gang of Four Has Spoken, But It Doesn't Understand US-China Reality," CNN Opinion, August 4, 2020.

34. See G. J. Meyer, *A World Undone: The Story of the Great War, 1914 to 1918* (New York: Random House, 2006); and Christopher Clark, *The Sleepwalkers: How Europe Went to War in 1914* (New York: HarperCollins, 2012).

35. See Allison, *Destined for War.*

36. See, for example, the latest best-selling thriller: Elliot Ackerman and Admiral James Stavridis, *2034: A Novel of the Next World War* (New York: Penguin Press, 2021).

37. See Joel Wuthnow and Phillip C. Saunders, *Chinese Military Reforms in the Age of Xi Jinping: Drivers, Challenges, and Implications,* Center for the Study of Chinese Military Affairs, National Defense University (Washington DC: National Defense University Press, March 2017).

38. See Office of the Secretary of Defense, *Military and Security Developments Involving the People's Republic of China: 2020,* Annual Report to Congress, Washington DC, September 2020.

39. See Shannon Bugos and Julia Masterson, "New Chinese Missile Silo Fields Discovered," *Arms Control Today,* Arms Control Association, September 2021.

40. See Demetri Sevastopulo and Kathrin Hille, "China Tests New Space Capability with Hypersonic Missile," *Financial Times,* October 16, 2021.

41. See Peter Martin, "U.S. General Likens China's Hypersonic Test to a 'Sputnik Moment,'" *Bloomberg,* October 27, 2021. However, it remains to be seen if this is, indeed, a threat on the order of magnitude that General Milley has suggested; see Fareed Zakaria, "It's Not a 'Sputnik Moment' and We Should Not Feed Cold War Paranoia," *Washington Post,* October 38, 2021. For its part, China has denied the report that it was testing a new missile technology; see Yew Lun Tian, "China Denies Report of Hypersonic Missile Test, Says Tested Space Vehicle," Reuters, October 18, 2021.

42. See, for example, Geir Lundestad, "'Imperial Overstretch,' Mikhail Gorbachev, and the End of the Cold War," *Cold War History* 1, no. 1 (2000); Joseph S. Nye, "The Dialectics of Rise and Decline: Russia in Global Affairs Since the End of the Cold War," *Russia in Global Affairs,* October/November 2011; and Fred Weir, "Specter of New Arms Race Has Russia Recalling Soviets' Fate," *Christian Science Monitor,* February 27, 2019.

43. See Paul Kennedy, "Whether China's Rise Means America's Fall," *The Economist,* September 1, 2021.

44. Curiously, and at odds with long-standing diplomatic protocol, as of this writing, the Chinese government has yet to release an English-language version of this agreement. The only such version available is that issued by the Russian government; see President of Russia, "Joint Statement of the Russian Federation and

the People's Republic of China on the International Relations Entering a New Era and the Global Sustainable Development," February 4, 2022, available at http://en.kremlin.ru/supplement/5770.

45. See Ken Moritsugu, "China Calls Russia Its Chief 'Strategic Partner' Despite War," AP News, March 7, 2022.

46. See Henry Kissinger, *On China* (New York: Penguin Books, 2011).

47. Putin's remarks were made on April 25, 2005, in an address to the Federal Assembly of the Russian Federation; see Andrew Kuchins, "Europe's Last Geopolitician?" *Profil*, Carnegie Endowment for International Peace, May 9, 2005.

48. See Sergey Radchenko, "Sergey Radchenko, an Expert on Russia's Foreign Relations, Writes on Its Evolving Friendship with China," *The Economist*, February 15, 2022.

49. See Ministry of Foreign Affairs of the People's Republic of China, "Treaty of Good-Neighborliness and Friendly Cooperation between the People's Republic of China and the Russian Federation," July 24, 2001, available at https://www.fmprc.gov.cn/mfa_eng/wjdt_665385/2649_665393/200107/t20010724_679026.html.

50. See Alison Smale and Michael D. Shear, "Russia Is Ousted from Group of 8 by U.S. and Allies," *New York Times*, March 24, 2014.

51. See Wen Jiabao, "Carrying Forward the Five Principles of Peaceful Coexistence in the Promotion of Peace and Development," Speech by the Premier of China at Rally Commemorating the Fiftieth Anniversary of the Five Principles of Peaceful Coexistence, June 28, 2004, available at https://www.mfa.gov.cn/ce/cetur/eng/xwdt/t140777.htm.

52. See Stephen Roach, "Only China Can Stop Russia," *Project Syndicate*, March 7, 2022.

53. See A. A. Smith, *Revolution and the People in Russia and China* (Cambridge: Cambridge University Press, 2021); Andrew Radin et al., *China-Russia Cooperation: Determining Factors, Future Trajectories, Implications for the United States* (Santa Monica, CA: RAND Corporation, 2021); and Michael M. Walker, *The 1929 Sino-Soviet War: The War Nobody Knew* (Lawrence, KS: University Press of Kansas, 2017).

54. See Sun Tzu, *The Art of War*, trans. Gary Gagliardi (Seattle, WA: Science of Strategy Institute/Clearbridge Publishing, 1999).

55. See Stephanie Segal, Matthew Reynolds, and Brooke Roberts, "Degrees of Separation: A Targeted Approach to U.S.-China Decoupling," A Report of the CSIS Economics Program, October 2021.

56. Source: US Department of Commerce (Bureau of Economic Analysis).

57. China and Japan have swapped places repeatedly over the past decade as the first or second largest foreign holder of US Treasury debt. Source: US Department of the Treasury (Treasury International Capital [TIC] System).

58. Source: US Department of State (Bureau of Consular Affairs), "Report of the Visa Office 2020," available at https://travel.state.gov/content/travel/en/legal/visa-law0/visa-statistics/annual-reports/report-of-the-visa-office-2020.html.

59. Source: International Student Enrollment Statistics, https://educationdata.org/international-student-enrollment-statistics.

60. See Eleanor Albert, "Will Easing of Student Visa Restrictions Rekindle China-US Exchanges?" *The Diplomat,* May 5, 2021.

61. See Daniel H. Rosen and Lauren Gloudeman, "Understanding US-China Decoupling: Macro Trends and Industry Impacts," Report of the Rhodium Group and US Chamber of Commerce China Center, February 2021.

62. Source: World Bank Development Indicators.

63. See Richard Baldwin, *The Great Convergence: Information Technology and the New Globalization* (Cambridge, MA: Harvard University Press, 2016).

64. See Stephen S. Roach, "The Myth of Global Decoupling," *Project Syndicate,* January 3, 2020.

65. See World Bank and World Trade Organization, *Global Value Chain Development Report 2019: Innovation, Supply Chain Trade, and Workers in a Globalized World* (Washington DC: World Bank, 2019).

66. See David Autor, David Dorn, and Gordon Hanson, "On the Persistence of the China Shock," *Brookings Papers on Economic Activity* 2021, no. 2 (2021).

67. See Roach, "The Myth of Global Decoupling."

68. Source: International Monetary Fund, *World Economic Outlook* database.

69. See M. Ayhan Kose and Marco E. Terrones, *Collapse and Revival: Understanding Global Recessions and Recoveries,* International Monetary Fund, Washington DC, December 2015.

70. The Covid shock of 2020 was the closest exception to the general rule that global recessions usually spare a significant number of countries from outright contraction; according to the World Bank, per capita output contracted for fully 93 percent of the world's economies in 2020, higher than the previous record of 84 percent in 1931 during the Great Depression and the highest incidence of contraction since records were established in 1870; over the five preceding global recessions—1958, 1975, 1982, 1991, and 2009—an average of 46 percent of the economies experienced outright contractions in per capita output. See World Bank, *Global Economic Prospects,* June 2020.

Chapter 7. From Trump to Biden—The Plot Thickens

1. See Glenn Kessler, "Trump's False or Misleading Claims Total 30,573 over 4 Years," *Washington Post,* January 24, 2021.

2. Source: FiveThirtyEight, https://projects.fivethirtyeight.com/trump-approval-ratings/; Laura Silver, Kat Devlin, and Christine Huang, "Most Americans Support Tough Stance toward China on Human Rights, Economic Issues," Pew Research Center, March 2021.

3. See Nancy Bernkopf Tucker, "Strategic Ambiguity or Strategic Clarity?" in *Dangerous Strait,* ed. Nancy Bernkopf Tucker (New York: Columbia University Press, 2005), especially 186–212.

4. While Donald Trump stressed "America First" in his inaugural speech in January 2017, the term long predates his tenure in office, with a most unfortunate anti-Semitic antecedent in the early 1940s as the United States was inching into war. See Donald Trump, "The Inauguration Speech," full text as published in *Politico*, January 20, 2017; and Krishnadev Calamur, "A Short History of 'America First,'" *The Atlantic*, January 21, 2017. Also see Richard Haass, "The Age of America First: Washington's Flawed New Foreign Policy Consensus," *Foreign Affairs*, November/December 2021.

5. For the US case of strategic naïveté with respect to China, see Kurt M. Campbell and Ely Ratner, "The China Reckoning: How Beijing Defied American Expectations," *Foreign Affairs*, March/April 2018; for a comparable argument regarding the equally naïve US and European approach to Russia, see Michael R. Gordon, Bojan Pancevski, Noemie Bisserbe, and Marcus Walker, "Vladimir Putin's 20-Year March to War in Ukraine—and How the West Mishandled It," *Wall Street Journal*, April 1, 2022.

6. See Donald J. Trump with Tony Schwartz, *Trump: The Art of the Deal* (New York: Ballantine Books, 1987).

7. Office of the US Trade Representative, Executive Office of the President, "Economic and Trade Agreement between the Government of the United States and the Government of the People's Republic of China," January 15, 2020, available at https://ustr.gov/about-us/policy-offices/press-office/press-releases/2020/january/economic-and-trade-agreement-between-government-united-states-and-government-peoples-republic-china.

8. Source: US Department of Commerce (Bureau of Economic Analysis).

9. See Robert E. Lighthizer, "The President's 2020 Trade Policy Agenda," Testimony Before the House Committee on Ways and Means, June 17, 2020.

10. See Chad P. Bown, "Anatomy of a Flop: Why Trump's US-China Phase One Trade Deal Fell Short," Peterson Institute for International Economics, *Trade and Investment Policy Watch* (blog), February 8, 2021.

11. See Chad P. Bown, "US-China Phase One Tracker: China's Purchases of US Goods," Peterson Institute for International Economics, November 24, 2021.

12. See Jim Tankersley and Mark Landler, "Trump's Love for Tariffs Began in Japan's '80s Boom," *New York Times*, May 15, 2019.

13. Source: US Department of Commerce (Bureau of Economic Analysis).

14. Trump repeatedly made the fallacious claim that China was paying the United States "billions and billions of dollars in tariffs" beginning in 2018 and continuing through 2020; see, for example, his US presidential debate with Joe Biden, October 22, 2020. The validity of this claim was drawn into sharp question and soundly disproved by academic research. See, for example, Mary Amiti, Stephen J. Redding, and David Weinstein, "The Impact of the 2018 Trade War on US Prices and Welfare," NBER Working Paper No. 25672, March 2019; Pablo D. Fajgelbaum, Pinelopi K. Goldberg, Patrick J. Kennedy, and Amit K. Khandelwal, "The Return to Protectionism," NBER Working Paper No. 25638, March 2019; Alberto

Cavallo, Gita Gopinath, Brent Neiman, and Jenny Tang, "Tariff Passthrough at the Border and at the Store: Evidence from US Trade Policy," University of Chicago BFI Working Paper, October 2019; and Aaron Flaaen and Justin Pierce, "Disentangling the Effects of the 2018–2019 Tariffs on a Globally Connected U.S. Manufacturing Sector," Federal Reserve Board, Finance and Discussion Series, December 2019.

15. See Katherine Tai, "New Approach to the U.S. China Trade Relationship," Remarks delivered to Center for Strategic and International Studies (CSIS), Washington DC, October 4, 2021. The only new wrinkle in USTR Tai's re-assessment was in the "targeted tariff exclusion process," which allowed for dispensation from tariffs for products that are not thought to be injurious to US producers or workers; currently some 549 exclusions remain in place—out of an original 2,200 that were initially granted—and the new USTR appears to be open to some additional extensions, to be determined on a case-by-case basis. See Office of the US Trade Representative, Executive Office of the President, "USTR Requests Comments on Reinstatement of Targeted Potential Exclusions of Products of China Subject to Section 301 Tariffs," October 5, 2021.

16. See US Department of State, "Secretary Antony J. Blinken, National Security Advisor Jake Sullivan, Director Yang and State Councilor Wang at the Top of Their Meeting," Anchorage, Alaska, March 18, 2001, available at https://www.state.gov /secretary-antony-j-blinken-national-security-advisor-jake-sullivan-chinese-director -of-the-office-of-the-central-commission-for-foreign-affairs-yang-jiechi-and-chinese -state-councilor-wang-yi-at-th/.

17. The "wolf warrior" concept comes from heroes in Chinese action movies—special forces in the People's Liberation Army who attack and vanquish foreign mercenaries. These cinematic military heroes—wolf warriors—have their counterparts in members of China's diplomatic corps who aggressively take on foreign adversaries. See Peter Martin, *China's Civilian Army: The Making of Wolf Warrior Diplomacy* (London: Oxford University Press, 2021).

18. See Thomas Wright, "The US and China Finally Get Real with Each Other," *Order from Chaos* (blog), Brookings Institution, March 22, 2021.

19. See Zhang Hui, "Chinese Diplomats Deal Vigorous Counterblows to Condescending US Representatives; Common Ground Hard to Reach on Contrasting Logistics," *Global Times* (China), March 19, 2021. China has long taken great umbrage to what it believes is the extreme hypocrisy of America's human rights allegations; see the State Council Information Office of the People's Republic of China, "The Report on Human Rights Violations in the United States in 2021," February 2022, available at http://english.scio.gov.cn/m/scionews/2022-02/28 /content_78076572.htm. In the PRC's 2021 report, special note is made of the apparent racial profiling of the "China Initiative" launched by the Trump administration in 2018 and since terminated by the Biden administration in 2022 as noted in Chapter 13.

20. Bipartisan enactment of the Uyghur Forced Labor Prevention Act in December

2021 dispels the notion that the Anchorage confrontation was just diplomatic posturing; see Felicia Sonmez, "Biden Signs Uyghur Forced Labor Prevention Act into Law," *Washington Post,* December 23, 2021.

21. See Stephen Roach, "Boxed In On China," *Project Syndicate,* March 23, 2021.

22. See Barack Obama, "The TPP Would Let America, Not China, Lead the Way on Global Trade," *Washington Post,* May 2, 2016; and Mireya Solis, "The Containment Fallacy: China and the TPP," *Brookings Up Front,* May 24, 2013.

23. The conceptual case for China's "peaceful rise" is widely associated with Zheng Bijian, currently chairman of the China Institute for Innovation and Development Strategy (CIIDS) and a leading Chinese figure in the globalization debate; see, for example, Zheng Bijian, *China's Peaceful Rise: Speeches of Zheng Bijian, 1997–2005* (Washington DC: Brookings Institution, 2005); and Zheng Bijian, "China's 'Peaceful Rise' to Great-Power Status," *Foreign Affairs,* September/October 2005. For a broader perspective on historical references to China's "peaceful rise," see C. Raja Mohan, "Debating China's 'Peaceful Rise': The Rhyme of the Ancient Mariner," *Economic and Political Weekly* (Mumbai), August 2004.

24. See Hillary Clinton, "America's Pacific Century," *Foreign Policy,* October 2011.

25. See Kurt M. Campbell, "Principles of US Engagement in the Asia-Pacific," testimony before the Subcommittee on East Asian and Pacific Affairs, Senate Foreign Relations Committee, US Congress, January 21, 2010.

26. See "China Formally Applies to Join Asia Trade Deal Trump Abandoned," *Bloomberg News,* September 16, 2021.

27. See Shannon Tiezzi, "Will China Actually Join the CPTPP?" *The Diplomat,* September 17, 2021.

28. See "China Must Win Over Canada and Australia before Trade Pact Talks Can Start," *Financial Times,* September 19, 2021.

29. In 2007, Campbell and Michelle Flournoy, a former senior Defense Department official in the Clinton and Obama administrations, co-founded the Center for a New American Security, a Washington DC–based think tank focusing on US national security issues. See Kurt M. Campbell, *The Pivot: The Future of American Statecraft in Asia* (New York: Hachette Book Group, 2016).

30. See Kurt M. Campbell and Jake Sullivan, "Competition without Catastrophe: How America Can Both Challenge and Coexist with China," *Foreign Affairs,* September/October 2019.

31. China's 2021 policy shifts—a regulatory re-set and "common prosperity"—while not targeted directly at the United States, have also been interpreted by some as a Chinese pivot; see Kevin Rudd, "Xi Jinping's Pivot to the State," an address to the Asia Society, New York, September 8, 2021.

32. See White House Briefing Room, "Joint Leaders Statement on AUKUS," September 15, 2021.

33. See, for example, David E. Sanger and Zolan Kanno-Youngs, "Biden Announces Defense Deal with Australia in a Bid to Counter China," *New York Times,* September 21, 2021; Walter Russell Mead, "Aukus Is the Indo-Pacific Pact of the Future,"

Wall Street Journal, September 27, 2021; and "AUKUS Reshapes the Strategic Landscape of the Indo-Pacific," Special Briefing, *The Economist,* September 25, 2021.

34. See Ryan Hass, Ryan McElveen, and Robert D. Williams, eds., "The Future of US Policy towards China: Recommendations for the Biden Administration," Brookings John L. Thornton China Center and Yale Law School's Paul Tsai China Center, November 2020.

35. See, for example, Stephen Ezell, "False Promises II: The Continuing Gap between China's WTO Commitments and Its Practices," International Technology & Innovation Foundation (ITIF), July 2021; Gregory Shaffer and Henry Gao, "China's Rise: How It Took on the U.S. at the WTO," *University of Illinois Law Review* 2018, no. 1 (January 2018); and Chad P. Bown, "China's WTO Entry: Antidumping, Safeguards, and Dispute Settlement," NBER Working Paper No. 13349, August 2007.

36. See US Department of State, "Secretary Antony J. Blinken, National Security Advisor Jake Sullivan, Director Yang and State Councilor Wang at the Top of Their Meeting."

37. The United States has long favored a label-like marketing approach to its China policies. Since the days of Richard Nixon, US administrations have dubbed China a *strategic partner* (Kissinger), a *strategic competitor* (George W. Bush), and a *responsible stakeholder* (Robert Zoellick). See Richard Baum, "From 'Strategic Partners' to 'Strategic Competitors': George W. Bush and the Politics of U.S. China Policy," *Journal of East Asian Studies* 1, no. 2 (August 2001); and Robert B. Zoellick, "Whither China: From Membership to Responsibility?" Remarks to National Committee on U.S.-China Relations, New York, September 21, 2005. During the Obama administration, the labeling became more cautious, focusing on the need for *strategic reassurance;* in retrospect, that was a hint of the Trump administration's far more aggressive characterization of China as a *revisionist power* posing an outright existential threat (Mike Pompeo). See James Steinberg, "The Obama Administration's Vision of the U.S.-China Relationship," speech before the Center for New American Security, Washington DC, September 24, 2009, and "National Security Strategy of the United States of America," White House, December 2017, as well as Pompeo, "Communist China."

38. From 1962 to 2008, a period that predates the outsize deficits triggered by the Global Financial Crisis, the federal budget deficit averaged 2.7 percent of GDP; see Congressional Budget Office, "The 2021 Long-Term Budget Outlook," March 2021.

39. See Congressional Budget Office, "An Evaluation of CBO's Past Revenue Projections," Congress of the United States, August 2020.

40. Source: US Department of Commerce (Bureau of Economic Analysis).

41. Source: Bank for International Settlements, Broad Real Effective Exchange Rates, available at https://www.bis.org/statistics/eer.htm?m=6%7C381%7C676.

42. See Stephen Roach, "A Crash in the Dollar Is Coming," *Bloomberg,* June 8, 2020.

43. Source: Bank for International Settlements, Broad Real Effective Exchange Rates.

44. See Stephen Roach, "The End of the Dollar's Exorbitant Privilege," *Financial Times,* October 4, 2020; Matthew C. Klein and Michael Pettis, *Trade Wars Are Class Wars* (New Haven, CT: Yale University Press, 2020), chapter 6; and Barry Eichengreen, *Exorbitant Privilege: The Rise and Fall of the Dollar and the Future of the International Monetary System* (New York: Oxford University Press, 2012). Recent research has pointed to early signs of a shift in global foreign exchange reserves into the Chinese renminbi; see Serkan Arslanalp, Barry Eichengreen, and Chima Simpson-Bell, "The Stealth Erosion of Dollar Dominance: Active Diversifiers and the Rise of Nontraditional Reserve Currencies," IMF Working Paper No. WP/22/58, March 2022.

45. See, for example, Robert Kagan, "Our Constitutional Crisis Is Already Here," *Washington Post,* September 23, 2021; Steven Levitsky and Daniel Ziblatt, *How Democracies Die* (New York: Crown, 2018); Martin Wolf, "The Strange Death of American Democracy," *Financial Times,* September 28, 2021; and Peter Grier, "'If You Can Keep It': Where Next for a Strained Democracy," *Christian Science Monitor,* March 29, 2021.

46. See Dan Zak, "Whataboutism: The Cold War Tactic, Thawed by Putin, Is Brandished by Donald Trump," *Washington Post,* August 18, 2017; Melissa Mehr, "When Politicians Resort to 'Whataboutism,'" *Christian Science Monitor,* February 4, 2021.

47. See Alexa Lardieri, "Just 16 Percent Says U.S. Democracy Is Working, Poll Finds," *U.S. News and World Report,* February 8, 2021.

48. See Elizabeth D. Samet, *Looking for the Good War: American Amnesia and the Violent Pursuit of Happiness* (New York: Farrar, Straus and Giroux, 2021).

49. See Steven Pinker, *The Blank Slate: The Modern Denial of Human Nature* (New York: Penguin Books, 2003); Otto Rank, "Love, Guilt, and the Denial of Feelings (1927)," chapter 11 in *A Psychology of Difference: The American Lectures,* ed. Robert Kramer (Princeton, NJ: Princeton University Press, 1996); and Andrew E. Monroe and E. Ashley Plant, "The Dark Side of Morality: Prioritizing Sanctity over Care Motivates Denial of Mind and Prejudice toward Sexual Outgroups," *Journal of Experimental Psychology* (American Psychological Association) 148, no. 2 (February 2019).

50. Source: US Department of Commerce (Bureau of Economic Analysis); for a review of the many explanations that have been offered to explain the declining labor share in the US economy, see Gene M. Grossman and Ezra Oberfeld, "The Elusive Explanation for the Declining Labor Share," NBER Working Paper No. 29165, August 2021.

51. See, for example, Aditya Aladangady and Kelsey O'Flaherty, "How Much Does Home Equity Extraction Matter for Spending?" *FEDS Notes,* Board of Governors of the Federal Reserve System, May 2020; John V. Duca and Anil Kumar, "Financial Literacy and Mortgage Equity Withdrawals," Federal Reserve Bank of Dallas, Working Paper No. 1110, August 2011; and Alan Greenspan and James Kennedy, "Sources and Uses of Equity Extracted from Homes," Finance and Economics

Discussion Series, Board of Governors of the Federal Reserve System, March 2007.

52. Source: US Department of Commerce (Bureau of Economic Analysis).

53. See Richard C. Koo, *Balance Sheet Recession: Japan's Struggle with Uncharted Economics and Its Global Implications* (New York: John Wiley & Sons, 2003).

54. See Congressional Budget Office, "The 2021 Long-Term Budget Outlook," March 2021.

55. On the eve of the Global Financial Crisis in 2007, Chuck Prince, then CEO of Citigroup, famously said in an interview in the *Financial Times,* "as long as the music is playing, you've got to get up and dance"; see Michiyo Nakamoto and David Wighton, "Citigroup Chief Stays Bullish on Buy-Outs," *Financial Times,* July 9, 2007. See Ronald W. Reagan, "Remarks at the Presentation Ceremony for the Presidential Medal of Freedom," White House, January 19, 1989.

56. See, for example, Robert Shapiro, "What the U.S. Loses When Americans Save Too Much," *The Atlantic,* June 26, 2021; Paul Krugman, "The Paradox of Thrift—For Real," *New York Times,* July 7, 2009; and E. Katarina Vermann, "Wait, Is Saving Good or Bad? The Paradox of Thrift," Federal Reserve Bank of St. Louis, *Page One Economics,* May 2012.

Chapter 8. Censorship as Conflict

1. See Anne Marie-Brady, "Guiding Hand: The Role of the CCP Central Propaganda Department in the Current Era," *Westminster Papers in Communication and Culture* 3, no. 1 (2006); also see David Shambaugh, "China's Propaganda System: Institutions, Processes and Efficacy," *China Journal,* January 2007.

2. See Katie Hunt and CY Xu, "China 'Employs 2 Million to Police the Internet,'" CNN, October 7, 2013.

3. One recent study estimates that as many as twenty-three separate Chinese organizations—spread across the Party, the State Council, and the PLA—are involved in the national propaganda effort; see Atlantic Council Digital Forensic Research Lab (DFRLab) and Scowcroft Center for Strategy and Security, "Chinese Discourse Power: China's Use of Information Manipulation in Regional and Global Competition," December 2020.

4. See, for example, Geremie R. Barme and Sang Ye, "The Great Firewall of China," *Wired,* June 1, 1997; James Griffiths, *The Great Firewall of China: How to Build and Control an Alternative Version of the Internet* (London: Zed Books, 2019).

5. Express News Service, "China Blocks Indian Media Websites, INS Seeks Govt Action," *Indian Express,* July 2, 2020.

6. See Freedom House, "China's Information Isolation, New Censorship Rules, Transnational Repression," China Media Bulletin 151, February 2021.

7. For each country in the Freedom House sample, the global freedom index consists of some twenty-five civil liberties and political rights indicators that are aimed at capturing personal, civil, and economic freedoms; see Sarah Repucci and Amy

Slipowitz, "Democracy under Siege," *Freedom in the World 2021* (New York: Freedom House, 2021).

8. In the early (pre–Xi Jinping) days, China's social media platforms allowed surprisingly vigorous exchanges of debate on many issues that would now be verboten, including sensitive political issues (i.e., riots, street violence, labor strikes, anti-Japan demonstrations) and allegations of corruption by local Party officials. That was the conclusion of an exhaustive empirical study of some 13.2 billion Sina Weibo posts from 2009–13 that covered about 95 percent of all posts on China's second largest social media platform (after WeChat); see Bei Qin, David Stromberg, and Yanhui Wu, "Why Does China Allow Freer Social Media? Protests versus Surveillance and Propaganda," *Journal of Economic Perspectives* 31, no. 1 (Winter 2017). The research, which covered the period through 2013, ended with the prescient observation "that the stricter regime [the Xi Jinping administration] has still found it not in its interest to fully censor posts about the sensitive topics that we study." That, of course, was about to change very shortly.

9. See Brendan Forde, "China's 'Mass Line' Campaign," *The Diplomat*, September 9, 2013.

10. Source: James Mulvenon, "'Comrade, Where's My Military Car?' Xi Jinping's Throwback Mass-Line Campaign to Curb PLA Corruption," *China Leadership Monitor*, no. 42 (Fall 2013); Noel Irwin Hentschel, "Good Guy Xi Jinping, President of China, Confronts Bad Habits and Ugly Vices: Calls for Virtues and Caring Hospitality, East and West," *Huffpost*, January 23, 2014; and Hou Wei, "The Mass Line and the Reconstruction of Legitimacy of the Communist Party of China in the New Era," *Advances in Social Science, Education, and Humanities Research* (Atlantis Press), vol. 345 (2019).

11. The United States has long been chastised for its excessively materialistic lifestyles. See, for example, John Kenneth Galbraith, *The Affluent Society* (New York: Houghton Mifflin, 1958); Juliet B. Schor, *The Overspent American: Why We Want What We Don't Need* (New York: Harper Perennial, 1998); and Rebecca Mead, "What Rampant Materialism Looks Like, and What It Costs," *New Yorker*, August 9, 2017.

12. See Dan Levin, "China Revives Mao-Era Self-Criticism, but This Kind Bruises Few Egos," *New York Times*, December 20, 2013; Shannon Tiezzi, "The Mass Line Campaign in the 21st Century," *The Diplomat*, December 27, 2013; Paul Gewirtz, "Xi, Mao, and China's Search for a Usable Past," *ChinaFile*, January 14, 2014.

13. See Elsa Kania, "The Right to Speak: Discourse and Chinese Power," Center for Advanced China Research, Washington DC, November 27, 2018.

14. See Atlantic Council Digital Forensic Research, "Chinese Discourse Power."

15. For a discussion of China's earlier uses of discourse power, see Wang Hung-jen, "Contextualizing China's Call for Discourse Power in International Politics," *China: An International Journal* 13, no. 3 (December 2015); also see Kejin Zhao, "China's Rise and Its Discursive Power Strategy," *Chinese Political Science Review* (2016).

16. See Marshall McLuhan, *Understanding Media: The Extensions of Man* (New York: McGraw Hill, 1964).

17. The BRI is not another Marshall Plan, nor was it original or even conceived in China. Asia's pan-regional infrastructure gap had, in fact, been stressed for years by the Asian Development Bank and the World Bank. Xi Jinping glommed on to the idea in early 2013 and turned the BRI into a personal statement of his vision and commitment to enhancing the Asian growth potential. This branded discourse was enhanced by the tandem launching of a financial infrastructure, the Silk Road Fund in 2014 and the Asian Infrastructure Investment Bank in 2016, both headquartered in Beijing. The AIIB is a multilateral institution, now involving more than one hundred members, which, apart from the refusal of the United States and Japan to join, provided something close to a global endorsement of the BRI. The glitz of periodic high-profile global BRI conferences added to the image-building of Xi's global brand. See "Will China's Belt and Road Initiative Outdo the Marshall Plan?" *The Economist*, March 10, 2018; Simon Chen and Wilson Chan, "A Comparative Study of the Belt and Road Initiative and the Marshall Plan," *Palgrave Communications* 4 (2018); Asian Development Bank, *Annual Report 2010: Volume 1*, Manila, 2011; Asian Development Bank, *Meeting Asia's Infrastructure Needs*, Manila, 2017; Luis Andres, Dan Biller, and Matias Herrera Dappe, "Reducing Poverty by Closing South Asia's Infrastructure Gap," World Bank, Washington DC, December 2013; and Jonathan E. Hillman, "A 'China Model?' Beijing's Promotion of Alternative Global Norms and Standards," testimony before the US-China Economic and Security Review Commission, Center for Strategic and International Studies (CSIS), March 13, 2020.

18. See Richard Turcsanyi and Eva Kachlikova, "The BRI and China's Soft Power in Europe: Why Chinese Narratives (Initially) Won," *Journal of Current Chinese Affairs* 49, no. 1 (2020).

19. See Julie T. Miao, "Understanding the Soft Power of China's Belt and Road Initiative through a Discourse Analysis in Europe," *Regional Studies, Regional Science* 8, no. 2 (2021).

20. See Madi Sarsenbayev and Nicolas Veron, "European versus American Perspectives on the Belt and Road Initiative," *China & World Economy* 28, no. 2 (2020).

21. See, for example, Policy Planning Staff, Office of the Secretary of State, "The Elements of the China Challenge," Washington DC, November 2020; Jacob J. Lew and Gary Roughead (Chairs), "China's Belt and Road: Implications for the United States," Council on Foreign Relations Independent Task Force Report No. 79, 2021; Parag Khanna, "Washington Is Dismissing China's Belt and Road. That's a Huge Mistake," *Politico Magazine*, April 30, 2019; and Syed Munir Khasru, "China Tries to Win Over Critics of the New Silk Road," World Economic Forum Global Agenda, May 29, 2019.

22. See, for example, Daniel R. Russel and Blake H. Berger, "Weaponizing the Belt and Road Initiative," Asia Society Policy Institute, September 2020; Christopher Mott, "China's Belt and Road Initiative: Is It Really a Threat?" *National Interest*,

February 18, 2020; Sara Hsu, "Is China's Belt and Road Initiative a Threat to the US?" *The Diplomat,* May 22, 2021.

23. The US response to the BRI has started to change in the early days of the Biden administration. At a G-7 meeting of leading global nations in Great Britain in early 2021, the United States took the lead in countering the BRI with a proposal dubbed "Build Back Better World." While vague in details it was aimed at addressing some $40 trillion in infrastructure needs for low- and middle-income nations. Like the earlier TPP that initially featured pan-regional Asia trade liberalization without China, the new Biden plan was apparently aimed at applying the same formula to addressing the developing world's infrastructure gap. See White House Briefing Room, "FACT SHEET: President Biden and G7 Leaders Launch Build Back Better World (B3W) Partnership," June 12, 2021, available at https://www.whitehouse .gov/briefing-room/statements-releases/2021/06/12/fact-sheet-president -biden-and-g7-leaders-launch-build-back-better-world-b3w-partnership/.

24. See Robert Greene and Paul Triolo, "Will China Control the Global Internet via Its Digital Silk Road?" Carnegie Endowment for International Peace, SUPCHINA, May 8, 2020.

25. See E. John Gregory, "Control Issues Are Feeding China's 'Discourse Power' Project," *National Interest,* August 2018.

26. See Eamon Barrett, "Broadcasting Rights, Ticket Sales, Sponsorships: NBA's Hong Kong Crisis Risks Its Massive China Business," *Fortune,* October 10, 2019.

27. At the same time, LeBron James has been accused of having a hyperreactive Twitter-finger response habit; see Candace Buckner, "LeBron James's Tweet on Glenn Consor: An Eagerness to Judge and a Reluctance to Think," *Washington Post,* January 7, 2022.

28. See Ben Cohen, "China Standoff Cost the NBA 'Hundreds of Millions,'" *Wall Street Journal,* February 16, 2020.

29. See William D. O'Connell, "Silencing the Crowd: China, the NBA, and Leveraging Market Size to Export Censorship," *Review of International Political Economy,* March 29, 2021. An interesting twist in this story appeared in October 2021, when China suspended livestreaming of Boston Celtics NBA basketball games after the Celtics center, Enes Kanter, directed derogatory remarks toward Xi Jinping; see Jacob Knutson, "China Pulls Celtic Games after Enes Kanter Criticizes Xi Jinping," *Axios,* October 21, 2021. Aside from pulling the plug on Celtics livestreaming, China's response to Kanter has been considerably less extreme than in the case of Daryl Morey. In a curious sequel to this incident, Chinese livestreaming of Celtics basketball games resumed in February 2022 after Kanter, who added "Freedom" to his name in November 2021, was cut from the team and, ironically, traded (temporarily) to the Houston Rockets; see Dan McLaughlin, "Chinese Media Gloat about PRC Influence on the NBA as Enes Kanter Freedom Is Cut," *National Review,* February 13, 2022.

30. See "Cambridge University Press Battles Censorship in China," *The Economist,* August 26, 2017.

31. See Simon Denyer, "Gap Apologizes to China over Map on T-shirt that Omits Taiwan, South China Sea," *Washington Post*, May 15, 2018.

32. See Bailey Vogt, "ESPN Memo Bans Discussion of Hong Kong Conflict in Wake of China, Houston Rockets Tensions," *Washington Post*, October 9, 2019.

33. See Tufayel Ahmed, "Batman Poster Accused of Supporting Hong Kong Protests, Chinese Fans Threaten DC Comics Boycott," *Newsweek*, November 28, 2019.

34. See Matt Apuzzo, "Pressured by China, E.U. Softens Report on Covid-19 Disinformation," *New York Times*, April 24, 2020.

35. See "H&M, Nike Face Boycotts in China as Xinjiang Dilemma Deepens," *Bloomberg News*, March 25, 2021.

36. See Liza Lin and Stu Woo, "It's China vs. Walmart, Latest Western Brand Entangled in Human Rights Dispute," *Wall Street Journal*, January 2, 2022.

37. See Tom Uren, Elise Thomas, and Dr. Jacob Wallis, "Tweeting through the Great Firewall: Preliminary Analysis of PRC-Linked Information Operations on the Hong Kong Protests," Australian Strategic Policy Institute, September 2019; and Atlantic Council Digital Forensic Research, "Chinese Discourse Power."

38. See Tom Cotton, "Coronavirus and the Laboratories in Wuhan," *Wall Street Journal*, April 21, 2020. Earlier and subsequent claims by Senator Cotton have provoked considerable controversy over the veracity of his original lab-leak allegations. See, for example, Paulina Firozi, "Tom Cotton Keeps Repeating a Coronavirus Fringe Theory that Scientists Have Disputed," *Washington Post*, February 17, 2020; Glenn Kessler, "Timeline: How the Wuhan Lab-Leak Theory Suddenly Became Credible," *Washington Post*, May 25, 2021; and Olafimihan Oshin, "Washington Post Issues Correction on 2020 Report on Tom Cotton, Lab-Leak Theory," *The Hill*, June 1, 2021.

39. See Jeff Kao and Mia Shuang, "How China Built a Twitter Propaganda Machine Then Let It Loose on Coronavirus," ProPublica, March 26, 2020.

40. See Atlantic Council Digital Forensic Research, "Chinese Discourse Power."

41. See Marcel Schliebs, Hannah Bailey, Jonathan Bright, and Philip N. Howard, "China's Public Diplomacy Operations: Understanding Engagement and Inauthentic Amplification of PRC Diplomats on Facebook and Twitter," DemTech Working Paper, Oxford Internet Institute, University of Oxford Programme on Democracy and Technology, May 2021.

42. See Jessica Batke and Mareike Ohlberg, "Message Control: How a New For-Profit Industry Helps China's Leaders 'Manage Public Opinion,'" *ChinaFile*, December 20, 2020.

43. See Gary King, Jennifer Pan, and Margaret E. Roberts, "How the Chinese Government Fabricates Social Media Posts for Strategic Distraction, Not Engaged Argument," *American Political Science Review* 111, no. 3 (2017).

44. See Xi Jinping, "Speech at a Ceremony Marking the Centenary of the Communist Party of China," July 1, 2021.

45. See Deng Xiaoping, "Emancipate the Mind, Seek Truth from Facts, Unite and Look Forward," speech before the Central Party Work Conference, December 13, 1978.

46. See Ann Florini, Hairong Lai, and Yeling Tan, *China Experiments: From Local In-novation to National Reform* (Washington DC: Brookings Institution, 2012).

47. See David Volodzko, "China's Biggest Taboos: The Three Ts," *The Diplomat,* June 23, 2015.

48. Apparently, Chinese censorship also aims to protect the personal sensitivities of Xi Jinping, especially online allusions to any resemblance to A. A. Milne's Winnie the Pooh character; see Benjamin Haas, "China Bans Winnie the Pooh Film after Comparisons to President Xi," *The Guardian,* August 6, 2018.

49. See Josh Ye, "China Tightens Great Firewall by Declaring Unauthorized VPN Services Illegal," *South China Morning Post,* January 23, 2017.

50. See, for example, Kerry Brown, "China and Self-Censorship," in Michael Natzler, ed., *UK Universities and China,* HEPI Report 132, July 2020; Simon K. Zhen, "An Explanation of Self-Censorship in China: The Enforcement of Social Control through a Panoptic Infrastructure," *Inquiries Journal/Student Pulse* 7, no. 9 (September 2015); and Jingrong Tong, "Press Self-Censorship in China: A Case Study of the Transformation of Discourse," *Discourse & Society* 20, no. 5 (September 2009).

51. See Richard McGregor, *The Party: The Secret World of China's Communist Rulers* (New York: HarperCollins, 2010).

52. There has been considerable debate in the West on the occasion of the July 2021 CCP centennial; unsurprisingly, the discussion boils down to a Xi-centric assessment of one hundred years of history. See, for example, Orville Schell, "Life of the Party: How Secure Is the CCP," *Foreign Affairs,* July/August 2021; Ian Johnson, "A Most Adaptable Party," *New York Review,* July 2021; and Isaac Chotiner, "Reconsidering the History of the Chinese Communist Party," *New Yorker,* July 22, 2021.

53. See, for example, Timothy Snyder, "The American Abyss," *New York Times Magazine,* January 9, 2021; John W. Dean and Bob Altemeyer, *Authoritarian Nightmare: Trump and His Followers* (New York: Melville House, 2020); and Karen Stenner and Jessica Stern, "How to Live with Authoritarians," *Foreign Policy,* February 11, 2021.

54. See, for example, Adrian Shahbaz, "Freedom on the Net 2018: The Rise of Digital Authoritarianism: Fake News, Data Collection, and the Challenge to Democracy," Freedom House, October 2018; Alina Polyakova and Chris Meserole, "Exporting Digital Authoritarianism: The Russian and Chinese Models," Brookings Institution, August 2019; Tiberiu Dragu and Yonatan Lupu, "Digital Authoritarianism and the Future of Human Rights," *International Organization* 75, no. 4 (February 2021).

55. See George Orwell, *Nineteen Eighty-Four* (London: Secker & Warburg, 1949).

56. See, for example, Quinn P. Dauer, "The Digital Polarization Initiative: Teaching History and Information Literacy," *Perspectives on History,* American Historical Association, October 2019; and Constella, "Polarization as an Emerging Source of Digital Risk: Case Study: Spain."

57. See, for example, Keith Hagey and Jeff Horwitz, "The Facebook Files: Facebook

Tried to Make Its Platform a Healthier Place. It Got Angrier Instead," *Wall Street Journal*, September 15, 2021; Paul M. Barrett, Justin Hendrix, and J. Grant Sims, "Fueling the Fire: How Social Media Intensifies U.S. Political Polarization—And What Can Be Done About It," NYU Stern Center for Business and Human Rights, September 2021; and Steve Rathje, Jay Van Bavel, and Sander van der Linden, "Why Facebook Really, Really Doesn't Want to Discourage Extremism," *Washington Post*, July 13, 2021.

58. See Aldous Huxley, *Brave New World* (London: Chatto & Windus, 1932).

Chapter 9. Consumerism and Animal Spirits

1. Source: Author's calculation based on data from the National Bureau of Statistics (China).
2. Source: International Monetary Fund, *World Economic Outlook* database.
3. Source: International Monetary Fund, *Fiscal Monitor*, October 2021, Methodological and Statistical Appendix.
4. Source: National Bureau of Statistics (China).
5. Source: US Department of Commerce (Bureau of Economic Analysis).
6. Source: World Bank Development Indicators.
7. See James S. Duesenberry, *Income, Saving, and the Theory of Consumer Behavior* (Cambridge, MA: Harvard University Press, 1949); and Milton Friedman, "The Permanent Income Hypothesis," in Milton Friedman, ed., *A Theory of the Consumption Function* (Princeton, NJ: Princeton University Press, 1957), 20–37.
8. Source: National Bureau of Statistics (China).
9. In 2019, the labor compensation share of GDP in China was about 6 percent higher than that for other BRICS—Brazil, Russia, India, and South Africa—whereas it was about 2 percent lower than in the United States, Japan, Germany, and the United Kingdom combined; source: Penn World Tables Version 10.0, available at www.ggdc.net/pwt.
10. See Alan Greenspan and James Kennedy, "Sources and Uses of Equity Extracted from Homes," Finance and Economics Discussion Series, Federal Reserve Board, March 2007.
11. Source: Author's calculations based on flow-of-funds data from the National Bureau of Statistics (China).
12. Source: Author's calculations based on data from the National Bureau of Statistics (China).
13. Source: National Bureau of Statistics (China) and World Bank Development Indicators.
14. Source: National Bureau of Statistics (China).
15. For a more critical assessment of the Chinese urbanization challenge, see Scott Rozelle and Natalie Hell, *Invisible China: How the Urban-Rural Divide Threatens China's Rise* (Chicago: University of Chicago Press, 2020).

16. In the autumn of 2012, before he became premier in 2013, then Vice Premier Li Keqiang stressed that "[t]he issues of urbanization and service industries are closely related." See Li Keqiang, "Promoting Coordinated Urbanization—An Important Strategic Choice for Achieving Modernization," speech delivered at a seminar sponsored by the National Development and Reform Commission, September 7, 2012.

17. Source: Flow-of-funds accounts, National Bureau of Statistics (China); and US Department of Commerce (Bureau of Economic Analysis).

18. See Longmei Zhang, Ray Brooks, Ding Ding, Hayan Ding, Hui He, Jing Lu, and Rui C. Mano, "China's High Saving: Drivers, Prospects, and Policies," IMF Working Paper No. 18/277, December 2018.

19. Source: International Monetary Fund, "People's Republic of China: Selected Issues," August 2017.

20. See Arthur Kennickell and Anamaria Lusardi, "Disentangling the Importance of the Precautionary Saving Motive," Federal Reserve Board Discussion Paper, November 2005; and Ricardo J. Caballero, "Consumption Puzzles and Precautionary Saving," *Journal of Monetary Economics* 58, no. 2 (1990).

21. See Dezhu Ye, Shuang Pan, Yujun Lian, and Yew-Kwang Ng, "Culture and Saving: Why Do Asians Save More?" *Singapore Economic Review* 66, no. 3 (February 2020).

22. See, for example, Junsen Zhang, "The Evolution of China's One-Child Policy and Its Effects on Family Outcomes," *Journal of Economic Perspectives* 31, no. 1 (Winter 2017); Gu Baochang, Wang Feng, Guo Zhigang, and Zhang Erli, "China's Local and National Fertility Policies at the End of the Twentieth Century," *Population and Development Review* 33, no. 1 (March 2007); and Barbara H. Settles and Xuewen Sheng, "The One-Child Policy and Its Impact on Chinese Families," based on a paper prepared for the XV World Congress of Sociology, Brisbane, Australia, July 7–13, 2002.

23. The projection of the 60 percent old-age dependency ratio is based on the "medium variant" extrapolation of UN demographers; see United Nations, *World Population Prospects 2019*, UN Department of Economic and Social Affairs, Population Division, 2019. The release of the 2021 population data for China was buried in the January 17, 2022, release of national economic statistics; the total population of 1,412.6 million was only 0.48 million (or 0.034%) above that of 2020, the fifth consecutive year of sharply declining growth in total Chinese population and the weakest annual growth rate since the −0.6% decline in 1961, which followed a −1.5% plunge in 1960—both of which occurred during the Great Famine; source: National Bureau of Statistics (China).

24. See, for example, Pat Howard, "Rice Bowls and Job Security: The Urban Contract Labour System," *Australian Journal of Chinese Affairs* 25 (January 1991); Larry Liu, "Capitalist Reform, the Dismantling of the Iron Rice Bowl and Land Expropriation in China: A Theory of Primitive Accumulation and State Power," *Sociology Mind* 5, no. 1 (January 2015); and Lein-Lein Chen and John Devereux, "The Iron

Rice Bowl: Chinese Living Standards 1952–1978," *Comparative Economic Studies* 59, no. 3 (September 2017).

25. See, for example, Hui He, Feng Huang, Zheng Liu, and Dongming Zhu, "Breaking the 'Iron Rice Bowl': Evidence of Precautionary Savings from the Chinese State-Owned Enterprises Reform," Federal Reserve Bank of San Francisco Working Paper Series, No. 2014-04, November 2017; Daniel Berkowitz, Hong Ma, and Shuichiro Nishioka, "Recasting the Iron Rice Bowl: The Reform of China's State-Owned Enterprises," *Review of Economics and Statistics* 99, no. 4 (October 2017); and Chang-Tai Hsieh and Zheng Song, "Grasp the Large, Let Go of the Small: The Transformation of the State Sector in China," *Brookings Papers on Economic Activity* 2015, no. 1 (2015).

26. On July 20, 2021, China formally lifted the restrictions on family size to three children; see Xinhua News Agency, "About Optimizing the Maternity Policy: The Decision to Promote the Long-term Balanced Development of the Population," June 26, 2021, decision of the Central Committee of the Communist Party of China and the State Council, available at http://www.xinhuanet.com/politics/zywj /2021-07/20/c_1127675462.htm.

27. See Waiyee Yip, "China: The Men Who Are Single and the Women Who Don't Want Kids," BBC News, May 25, 2021. Sensitive to concerns that the cost of child rearing has been a major constraint on the expansion of family size, the Chinese government has recently enacted policies encouraging as many as three births and providing tax deductions for childcare expenses for children under the age of three; see Yew Lun Tian, "China to Allow Tax Deduction for Care of Small Children to Help Boost Births," Reuters, July 20, 2021.

28. Under the "high-variant alternative"—which is modeled off a total fertility rate that is 0.5 children above the UN's so-called medium variant baseline—China's old-age dependency ratio (sixty-five years and older relative to the twenty- to sixty-four-year-old cohort) would start to fall short of the baseline trajectory and peak in 2055; author's calculations based on United Nations, *World Population Prospects 2019*.

29. See Rozelle and Hell, *Invisible China*.

30. In 2016, China's State Council announced the consolidation of three public healthcare insurance programs—Urban Employee Basic Medical Insurance, Newly Cooperative Medical Scheme for rural residents, and a voluntary Urban Resident Basic Medical Insurance plan to cover urban residents without formal jobs (i.e., children, the elderly, and self-employed workers). More than 95 percent of the population is covered by one of the three plans. See Julie Shi and Gordon Liu, "Health Insurance and Payment System Reform in China," chapter 9 in Thomas G. McGuire and Richard C. van Kleef, eds., *Risk Adjustment, Risk Sharing and Premium Regulation in Health Insurance Markets: Theory and Practice* (Elsevier, 2018); also see Xiong-Fei Pan and Jin Xu, "Integrating Social Health Insurance Systems in China," *The Lancet* 387, no. 10025 (March 2016).

31. The $385 figure is for the 2014 average payout of the urban basic medical plan— fully four to five times the average benefits of China's other healthcare plans for

rural workers and urban workers not covered in the basic plan; see Shi and Liu, "Health Insurance and Payment System Reform."

32. Research studies based on data from the China Health and Retirement Longitudinal Survey estimate that the rate of "red envelope" payments in China has varied between 54 percent and 76 percent of total medical expenses; see Ning Liu, Guoxian Bao, and Alex Jingwei He, "Does Health Insurance Coverage Reduce Informal Payments? Evidence from the 'Red Envelopes' of China," BMC Health Services Research, 2020.

33. For an overview of China's government-sponsored retirement system, see "China's Social Security System," *China Labour Bulletin*, June 30, 2021. The lack of private pension funds, long a major shortcoming in China's retirement safety net, may now be changing—albeit very slowly; see Thomas Hale and Josephine Cumbo, "China to Launch Private Pensions in Bid to Unlock Vast Savings Stockpile," *Financial Times*, April 21, 2022.

34. At the end of 2020, China's National Social Security Fund reported RMB2.9 trillion of assets under management. That works out to USD$447.5 billion, or $596 per worker in China. See Twinkle Zhou, "Equities Lift China's Social Security Fund Return to 11-Year High," *Asia Investor*, August 19, 2021; and "National Council for Social Security of the People's Republic of China (NSSF)," Sovereign Wealth Fund Institute (SWFI), available at https://www.swfinstitute.org/profile/598cdaa60124e9fd2d05b8ce.

35. See Premier Li Keqiang, "Report on the Work of the Government," delivered at the Fifth Session of the Thirteenth National People's Congress of the People's Republic of China, March 5, 2022.

36. The "dual circulation" strategy was first announced at a May 14, 2020, meeting of the Standing Committee of the Chinese Politburo, http://www.gov.cn/xinwen/2020-05/14/content_5511638.htm. See Zhong Jingwen, "Deeply Grasp the Essence of Accelerating the Formation of a New Development Pattern," *Economic Daily* (China), August 19, 2020, http://www.ce.cn/xwzx/gnsz/gdxw/202008/19/t20200819_35552027.shtml; Jude Blanchette and Andrew Polk, "Dual Circulation and China's New Hedged Integration Strategy," Center for Strategic and International Studies, August 24, 2020; and Bert Hoffman, "China Has a Plan for That," East Asian Institute, National University of Singapore, 2020.

37. See Nicholas R. Lardy and Tianlei Huang, "China's Weak Social Safety Net Will Dampen Its Economic Recovery," *China Economic Watch* (blog), Peterson Institute for International Economics, May 4, 2020; and Brad Hebert, "Is Reform on the Horizon for China's Weak Social Safety Net?" Center for International Strategic and International Studies (CSIS), September 9, 2020.

38. Source: National Council for Social Security Fund (China) and National Bureau of Statistics (China).

39. Source: China Social Health Insurance Fund Annual Spending, Boston Healthcare Associates.

40. The inference that China will grow old before it gets rich is attributed to Professor

Cai Fang, director of the Institute of Population and Labor Economics, CASS; for a discussion of this point, as well as a counterargument, see Baozhen Luo, "China Will Get Rich Before It Grows Old," *Foreign Affairs*, May/June 2015.

41. See George A. Akerlof and Robert J. Shiller, *Animal Sprits: How Human Psychology Drives the Economy, and Why It Matters for Global Capitalism* (Princeton, NJ: Princeton University Press, 2009).

42. See John Maynard Keynes, *The General Theory of Employment, Interest, and Money* (London: Macmillan, 1936).

43. The emphasis of Akerlof and Shiller is couched in the behavioral aspects of economic decision making; like confidence, the story, or the narrative, plays an important role in the framing of their theory of animal spirits. This foreshadows the arguments of Shiller's later work on narrative economics discussed earlier in Chapter 3. See Robert J. Shiller, *Narrative Economics: How Stories Go Viral & Drive Major Economic Events* (Princeton, NJ: Princeton University Press, 2019).

44. Columbia economics professor and Nobel laureate Edmund Phelps has long focused on the theory of practice of indigenous innovation, with special emphasis on applications to Chinese economic development; for many years he has been encouraged over the possibilities of indigenous innovation in China, provided progress shifts to the creative talent pool and the related generation of original (indigenous) breakthroughs. See Edmund S. Phelps, "Achieving Economic Dynamism in China," in Huiyao Wang and Alistair Michie, eds., *Consensus or Conflict? China and Globalization in the 21st Century* (Singapore: Springer, September 2021); Edmund S. Phelps, "Will China Out-Innovate the West?" *Project Syndicate*, March 5, 2018; and Edmund S. Phelps, "The Dynamism of Nations: Toward a Theory of Indigenous Innovation," *Capitalism and Society* 12, no. 1 (May 2017). However, in a March 2022 telephone conversation with the author, Phelps expressed great concern over the prospects of Chinese dynamism in light of the common prosperity and regulatory policy shifts that occurred in 2021 as discussed above.

45. See Stephen S. Roach, "China's Animal Spirits Deficit," *Project Syndicate*, July 27, 2021.

46. See Kai-Fu Lee, *AI Super-Powers: China, Silicon Valley, and the New World Order* (Boston: Houghton Mifflin Harcourt, 2018).

47. See "Xi Jinping Chairs Collective Study Session of Politburo on National Big Data Strategy," Xinhua News Service (China), December 9, 2017.

48. For a comprehensive assessment of Chinese surveillance and its implications for personal privacy and state-directed social control, see Josh Chin and Liza Lin, *Surveillance State: Inside China's Quest to Launch a New Era of Social Control* (New York: St. Martin's Press, September 2022). For a description of the 2021 enactment of the PRC's new privacy law, see Alexa Lee, Mingli Shi, Qiheng Chen, et al., "Seven Major Changes in China's Finalized Personal Information Protection Law," Brookings and *DigiChina*, August 23, 2021.

49. See Diego A. Cerdeiro and Cian Ruane, "China's Declining Business Dynamism," IMF Working Paper, WP/22/32, January 2022; despite this shifting policy climate,

some argue that China's private sector dynamism remains intact; see Tianiei Huang and Nicolas Véron, "The Private Sector Advances in China: The Evolving Ownership Structures of the Largest Companies in the Xi Jinping Era," Peterson Institute for International Economics, Working Paper 22-3, March 2022.

50. See "Xi Stresses Promoting Common Prosperity amid High-Quality Development, Forestalling Major Financial Risks," Xinhua News Service (China), August 18, 2021.

51. This has become a matter of intense debate that harkens back to many of the issues that arose during China's tumultuous Cultural Revolution from 1966 to 1976—a comparison that most Western observers reject as being out of step with the forty-five years of extraordinary progress that has been made since those dark days ended. See, for example, "Xi Jinping's Campaign: China's New Reality Is Rife with Danger," Leaders, *The Economist*, October 2, 2021; Lingling Wei, "Xi Jinping Aims to Rein In Chinese Capitalism, Hew to Mao's Socialist Vision," *Wall Street Journal*, September 20, 2021; and Yuen Yuen Ang, "Can Xi End China's Gilded Age?" *Project Syndicate*, September 21, 2021.

52. See Stephen S. Roach, "Connecting the Dots in China," *Project Syndicate*, September 27, 2021.

53. See Saad Ahmed Javed, Yu Bo, Liangyan Tao, et al., "The 'Dual Circulation' Development Model of China: Background and Insights," *Rajagiri Management Journal*, published ahead of print, April 2021; also see Bert Hofman, "China's Economic Policy of Dual Circulation," Hinrich Foundation, June 8, 2021; and Blanchette and Polk, "Dual Circulation and China's New Hedged Integration Strategy."

54. By "efficient external circulation," dual circulation also emphasizes a focus on global supply-chain efficiencies as well as productivity enhancements of China's previously announced "supply-side structural reforms"; see Xi Jinping, "Understanding the New Development Stage, Applying the New Development Philosophy, and Creating a New Development Dynamic," July 8, 2021.

55. See Stephen Roach, *Unbalanced: The Codependency of America and China* (New Haven, CT: Yale University Press, 2014), chapter 12.

56. The 2017 appointment of Wang Huning to the Standing Committee of the Politburo, making him one of the seven top members of the elite CCP leadership team, adds credence to the view that Xi Jinping's ideological tilt should be interpreted as an outgrowth of a long-simmering conservative backlash. Wang's pedigree as the Party's senior ideological theorist is unquestionable, borne out by the important role he played in the formulation of Jiang Zemin's "Three Representatives," Hu Jintao's "Scientific Development," Xi's Chinese Dream, his signature ideological contribution of Xi Jinping Thought, and the recent common prosperity campaign. Wang's elevation to the Standing Committee in 2017—the same year that Xi Jinping Thought was incorporated into the CCP constitution at the Nineteenth Party Congress—underscores the ascendancy of ideology in China's "fifth generation" leadership team. For a discussion of the ideological influence and thrust of Wang Huning, see N. S. Lyons, "The Triumph and Terror of Wang

Huning," *Palladium: Governance Futurism,* October 11, 2021; also see Matthew D. Johnson, "Introduction to Wang Huning's 1988 essay "The Structure of China's Changing Political Culture," 王沪宁, "转变中的中国政治文化结构," 复旦学报 (社会科学版), 1988.3: 55–64. China's recent conservative ideological backlash was also underscored by a notorious memo written in late 2013 by "senior Party leaders" to the general CCP leadership known as Document No. 9 that was leaked by a now imprisoned journalist, Gao Yu. See *ChinaFile,* "Document 9: A China-File Translation," November 8, 2013; Stanley Lubman, "Document No. 9: The Party Attacks Western Democratic Ideals," *Wall Street Journal,* August 27, 2013; and John Lanchester, "Document Number Nine," *London Review of Books* 41, no. 19 (October 10, 2019).

57. See Wang Huning, *America against America* (1991; independently republished, February 2022); and Yi Wang, "Meet the Mastermind behind Xi Jinping's Power," *Washington Post,* November 6, 2017.

Chapter 10. China with American Characteristics

1. See Jinglian Wu, "Improving the Socialist Market Economy, Building Inclusive Economic Systems," in *Facing the Era of Great Transformation* (Singapore: Palgrave Macmillan, 2021); and Kjeld Erik Brødsgaard and Koen Rutten, *From Accelerated Accumulation to Socialist Market Economy in China: Economic Discourse and Development from 1953 to the Present* (Netherlands: Brill, 2017).

2. See Yiping Huang & K. P. Kalirajan, "Enterprise Reform and Technical Efficiency of China's State-Owned Enterprises," *Applied Economics* 30, no. 5 (1998).

3. This decision was promulgated in 1993 during the Third Plenary Session of the Fourteenth Central Committee; see http://www.bjreview.com.cn/special/2013-10/23/content_574000_2.htm.

4. See, for example, Yongshun Cai, "The Resistance of Chinese Laid-Off Workers in the Reform Period," *China Quarterly* 170 (2002); Louis Putterman and Xiao-Yuan Dong, "China's State-Owned Enterprises: Their Role, Job Creation and Efficiency in Long-Term Perspective," *Modern China* 26, no. 4 (October 2000); and Mary E. Gallagher, "Reform and Openness: Why China's Economic Reforms Have Delayed Democracy," *World Politics* 54, no. 3 (2002).

5. See Stephen Roach, *Unbalanced: The Codependency of America and China* (New Haven, CT: Yale University Press, 2014), chapter 3; for the original Chinese source on the Fifteenth Party Congress, also see http://cpc.people.com.cn/GB/64162/64168/64568/index.html.

6. See Joseph Schumpeter, *Capitalism, Socialism, and Democracy* (New York: Harper & Brothers, 1942).

7. See Shahid Yusuf, Kaoru Nabeshima, and Dwight H. Perkins, *Under New Ownership: Privatizing China's State-Owned Enterprises* (Washington DC: World Bank and Stanford University Press, 2006).

8. See "Law of the People's Republic of China on State-Owned Assets in Enterprises,"

adopted at the Fifth Meeting of the Standing Committee of the Eleventh National People's Congress on October 28, 2008, available at http://www.npc.gov.cn/zgrdw /englishnpc/Law/2011-02/15/content_1620615.htm.

9. See "Communiqué of the Third Plenary Session of the 18th Central Committee of the Communist Party of China," November 12, 2013, available at http://www .china.org.cn/china/third_plenary_session/2014-01/15/content_31203056.htm.

10. See Premier Li Keqiang, "Report on the Work of the Government," presented to the National People's Congress," March 13, 2014, available at http://english.www.gov .cn/archive/publications/2014/08/23/content_281474982987826.htm. There has been a vigorous debate over the efficacy of China's mixed ownership SOE reform strategy, with the consensus coming out more on the critical side. See, for example, Curtis J. Milhaupt and Wentong Zheng, "Why Mixed-Ownership Reforms Cannot Fix China's State Sector," Paulson Institute, Paulson Policy Memorandum, January 2016; Nicholas R. Lardy, "China's SOE Reform—The Wrong Path," Peterson Institute for International Economics, *China Economic Watch,* July 28, 2016; Henny Sender, "China's State-Owned Business Reform a Step in the Wrong Direction," *Financial Times,* September 25, 2017; Jiang Yu Wang and Cheng Han Tan, "Mixed Ownership Reform and Corporate Governance in China's State-Owned Enterprises," *Vanderbilt Journal of Transnational Law* 53, no. 3 (October 2019); and Ann Listerud, "MOR Money MOR Problems: China's Mixed Ownership Reforms in Practice," Center for Strategic International Studies (CSIS), October 2019.

11. See Nicholas R. Lardy, *Markets over Mao: The Rise of Private Business in China* (Washington DC: Peterson Institute for International Economics, 2014) and Nicholas R. Lardy, *The State Strikes Back: The End of Economic Reform in China?* (Washington DC: Peterson Institute for International Economics, 2019). Curiously, in October 2021, amid the intense debate over common prosperity and China's newest round of regulatory actions, Lardy hinted at yet another swing in his own pendulum in a stirring defense of China's private sector that he was starting to doubt in his 2019 book; see Tianlei Huang and Nicholas R. Lardy, "Is the Sky Really Falling for Private Firms in China?" Peterson Institute for International Economics, *China Economic Watch* (blog), October 14, 2021.

12. See Deborah Petrara, "Ranked Network Operator Leaders Providing Enterprise 5G Connectivity," ABI Research, July 8, 2021; and https://en.wikipedia.org/wiki /List_of_mobile_network_operators.

13. See China Unicom, "China Unicom's Mixed-Ownership Reform Leaps Forward in Business Cooperation with Tencent," press release, October 23, 2017.

14. See Dan Strumpf, "Tencent, Alibaba in Group Buying $11.7 Billion Stake in State-Owned Telecom," *Wall Street Journal,* August 16, 2017.

15. See Eric Ng, "China Unicom Gets Funding and Stake Boost from Patent in 'Mixed Ownership Reform,'" *South China Morning Post,* August 23, 2017; and Huang Kaixi, Qin Min, Jiang Bowen, and Han Wei, "China Unicom Dials Up Private Capital in Ownership Reform," *Caixin,* August 27, 2017.

16. See R. Ashie Baxter, "Japan's Cross-Shareholding Legacy: The Financial Impact on Banks," *Asia Focus,* Federal Reserve Bank of San Francisco, August 2009.

17. See Alan G. Ahearne and Naoki Shinada, "Zombie Firms and Economic Stagnation in Japan," *International Economics and Economic Policy* 2, no. 4 (December 2005).

18. See Stephen S. Roach, "Technology and the Services Sector: The Hidden Competitive Challenge," *Technological Forecasting and Social Change* 34, no. 4 (December 1988); Stijn Claessens, Daniela Klingebiel, and Luc Laeven, "Financial Restructuring in Banking and Corporate Sector Crises: What Policies to Pursue?" NBER Working Paper No. 8386, July 2001; and Dani Rodrik and Arvind Subramanian, "Why Did Financial Globalization Disappoint?" *IMF Staff Papers* 56, no. 1 (January 2009).

19. See Daniel Ren, "Premier Li Keqiang Vows to Kill Off China's 'Zombie Firms,'" *South China Morning Post,* December 3, 2015.

20. There was some modest improvement in China's corporate debt problem in 2021; by the third quarter of the year, nonfinancial corporate debt had fallen to 155.5 percent, slightly below the peak reading of 163.3 percent hit in the second quarter of 2020 but still well above the low of 93.9 percent recorded at the end of 2008. Source: Bank for International Settlements, Credit to the Nonfinancial Sector, available at https://www.bis.org/statistics/totcredit.htm?m=6%7C380%7 C669.

21. See Ricardo J. Caballero, Takeo Hoshi, and Anil K. Kashyap, "Zombie Lending and Depressed Restructuring in Japan," *American Economic Review* 98, no. 5 (December 2008).

22. See W. Raphael Lam and Alfred Schipke, "State-Owned Enterprise Reform," chapter 11 in W. R. Lam, M. Rodlauer, and A. Schipke, *Modernizing China: Investing in Soft Infrastructure* (Washington DC: International Monetary Fund, January 2017).

23. See "China Cannot Accelerate Economic Growth by Increasing Leverage, Says 'Authoritative Insider,'" *People's Daily Online,* May 10, 2016; also see "China's 'Authoritative' Warning on Debt: People's Daily Excerpts," *Bloomberg News,* May 9, 2016.

24. The widely used metaphor of the financial circulatory system was particularly apt during the Global Financial Crisis of 2008–9, when a near breakdown of the global financial system pushed the world economy to the brink of collapse; see, for example, Alan S. Blinder, *After the Music Stopped: The Financial Crisis, the Response, and the Work Ahead* (New York: Penguin Press, 2013).

25. See Lawrence H. Summers, "International Financial Crises: Causes, Prevention, and Cures," Richard T. Ely Lecture, *American Economic Review* 90, no. 2 (May 2000).

26. Source: International Monetary Fund, "Financial Development Index Database," available at https://data.imf.org/?sk=F8032E80-B36C-43B1-AC26-493C5B1CD33B.

27. See International Monetary Fund, *Global Financial Stability Report: COVID-19,*

Crypto, and Climate: Navigating Challenging Transitions (Washington DC: IMF, October 2021).

28. I am indebted to my former colleagues from the Morgan Stanley economics team, Richard Berner and David Greenlaw, for updating this calculation of the US banking share of credit intermediation, which is based on Federal Reserve flow-of-funds data; the Chinese calculation is based on data from the Bank for International Settlements, Credit to the Nonfinancial Sector, available at https://www.bis.org/statistics/totcredit.htm?m=6%7C380%7C669.

29. See David Feliba and Rehn Ahmad, "The World's 100 Largest Banks, 2021," *S&P Global Market Intelligence*, April 12, 2021; R. Taggart Murphy, "Power without Purpose: The Crisis of Japan's Global Financial Dominance," *Harvard Business Review*, March–April 1989; and Douglas Frantz, "Top 8 Banking Firms in Japan, Magazine Says," *Los Angeles Times*, June 15, 1989.

30. Source: Flow-of-funds accounts, National Bureau of Statistics (China).

31. See Torsten Ehlers, Steven Kong, and Feng Zhu, "Mapping Shadow Banking in China: Structure and Dynamics," Bank for International Settlements, BIS Working Paper No. 701, February 2018.

32. See Financial Stability Board, "Global Monitoring Report on Non-Bank Financial Intermediation: 2020," December 16, 2020.

33. See Fitch Ratings, "China's Shadow Financing Under Pressure," *Special Report*, April 28, 2020.

34. See Sofia Horta e Costa and Rebecca Choong Wilkins, "Evergrande 76% Haircut Is Now a Base Case for Bond Analysts," *Bloomberg*, September 12, 2021.

35. See Harriet Agnew, "Evergrande Fallout Could Be Worse than Lehman for China, Warns Jim Chanos," *Financial Times*, September 22, 2021; and John Authers, "China's Evergrande Moment Is Looking More LTCM than Minsky," *Bloomberg Opinion*, September 20, 2021.

36. See Tian Chen and Tania Chen, "China Injects $18.6 Billion into Banking System during Evergrande Crisis," *Bloomberg*, September 21, 2021.

37. See Nassim Nicholas Taleb, *The Black Swan: The Impact of the Highly Improbable* (New York: Random House, 2007).

38. Source: United Nations, World Urbanization Prospects 2018, available at: https://population.un.org/wup/.

39. See Ying Long and Shuqi Gao, "Shrinking Cities in China: The Overall Profile and Paradox in Planning," in Ying Long and Shuqi Gao, eds., *Shrinking Cities in China: The Other Facet of Urbanization* (New York: Springer, 2019); and Iori Kawate, "China's Largest 'Ghost City' Booms Again Thanks to Education Fever," *Nikkei Asia*, April 19, 2021.

40. The nonlabor income portion of Chinese disposable household income is derived from the flow-of-funds accounts of the National Bureau of Statistics (China); the comparable measure for the United States is derived from the national income and product accounts of the US Department of Commerce (Bureau of Economic Analysis).

41. "Higher-level opening up" is a key theme of China's latest five-year plan, the Fourteenth Five-Year Plan of 2021–25; see "China's New Development Blueprint Heralds Opening-Up at Higher Level," Xinhua News (China), March 14, 2021.

42. See China Securities Regulatory Commission, *China Capital Markets Development Report* (Beijing: China Financial Publishing House, 2008); National Equities Exchange and Quotations (NEEQ), available at http://www.neeq.com.cn/en/about_neeq/introduction.html; and the development of the STAR Market, available at http://star.sse.com.cn/en/. In September 2021, Xi Jinping announced the proposed establishment of a Beijing stock exchange aimed at "innovations-oriented small and medium sized enterprises (SMEs)"; see "Xi Says China to Set Up Beijing Stock Exchange for SMEs," Reuters, September 2, 2021.

43. In an April 2022 speech, Yi Huiman, chairman of China's Securities Regulatory Commission (CSRC), indicated that China was willing to move into closer alignment with listing requirements of US regulators, breaking an increasingly worrisome standoff that was inhibiting offshore capital raising of Chinese companies. See Zhang Hongpei, "China to Keep Offshore Listing Channels Open, Accelerate Launch of New Rules: Official," *Global Times* (China), April 10, 2022; also see "China's CSRC Calls for New Overseas Listing Rule to Take Effect," *Bloomberg News,* April 9, 2022. For a discussion of pre-WTO Chinese financial reforms, see Nicholas R. Lardy, "Issues in China's WTO Accession," testimony before the US-China Security Review Commission, May 9, 2001.

44. See Franklin Allen, Xian Gu, and Jun Qian, "People's Bank of China: History, Current Operations and Future Outlook," Riksbank Summer Institute of Finance Conference 2017, October 2017.

45. See James Stent, *China's Banking Transformation: The Untold Story* (London: Oxford University Press, 2017).

46. See Jun Zhu, "Closure of Financial Institutions in China," in Bank for International Settlements, *Strengthening the Banking System in China: Issues and Experience,* proceedings of a joint BIS/PBC Conference, Beijing, March 1–2, 1999; and Douglas J. Elliott and Kai Yan, "The Chinese Financial System: An Introduction and Overview," Brookings Institution, John L. Thornton China Center Monograph Series No. 6, July 2013.

47. See Weitseng Chen, "WTO: Time's Up for Chinese Banks—China's Banking Reform and Non-Performing Loan Disposal," *Chicago Journal of International Law* 7, no. 1 (2006).

48. See Allen et al., "People's Bank of China."

49. See Stephen Roach, "The Boss and the Maestro," chapter 3 in *Unbalanced.*

50. In 2018, consolidation of the CBRC and CIRC occurred, and a super-regulatory oversight function was created, the China Banking and Insurance Regulatory Commission (CBIRC), headed by Guo Shuqing. Guo, an economist and lawyer by training, has risen through the ranks with an impressive portfolio of operational and Party experience. He held a number of senior positions in banking (as chairman of the China Construction Bank), regulatory oversight (as chairman of the

CSRC), and policy (as director of the State Administration of Foreign Exchange and PBC vice governor); in 2013 he was appointed governor of Shandong Province, and he has been a full member of the CCP Central Committee of senior leaders since 2017.

51. See Alberto Alesina and Lawrence H. Summers, "Central Bank Independence and Macroeconomic Performance: Some Comparative Evidence," *Journal of Money, Credit and Banking* 25, no. 2 (May 1993); Christopher A. Sims, "Fiscal Policy, Monetary Policy and Central Bank Independence," Jackson Hole Symposium, Federal Reserve Bank of Kansas City, August 2016; Athanasios Orphanides, "The Boundaries of Central Bank Independence: Lessons from Unconventional Times," Bank of Japan IMES Discussion Paper, August 2018.

52. See Zhou Xiaochuan, "Managing Multi-Objective Monetary Policy from the Perspective of the Transitioning Chinese Economy," Michel Camdessus Central Banking Lecture, International Monetary Fund, Washington DC, June 24, 2016.

53. In 2021, the IMF's US-dollar-based estimate of nominal GDP in China was 73 percent of that in the United States. The IMF's October 2021 forecast calls for a steady deceleration of nominal GDP growth in China from 8.2 percent in 2022 to 7.3 percent by 2026. To assess the prospects of convergence with the United States, Chinese GDP was extrapolated forward by allowing for an additional modest deceleration down to 6.1 percent nominal GDP growth by 2032. The US growth trajectory reflects an extrapolation of 3.5 percent gains in nominal GDP growth off the IMF's baseline forecast ending in 2026. On the basis of these trajectories, Chinese and US nominal GDP should converge in 2030. One important caveat to this calculation: significant shifts in the foreign exchange rate between the US dollar and the Chinese renminbi could have a material impact on the stipulated convergence trajectory; an acceleration of RMB appreciation could lead to a commensurate acceleration in GDP convergence between the United States and China. Source: Author's calculations based on data from the International Monetary Fund, *World Economic Outlook* database.

54. Purchasing-power parity (PPP) is a widely accepted comparative metric, which adjusts for cross-country disparities in price levels. According to the IMF, world GDP shares of the United States and China hit parity on a PPP basis in 2016; by 2021, the IMF estimated that China's share of 18.6 percent was nearly three percentage points larger than the US share of 15.7 percent. Source: IMF *World Economic Outlook* database.

55. Growth in GDP per capita averaged 9.7 percent in China from 1981 to 2020 and 4.2 percent in the United States over the same period. Extrapolating the 2021 level of $11,819 in China versus the $68,309 level in the United States results in per capita convergence by 2055. Source: Author's calculations based on data from the International Monetary Fund, *World Economic Outlook* database.

56. Ezra F. Vogel, *Japan as Number One: Lessons for America* (Cambridge, MA: Harvard University Press, 1979).

57. Source: International Monetary Fund, *World Economic Outlook* database.

58. See James Fallows, "Containing Japan," *The Atlantic,* May 1989; Clyde V. Presto-witz, *Trading Places: How We Are Giving Our Future to Japan & How to Reclaim It* (New York: Basic Books, 1990); Paul Kennedy, *The Rise and Fall of the Great Powers: Economic Change and Military Conflict from 1500 to 2000* (New York: Random House, 1987); and Stephen Roach, "Japan Then, China Now," *Project Syndicate,* May 2019.

59. See, for example, Donald J. Trump, "National Security Strategy of the United States of America," White House, December 2017; Anthony H. Cordesman, "President Trump's New National Security Strategy," Center for Strategic & International Studies (CSIS), December 18, 2017; and James Fallows, "China's Great Leap Backwards," *The Atlantic,* December 2016.

60. See M. Nakamura, S. Sakakibara, and R. Schroeder, "Adoption of Just-in-Time Manufacturing Methods at US- and Japanese-Owned Plants: Some Empirical Evidence," *IEEE Transactions on Engineering Management* 45, no. 3 (August 1998); and John F. Krafcik, "Triumph of the Lean Production System," *Sloan Management Review* 30 (Fall 1988).

Chapter 11. A New Model of Major Country Relationships

1. See Denise Chao, "The Snake in Chinese Belief," *Folklore* 90, no. 2 (1979).

2. See Xi Jinping, "Build a New Model of Major-Country Relationship between China and the United States"; the Chinese version of Xi's comments to the press on June 8, 2013, can be found in volume 1 of Xi Jinping, *The Governance of China,* updated edition (Shanghai: Foreign Language Press, January 20, 2021).

3. See Vice Premier Wang Yang and State Councilor Yang Jiechi, "Joint Comments to U.S.-China Strategic and Economic Dialogue Opening Session," Washington DC, July 19, 2013; also see Wang Yi, "Toward a New Model of Major-Country Relations between China and the United States," speech delivered to the Brookings Institution, Washington DC, September 30, 2013.

4. See Sun Tzu, *The Art of War,* trans. Gary Gagliardi (Seattle, WA: Science of Strategy Institute/Clearbridge Publishing, 1999).

5. See Office of the White House Press Secretary, "Remarks by President Obama and President Xi Jinping of the People's Republic of China after Bilateral Meeting," Sunnylands Retreat, Rancho Mirage, California, June 8, 2013.

6. See Yang Jiechi, "A New Type of International Relations: Writing a New Chapter of Win-Win Cooperation," *Horizons,* Summer 2015.

7. See Dean P. Chen, *U.S. Taiwan Strait Policy: The Origins of Strategic Ambiguity* (Boulder, CO: First Forum Press, 2012). Recently there has been a growing dissatisfaction with strategic ambiguity in an era of greater Chinese assertiveness, arguing that it is time for the United States and Taiwan to embrace a more clear-cut commitment of strategic clarity; see Richard Haass and David Sacks, "American Support for Taiwan Must Be Unambiguous," *Foreign Affairs,* September 2020.

8. See Office of the White House Press Secretary, "Remarks by President Obama and

President Xi Jinping." This is consistent with views expressed prior to Sunny-lands by several of Obama's senior advisors, including then Secretary of State Hillary Clinton and former National Security Advisor Tom Donilon; see Emily Rauhala, "Hillary Clinton's Long—and Complicated—Relationship with China," *Washington Post*, October 12, 2015, and Tom Donilon, "The United States and the Asia-Pacific in 2013," remarks to the Asia Society, March 11, 2013.

9. That was particularly the case for Stephen Hadley, former national security advisor for President George W. Bush from 2005 to 2009 and a seasoned China expert; see Stephen Hadley, "America, China and the 'New Model of Great-Power Relations,'" speech before the Lowy Institute, Sydney, Australia, November 5, 2014. Also see Caitlin Campbell and Craig Murray, "China Seeks a 'New Type of Major-Country Relationship' with the United States," US-China Economic and Security Review Commission Staff Research Backgrounder, June 25, 2013. For a prominent assessment of the Chinese perspective, see Dai Bingguo, "On Building a New Model of Major-Country Relations between China and the United States," dialogue with Henry Kissinger before the China Development Forum, Beijing, March 2016; also see Cheng-yi Lin, "Xi Jinping, the U.S., and the New Model of Major Country Relations," *Prospect Journal* (Taiwan), 2015.

10. David Lampton, professor at Johns Hopkins University, offered the most detailed action plan for bringing the new model to life, stressing concrete proposals on joint foreign direct investment, a new bilateral dialogue mechanism, and enhanced military-to-military cooperation; see David M. Lampton, "A New Type of Major-Power Relationship: Seeking a Durable Foundation for US-China Ties," *Asia Policy*, July 2013. The Chinese perspective was best articulated in Dai Bingguo's dialogue with Henry Kissinger, "On Building a New Model of Major-Country Relations."

11. The term "co-opetition" was used by Fu Ying, China's former vice minister for foreign affairs, to convey the sense of a cooperative competition between the United States and China—making certain to address each other's concerns in their economic and foreign policy relationship; see Fu Ying, "China and the US Should Prepare for an Era of 'Co-opetition,'" *Financial Times*, November 6, 2019.

12. The ever-creative punditry has gone even further in its attempts to characterize the US-China relationship. Fred Bergsten was first to stress the "G-2" shared global leadership construct; see C. Fred Bergsten, *The United States and the World Economy: Foreign Economic Policy for the Next Decade* (New York: Columbia University Press, 2005); also see Zbigniew Brzezinski, "The Group of Two that Could Change the World," *Financial Times*, January 13, 2009. Then there were those who alluded to a functional merger between two systems dubbed "Chimerica." See Niall Ferguson and Moritz Schularick, "Chimerica and Global Asset Markets," *International Finance* 10, vol. 3 (2007). Curiously, in the aftermath of the Global Financial Crisis of 2008–9, Ferguson and Schularick were quick to reverse their views on the US-China symbiosis; see Niall Ferguson and Moritz Schularick, "The End of Chimerica," Harvard Business School Working Paper No. 10–037,

October 2009. And then there are those, of course, who have droned on about US-China codependency.

13. The economics profession has long had the unfortunate penchant for modeling behavioral social science relationships with the mathematical precision of engineering and the physical sciences; some leading economists, including Nobel Prize winner Paul Romer, believe this trend has gone too far; see Paul M. Romer, "Mathiness in the Theory of Economic Growth," *American Economic Review: Papers and Proceedings* 105, no. 5 (May 2015).

14. Financial market traders have a name for this: "marking to market" is the true test of examining trading strategies relative to shifting security valuations. See, for example, Committee on the Global Financial System, "Market-Making and Proprietary Trading: Industry Trends, Drivers, and Policy Implications," Bank for International Settlements, CGFS Papers No. 52, November 2014.

15. See Ian Bremmer and Nouriel Roubini, "A G-Zero World: The New Economic Club Will Produce Conflict, Not Cooperation," *Foreign Affairs*, March/April 2011.

16. Source: World Bank Development Indicators.

17. Source: Author's calculation based on World Bank Development Indicators.

18. Source: Author's calculation based on World Bank Development Indicators.

19. See Matthew P. Funaiole and Brian Hart, "Understanding China's 2021 Defense Budget," Center for Strategic and International Studies (CSIS), March 5, 2021.

20. See, for example, the State Council Information Office of the People's Republic of China, "China's National Defense in the New Era," white paper (Beijing: Foreign Language Press Co. Ltd., July 2019); Edmund J. Burke, Kristen Gunness, et al., "People's Liberation Army Operational Concepts," RAND Corporation Research Report, 2020; and Demetri Sevastopulo, "China Conducted Two Hypersonic Weapons Tests This Summer," *Financial Times*, October 20, 2021.

21. See Office of the Secretary of Defense, *Military and Security Developments Involving the People's Republic of China: 2020*, Annual Report to Congress, Washington DC, September 2020.

22. Calculations assume that China stays on its nominal GDP growth trajectory through 2026 based on IMF projections and then continues to expand at a 7.4 percent annual pace through 2035; US nominal GDP trajectory is also taken from IMF projections through 2026 and then extrapolated out by 3.8 percent per year. Military spending share of GDP for both nations is held constant at the 2020 actual as per World Bank Development Indicators—1.7 percent for China and 3.7 percent for the United States. Under those assumptions, Chinese military outlays would exceed those of the United States in late 2032 or early 2033. Source: Author's calculation based on World Bank Development Indicators and IMF *World Economic Outlook* database.

23. Between 1980 and 2021, China's nominal GDP increased fifty-five-fold, well in excess of the thirty-five-fold increase in per capita GDP over the same period; source: author's calculations based on International Monetary Fund, *World Economic Outlook* database.

24. This ranking of per capita GDP, expressed in purchasing-power parity, reflects an average of estimates from the International Monetary Fund, the World Bank, and America's Central Intelligence Agency; see https://en.wikipedia.org/wiki/List _of_countries_by_GDP_(PPP)_per_capita.

25. See Paul Kennedy, *The Rise and Fall of Great Powers: Economic Change and Military Conflict from 1500 to 2000* (New York: Random House, 1987). Italic emphasis as per Kennedy.

26. In his 1987 book, *The Rise and Fall of Great Powers*, Kennedy used this same conclusion to argue that the United States might also be guilty of such over-stretch, with an outsize military budget that far outstripped the domestic capacity of a then weakened and more slowly growing US economy. In the aftermath of the 2001 terrorist attacks on the United States, he subsequently reversed that view; see Paul Kennedy, "The Eagle Has Landed," *Financial Times*, February 2–3, 2002.

27. See Anton Cheremukhin, Mikhail Golosov, Sergei Guriev, and Aleh Tsyvinski, "Was Stalin Necessary for Russia's Economic Development?" NBER Working Paper No. 19425, September 2013.

28. See Susan E. Rice, "America's Future in Asia," remarks at Georgetown University, Washington DC, November 30, 2013.

29. See Donilon, "United States and the Asia-Pacific."

30. See Hillary Clinton, "America's Pacific Century," *Foreign Policy*, October 11, 2011; also see Geoff Dyer and Tim Mitchell, "Hillary Clinton: The China Hawk," *Financial Times*, September 5, 2016.

31. As pointed out in Chapter 7, any doubts of US resolve on a China containment strategy were dispelled by the AUKUS trilateral security arrangement of 2021 between Australia, the United Kingdom, and the United States. See David E. Sanger and Zolan Kanno-Youngs, "Biden Announces Defense Deal with Australia in a Bid to Counter China," *New York Times*, September 21, 2021; and "AUKUS Reshapes the Strategic Landscape of the Indo-Pacific," *The Economist*, September 25, 2021.

32. See Charles L. Glaser, "A U.S.-China Grand Bargain? The Hard Choice between Military Competition and Accommodation," *International Security* 39, no. 4 (Spring 2015).

33. See James B. Steinberg, "U.S.-China Relations at a Crossroad: Can History Guide the Path Forward?" Ernest May Memorial Lecture in Leah Bitounis and Jonathon Price, eds., *The Struggle for Power: U.S.-China Relations in the 21st Century* (Washington DC: Aspen Institute, 2020).

34. See Office of the White House Press Secretary, "FACT SHEET: President Xi Jinping's State Visit to the United States," September 25, 2015.

35. Source: Author's calculations based on data from the US Department of Commerce (Bureau of Economic Analysis).

36. Source: Author's calculations based on data from the National Bureau of Statistics (China).

37. Source: Author's calculations based on data from the US Department of Commerce (Bureau of Economic Analysis).

38. Source: Author's calculations based on data from the US Department of Commerce (Bureau of Economic Analysis).

39. See Congressional Budget Office, "The Distribution of Household Income, 2017," October 2020; also see Board of Governors of the Federal Reserve System, "Distribution of Household Wealth in the U.S. since 1989," Distributional Financial Accounts, June 2021.

40. See Office of the White House Press Secretary, "Remarks by President Obama and President Xi of the People's Republic of China in Joint Press Conference," Washington DC, September 25, 2015.

41. See Asia Maritime Transparency Initiative, "China's New Spratly Island Defenses," December 13, 2016, available at: https://amti.csis.org/chinas-new-spratly-island-defenses/.

42. See Asia Maritime Transparency Initiative, "China's New Spratly Island Defenses."

43. See Ankit Panda, "It's Official: Xi Jinping Breaks His Non-Militarization Pledge in the Spratlys," *The Diplomat*, December 16, 2016.

44. See Jeffrey A. Bader, "The U.S. and China's Nine-Dash Line: Ending the Ambiguity," op-ed, Brookings Institution, February 6, 2014.

45. See Sheila A. Smith, "A Sino-Japanese Clash in the East China Sea," Council on Foreign Relations Contingency Planning Memorandum No. 18, April 2013.

46. See Robert D. Williams, "Tribunal Issues Landmark Ruling in South China Sea Arbitration," *Lawfare*, July 12, 2016.

47. See "China's Claims in the South China Sea Rejected," A *ChinaFile* Conversation, July 12, 2016; for a contrary view, which argues that China's territorial claims in the South China Sea are little different from the claims of Taiwan, see Weijian Shan, "Beijing and Taipei Are United—in Their South China Sea Claims," *South China Morning Post*, January 9, 2022.

48. See Murray Hiebert, Phuong Nguyen, and Gregory B. Poling, eds., *Perspectives on the South China Sea: Diplomatic, Legal, and Security Dimensions of the Dispute, A Report of the CSIS Sumitro Chair for Southeast Asia Studies*, Center for Strategic & International Studies (Lanham, MD: Rowman & Littlefield: September 2014). In early 2022, there were signs that the United States was becoming increasingly concerned about potential Chinese military presence in the Solomon Islands, strategically located in the South Pacific to the east of Papua New Guinea and nowhere near China's nine-dash line. Following a new China–Solomon Islands security pact signed in April 2022, Kurt Campbell, Asia coordinator for the Biden administration's National Security Council and identified in Chapter 7 as the architect of America's Asia pivot, was quickly dispatched on a high-level mission to the Solomon Islands to address this issue; see Damien Cave, "Why China's Security Pact with the Solomon Islands Is a Threat," *New York Times*, April 21, 2022.

49. See National Institute for Defense Studies, *NIDS China Security Report 2021: China's Military Strategy in the New Era* (Tokyo: National Institute for Defense Studies, 2021).

50. See, for example, Jeffrey B. Jones, "Confronting China's Efforts to Steal Defense Information," Belfer Center, Harvard Kennedy School, May 2020; James Millward and Dahlia Peterson, "China's System of Oppression in Xinjiang: How It Developed and How to Cure It," Global China, Brookings Institution, September 2020; Oriana Skylar Mastro, "China's Dangerous Double Game in North Korea," *Foreign Affairs*, April 2, 2021; and Will Green, "China-Iran Relations: A Limited but Enduring Strategic Partnership," US-China Economic and Security Review Commission Staff Research Report, June 28, 2021.

51. From time to time, senior US and Chinese officials would attend lectures in my Yale class, "The Next China." On one of those occasions, a former high-ranking US policy advisor happened to be in attendance for my overview lecture on US-China codependency and what it implied for mounting tensions in the South China Sea. The polite response from the US official after class: "I never thought of it in this way. We never gave much consideration to the two-way aspects of this relationship conflict."

52. Published by China's CITIC Press in 2015 as a Chinese-language translation of my 2014 book, *Unbalanced: The Codependency of America and China*, the title of the Chinese version, 失衡—全球经济危机下的再平衡, roughly translates as "Loss of Balance: Rebalancing in the Global Economic Crisis." In addition to getting the translation of the title wrong, the Chinese edition failed to include any of the 438 endnotes in the original English-language text; when I asked for an explanation of this shocking omission, CITIC Press replied, "We don't do that with popular books like yours."

53. See American Psychiatric Association, *Diagnostic and Statistical Manual of Mental Disorders*, 4th and 5th eds. (Washington DC: American Psychiatric Publishing, 2003 and 2013).

54. The political economy of the European Union has been a subject of intense debate over the years—especially the sub-optimal currency union long hampered by the lack of a pan-regional fiscal policy. For the political economy debate, see Albert Alesina, Guido Tabellini, and Francesco Trebbi, "Is Europe an Optimal Political Area?" *Brookings Papers on Economic Activity* 2017, no. 1 (March 2017); for the shifting fiscal policy debate, especially in the aftermath of the recent pan-European fiscal initiative, the Next Generation EU fund, see Lorenzo Codogno and Paul van den Noord, "Assessing Next Generation EU," London School of Economics, "Europe in Question" Discussion Paper Series No. 166/2020, February 2021.

55. See Anonymous, "The Longer Telegram: Toward a New American China Strategy," Atlantic Center, Scowcroft Center for Strategy and Security, January 2021.

56. See Wang Huning, *America against America* (1991; republished independently, February 2022).

57. See Zhang Jian, "Behind the Political Chaos: The Decline of American Values," *Guangming Daily* (China), January 12, 2021; Li Yunlong, "'American Democracy'—The End of the Myth," *People's Daily* (China), January 13, 2021; Zhang Shuhua,

"The Deterioration of Western Politics Further Harms the World," *Global Times* (China), May 19, 2021; and Jude Blanchette and Seth G. Jones, "Beijing's New Narrative of U.S. Decline," A CSIS Open Source Project, Center for Strategic and International Studies (CSIS), July 2021.

58. See Rush Doshi, *The Long Game: China's Grand Strategy to Displace American Power* (New York: Oxford University Press, 2021); also see "Elites in Beijing See America in Decline, Hastened by Trump," *The Economist,* June 13, 2020.

59. See, for example, Feng Zhongping and Huang Jing, "China's Strategic Partnership Diplomacy: Engaging with a Changing World," European Strategic Partnership Observatory, Working Paper 8, June 2014; Shengsong Yue, "Towards a Global Partnership Network: Implications, Evolution and Prospects of China's Partnership Diplomacy," *Copenhagen Journal of Asian Studies* 36, no. 2 (2018); and Helena Legarda, "From Marriage of Convenience to Strategic Partnership: China-Russia Relations and the Fight for Global Influence," *Merics,* August 24, 2021.

60. Source: International Monetary Fund, *World Economic Outlook* database.

61. In fact, the China-Russia partnership agreement of February 4, 2022, contained explicit language emphasizing that both "sides oppose further enlargement of NATO"; see President of Russia, "Joint Statement of the Russian Federation and the People's Republic of China on the International Relations Entering a New Era and the Global Sustainable Development," February 4, 2022, available at http://en.kremlin.ru/supplement/5770. Moreover, there were respected academics inside of China making a strong case in support of the Russian rationale for the invasion of Ukraine; see Zheng Yongnian, "Will the War in Ukraine Lead to the Reconstruction of the World Order?" *Beijing Cultural Review,* February 25, 2022.

62. See Edward Wong and Julian E. Barnes, "China Asked Russia to Delay Ukraine War Until After Olympics, US Officials Say," *New York Times,* March 2, 2022; and Mark Magnier, "China, Told of Ukraine Move in Advance, Asked Russia to Wait Until Olympics Ended: Sources," *South China Morning Post,* March 3, 2022.

63. See Christopher F. Schuetze, "Russia's Invasion Prompts Germany to Beef Up Military Funding," *New York Times,* February 27, 2022.

64. See Stephen Roach, "Only China Can Stop Russia," *Project Syndicate,* March 7, 2022.

65. See "China Says It Wants to Avoid US Sanctions over Russia's War," *Bloomberg News,* March 14, 2022.

66. See Michelle Nichols and Humeyra Pamuk, "Russia Vetoes UN Security Action on Ukraine as China Abstains," *Reuters News,* February 25, 2022.

67. See Phoebe Zhang, "Ukraine War: China Is on the Right Side of History, Foreign Minister Says," *South China Morning Post,* March 20, 2022; and Christian Shepherd, "China and Russia's Military Relationship Likely to Deepen with Ukraine War," *Washington Post,* March 21, 2022. Moreover, there are reports that the CCP has launched an aggressive new pro-Russia propaganda effort; see Chris Buckley, "Bristling Against the West, China Rallies Domestic Sympathy for Russia," *New York Times,* April 4, 2022.

68. See Ministry of Foreign Affairs of the People's Republic of China, "State Councilor and Foreign Minister Wang Yi Meets the Press," March 7, 2022, available at https://www.fmprc.gov.cn/eng/zxxx_662805/202203/t20220308_10649559 .html; Ken Moritsugu, "China Calls Russia Its Chief 'Strategic Partner' Despite War," AP News, March 7, 2022; and Wang Qi and Xu Yelu, "Wang Meets Lavrov in China, Hails Ties as Withstanding Test of Changing Intl Situation," *Global Times* (China), March 30, 2022.

69. See Stephen Roach, Paul De Grauwe, Sergei Guriev, and Odd Arne Westad, "China's Time for Global Leadership," *Project Syndicate,* March 17, 2022.

70. As the architect of US-led global sanctions imposed on Russia, US Treasury Secretary Janet Yellen has been direct in warning China and others of the consequences of "sitting on the fence" as war rages in Ukraine. In a mid-April 2022 speech, she said, "The world's attitude towards China and its willingness to embrace further economic integration may well be affected by China's reaction to our call for resolute action on Russia." See "Remarks by Secretary of the Treasury Janet L. Yellen on Way Forward for the Global Economy," speech before the Atlantic Council, April 13, 2022.

Chapter 12. Accidental Conflict

1. Notwithstanding the sharp deterioration in the US-China relationship since 2018, the broad consensus in the policy communities of both nations has fixated on preemptive actions aimed at forestalling conflict. For the US perspective, see Robert D. Blackwill and Ashley J. Tellis, "Revising U.S. Grand Strategy toward China," Council on Foreign Relations, Council Special Report No. 72, March 2015; The Policy Planning Staff, Office of the Secretary of State, "The Elements of the China Challenge," US State Department, November 2020; Michael D. Swaine, "China Doesn't Pose an Existential Threat for America," *Foreign Policy,* April 2021; and Minxin Pei, "The China Threat Is Being Overhyped," *Bloomberg Opinion,* May 2021. For the Chinese perspective, see Wang Yi, "Interview on International Situation and China's Diplomacy in 2020," Xinhua News Agency and China Media Group, January 2, 2021; Yang Jiechi, "Dialogue with National Committee on U.S.-China Relations," Ministry of Foreign Affairs of the People's Republic of China, February 2, 2021.

2. In economic policy debates, the term *paranoia* has been used to refer to the focus on the *motives* of the debaters rather than the substance of their arguments; see Raghuram G. Rajan, "Why Paranoia Reigns in Economics," *World Economic Forum Global Agenda,* August 12, 2013; also see Rafael Di Tella and Julio T. Rotemberg, "Populism and the Return of the 'Paranoid Style': Some Evidence and a Simple Model of Demand for Incompetence as Insurance against Elite Betrayal," Harvard Business School, Working Paper 17-056, December 2016.

3. See, for example, Barbara W. Tuchman, *The Guns of August* (New York: Ballantine Books, 1962); David Stevenson, *1914–1918: The History of the First World War* (Lon-

don: Gardners Books, 2004); and Greg King and Sue Woolmans, *The Assassination of the Archduke: Sarajevo 1914 and the Romance that Changed the World* (New York: St. Martin's Press, 2013).

4. See, for example, Lawrence E. Blume, "Duality," for *The New Palgrave Dictionary of Economics,* 2nd ed. (New York: Palgrave MacMillan, 2008); William A. Jackson, "Dualism, Duality and the Complexity of Economic Institutions," *International Journal of Social Economics* 26, no. 4 (April 1999); and Stephen R. Lewis Jr., "Some Problems in the Analysis of the Dual Economy," *Pakistan Development Review* 3, no. 4 (Winter 1963).

5. In economics, another well-known example of duality is the "shadow pricing" embedded in classic linear programing problems; in effect, shadow prices are the implicit price of a nonmarketable item as derived from the solution to a linear programing problem. See Robert Dorfman, Paul A. Samuelson, and Robert M. Solow, *Linear Programming and Economic Analysis* (New York: McGraw-Hill, 1958). The duality of shadow pricing was, in fact, used to approximate the implicit price structure embedded in the input-output models of Soviet-style central planning; see John M. Montias, *Central Planning in Poland* (New Haven, CT: Yale University Press, 1962), and Alec Nove, *The Economics of Feasible Socialism Revisited* (London: HarperCollins Academic, 1991).

6. The case for trade diversion of a savings-short US economy was developed earlier in Chapter 4, which underscored that the tariff-related narrowing of the US-China bilateral trade deficit has been more than offset by a widening of US trade deficits with Mexico, Vietnam, Hong Kong, Singapore, South Korea, and India; see also Stephen S. Roach, "The Myth of Global Decoupling," *Project Syndicate,* January 3, 2020.

7. The United States has been especially prominent in generating a continuum of asset bubbles since the late 1990s, as the excesses of post-bubble monetary accommodation have repeatedly fueled subsequent asset and credit bubbles; see Stephen S. Roach, "Double Bubble Trouble," *New York Times,* March 5, 2008.

8. Source: Based on data from World Integrated Trade Solution (WITS), World Bank.

9. This follows from our earlier discussion of the human relationship characteristics of codependency in Chapter 2; see Timmen L. Cermak, *Diagnosing and Treating Co-Dependence* (Minneapolis: Johnson Institute Books, 1986).

10. See, for example, Karen M. Sutter, "'Made in China 2025' Industrial Policies: Issues for Congress," Congressional Research Service, August 11, 2020; Marco Rubio, "Made in China 2025 and the Future of American Industry," US Senate Committee on Small Business and Entrepreneurship Project for Strong Labor Markets and National Development, February 2019; and USTR Section 301 report.

11. See Marcy E. Gallo, "Defense Advanced Research Projects Agency: Overview and Issues for Congress," Congressional Research Service, August 19, 2021; US Chamber of Commerce, "Q&A on 'Buy American' Policies," January 25, 2021; Executive Office of the President, "Buy American and Hire American," Executive Order 13788, April 18, 2017 (Trump), and "Ensuring the Future Is Made in All of

America by All of America's Workers," Executive Order 14005, January 25, 2021 (Biden); and Julian M. Alston, "Benefits and Beneficiaries from U.S. Farm Subsidies," paper prepared for the American Enterprise Institute Project on Agricultural Policy, May 5, 2007. The "US Innovation and Competition Act," passed by the Senate in June 2021 but stuck in the US House of Representatives as of this writing, contains the $52 billion "CHIPS for America Act" that would provide major incentives for domestic US producers of high-end microchips; see Steven Overly, "Frustration Builds over Stalled China Competition Bill," *Politico Weekly Trade*, October 25, 2021.

12. See Nicholas Lardy, *The State Strikes Back: The End of Economic Reform in China?* (Washington DC: Peterson Institute for International Economics, 2019).

13. See Anshu Siripurapu, "Is Industrial Policy Making a Comeback?" Council on Foreign Relations Backgrounder, March 2021; also see Jared Bernstein, "The Time for America to Embrace Industrial Policy Has Arrived," *Foreign Policy*, July 22, 2020.

14. See Serena Ng and Nick Timiraos, "Covid Supercharges Federal Reserve as Backup Lender to the World," *Wall Street Journal*, August 3, 2020; and Paul Tucker, "The Lender of Last Resort and Modern Central Banking: Principles and Reconstruction," Bank for International Settlements, BIS Working Paper No. 79, September 2014. For a discussion of the global role of lenders of last resort, see Maurice Obstfeld, "Lenders of Last Resort in a Globalized World," keynote address for 2009 International Conference, Institute for Monetary and Economic Studies, Bank of Japan, Tokyo, May 27–28, 2009; also see Charles Calomiris, Marc Flandreau, and Luc Laeven, "Political Foundations of the Lender of Last Resort," VoxEU, Centre for Economic and Policy Research (CEPR), September 19, 2016.

15. See, for example, Stephen S. Roach, "The Perils of Fed Gradualism," *Project Syndicate*, December 23, 2015; James Grant, "The High Cost of Low Interest Rates," *Wall Street Journal*, April 1, 2020; and Lorie Logan and Ulrich Bindseil, "Large Central Bank Balance Sheets and Market Functioning," report prepared by a BIS Study Group, October 2019.

16. There is considerable debate over the Chinese view of an America in decline in the twenty-first century; see, for example, Li Yunlong, "American Democracy—The End of the Myth," *People's Daily* (China), January 13, 2021; Rush Doshi, *The Long Game: China's Grand Strategy to Displace American Power* (New York: Oxford University Press, 2021); "Elites in Beijing See America in Decline, Hastened by Trump," *The Economist*, June 13, 2020; and Julian Gewirtz, "China Thinks America Is Losing," *Foreign Affairs* (November/December 2020).

17. See Matthew P. Goodman and David A. Parker, "Navigating Choppy Waters: China's Economic Decision-Making at a Time of Transition," Center for Strategic & International Studies (CSIS), March 2015; Alice Miller, "How Strong Is Xi Jinping?" *China Leadership Monitor*, no. 43 (March 2014); and Daniel H. Rosen, *Avoiding the Blind Alley: China's Economic Overhaul and Its Global Implications*, An Asia Society Policy Institute Report (New York: Asia Society, October 2014).

18. Bailouts during the Global Financial Crisis of 2008–9 sparked a vigorous debate over the perils of moral hazard—in effect, a philosophical critique of a culture of government support of bad conduct by corporate borrowers and investors. See, for example, Peter L. Bernstein, "The Moral Hazard Economy," *Harvard Business Review,* July–August 2009; Emmanuel Farhi and Jean Tirole, "Collective Moral Hazard, Maturity Mismatch and Systemic Bailouts, NBER Working Paper No. 15138, July 2009; and Javier Bianchi, "Efficient Bailouts?" *American Economic Review* 106, no. 12 (December 2016).

19. While Xi Jinping has stressed the objective of common prosperity since November 2012, when he first ascended to Party leadership, attention increased dramatically in the summer of 2021. Xi's July 2021 article in the Party journal, *Qiushi,* followed by his speech to the Central Committee for Financial and Economic Affairs in August, left little doubt of a new CCP ideological campaign. See Xi Jinping, "Understanding the New Development Stage, Applying the New Development Philosophy, and Creating a New Development Dynamic," *Qiushi Journal* (China), July 8, 2021; also see "Xi Stresses Promoting Common Prosperity amid High-Quality Development, Forestalling Major Financial Risks," Xinhua News Service (China), August 18, 2021; Ryan Hass, "Assessing China's 'Common Prosperity' Campaign," *Order from Chaos* (blog), Brookings Institution, September 9, 2021; and Dexter Tiff Roberts, "What Is 'Common Prosperity' and How Will It Change China and Its Relationship with the World?" Atlantic Council Issue Brief, December 2021.

20. See Stephen S. Roach, "China's Animal Spirits Deficit," *Project Syndicate,* July 27, 2021.

21. See Jeanny Yu and Ishika Mookerjee, "Even after $1.5 Trillion Rout, China Tech Traders See More Pain," *Bloomberg,* August 20, 2021.

22. The modern Chinese strain of egalitarianism is very different from that which was first articulated as a "class struggle" under Mao Zedong; see Kerry Brown and Una Aleksandra Berzina-Cerenkova, "Ideology in the Era of Xi Jinping," *Journal of Chinese Political Science* 23, no. 3 (2018).

23. This point has been stressed by Bert Hofman, formerly China director at the World Bank and currently director, East Asian Institute, National University of Singapore, in tying Xi Jinping's common prosperity campaign to this famous statement by Deng Xiaoping on the occasion of the 1986 launch of the Coastal Development Strategy; see Bert Hofman, "China's Common Prosperity Drive," *EAI Commentary,* National University of Singapore, September 3, 2021. There has also been debate over the role that AI can play in tempering regional income and wealth disparities—in effect, using scalable AI-enabled applications to spread the benefits, implicitly addressing the "uncoordinated" critique of Wen Jiabao's "four uns"; see Shiyuan Li and Miao Hao, "Can Artificial Intelligence Reduce Income Inequality? Evidence from China," *Munich Personal RePEc Archive,* MPRA Paper No. 110973, October 2021.

24. See "Xi Jinping's Talk of 'Common Prosperity' Spooks the Prosperous," Free Exchange, *The Economist*, August 28, 2021.

25. See, for example, Macabe Keliher and Hsinchao Wu, "Corruption, Anticorruption, and the Transformation of Political Culture in Contemporary China," *Journal of Asian Studies* 75, no. 1 (February 2016); Melanie Manion, "Taking China's Anticorruption Campaign Seriously," *Economic and Political Studies* 4, no. 1 (May 2016); Jiangnan Zhu, Dong Zhang, and Huang Huang, "'Big Tigers, Big Data': Learning Social Reactions to China's Anticorruption Campaign through Online Feedback," *Public Administration Review* 79, no. 4 (July/August 2019); and Yuen Yuen Ang, *China's Gilded Age: The Paradox of Economic Boom and Vast Corruption* (London: Cambridge University Press, 2020).

26. See, for example, Steven Levitsky and Daniel Ziblatt, *How Democracies Die* (New York: Crown, 2018); Sarah Smarsh, *Heartland: A Memoir of Working Hard and Being Broke in the Richest Country on Earth* (New York: Scribner, 2018); Timothy Snyder, *On Tyranny: Twenty Lessons from the Twentieth Century* (New York: Random House Crown, 2017); and J. D. Vance, *Hillbilly Elegy: A Memoir of Family and Culture in Crisis* (New York: HarperCollins, 2016). For an overview of some 150 books assessing the Trump presidency and its origins, see Carlos Lozada, *What Were We Thinking: A Brief Intellectual History of the Trump Era* (New York: Simon & Schuster, 2020).

27. Nobel Prize–winning economist Robert M. Solow is generally credited with framing the role of productivity in the context of modern economic growth theory; see Robert M. Solow, "A Contribution to the Theory of Economic Growth," *Quarterly Journal of Economics* 70, no. 1 (February 1956). Over the years, the debate has shifted to the sources of productivity growth, especially indigenous innovation; see, for example, Edmund S. Phelps, "The Dynamism of Nations: Toward a Theory of Indigenous Innovation," *Capitalism and Society* 12, no. 1 (May 2017); and Edmund Phelps, Raicho Bojilov, Hian Teck Hoon, and Gylfi Zoega, *Dynamism: The Values That Drive Innovation, Job Satisfaction, and Economic Growth* (Cambridge, MA: Harvard University Press, 2020). Also see Stephen S. Roach, "The Sino-American Innovation Dilemma: A Conflict with Deep Roots and Tough Solutions," *Asia-Pacific Journal* 16, no. 20 (October 2018).

28. The trend toward US and Chinese R&D convergence was discussed previously in Chapter 5. STEM refers to studies in Science, Technology, Engineering, and Mathematics; for a discussion of the coming US-China STEM convergence, see Remco Zwetsloot, Jack Corrigan, Emily Weinstein, et al., "China Is Fast Outpacing U.S. STEM PhD Growth," CSET Data Brief, Center for Security and Economic Policy, August 2021.

29. As noted in Chapter 4, former Trump administration advisor Peter Navarro took the lead in delivering this message; see his June 19, 2018, CNBC interview, as well as the June 2018 white paper produced by Navarro's White House Office of Trade and Manufacturing Policy, "How China's Economic Aggression Threatens

the Technologies and Intellectual Property of the United States and the World," June 2018. Former USTR Robert Lighthizer has continued the saber-rattling on this same point after returning to civilian life following the November 2020 defeat of his patron, Donald Trump; see Robert Lighthizer, "America Shouldn't Compete against China with One Arm Tied Behind Its Back," *New York Times,* July 27, 2021. Nor is this just a Republican position—leading members of the Democratic Party have also expressed similar anti-China sentiments regarding the existential character of the China technology threat. See Maggie Miller, "Senators Warn of Chinese Technology Threats Ahead of International Meeting," *The Hill,* October 4, 2021; also see Vincent Ni, "China Denounces US Senate's $250bn Move to Boost Tech and Manufacturing," *The Guardian,* June 9, 2021.

30. See Ha-Joon Chang, *Bad Samaritans: The Myth of Free Trade and the Secret History of Capitalism* (New York: Bloomsbury Press, 2010).

31. The point made earlier in Chapter 5 on the arrogance of Huawei's Chairman Ren Zhengfei bears repeating; when confronted by evidence supporting Cisco's 2007 charges of software piracy embedded in one of its routers, Ren's one-word retort said it all, "Coincidence." See Chuin-Wei Yap and Dan Strumpf, "Huawei's Years-long Rise Is Littered with Accusations of Theft and Dubious Ethics," *Wall Street Journal,* May 25, 2019.

32. See Mark Scott, Laura Kayali, and Laurens Cerulus, "European Commission Accuses China of Peddling Disinformation," *Politico,* June 10, 2020; Kuni Mayake, "China's Information Warfare Is Failing Again," *Japan Times,* March 16, 2020; and Ruth Levush, "Government Responses to Disinformation on Social Media Platforms," Law Library of Congress, Global Legal Research Directorate, September 2019.

33. See Pew Research Center, "Most Americans Have 'Cold' Views of China. Here's What They Think about China, in Their Own Words," June 30, 2021.

34. See Globely staff, "How Do the Chinese People View America?" *Globely News,* March 17, 2022; Ilaria Mazzocco and Scott Kennedy, "Public Opinion in China: A Liberal Silent Majority?" *Big Data China,* Center for Strategic and International Studies (CSIS), February 9, 2022; Kaiser Kuo, "How Do Chinese People View the United States?" SupChina Sinica podcast with Yaswei Liu and Michael Cerny, November 26, 2021; and Adam Y. Liu, Xiaojun Li, and Songyin Fang, "What Do Chinese People Think of Developed Countries? 2021 Edition," *The Diplomat,* March 13, 2021.

35. On Frances Haugen's revelations about Facebook, see "Statement of Frances Haugen," testimony before the US Senate Committee on Commerce, Science, and Transportation, Sub-Committee on Consumer Protection, Product Safety, and Data Security," October 4, 2021. Also see Jeff Horwitz, "The Facebook Whistleblower, Frances Haugen, Says She Wants to Fix the Company, Not Harm It," *Wall Street Journal,* October 3, 2021; Ryan Mac and Cecilia Kang, "Whistleblower Says Facebook 'Chooses Profits over Safety,'" *New York Times,* October 3, 2021; and Scott Pelley, "Whistleblower: Facebook Is Misleading the Public on Progress against

Hate Speech, Violence, Misinformation," *CBS Sixty Minutes*, October 4, 2021. On former President Obama's speech on the perils to democracy posed by social media, see Barack Obama, "Disinformation Is a Threat to Our Democracy," speech before Stanford University Symposium on Challenges to Democracy in the Digital Information Realm, April 21, 2022.

36. See Stephen Roach, "Codependency, the Internet, and a Dual Identity Crisis," chapter 13 in *Unbalanced: The Codependency of America and China* (New Haven, CT: Yale University Press, 2014).

37. See Daniel H. Rosen and Lauren Gloudeman, "Understanding US-China Decoupling: Macro Trends and Industry Impacts," Report of the Rhodium Group and US Chamber of Commerce China Center, February 2021. Also see Keith Johnson and Robbie Gramer, "The Great Decoupling," *Foreign Policy*, May 14, 2020; and Stephanie Segal, "Degrees of Separation: A Targeted Approach to U.S.-China Decoupling—Final Report," A Report of the CSIS Economics Program, Center for International and Strategic Studies, October 2021.

38. See Graham Allison, *Destined for War: Can America and China Escape Thucydides's Trap?* (New York: Mariner Books, 2017).

39. Considerable attention has been drawn to the increased risks of a US-China hot war in Asia; see Minxin Pei, "China and the US Dash toward Another MAD Arms Race," *Nikkei Asia*, May 16, 2021; also see David C. Gompert, Astrid Stuth Cevallos, and Cristina L. Garafola, *War with China: Thinking Through the Unthinkable* (Santa Monica: The RAND Corporation, 2016). On the South China Sea, see Oriana Skylar Mastro, "Military Confrontation in the South China Sea," Council on Foreign Relations Contingency Planning Memorandum No. 36, May 21, 2020; and Edith M. Lederer, "US and China Clash at UN over South China Sea Disputes," *Military Times*, August 9, 2021. On Taiwan, see Lindsay Maizland, "Why China-Taiwan Relations Are So Tense," Council on Foreign Relations Backgrounder, May 10, 2021; Alastair Gale and Chieko Tsuneoka, "As China-Taiwan Tensions Rise, Japan Begins Preparing for Possible Conflict," *Wall Street Journal*, August 27, 2021; and Economist Intelligence Unit, "Is War between China and Taiwan Inevitable?" Economist Group, June 16, 2021. Vladimir Putin's nuclear threats that have arisen out of the Russo-Ukrainian War are even more disturbing; see Uri Friedman, "Putin's Nuclear Threats Are a Wake-Up Call for the World," *The Atlantic*, March 15, 2022; Steven Simon and Jonathan Stevenson, "Why Putin Went Straight for the Nuclear Threat," *New York Times*, April 1, 2022; Matthew Kroemig, Mark J. Massa, and Alyxandra Marine, "To Decipher Putin's Nuclear Threats, Watch What He Does—Not What He Says," *New Atlanticist* (Atlantic Council, March 4, 2022).

40. See Office of the Secretary of Defense, *Military and Security Developments Involving the People's Republic of China: 2020*, Annual Report to Congress, Washington DC, September 2020; and Anthony H. Cordesman, "Chinese Strategy and Military Forces in 2021: A Graphic Net Assessment," Center for Strategic and International Studies, August 2021.

41. This point was developed earlier in Chapter 6; see Paul Kennedy, *The Rise and Fall of the Great Powers: Economic Change and Military Conflict from 1500 to 2000* (New York: Random House, 1987).

42. See Gloria Cowan, Mimi Bommersbach, and Sheri R. Curtis, "Codependency, Loss of Self, and Power," *Psychology of Women Quarterly* 19, no. 2 (June 1995); Marolyn Wells, Cheryl Glickauf-Hughes, and Rebecca Jones, "Codependency: A Grass Roots Construct's Relationship to Shame-Proneness, Low Self-Esteem, and Childhood Parentification," *American Journal of Family Therapy* 27, no. 1 (1999).

43. See Alison Favorini, "Concept of Codependency: Blaming the Victim or Pathway to Recovery?" *Social Work* 40, no. 6 (November 1995); Ofer Zur, "Rethinking 'Don't Blame the Victim': The Psychology of Victimhood," *Journal of Couples Therapy* 4, no. 3–4 (1995).

44. See Jimmy Carter, "Energy and National Goals: Address to the Nation," July 15, 1979, Jimmy Carter Presidential Library and Museum, https://www.jimmycarter library.gov/assets/documents/speeches/energy-crisis.phtml.

45. See Stephen S. Roach, "Japan Then, China Now," *Project Syndicate,* May 2019.

46. See Jude Blanchette, "Xi's Gamble: The Race to Consolidate Power and Stave Off Disaster," *Foreign Affairs,* July/August 2021; Dexter Tiff Roberts, "Xi Jinping's Politics in Command Economy," Scowcroft Center for Strategy and Security, Atlantic Council Issue Brief, July 2021; and Susan L. Shirk, "China in Xi's 'New Era': The Return to Personalistic Rule," *Journal of Democracy* 29, no. 2 (April 2018).

Chapter 13. From Distrust to Trust

1. See, for example, David S. Mason, "Glasnost, Perestroika and Eastern Europe," *International Affairs* 64, no. 3 (Summer 1988); Lilita Dzirkals, "Glasnost and Soviet Foreign Policy," RAND Note, Rand Corporation, January 1990; and George A. Carver Jr., "Intelligence in the Ages of Glasnost," *Foreign Affairs,* Summer 1990.

2. See Chris Buckley, "China Sees 'Trust Deficit' before Xi's US Trip," Reuters, February 7, 2012. For a comparison of long-standing Chinese and American perspectives of strategic distrust, see Kenneth Lieberthal and Wang Jisi, "Addressing U.S.-China Strategic Distrust," John L. Thornton China Center Monograph Series, Number 4 (Washington DC: Brookings Institution, March 2012).

3. Cui Tiankai did postgraduate work at Johns Hopkins University, and had a twenty-year career in China's Ministry of Foreign Affairs, including three years as ambassador to Japan from 2007–9, before he became ambassador to the United States in 2013; see "Biography of Ambassador Cui Tiankai," Embassy of the People's Republic of China in the United States of America, available at http://www .china-embassy.org/eng/sgxx/ctk/boa/.

4. See Jonathan D. Spence, *The Chan's Great Continent: China in Western Minds* (New York: W. W. Norton & Company, Inc.: 1998).

5. See Phoebe Scott, "Mimesis to Mockery: Chinoiserie Ornament in the Social Space of Eighteenth-Century France," *Philament* 5 (January 2005).

6. See Spence, *The Chan's Great Continent*, 16.

7. See Jonathan D. Spence, "Kissinger and China," *New York Review*, June 9, 2011.

8. The "China Initiative" was launched by the Trump administration in November 2018 allegedly to counter threats from Chinese espionage that posed risks to US national security. The US Department of Justice (DOJ) quickly shifted the focus of this effort away from economic espionage and cyberhacking toward questions of "research integrity"—specifically focusing on failures by some academics to disclose Chinese sources of funding for their research programs. According to a detailed assessment published in the *MIT Technology Review*, almost 90 percent of the nearly 150 individuals charged under the initiative are of Chinese heritage. Large faculty groups from several US universities have written letters to US Attorney General Merrick Garland protesting the abuses of the China Initiative and demanding its immediate termination; I was one of 193 signatories to the Yale University letter sent to AG Garland in January 2022. See Eileen Guo, Jess Aloe, and Karen Hao, "The US Crackdown on Chinese Economic Espionage Is a Mess. We Have the Data to Show It," *MIT Technology Review*, December 2, 2021; and Isaac Yu, "'A Chilling Hostile Environment': Faculty Protest China Initiative as Tensions Continue to Disrupt Research," *Yale Daily News*, December 2, 2021. In response to increasingly widespread criticism, the China Initiative was formally ended by the Biden administration in February 2022, with espionage cases against China folded back into the DOJ's national security division; see Katie Benner, "Justice Dept. to end Trump-Era Initiative to Deter Chinese Threats," *New York Times*, February 23, 2022.

9. See Tamim Bayoumi and Yunhui Zhao, "Incomplete Financial Markets and the Booming Housing Sector in China," International Monetary Fund Working Paper No. 2020/265, December 2020; Kenneth S. Rogoff and Yuanchen Yang, "Peak China Housing," NBER Working Paper 27967, August 2020; Stella Yifan Xie and Mike Bird, "The $52 Trillion Bubble: China Grapples with Epic Property Boom," *Wall Street Journal*, July 16, 2020; and Maya Bhandari et al., "If the Chinese Bubble Bursts: The Views of 30 Experts," *International Economy*, Fall 2019. For contrary views, see Thomas Orlick, *China: The Bubble that Never Pops* (New York: Oxford University Press, 2020); Hanming Fang, Quanlin Gu, Wei Xiong, and Li-An Zhou, "Demystifying the Chinese Housing Boom," NBER Working Paper No. 21112, April 2015. For a discussion of concerns over the parallels between China's Evergrande failure of 2021–2 and the bankruptcy of America's Lehman Brothers in 2008, see Martin Farrer and Vincent Ni, "China's Lehman Brothers Moment? Evergrande Crisis Rattles Economy," *Guardian*, September 17, 2021; and Desmond Lachman, "Is This China's Lehman Brothers Moment?" *The Hill*, September 21, 2011.

10. See Dinny McMahon, *China's Great Wall of Debt: Shadow Banks, Ghost Cities, Massive Loans, and the End of the Chinese Miracle* (New York: Houghton Mifflin Harcourt, 2018); Wojciech Maliszewski et al., "Resolving China's Corporate Debt Problem," IMF Working Paper No. 16/203, October 2016; and Yukon Huang and

Canyon Bosler, "China's Debt Dilemma: Deleveraging While Generating Growth," Carnegie Endowment for International Peace, September 2014.

11. See Stephen S. Roach, "Deciphering China's Economic Resilience," *Project Syndicate,* July 25, 2017; and Barry Naughton, "Two Trains Running: Supply-Side Reform, SOE Reform and the Authoritative Personage," *China Leadership Monitor,* August 2016.

12. The Washington establishment has long been sympathetic to the broken-promise narrative of China's WTO compliance; see "The Broken Promises of China's WTO Accession: Reprioritizing Human Rights," Hearing Before the Congressional-Executive Commission on China, March 2017; and Elizabeth Economy, "Trade: Parade of Broken Promises," *Democracy: A Journal of Ideas,* no. 52 (Spring 2019). This view is well aligned with the influential Modernization Theory linking economic development to democracy; see, for example, Seymour M. Lipset, "Some Social Requisites of Democracy: Economic Development and Political Legitimacy," *American Political Science Review* 53, no. 1 (1959); and Samuel P. Huntington, *The Third Wave: Democratization in the Late Twentieth Century* (Norman, OK: University of Oklahoma Press, 1961). An extraordinary 2008 empirical study by four economists raised serious questions of spurious causality in this thesis; see Daron Acemoglu, Simon Johnson, James A. Robinson, and Pierre Yared, "Income and Democracy," *American Economic Review* 98, no. 3 (June 2008).

13. See Joe Renquard, "The Nixon-Mao Summit: A Week that Changed the World?" *US, Asia, and the World: 1914–2012* 17, no. 3 (Winter 2012).

14. See "The Shanghai Communiqué, February 28, 1972," *Foreign Policy Bulletin* 8, no. 2 (1997).

15. Henry Kissinger is widely credited with the application of ambiguity to US foreign policy, both in Middle East and in China-Taiwan negotiations. See, for example, Robert D. Blackwill and Philip Zelikow, "The United States, China, and Taiwan: A Strategy to Prevent War," Council on Foreign Relations, Council Special Report No. 90, February 2021; Joel Singer, "The Use of Constructive Ambiguity in Israeli-Arab Peace Negotiations," in Yoram Dinstein, ed., *Israeli Yearbook on Human Rights,* vol. 50 (Leiden and Boston: Brill Nijhoff, 2020); and Khaled Elgindy, "When Ambiguity Is Destructive," op-ed, *Brookings,* January 22, 2014.

16. See Henry Kissinger, *On China* (New York: Penguin Press, 2011).

17. In a lengthy November 19, 1973, memorandum from Henry Kissinger to Richard Nixon summarizing his just-completed mission to China, Kissinger described the Liaison Offices as supporting "larger missions performing wider tasks. They are becoming embassies in all but name." See Office of the Historian, *Foreign Relations of the United States, 1969–1976,* Volume XVIII, China, 1973–1976, Document No. 62.

18. Source: World Bank Development Indicators.

19. See Nicholas R. Lardy, *Integrating China into the Global Economy* (Washington DC: Brookings Institution, 2002); US Congress, "Normal Trade Relations for the People's Republic of China," Public Law 106-286, October 10, 2000; and Gary C.

Hufbauer and Daniel H. Rosen, "American Access to China's Market: The Congressional Vote on PNTR," International Economic Policy Briefs, Institute for International Economics, May 2000.

20. See World Trade Organization, "Protocol on the Accession of the People's Republic of China," decision of November 10, 2001.

21. See Bill Clinton, "Speech on China Trade Bill," before the Paul H. Nitze School of Advanced International Studies, Johns Hopkins University, Washington DC, March 9, 2000.

22. Clinton, "Speech on China Trade Bill."

23. Clinton, "Speech on China Trade Bill."

24. China is far from the major target of WTO complaints; over the 1995 to 2021 history of the WTO, fully 178 complaints have been filed against the United States and 101 have been lodged against the European Union—well in excess of the forty-nine complaints against China in an admittedly shorter period of time (2001–21); see World Trade Organization Dispute Settlement Database, available at https://www.wto.org/english/tratop_e/dispu_e/dispu_by_country_e.htm. Also see James Bacchus, Simon Lester, and Huan Zhu, "Disciplining China's Trade Practices at the WTO," Cato Institute Policy Analysis No. 856, November 15, 2018.

25. See US Trade Representative, "2020 Report to Congress on China's WTO Compliance," January 2021.

26. Katherine Tai, the new USTR of the Biden administration, has kept up the pressure on China over concerns of unfair industrial policy subsidies; see David Lawder and Andrea Shalal, "U.S. Trade Chief Tai Seeks Talks with China, Won't Rule Out New Tariff Actions," Reuters, October 4, 2021.

27. See US Department of Commerce, "U.S.-China Joint Commission on Commerce and Trade (JCCT)," available at https://2014-2017.commerce.gov/tags/us-china -joint-commission-commerce-and-trade-jcct.html.

28. See Tiffany Barron et. al., *Engagement Revisited: Progress Made and Lessons Learned from the US-China Strategic and Economic Dialogue*, National Committee on American Foreign Policy, September 2021.

29. See US Department of the Treasury, "U.S.-China Comprehensive Economic Dialogue: 2017," available at https://www.treasury.gov/initiatives/pages/china.aspx.

30. See charter of the US-China Economic and Security Review Commission, available at https://www.uscc.gov/charter.

31. The Chinese foreign policy establishment has long expressed concerns over the USCESRC's anti-China biases; in 2017, Chinese Foreign Ministry spokesman Geng Shuang commented, "This commission [USCESRC] . . . has always been full of prejudice on China-related issues." See Reuters staff, "China Denounces U.S. Call to Register Chinese Journalists as Agents," Reuters, November 16, 2017; and Tom O'Connor, "China Says US Report to Congress Filled with 'Conspiracies, Pitfalls, Threats,'" *Newsweek*, December 2, 2020. This view has been echoed by others. See "U.S. Urged to Do More against Rising Threat of Assertive China," *Bloomberg News*, December 1, 2020; and Government of the Hong Kong Special

Administrative Region, "HKSARG Vehemently Refutes Groundless Accusations by the United States-China Economic and Security Review Commission," press release, December 2, 2020.

32. See US-China Economic and Security Review Commission, *2020 Report to Congress*, Washington DC, December 2020. In 2022, Clyde Prestowitz, founder and president of the Economic Strategy Institute, presented testimony and argued to the USCESRC that both Tim Cook, CEO of Apple, and Ray Dalio, founder and co-chairman of Bridgewater, should be required to register as foreign agents in light of their repeated corporate "kowtowing" to China in order to seek favorable commercial treatment for the companies they headed. See Clyde Prestowitz, "Testimony Before the U.S.-China Economic and Security Review Commission," April 6, 2022; also see Robert Delaney and Joshua Cartwright, "Tim Cook of Apple and Financier Ray Dalio Should Register as Foreign Agents for China, US Panel Hears," *South China Morning Post,* April 15, 2022.

33. See Stephen S. Roach, "Chinese Rebalancing: Transitioning from the 12th to the 13th Five-Year Plan," testimony before the USCESRC, April 22, 2015; Stephen S. Roach, "A Wake-Up Call for the US and China: Stress Testing a Symbiotic Relationship," testimony before the USCESRC, February 15, 2009; and Stephen S. Roach, "Getting China Right," testimony before the USCESRC, September 25, 2003. The line of questioning following each of my testimonies illustrates the anti-China biases of commission members; Q&A sessions for each such appearance can be found at https://www.uscc.gov/hearings.

34. See China Development Forum website for meeting agendas from 2000 to 2021, available at https://www.cdf.org.cn/cdf2021/index.jhtml.

35. After missing the first meeting of the China Development Forum in 2000, I have attended and spoken at every subsequent session of the CDF since 2001, including virtual participation in 2021 and a webinar in 2022 following another Covid-related cancellation; no senior officials of the Trump administration attended the CDF from 2017 to 2020.

36. See https://english.boaoforum.org/; https://www.weforum.org/about/new-champions; http://english.cciee.org.cn/; http://www.ciids.cn/node_64908.htm; and http://new.cf40.org.cn/index_en.php.

37. While there is a long history of Track II dialogues as an ancillary mechanism of diplomacy, the first "high-level" Track II was held in Beijing in October 2009 featuring Premier Wen Jiabao on the Chinese side along with Henry Kissinger, George Schultz, Robert Rubin, and William Perry from the US side; I have participated in several Track II dialogues over the years and have a long association with one sponsored by the National Committee on US-China Relations. Also see Charles Homans, "Track II Diplomacy: A Short History," *Foreign Policy,* June 20, 2011; Jennifer Staats, "A Primer on Multi-Track Diplomacy: How Does It Work?" United States Institute of Peace, July 31, 2019; and Jiao Liu, "China-US Track Two Diplomacy Injecting Huge Positive Energy," *China Daily,* November 7, 2018.

38. See Henry Kissinger, *On China* (New York: Penguin Books, 2011); also see "Kis-

singer among Featured Speakers at Johnson Center's First Annual Conference," *Yale News,* April 1, 2012.

39. The hot line stumbling point in the 1973 US-China negotiations had been referenced earlier in US diplomatic archival material. See Office of the Historian, *Foreign Relations of the United States, 1969–1976,* Volume XVIII, China, 1973–1976, Document No. 55; and Kazushi Minami, "Re-examining the End of Mao's Revolution: China's Changing Statecraft and Sino-American Relations, 1973–1978," *Cold War History* 16, no. 4 (2016).

40. In earlier research, Professor Chen hinted of Mao's destabilizing impact on US-China negotiations in the 1970s; see Chen Jian, *Mao's China and the Cold War* (Chapel Hill: University of North Carolina Press, 2001). Chen's forthcoming biography of Zhou Enlai, which draws on the newly available Chinese archival data that he discussed at the Yale conference in 2012, apparently confirms his earlier suspicions.

41. I am indebted to Richard Levin, former president of Yale University, for corroborating this account of the 2012 Yale symposium.

42. See Matt Bevan, "Xi Jinping discussed the Thucydides Trap with Malcolm Turnbull, Revealing His View of the World Today," ABC News Australia, July 5, 2021; "China Generals Urge More Spending for U.S. Conflict 'Trap,'" *Bloomberg News,* March 8, 2021; Michael Crowley, "Why the White House Is Reading Greek History," *Politico Magazine,* June 21, 2017; and Ministry of Foreign Affairs of the People's Republic of China, "Transcript of Ambassador Cui Tiankai's Dialogue with Professor Graham Allison at the Annual Conference of the Institute for China-American Studies," Washington DC, December 5, 2020.

43. See Intergovernmental Panel on Climate Change, *Climate Change 2021: The Physical Science Basis,* Contribution of Working Group I to the Sixth Assessment Report of the IPCC (Cambridge: Cambridge University Press, August 2021).

44. See Our World in Data, "Coronavirus (Covid-19) Vaccinations," available at http://new.cf40.org.cn/index_en.php.

45. See Peter J. Hotez, *Preventing the Next Pandemic: Vaccine Diplomacy in a Time of Anti-science* (Baltimore, MD: Johns Hopkins University Press, 2021); and Gina Kolata, "Fauci Wants to Make Vaccines for the Next Pandemic Before It Hits," *New York Times,* July 25, 2021.

46. See Matt Warren, "Ransomware: A Global Problem," *RMIT Australia,* July 5, 2021; and Enrique Dans, "Ransomware Is a Global Threat That Requires a Coordinated Global Response," *Forbes,* August 5, 2021.

47. See Derek Kortepeter, "Shipping Giant COSCO Brutalized by Ransomware Attack," *TechGenix,* August 3, 2018; "The Latest: 29,000 Chinese Institutions Hit by Cyberattack," Associated Press, May 15, 2017; and Naveen Goud, "Over 20K Chinese PCs Infected with a New Ransomware Variant," *Cybersecurity Insiders,* December 2016.

48. See Joseph R. Biden, "Paris Climate Agreement," White House Briefing Room, January 20, 2021.

49. See US Department of State, Leaders' Summit on Climate, https://www.state.gov /leaders-summit-on-climate/; also see UN Climate Change Conference (COP26): UK 2021, https://ukcop26.org/.

50. See Chris Buckley, "China Opened a National Carbon Market. Here's Why It Matters," *New York Times*, July 16, 2021; also see Bianca Nogardy, "China Launches World's Largest Carbon Market: But Is It Ambitious Enough?" *Nature*, July 29, 2021.

51. US Department of State, "U.S.-China Joint Statement Addressing the Climate Crisis," Media Note, Office of the Spokesperson, April 17, 2021.

52. John Kerry, who has expressed the view that COP26 was a serious starting point for US-China leadership in addressing global climate change, has continued to push ahead post-Glasgow with his Chinese counterparts. See Steven Mufson, Brady Dennis, and Michael Birnbaum, "Beyond Glasgow, Kerry Pushes to Close Emission Gaps," *Washington Post*, December 30, 2021; also see Tripti Lahiri, "An Old Friendship Is Behind the Surprise US-China COP26 Announcement," *Quartz*, November 11, 2021. At the same time, preliminary data pointed to a surprisingly sharp increase in 2021 greenhouse emissions, making a closing of the COP26 emissions gap look all the more daunting; see Alfredo Rivera, Kate Larsen, Hannah Pitt, and Shweta Movalia, "Preliminary US Greenhouse Emissions Estimates for 2021," Rhodium Group Note, January 10, 2022. For a discussion of the upsurge in coal demand in response to a war-related surge of energy prices in early 2022, see Darrell Proctor, "Coal Use Rises, Prices Soar as War Impacts Energy Markets," *Power*, March 8, 2022; and Ajit Niranjan, "Russia-Ukraine War Risks Greater Carbon Pollution Despite Boost to Clean Energy," DW Akademie (Germany), March 15, 2022.

53. See White House Briefing Room, "Statement by President Joe Biden on the Investigations into the Origins of COVID-19," May 26, 2021.

54. See Office of the Director of National Intelligence, "Unclassified Summary of Assessment on COVID-19 Origins," Intelligence Community Assessment, August 27, 2021, available at https://www.dni.gov/index.php/newsroom/reports -publications/reports-publications-2021/item/2236-unclassified-summary-of -assessment-on-covid-19-origins; Michael Worobey, Joshua I. Levy, Lorena M. Malpica Serrano, et al., "The Huanan Market Was the Epicenter of SARS-Cov-2 Emergence," *Zenodo*, February 26, 2022, available at https://doi.org/10.5281 /zenodo.6299116; and Jonathan E. Pekar, Andrew Magee, Edyth Parjer, et al., "SARS-CoV-2 Emergence Very Likely Resulted from Two Zoonotic Events," *Zenodo*, February 26, 2022, https://doi.org/10.5281/zenodo.6291628.

55. See White House Briefing Room, "Statement by President Joe Biden on the Investigations into the Origins of COVID-19," August 27, 2021, available at https://www .whitehouse.gov/briefing-room/statements-releases/2021/08/27/statement -by-president-joe-biden-on-the-investigation-into-the-origins-of-covid-%E2%81 %A019/.

56. See White House Briefing Room, "Statement by President Joe Biden on the Investigations into the Origins of COVID-19," May 26, 2021.

57. See Chao Deng, "China Rejects WHO Proposal for Second Phase of Covid-19 Origins Probe," *Wall Street Journal*, July 22, 2021.

58. See Raymond Zhong, Paul Mozur, and Aaron Krolik, "No 'Negative' News: How China Censored the Coronavirus," *New York Times*, January 13, 2021.

59. See Embassy of the PRC in the United States of America, "Statement by the Chinese Embassy in the United States on the 'COVID-19 Origin-Tracing' Report of the U.S. Side," August 27, 2021; also see Ministry of Foreign Affairs of the PRC, "Remarks by Ambassador Chen Xiaodong at Press Briefing on COVID-19 Origin-Tracing," Chinese Embassy in South Africa, August 30, 2021.

60. See White House Briefing Room, "Background Press Call by Senior Administration Officials on Malicious Cyber Activity Attributable to the People's Republic of China," July 19, 2021; also see Zolan Kanno-Youngs and David E. Sanger, "U.S. Accuses China of Hacking Microsoft," *New York Times*, July 19, 2021.

61. See Office of the Secretary of Defense, *Military and Security Developments Involving the People's Republic of China: 2020*, Annual Report to Congress, Washington DC, September 2020; and Office of the Attorney General, "U.S. Charges Five Chinese Military Hackers for Cyber Espionage against U.S. Corporations and a Labor Organization for Commercial Advantage," Office of Public Affairs, Department of Justice, May 19, 2014. US press reports stressed that "the move makes for good publicity, but will do little to deter hackers"; also see Jaikumar Vijayan, "Hacker Indictments against China's Military Unlikely to Change Anything," *Computerworld*, May 19, 2014. While the as yet unprosecuted 2014 criminal charges were the first such actions filed against state actors for hacking, the DOJ followed up with another effort in July 2021 by indicting four more Chinese nationals for global cyberhacking aimed at companies, universities, and government agencies in the United States and around the world. See Office of the Attorney General, "Four Chinese Nationals Working with the Ministry of State Security Charged with Global Computer Intrusion Campaign Targeting Intellectual Property and Confidential Business Information, Including Infectious Disease Research," Office of Public Affairs, Department of Justice, July 19, 2021; also see Katie Benner, "U.S. Accuses Chinese Officials of Running Data Theft Ring," *New York Times*, July 19, 2021.

62. See Teddy Ng and Echo Xie, "China Confirms Xi Jinping Will Attend Biden's Earth Day Climate Summit," *South China Morning Post*, April 21, 2021. Nor did Xi attend the COP26 global climate summit in Glasgow in November 2021, maintaining his record for not having left China since the outbreak of Covid-19.

63. See, for example, Ma Jun, *The Economics of Air Pollution in China: Achieving Better and Cleaner Growth* (New York: Columbia University Press, 2017); Angang Hu and Qingyou Guan, *China: Tackle the Challenge of Global Climate Change (China Perspectives)* (New York and Beijing: Routledge and Tsinghua University Press, 2017);

and Weiguang Wang and Guoguang Zheng, eds., *China's Climate Change Policies* (New York: Routledge, 2012).

64. See Stephen Roach, "Time for the U.S. and China to Collaborate, Not Complain," *Bloomberg Opinion*, March 30, 2020.

65. The scale of China's global vaccine distribution pledge (two billion doses in 2021) far outstrips the foreign distribution plans by the United States (1.2 billion doses with over 400 million doses shipped to 112 countries as of February 2022); there are, however, important questions about the relative efficacy of the two vaccines, especially in coping with the highly transmissible Omicron variant. See White House Briefing Room, "FACT SHEET: The Biden Administration's Commitment to Global Health," February 2, 2022; Liu Zhen, "Xi Jinping Says China Promises 2 Billion Covid-19 Vaccine Doses to Other Countries in 2021," *South China Morning Post*, August 6, 2021; and Smriti Mallapaty, "China's COVID Vaccines Are Going Global—But Questions Remain," *Nature*, May 12, 2021.

66. See Sam Meredith, "Dr. Fauci Says U.S. Will Remain a WHO Member and Join Global Covid Vaccine Plan," CNBC, January 21, 2021.

67. For a discussion of China's role in global health leadership in addressing the current pandemic, see Yanzhong Huang, "The COVID-19 Pandemic and China's Global Health Leadership," Council on Foreign Relations, Council Special Report No. 92, January 2022; on the potential for US-China Covid-19 collaboration, see Stephen Roach, "Time for the U.S. and China to Collaborate, Not Complain," *Bloomberg Opinion*, March 30, 2020.

68. The Chinese Center for Disease Control and Prevention (CDC) was set up in 2002 following the outbreak of SARS in 2001; organizationally, it is part the National Health Commission of the PRC. The US Centers for Disease Control and Prevention was set up in 1946, and the National Institutes of Health (NIH), the largest biomedical research agency in the world, was set up in 1887; organizationally, both are part of the US Department of Health and Human Services. See "U.S.-China Dialogue on Global Health," Background Report of the Georgetown University Institute for US China Dialogue, April 2017.

69. See, for example, Stephen Orlins, "How Joe Biden's America and China Can Turn the Page on a Rocky Relationship," *South China Morning Post*, January 14, 2021.

70. Prominent examples of easing restraints on NGO activity might include relaxing pressure on China's Confucius Institutes in the United States and the American Bar Association's now-shuttered activities in China. See, for example, Jessica Batke, "'The New Normal' for Foreign NGOs in 2020," *ChinaFile*, The China NGO Project, January 3, 2020; Elizabeth Knup, "The Role of American NGOs and Civil Society Actors in an Evolving US-China Relationship," Carter Center China Program, 2019; and Yawei Liu, Susan Thornton, and Robert A. Kapp, "Finding Firmer Ground: The Role of Civil Society and NGOs in U.S.-China Relations," A Report on US-China Relations Produced by the Carter Center, 2021. On the subject of US listings of Chinese firms, see "How the Delisting of Chinese Firms on American Exchanges Might Play Out," Buttonwood's Notebook, *The Economist*, August

14, 2021; Paul Kiernan, "SEC to Set New Disclosure Requirements for Chinese Company IPOs," *Wall Street Journal*, July 30, 2021; and Keith Zhai, "China Plans to Ban U.S. IPOs for Data-Heavy Tech Firms," *Wall Street Journal*, August 27, 2021. For a discussion of CIFIUS expansion, see Alan Rappeport, "U.S. Outlines Plans to Scrutinize Chinese and Other Foreign Investment," *New York Times*, September 17, 2019. On the subject of blacklisting via the "entity list," see Eversheds Sutherland LLP, "US Maximizes Sanctions Pressure on China with 'Entity Listing' of 59 Chinese Entities," *JD Supra*, December 22, 2020.

Chapter 14. A Path to Interdependency

1. Source: US Department of Commerce (Bureau of Economic Analysis).
2. See the Conference Board, "The China Trade Challenge: Phase II," *Solution Briefs*, July 2020.
3. Phase I compliance was assiduously monitored by Chad P. Bown of the Peterson Institute for International Economics; see Chad P. Bown, "US-China Phase One Tracker: China's Purchases of US Goods," Peterson Institute for International Economics, March 11, 2022. For Bown's stunning recap of the deal's ultimate failure, see Chad P. Bown. "China Bought None of the Extra $200 Billion of US Exports in Trump's Trade Deal," Peterson Institute for International Economics, March 8, 2022. In public statements, USTR Katherine Tai has been quite vocal in continuing to hold China accountable for its failed Phase I compliance; see David Lawler, "U.S. Trade Chief Tai Says Getting 'Traction' with China in 'Phase I' Deal Talks," Reuters, November 10, 2021; also see "Testimony of Ambassador Katherine Tai Before the House Ways & Means Committee on the President's 2022 Trade Policy Agenda," March 30, 2022, available at https://ustr.gov/about-us/policy-offices/press-office/speeches-and-remarks/2022/march/testimony-ambassador-katherine-tai-house-ways-means-committee-hearing-presidents-2022-trade-policy.
4. See Chad P. Bown, "US-China Trade War Tariffs," Peterson Institute for International Economics, March 26, 2021; also see Erica York, "Tracking the Economic Impact of U.S. Tariffs and Retaliatory Actions," Tax Foundation Tariff Tracker, September 18, 2020.
5. The estimated $65 billion "tariff tax" that would be eliminated by the full rollback of both US and Chinese tariffs to levels prevailing in January 2018 was calculated as follows: US tariff rates on some 66 percent of Chinese imports were increased from 3.1 percent in January 2018 to 19.3 percent through January 2021; rolling back this 16.2 percentage point tariff hike works out to about $54 billion of annualized saving. A comparable rollback of the 12.7 percentage point increase of Chinese tariff rates (from 8 percent in January 2018 to 20.7 percent in January 2021) imposed on the 58 percent of US exports covered by Chinese tariff hikes works out to another $11 billion in annualized saving. The sum of the two—$54 billion of US tariffs and $11 billion in Chinese tariffs—adds up to $65 billion in joint saving by tariff rollbacks in the US and China, combined. Source: Author's calculation

based on data from Chad Bown, PIIE (October 2021) and the US Department of Commerce (BEA).

6. See, for example, David Wessel, "How Worried Should You Be about the Federal Deficit and Debt?" Brookings Voter Vitals, July 8, 2020; Douglas W. Elmendorf, "Why We Should Not Reduce Budget Deficits Now," remarks delivered at a conference at Princeton University, Princeton, NJ, February 22, 2020; and Desmond Lachman, "With Low Interest Rates, Should We Really Ignore Budget Deficits?" American Enterprise Institute, June 8, 2020.

7. See Stephen S. Roach, "The Fed Must Think Creatively Again," *Project Syndicate,* November 22, 2021.

8. See "Pelosi-Schumer Remarks at Press Conference on Trump FY2021 Budget," February 11, 2020, available at https://www.speaker.gov/newsroom/21120-0; and Mitch McConnell, "President Biden's Budget 'Would Drown American Families in Debt, Deficits, and Inflation,'" press release, May 28, 2021, available at https://www.republicanleader.senate.gov/newsroom/press-releases/mcconnell-president-bidens-budget-would-drown-american-families-in-debt-deficits-and-inflation-. Also see Kevin L. Kliesen, "Do We Have a Saving Crisis?" *Regional Economist,* St. Louis Federal Reserve Bank, July 2005; Daniel J. Mitchell, "How Government Policies Discourage Savings," *Heritage Foundation Backgrounder* No. 1185, June 2, 1998; and George Packer, "America's Plastic Hour Is Upon Us," *The Atlantic,* October 2020.

9. The critique on saving policy is typically framed in the context of the long-standing US policy debate over the potential impacts of outsize budget deficits. Nobel Prize–winning economist Paul Krugman has long been one of the more high-profile critics of what he has dubbed the misdirected advice of "deficit scolds"; for one of his earliest diatribes, see Paul Krugman, "What the Deficit Scolds Won't Say about the Fiscal Cliff," *Akron Beacon Journal,* November 13, 2012. Also see Jason Furman and Lawrence H. Summers, "Who's Afraid of Budget Deficits?" *Foreign Affairs,* March/April 2019; and James McBride and Andrew Chatzky, "The U.S. Trade Deficit: How Much Does It Matter?" Council on Foreign Relations Backgrounder, March 8, 2019. Deficit and saving denial have also crept into the recent debate over "modern monetary theory"; see Stephanie Kelton, *The Deficit Myth: Modern Monetary Theory and the Birth of the People's Economy* (New York: Public Affairs, 2020).

10. While former presidential counselor Kellyanne Conway is widely credited for originating the catchy phrase "alternative facts," this quickly became an operative protocol for the Trump administration and its supporters in the Republican Party; see Aaron Blake, "Kellyanne Conway's Legacy: The 'Alternative Facts'-ification of the GOP," *Washington Post,* August 24, 2020.

11. See, for example, Jyh-An Lee, "Forced Technology Transfer in the Case of China," *Journal of Science & Technology Law* 6, no. 2 (August 2020); Anton Malkin, "Beyond 'Forced' Technology Transfers: Analysis of and Recommendations on Intangible Economy Governance in China," Center for International Governance Innovation,

CIGI Papers No. 239, March 2020; Julia Ya Qin, "Forced Technology Transfer and the US-China Trade War: Implications for International Economic Law," *Journal of International Economic Law* 22, no. 4 (December 2019).

12. As noted in Chapter 4, there is also a perfectly legal intermediate technology transfer mechanism, whereby foreign companies pay licensing fees and royalties for the legitimate acquisition of foreign intellectual property. Most countries, including the United States and China, engage in this legal form of tech transfer in the normal course of doing business. Significantly, while Chinese payments for the use of foreign intellectual property have increased sharply in recent years, they remain well behind those of Ireland, the Netherlands, and, yes, the United States. This legal form of tech transfer is widely overlooked in demonizing China as the villain in the trade war; see Nicholas R. Lardy, "China: Forced Technology Transfer and Theft?" *China Economic Watch* (blog), Peterson Institute for International Economics, April 29, 2018.

13. See Rappeport, "U.S. Outlines Plans to Scrutinize Chinese and Other Foreign Investment."

14. See Nicolas F. Runnels, "Securing Liberalization: China's New Foreign Investment Law," *Journal of International Law and Politics,* December 6, 2020; Jia Sheng, Chunbin Xu, and Wenjun Cai, "Implementing China's New Foreign Investment Law," Emerging Trends, Pillsbury Law, July 2020; Maurits Elen, "What's Missing in China's Foreign Investment Law?" Interview in *The Diplomat,* January 22, 2020; and Yawen Zheng, "China's New Foreign Investment Law and Its Contribution towards the Country's Development Goals," *Journal of World Investment and Trade* 22, no. 3 (June 2021). Also see US Department of State, "2021 Investment Climate Statements: China," available at https://www.state.gov/reports/2021-investment-climate-statements/china/.

15. In the summer of 2021, there was a growing sense of impatience over the Biden administration's foot-dragging on its long-promised review of US trade policies toward China; there were also hints of new US actions aimed at Chinese industrial policies and related subsidies for China's state-owned enterprises. See Gavin Bade, "'Lay Out the Strategy': Corporate America Grows Impatient on Biden's China Trade Review," *Politico,* August 16, 2021; and Bob Davis and Lingling Wei, "Biden Administration Takes Aim at China's Industrial Subsidies," *Wall Street Journal,* September 11, 2021.

16. See Petros C. Mavroidis and Andre Sapir, "China and the WTO: An Uneasy Relationship," VoxEU, April 29, 2021; Romi Jain, "China's Compliance with the WTO: A Critical Examination," *Indian Journal of Asian Affairs* 29, no. 1/2 (June–December, 2016); and US Trade Representative, "2020 Report to Congress on China's WTO Compliance," January 2021.

17. See Todd Allee and Clint Peinhardt, "Evaluating Three Explanations for the Design of Bilateral Investment Treaties," *World Politics* 66, no. 1 (January 2014).

18. Previously signed US BITs with Bolivia and Ecuador have subsequently been terminated; six additional BITs—with Belarus, El Salvador, Haiti, Nicaragua, Russia,

and Uzbekistan—have been signed but have yet to be ratified and put in force. Source: https://www.state.gov/investment-affairs/bilateral-investment-treaties-and -related-agreements/united-states-bilateral-investment-treaties/.

19. See Michael Froman, "Trump Needs a Comprehensive Trade Deal with China. Luckily, He Has This to Build On," *WorldPost*, February 4, 2019.

20. Source: The BIT tab of the website of the Office of the US Trade Representative, Executive Office of the President, available at https://ustr.gov/trade-agreements /bilateral-investment-treaties.

21. The template for the 2012 US Model Bilateral Investment Treaty can be found at https://www.state.gov/investment-affairs/bilateral-investment-treaties-and -related-agreements/.

22. Source: The BIT tab of the US State Department website, available at https:// www.state.gov/investment-affairs/bilateral-investment-treaties-and-related -agreements/united-states-bilateral-investment-treaties/.

23. See Peter Carberry, "China's Fourth Model Bilateral Investment Treaty," *European Guanxi*, November 15, 2020; Arendse Huld, "China BITs: How to Use Investment Agreements," *China Briefing*, Dezan, Shira & Associates, August 17, 2021, available at https://www.china-briefing.com/news/china-bits-how-to-use-bilateral -investment-treaties/; and https://tcc.export.gov/Trade_Agreements/Bilateral_ Investment_Treaties/index.asp.

24. See Huld, "China BITs."

25. For example, the US-Egypt BIT, the first treaty signed under the US program initiated in 1981, had special provisions to protect Egypt's foreign exchange reserves; it also had an extensive "negative list" of excluded industries, especially in the distribution sectors (i.e., wholesaling, retail, and import and export activities) but also for investment banks, merchant banks, and reinsurance companies. The BIT with Poland was expanded to include significant modifications that took the "different landscape of Eastern Europe" into account; as the first such effort to expand the BIT beyond its original focus on the developing world, it was dubbed a "Business and Economic Relations Treaty." See "Egypt Bilateral Investment Treaty," Senate Treaty Doc. 99–24, signed March 11, 1986 (modified); "Argentina Bilateral Investment Treaty," Senate Treaty Doc. 103–1, signed November 14, 1991; "Poland Business and Economic Relations Treaty," Senate Treaty Doc. 101–18, signed March 21, 1990; "Turkey Bilateral Investment Treaty," Senate Treaty Doc. 99–19, signed December 3, 1985; "Uruguay Bilateral Investment Treaty," Senate Treaty Doc. 109–9, signed November 4, 2005; and "Rwanda Bilateral Investment Treaty," Senate Treaty Doc. 110–23, signed February 19, 2008. The treaties are available on the USTR website at https://tcc.export.gov/Trade_Agreements/Bilateral_Investment _Treaties/index.asp.

26. See Gisela Grieger, "EU-China Comprehensive Agreement on Investment: Levelling the Playing Field with China," Briefing, European Parliament, March 2021; Alicia Garcia-Herrero, "The EU-China Investment Deal May Be Anachronic in

a Bifurcating World," *China-US Focus*, March 2021; and Weinian Hu, "The EU-China Comprehensive Agreement on Investment," *CEPS Policy Insight*, May 2021.

27. See Alexander Chipman Koty, "European Parliament Votes to Freeze the EU-China Comprehensive Agreement on Investment," *China Briefing*, Dezan, Shira & Associates, May 27, 2021; and "China's Embrace of Sanctions Costs It an Investment Deal with the EU," *Bloomberg News*, May 20, 2021.

28. See Jonathan T. Stoel and Michael Jacobson, "U.S. Free Trade Agreements and Bilateral Investment Treaties: How Does Ratification Differ?" *Kluwer Arbitration Blog*, Wolters Kluwer, October 28, 2014; and Jane M. Smith, Daniel T. Shedd, and Brandon J. Murrill, "Why Certain Trade Agreements Are Approved as Congressional-Executive Agreements Rather than Treaties," Congressional Research Service, April 15, 2013.

29. The North American Free Trade Agreement (NAFTA) passed the House by a vote of 234 to 200 and the Senate by a vote of 61 to 38—slightly less than a two-thirds majority in the Senate—in November 1993; the United States-Mexico-Canada Agreement (USMCA) passed the House by a vote of 385 to 41 in 2019 and the Senate by 89 to 10 in 2020. Source: Clerk, US House of Representatives, https://clerk.house.gov/Votes; and US Senate, "Legislation and Records," https://www.senate.gov/legislative/votes_new.htm.

30. The literature on international secretariats identifies five key functions of these organizations: service, intercommunication, synthesis, negotiation, and keeper of the collective conscience; see Anne Winslow, "Functions of an International Secretariat," *Public Administration Review* 30, no. 3 (May–June 1970). Also see Charles Winchmore, "The Secretariat: Retrospect and Prospect," *International Organization* 19, no. 3 (Summer 1965).

31. David Loevinger, the US Treasury's senior coordinator for China and the S&ED from 2009 to 2012, headed up a Washington DC–based staff of five professionals dedicated to annual S&ED preparation. According to a September 2021 email exchange between Loevinger and the author, as the annual S&ED meeting approached, staffing expanded to "literally hundreds of people including most of the sections of the US embassy [in Beijing] and advance teams from all participating agencies [including the US State Department and the White House National Security Council]." Loevinger went on to echo the point that "the annual or semi-annual pageantry meetings were the least important part of our engagement." He stressed that the bulk of the US Treasury's official engagement with China took place on an ongoing basis within a relatively small group of senior US officials and their Chinese counterparts.

32. See Stephen Roach, "Time for the U.S. and China to Collaborate, Not Complain," *Bloomberg Opinion*, March 30, 2020.

33. US insistence on WTO reform has led to blockage of appointments of WTO appeals judges since 2018, putting a major crimp in the dispute mechanism process. The WTO still prides itself on having "one of the most active international

dispute mechanisms in the world"; since the inception of the WTO in 1995, it has issued over 350 rulings resolving some 606 disputes. See https://www.wto.org /english/tratop_e/dispu_e/dispu_e.htm. Also see Jeongho Nam, "Model BIT: An Ideal Prototype or a Tool for Efficient Breach?" *Georgetown Journal of International Law* 48, no. 4 (Summer 2017).

ACKNOWLEDGMENTS

THIS HAS BASICALLY BEEN a thirteen-year book project—an outgrowth of the "Next China" course that I developed and have been privileged to teach at Yale since 2010. Over that period, some 1,400 students have taken the course, the bulk of them in the form of a lecture class that, due to Covid, was downsized to a seminar in 2020–22. Feedback from my students has been invaluable over this period as I have used the classroom as a laboratory to peer into the deep recesses of the US-China relationship. This book is dedicated to them.

My spring 2022 seminar deserves special mention. Unknowingly, twenty-two students enrolled as guinea pigs, offering the perfect stress test for most of the ideas in this book. By then, a third draft was well along in the final stages of editing. Yet there were many evenings after class, when seminar discussions sent me scurrying back to the manuscript to tweak an idea, add a citation, or even rethink a chapter. In the true spirit of a critical thinking seminar, these amazing students were all engaging, inquisitive, hardworking, and never reluctant to challenge their professor. I thanked them in class and do so again on these pages.

The broader Yale community has offered great support to my teaching, in general, and to this book, in particular. Special thanks to former president Richard Levin who persuaded me to join the faculty of a new start-up, the Jackson Institute for Global Affairs, at its inception in 2010. It was hardly a tough sell. Rick has been a tireless supporter of my work on China over the years, gave several guest lectures in my Next China class, and offered very helpful comments on several aspects of this book. I am also immensely grateful to John and Susan Jackson for their vision and generosity in bringing the Jackson Institute (now a full-fledged Yale school) to life, as well as to Jim Levinsohn, director and now dean of Jackson. Yale has a long tradition of excellence in so many diverse aspects of global affairs. Pulling them together under the Jackson umbrella is one of Rick Levin's many great legacies.

Publication of this book marks an important milestone in my Yale affiliation, as I now depart Jackson after nearly thirteen years and join the Paul Tsai China Center at the Yale Law School. I will miss the students and the energy and engagement of full-time teaching but am eager to participate in the exciting program of the China Center under the direction of my good friend and colleague, Paul Gewirtz.

From the start, my Yale career was heavily influenced by Jonathan Spence, a towering force in Sinology who passed away on Christmas 2021. When I came to Yale in 2010, Spence, who had retired as a professor a couple of years earlier, was warm and welcoming. I invited him to give a guest lecture in my new class, but he graciously declined. He offered a not-too-subtle hint that it was best I did this on my own (gulp). Over the years, I saw him in the audience at many of my campus presentations on China, and I had the honor of sharing several speaking platforms with him. He was never bashful about offering feedback, which at times caused me to rethink my own views on China. His curiosity was insatiable, his scholarship impeccable, his creative genius extraordinary. I thank him in memoriam for his inspiration, which shows up in Chapter 13 of this book.

I owe special thanks to a number of my other Yale colleagues who provided support, counsel, and insight during the long period of research and writing of this book. These include Paul Gewirtz, Robert Shiller (for his influential work on the behavioral aspects of narratives, dreams, and animal spirits, as well as his tips on Google Ngrams), Odd Arne Westad, Emma Sky, Carol Li Rafferty, Jeffrey Sonnenfeld, Aleh Tsyvinski, Jing Tsu, and Ted Wittenstein. I am also grateful for the inspirational and intellectual contagion of John Lewis Gaddis (on cold wars), Paul Kennedy (on great power rivalries), and Timothy Snyder (on fragile democracies), all whose prodigious scholarship had an important bearing on many of the themes in *Accidental Conflict*.

Over the years, a number of my Yale teaching fellows provided generous assistance for the research behind this book. I am especially grateful to those who toiled in that capacity from 2016–22: Drew D'Alelio, Douglas Gledhill, Eunsun Cho, Caroline Agsten, Ben Ditchfield, Lissa Kryska, Yi Wang, Yue (Hans) Zhu, Christian Marin, Gregor Novak, Andrea Chen, Tamara Grbusic, Shixue Hu, Agnivesh Mishra, Zongzhong Tang, Minghao Li, Kathleen Devlin, James Gorby, Chen Wang, and Yang Zhang.

I would also like to thank those who assisted me in tackling topic-specific issues covered in this book: Richard Berner and David Greenlaw (US credit intermediation), Nick Lardy (technology transfer), David Loevinger (Strategic & Economic Dialogues), Edmund Phelps (dynamism and indigenous innovation), Kai-Fu Lee (artificial intelligence), Hans Zhu (Chinese SOE reforms), Hugo Chung (Chinese censorship, joint ventures, and the US entity list), Carla Hills (Chinese WTO accession), and Liza Lin (Chinese surveillance). Thanks also to a network of good friends who, over the years, have offered camaraderie, support, and feedback during various phases of this project—especially Jim Fralick, Dick Berner, Robert Lunn, Ruth Porat, Rakesh Mohan, CH Tung, KS-Li, Lu Mai, Shan Weijian, Fang Xinghai, Gao Xiqing, Zhu Min, and Markus Rodlauer (d. 2021 and a tireless supporter of the Next China with nine years of guest lectures on the IMF China perspective).

I am particularly grateful to Ken Murphy and the *Project Syndicate* team for inviting me to join their effort in 2011; I have floated many of the views contained in this book as op-ed trial balloons on their extraordinary global platform. Vigorous feedback and debate from their far-flung global readership community has been invaluable in crystallizing my thinking on many themes in this book.

Special thanks also to my colleagues on a US-China Track II dialogue on economic issues sponsored by the National Committee on US-China Relations and the National School of Development at Peking University. Over the course of our meetings during the past twelve years, this group has provided a vigorous sounding board for many of my views on the US-China conflict. On the US side that includes Stephen Orlins, Carla Hills, Robert

Dohner, Haini Guo, Constance Hunter, Dino Kos, Nicholas Lardy, Jacob Lew, Catherine Mann, Barry Naughton, Daniel Rosen, Robert Rubin, Kim Schoenholtz, Ernie Thrasher, Jan van Eck, and Mark Zandi; on the Chinese side, my equal appreciation to Qin Xiao, Ding Anhua, Gao Shanwen, Hu Yifan, Huang Haizhou, Huang Yiping, Liang Hong, Lin Yifu, Lu Feng, Xu Gao, Yao Yang, and Zha Daojiong. We didn't always agree, but there was enormous value in our exchange of views.

I fully recognize that there may be considerable controversy over some of the arguments presented and positions taken in *Accidental Conflict*. The standard disclaimer rule is more than appropriate in this case: None of the above can or should be implicated in any of the conclusions of this book. Blame falls entirely on me.

Editors bring books to life. The team at Yale University Press has no peers. This is my second book with Bill Frucht, who once again added immeasurably to its structure and clarity—from conception to manuscript to polished final product. Bill forced me to think and rethink a number of key arguments and pushed me repeatedly to ponder long and hard over thematic resolution—specifically, in this book, US-China conflict resolution. While this is a complex book in many respects, Bill added focus, simplicity, and efficiency of expression when I needed it most. Erica Hanson was equally masterful in taking the manuscript to the finish line, leaving no stone unturned in stylistic rigor, clarity of expression, and laser-like attention to the extraordinary details required of more than 750 endnotes. Her tolerance of my endless "final" revisions makes the patience of Job look impulsive. My deepest gratitude to both as true partners in this book. Special thanks also to Enid Zafran for leaving no stone unturned in her masterful work on the index.

Finally, my family has always been willing to cut me slack as I disappear into yet another deep-dive project. One silver lining of the Covid era is that those disappearances did not involve any travel during the past couple of years—just interminable lockdowns in my home office. Deepest thanks always to Katie, my partner in life, for her understanding and encouragement during this latest book writing binge. Our large family, with its abundance of energy and curiosity, has truly been the ultimate support system for a life filled with next chapters.

INDEX

Figures and tables are indicated by page number followed by *f* and *t*, respectively.